Old Calabria

Old Calabria

NORMAN DOUGLAS

COSIMOCLASSICS

NEW YORK

Old Calabria
Cover © 2007 Cosimo, Inc.

For information, address:

Cosimo, P.O. Box 416
Old Chelsea Station
New York, NY 10113-0416

or visit our website at:
www.cosimobooks.com

Old Calabria was originally published in 1915.

Cover design by www.kerndesign.net

ISBN: 978-1-60206-376-1

Speaking of the weather, the landlady further told me that the wind blew so hard three months ago——"during that big storm in the winter, don't you remember?"——that it broke all the iron lamp-posts between the town and the station. Now here was a statement sounding even more improbable than her other one about Castel del Monte, but admitting of verification. Wheezing and sneezing, I crawled forth, and found it correct. It must have been a respectable gale, since the cast-iron supports are snapped in half, every one of them.

——from Chapter 2: "Manfred's Town"

CONTENTS

I

SARACEN LUCERA

I FIND it hard to sum up in one word the character of Lucera—the effect it produces on the mind; one sees so many towns that the freshness of their images becomes blurred. The houses are low but not undignified; the streets regular and clean; there is electric light and somewhat indifferent accommodation for travellers; an infinity of barbers and chemists. Nothing remarkable in all this. Yet the character is there, if one could but seize upon it, since every place has its genius. Perhaps it lies in a certain feeling of aloofness that never leaves one here. We are on a hill—a mere wave of ground; a kind of spur, rather, rising up from the south—quite an absurd little hill, but sufficiently high to dominate the wide Apulian plain. And the nakedness of the land stimulates this aerial sense.

There are some trees in the "Belvedere" or public garden that lies on the highest part of the spur and affords a fine view north and eastwards. But the greater part were only planted a few years ago, and those stretches of brown earth, those half-finished walks and straggling pigmy shrubs, give the place a crude and embryonic appearance. One thinks that the designers might have done more in the way of variety; there are no conifers excepting a few cryptomerias and yews which will all be dead in a couple of years, and as for those yuccas, beloved of Italian municipalities, they will have grown more dyspeptic-looking than ever. None the less, the garden will be a pleasant spot when the ilex shall have grown higher; even now it is the favourite evening walk of the citizens. Altogether, these public parks, which are now being planted all over south Italy, testify to renascent taste; they and the burial-places are often the only spots where the deafened and light-bedazzled stranger may find a little green content; the content, respectively, of *L'Allegro* and *Il Penseroso*. So the cemetery of Lucera, with its ordered walks drowned in the shade of cypress—roses and gleaming marble monuments in between—is a charming retreat, not only for the dead.

The Belvedere, however, is not my promenade. My promenade

lies yonder, on the other side of the valley, where the grave old Suabian castle sits on its emerald slope. It does not frown; it reposes firmly, with an air of tranquil and assured domination; "it has found its place," as an Italian observed to me. Long before Frederick Barbarossa made it the centre of his southern dominions, long before the Romans had their fortress on the site, this eminence must have been regarded as the key of Apulia. All round the outside of those turreted walls (they are nearly a mile in circumference; the enclosure, they say, held sixty thousand people) there runs a level space. This is my promenade, at all hours of the day. Falcons are fluttering with wild cries overhead; down below, a long unimpeded vista of velvety green, flecked by a few trees and sullen streamlets and white farmhouses—the whole vision framed in a ring of distant Apennines. The volcanic cone of Mount Vulture, land of Horace, can be detected on clear days; it tempts me to explore those regions. But eastward rises up the promontory of Mount Gargano, and on the summit of its nearest hill one perceives a cheerful building, some village or convent, that beckons imperiously across the intervening lowlands. Yonder lies the venerable shrine of the archangel Michael, and Manfred's town. . . .

This castle being a *national monument*, they have appointed a custodian to take charge of it; a worthless old fellow, full of untruthful information which he imparts with the hushed and conscience-stricken air of a man who is selling State secrets.

"That corner tower, sir, is the King's tower. It was built by the King."

"But you said just now that it was the Queen's tower."

"So it is. The Queen—she built it."

"What Queen?"

"What Queen? Why, the Queen—the Queen the German professor was talking about three years ago. But I must show you some skulls which we found (*sotto voce*) in a subterranean crypt. They used to throw the poor dead folk in here by hundreds; and under the Bourbons the criminals were hanged here, thousands of them. The blessed times! And this tower is the Queen's tower."

"But you called it the King's tower just now."

"Just so. That is because the King built it."

"What King?"

"Ah, sir, how can I remember the names of all those gentlemen? I haven't so much as set eyes on them! But I must now show you some round sling-stones which we excavated (*sotto voce*) in a subterranean crypt——"

One or two relics from this castle are preserved in the small municipal museum, founded about five years ago. Here are also a respectable collection of coins, a few prehistoric flints from Gargano, some quaint early bronze figurines and mutilated busts of Roman celebrities carved in marble or the recalcitrant local limestone. A dignified old lion—one of a pair (the other was stolen) that adorned the tomb of Aurelius, prætor of the Roman Colony of Luceria—has sought a refuge here, as well as many inscriptions, lamps, vases, and a miscellaneous collection of modern rubbish. A plaster cast of a Mussulman funereal stone, found near Foggia, will attract your eye; contrasted with the fulsome epitaphs of contemporary Christianity, it breathes a spirit of noble resignation:—

"In the name of Allah, the Merciful, the Compassionate. May God show kindness to Mahomet and his kinsfolk, fostering them by his favours! This is the tomb of the captain Jacchia Albosasso. God be merciful to him. He passed away towards noon on Saturday in the five days of the month Moharram of the year 745 (5th April, 1348). May Allah likewise show mercy to him who reads."

One cannot be at Lucera without thinking of that colony of twenty thousand Saracens, the escort of Frederick and his son, who lived here for nearly eighty years, and sheltered Manfred in his hour of danger. The chronicler Spinelli* has preserved an anecdote which shows Manfred's infatuation for these loyal aliens. In the year 1252 and in the sovereign's presence, a Saracen official gave a blow to a Neapolitan knight—a blow which was immediately returned; there was a tumult, and the upshot of it was that the Italian was condemned to lose his hand; all that the Neapolitan nobles could obtain from Manfred was that his left hand should be amputated instead of his right; the Arab, the cause of all, was merely relieved of his office. Nowadays, all memory of Saracens has been swept out of the land. In default of anything better, they are printing a local halfpenny paper called "Il Saraceno"—a very innocuous pagan, to judge by a copy which I bought in a reckless moment.

This museum also contains a buxom angel of stucco known as the "Genius of Bourbonism." In the good old days it used to ornament the town hall, fronting the entrance; but now, degraded to a mu-

* These journals are now admitted to have been manufactured in the sixteenth century by the historian Costanzo for certain genealogical purposes of his own. Professor Bernhardi doubted their authenticity in 1869, and his doubts have been confirmed by Capasso.

seum curiosity, it presents to the public its back of ample proportions, and the curator intimated that he considered this attitude quite appropriate—historically speaking, of course. Furthermore, they have carted hither, from the Chamber of Deputies in Rome, the chair once occupied by Ruggiero Bonghi. Dear Bonghi! From a sense of duty he used to visit a certain dull and pompous house in the capital and forthwith fall asleep on the nearest sofa; he slept sometimes for two hours at a stretch, while all the other visitors were solemnly marched to the spot to observe him—behold the great Bonghi: he slumbers! There is a statue erected to him here, and a street has likewise been named after another celebrity, Giovanni Bovio. If I informed the townsmen of my former acquaintance with these two heroes, they would perhaps put up a marble tablet commemorating the fact. For the place is infected with the patriotic disease of monumentomania. The drawback is that with every change of administration the streets are re-baptized and the status shifted to make room for new favourites; so the civic landmarks come and go, with the swiftness of a cinematograph.

Frederick II also has his street, and so has Pietro Giannone. This smacks of anti-clericalism. But to judge by the number of priests and the daily hordes of devout and dirty pilgrims that pour into the town from the fanatical fastnesses of the Abruzzi—picturesque, I suppose we should call them—the country is sufficiently orthodox. Every self respecting family, they tell me, has its pet priest, who lives on them in return for spiritual consolations.

There was a religious festival some nights ago in honour of Saint Espedito. No one could tell me more about this holy man than that he was a kind of pilgrim-warrior, and that his cult here is of a recent date; it was imported or manufactured some four years ago by a rich merchant who, tired of the old local saints, built a church in honour of this new one, and thereby enrolled him among the city gods.

On this occasion the square was seething with people: few women, and the men mostly in dark clothes; we are already under Moorish and Spanish influences. A young boy addressed me with the polite question whether I could tell him the precise number of the population of London.

That depended, I said, on what one described as London. There was what they called greater London——

It depended! That was what he had always been given to understand. . . . And how did I like Lucera? Rather a dull little place, was it not? Nothing like Paris, of course. Still, if I could delay my departure for some days longer, they would have the trial of a man who had murdered three people: it might be quite good fun. He was informed that they hanged such persons in England, as they used to do hereabouts; it seemed rather barbaric, because, naturally, nobody is ever responsible for his actions; but in England, no doubt——

That is the normal attitude of these folks towards us and our institutions. We are savages, hopeless savages; but a little savagery, after all, is quite endurable. Everything is endurable if you have lots of money, like these English.

As for myself, wandering among that crowd of unshaven creatures, that rustic population, fiercely gesticulating and dressed in slovenly hats and garments, I realized once again what the average Anglo-Saxon would ask himself: Are they *all* brigands, or only some of them? That music, too—what is it that makes this stuff so utterly unpalatable to a civilized northerner? A soulless cult of rhythm, and then, when the simplest of melodies emerges, they cling to it with the passionate delight of a child who has discovered the moon. These men are still in the age of platitudes, so far as music is concerned; an infantile aria is to them what some foolish rhymed proverb is to the Arabs: a thing of God, a portent, a joy for ever.

You may visit the cathedral; there is a fine *verde antico* column on either side of the sumptuous main portal. I am weary, just now, of these structures; the spirit of pagan Lucera—"Lucera dei Pagani" it used to be called—has descended upon me; I feel inclined to echo Carducci's "*Addio, nume semitico!*" One sees so many of these sombre churches, and they are all alike in their stony elaboration of mysticism and wrong-headedness; besides, they have been described, over and over again, by enthusiastic connaisseurs who dwell lovingly upon their artistic quaintnesses but forget the grovelling herd that reared them, with the lash at their backs, or the odd type of humanity—the gargoyle type—that has since grown up under their shadow and influence. I prefer to return to the sun and stars, to my promenade beside the castle walls.

But for the absence of trees and hedges, one might take this to be some English prospect of the drowsy Midland counties—so green it is, so golden-grey the sky. The sunlight peers down dispersedly through windows in this firmament of clouded amber, alighting on some mouldering tower, some patch of ripening corn or distant city—Troia, lapped in Byzantine slumber, or San Severo famed in war. This in spring. But what days of glistering summer heat, when the earth is burnt to cinders under a heavenly dome that glows like a brazier of molten copper! For this country is the Sahara of Italy.

One is glad, meanwhile, that the castle does not lie in the natal land of the Hohenstaufen. The interior is quite deserted, to be sure; they have built half the town of Lucera with its stones, even as Frederick quarried them out of the early Roman citadel beneath; but it is at least a harmonious desolation. There are no wire-fenced walks among the ruins, no feeding-booths and cheap reconstructions of draw-bridges and police-notices at every corner; no gaudy women scribbling to their friends in the "Residenzstadt" post cards illustrative of the "Burgruine," while their husbands perspire over mastodontic beer-jugs. There is only peace.

These are the delights of Lucera: to sit under those old walls and watch the gracious cloud-shadows dappling the plain, oblivious of yonder assemblage of barbers and politicians. As for those who can reconstruct the vanished glories of such a place—happy they! I find the task increasingly difficult. One outgrows the youthful age of hero-worship; next, our really keen edges are so soon worn off by mundane trivialities and vexations that one is glad to take refuge in simpler pleasures once more—to return to primitive emotionalism. There are so many Emperors of past days! And like the old custodian, I have not so much as set eyes on them.

Yet this Frederick is no dim figure; he looms grandly through the intervening haze. How well one understands that craving for the East, nowadays; how modern they were, he and his son the "Sultan of Lucera," and their friends and counsellors, who planted this garden of exotic culture! Was it some after-glow of the luminous world that had sunk below the horizon, or a pale streak of the coming dawn? And if you now glance down into this enclosure that once echoed with the song of minstrels and the soft laughter of women, with the discourse of wits, artists and philosophers, and the clang of arms—if you look, you will behold nothing but a green lake, a waving field of grass. No matter. The ambitions of these men are fairly realized, and every one of us may keep a body-guard of pagans, an't please him; and a harem likewise—to judge by the newspapers.

For he took his Orientalism seriously; he had a harem, with eunuchs, etc., all proper, and was pleased to give an Eastern colour to his entertainments. Matthew Paris relates how Frederick's brother-in-law, returning from the Holy Land, rested awhile at his Italian court, and saw, among other diversions, "duas puellas Saracenicas formosas, quæ in pavimenti planitie binis globis insisterent, volutisque globis huo illucque ferrentur canentes, cymbala manibus collidentes, corporaque secundum modulos motantes atque flectentes." I wish I had been there. . . .

I walked to the castle yesterday evening on the chance of seeing an eclipse of the moon which never came, having taken place at quite another hour. A cloudless night, dripping with moisture, the electric lights of distant Foggia gleaming in the plain. There are brick-kilns at the foot of the incline, and from some pools in the neighbourhood issued a loud croaking of frogs, while the pallid smoke of the furnaces, pressed down by the evening dew, trailed earthward in a long twisted wreath, like a dragon crawling sulkily to his den. But on the north side one could hear the nightingales singing in the gardens below. The dark mass of Mount Gargano rose up clearly in the moonlight, and I began to sketch out some itinerary of my wanderings on that soil. There was Sant' Angelo, the archangel's abode; and the forest region; and Lesina with its lake; and Vieste the remote, the end of all things. . . .

Then my thoughts wandered to the Hohenstaufen and the conspiracy whereby their fate was avenged. The romantic figures of Manfred and Conradin; their relentless enemy Charles; Costanza, her brow crowned with a poetic nimbus (that melted, towards the end, into an aureole of bigotry); Frangipani, huge in villainy; the princess Beatrix, tottering from the dungeon where she had been confined for nearly twenty years; her deliverer Roger de Lauria, without whose resourcefulness and audacity it might have gone ill with Aragon; Popes and Palæologus—brilliant colour effects; the king of England and Saint Louis of France; in the background, dimly discernible, the colossal shades of Frederick and Innocent, locked in deadly embrace; and the whole congress of figures enlivened and interpenetrated as by some electric fluid—the personality of John of Procida. That the element of farce might not be lacking, fate contrived that exquisite royal duel at Bordeaux where the two mighty potentates, calling each other by a variety of unkingly epithets, enacted a prodigiously fine piece of foolery for the delectation of Europe.

From this terrace one can overlook both Foggia and Castel Fiorentino—the beginning and end of the drama; and one follows the march of this magnificent retribution without a shred of compassion for the gloomy papal hireling. Disaster follows disaster with mathematical precision, till at last he perishes miserably, consumed by rage and despair. Then our satisfaction is complete.

No; not quite complete. For in one point the stupendous plot seems to have been imperfectly achieved. Why did Roger de Lauria not profit by his victory to insist upon the restitution of the young brothers of Beatrix, of those unhappy princes who had been confined as infants in 1266, and whose very existence seems to have faded from the memory of historians? Or why did Costanza, who might have dealt with her enemy's son even as Conradin had been dealt with, not round her magnanimity by claiming her own flesh and blood, the last scions of a great house? Why were they not released during the subsequent peace, or at least in 1302? The reason is as plain as it is unlovely; nobody knew what to do with them. Political reasons counselled their effacement, their non-existence. Horrible thought, that the sunny world should be too small for three orphan children! In their Apulian fastness they remained—in chains. A royal rescript of 1295 orders that they be freed from their fetters. Thirty years in fetters! Their fate is unknown; the night of mediæ-valism closes in upon them once more. . . .

Further musings were interrupted by the appearance of a shape which approached from round the corner of one of the towers. It came nearer stealthily, pausing every now and then. Had I evoked, willy-nilly, some phantom of the buried past?

It was only the custodian, leading his dog Musolino. After a shower of compliments and apologies, he gave me to understand that it was his duty, among other things, to see that no one should endeavour to raise the treasure which was hidden under these ruins; several people, he explained, had already made the attempt by night. For the rest, I was quite at liberty to take my pleasure about the castle at all hours. But as to touching the buried hoard, it was *proibito*—forbidden!

I was glad of the incident, which conjured up for me the Oriental mood with its genii and subterranean wealth. Straightway this incongruous and irresponsible old buffoon was invested with a new dignity; transformed into a threatening Ifrit, the guardian of the gold, or—who knows?—Iblis incarnate. The gods take wondrous shapes, sometimes.

II

MANFRED'S TOWN

AS the train moved from Lucera to Foggia and thence onwards, I had enjoyed myself rationally, gazing at the emerald plain of Apulia, soon to be scorched to ashes, but now richly dight with the yellow flowers of the giant fennel, with patches of ruby-red poppy and asphodels pale and shadowy, past their prime. I had thought upon the history of this immense tract of country—upon all the floods of legislation and theorizings to which its immemorial customs of pasturage have given birth. . . .

Then, suddenly, the aspect of life seemed to change. I felt unwell, and so swift was the transition from health that I had wantonly thrown out of the window, beyond recall, a burning cigar ere realizing that it was only a little more than half smoked. We were crossing the Calendaro, a sluggish stream which carefully collects all the waters of this region only to lose them again in a swamp not far distant; and it was positively as if some impish sprite had leapt out of those noisome waves, boarded the train, and flung himself into me, after the fashion of the "Horla" in the immortal tale.

Doses of quinine such as would make an English doctor raise his eyebrows have hitherto only succeeded in provoking the Calendaro microbe to more virulent activity. Nevertheless, *on s'y fait.* I am studying him and, despite his protean manifestations, have discovered three principal ingredients: malaria, bronchitis and hay-fever—not your ordinary hay-fever, oh, no! but such as a mammoth might conceivably catch, if thrust back from his germless, frozen tundras into the damply blossoming Miocene.

The landlady of this establishment has a more commonplace name for the distemper. She calls it "scirocco." And certainly this pest of the south blows incessantly; the mountain-line of Gargano is veiled, the sea's horizon veiled, the coast-lands of Apulia veiled by its tepid and unwholesome breath. To cheer me up, she says that on clear days one can see Castel del Monte, the Hohenstaufen eyrie, shining yonder above Barletta, forty miles distant. It sounds rather improbable; still, yesterday evening there arose a sudden vision of a white town in that direction, remote and dream-like, far across the water. Was it Barletta? Or Margherita? It lingered awhile, poised on an errant sunbeam; then sank into the deep.

From this window I look into the little harbour whose beach is dotted with fishing-boats. Some twenty or thirty sailing-vessels are riding at anchor; in the early morning they unfurl their canvas and sally forth, in amicable couples, to scour the azure deep—it is greenish-yellow at this moment—returning at nightfall with the spoils of ocean, mostly young sharks, to judge by the display in the market. Their white sails bear fabulous devices in golden colour of moons and crescents and dolphins; some are marked like the "orange-tip" butterfly. A gunboat is now stationed here on a mysterious errand connected with the Albanian rising on the other side of the Adriatic. There has been whispered talk of illicit volunteering among the youth on this side, which the government is anxious to prevent. And to enliven the scene, a steamer calls every now and then to take passengers to the Tremiti islands. One would like to visit them, if only in memory of those martyrs of Bourbonism, who were sent in hundreds to these rocks and cast into dungeons to perish. I have seen such places; they are vast caverns artificially excavated below the surface of the earth; into these the unfortunates were lowered and left to crawl about and rot, the living mingled with the dead. To this day they find mouldering skeletons, loaded with heavy iron chains and ball-weights.

A copious spring gushes up on this beach and flows into the sea. It is sadly neglected. Were I tyrant of Manfredonia, I would build me a fair marble fountain here, with a carven assemblage of nymphs and sea-monsters spouting water from their lusty throats, and plashing in its rivulets. It may well be that the existence of this fount helped to decide Manfred in his choice of a site for his city; such springs are rare in this waterless land. And from this same source, very likely, is derived the local legend of Saint Lorenzo and the Dragon, which is quite independent of that of Saint Michael the dragon-killer on the heights above us. These venerable water-spirits, these *dracs*, are interesting beasts who went through many metamorphoses ere attaining their present shape.

Manfredonia lies on a plain sloping very gently seawards—practically a dead level, and in one of the hottest districts of Italy. Yet, for some obscure reason, there is no street along the sea itself; the cross-roads end in abrupt squalor at the shore. One wonders what considerations—political, æsthetic or hygienic—prevented the designers of the town from carrying out its general principles of construction and building a decent promenade by the waves, where the ten thousand citizens could take the air in the breathless summer evenings, instead of being cooped up, as they now are, within stifling hot walls. The choice of Manfredonia as a port does not testify to any great foresight on the part of its founder—peace to his shade! It will for ever slumber in its bay, while commerce passes beyond its reach; it will for ever be malarious with the marshes of Sipontum at its edges. But this particular defect of the place is not Manfred's fault, since the city was razed to the ground by the Turks in 1620, and then built up anew; built up, says Lenormant, according to the design of the old city. Perhaps a fear of other Corsair raids induced the constructors to adhere to the old plan, by which the place could be more easily defended. Not much of Manfredonia seems to have been completed when Pacicchelli's view (1703) was engraved.

Speaking of the weather, the landlady further told me that the wind blew so hard three months ago—"during that big storm in the winter, don't you remember?"—that it broke all the iron lamp-posts between the town and the station. Now here was a statement sounding even more improbable than her other one about Castel del Monte, but admitting of verification. Wheezing and sneezing, I crawled forth, and found it correct. It must have been a respectable gale, since the cast-iron supports are snapped in half, every one of them.

Those Turks, by the way, burnt the town on that memorable occasion. That was a common occurrence in those days. Read any account of their incursions into Italy during this and the preceding centuries, and you will find that the corsairs burnt the towns whenever they had time to set them alight. They could not burn them nowadays, and this points to a total change in economic conditions. Wood was cut down so heedlessly that it became too scarce for building purposes, and stone took its place. This has altered domestic architecture; it has changed the landscape, denuding the hillsides that were once covered with timber; it has impoverished the country by converting fruitful plains into marshes or arid tracts of stone swept by irregular and intermittent floods; it has modified, if I mistake not, the very character of the people. The desiccation of the climate has entailed a desiccation of national humour.

Muratori has a passage somewhere in his "Antiquities" regarding the old method of construction and the wooden shingles, *scandulæ*, in use for roofing—I must look it up, if ever I reach civilized regions again.

At the municipality, which occupies the spacious apartments of a former Dominican convent, they will show you the picture of a young girl, one of the Beccarini family, who was carried off at a tender age in one of these Turkish raids, and subsequently became "Sultana." Such captive girls generally married sultans—or ought to have married them; the wish being father to the thought. But the story is disputed; rightly, I think. For the portrait is painted in the French manner, and it is hardly likely that a harem-lady would have been exhibited to a European artist. The legend goes on to say that she was afterwards liberated by the Knights of Malta, together with her Turkish son who, as was meet and proper, became converted to Christianity and died a monk. The Beccarini family (of Siena, I fancy) might find some traces of her in their archives. *Ben trovato*, at all events. When one looks at the pretty portrait, one cannot blame any kind of "Sultan" for feeling well-disposed towards the original.

The weather has shown some signs of improvement and tempted me, despite the persistent "scirocco" mood, to a few excursions into the neighbourhood. But there seem to be no walks hereabouts, and the hills, three miles distant, are too remote for my reduced vitality. The intervening region is a plain of rock carved so smoothly, in places, as to appear artificially levelled with the chisel; large tracts of it are covered with the Indian fig (cactus). In the shade of these grotesque growths lives a dainty flora: trembling grasses of many kinds, rue, asphodel, thyme, the wild asparagus, a diminutive blue iris, as well as patches of saxifrage that deck the stone with a brilliant enamel of red and yellow. This wild beauty makes one think how much better the graceful wrought-iron balconies of the town would look if enlivened with blossoms, with pendent carnations or pelargonium; but there is no great display of these things; the deficiency of water is a characteristic of the place; it is a flowerless and songless city. The only good drinking-water is that which is bottled at the mineral springs of Monte Vulture and sold cheaply enough all over the county. And the mass of the country people have small charm of feature. Their faces seem to have been chopped with a hatchet into masks of sombre virility; a hard life amid burning limestone deserts is reflected in their countenances.

None the less, they have a public garden; even more immature than that of Lucera, but testifying to greater taste. Its situation, covering a forlorn semicircular tract of ground about the old Anjou castle, is *a priori* a good one. But when the trees are fully grown, it will be impossible to see this fine ruin save at quite close quarters—just across the moat.

I lamented this fact to a solitary gentleman who was strolling about here and who replied, upon due deliberation:

"One cannot have everything."

Then he added, as a suggestive afterthought:

"Inasmuch as one thing sometimes excludes another."

I pause, to observe parenthetically that this habit of uttering platitudes in the grand manner as though disclosing an idea of vital novelty (which Charles Lamb, poor fellow, thought peculiar to natives of Scotland) is as common among Italians as among Englishmen. But veiled in sonorous Latinisms, the staleness of such remarks assumes an air of profundity.

"For my part," he went on, warming to his theme, "I am thoroughly satisfied. Who will complain of the trees? Only a few makers of bad pictures. They can go elsewhere. Our country, dear sir, is *encrusted* with old castles and other feudal absurdities, and if I had the management of things——"

The sentence was not concluded, for at that moment his hat was blown off by a violent gust of wind, and flew merrily over beds of flowering marguerites in the direction of the main street, while he raced after it, vanishing in a cloud of dust. The chase must have been long and arduous; he never returned.

Wandering about the upper regions of this fortress whose chambers are now used as a factory of cement goods and a refuge for some poor families, I espied a good pre-renaissance relief of Saint Michael and the dragon immured in the masonry, and overhung by the green leaves of an exuberant wild fig that has thrust its roots into the sturdy old walls. Here, at Manfredonia, we are already under the shadow of the holy mountain and the archangel's wings, but the usual representations of him are childishly emasculate—the negation of his divine and heroic character. This one portrays a genuine warrior-angel of the old type: grave and grim. Beyond this castle and the town-walls, which are best preserved on the north side, nothing in Manfredonia is older than 1620. There is a fine *campanile*, but the cathedral looks like a shed for disused omnibuses.

Along the streets, little red flags are hanging out of the houses, at frequent intervals: signals of harbourage for the parched wayfarer. Within, you behold a picturesque confusion of rude chairs set among barrels and vats full of dark red wine where, amid Rembrandtesque surroundings, you can get as drunk as a lord for sixpence. Blithe oases! It must be delightful, in summer, to while away the sultry hours in their hospitable twilight; even at this season they seem to be extremely popular resorts, throwing a new light on those allusions by classical authors to "thirsty Apulia."

But on many of the dwellings I noticed another symbol: an ominous blue metal tablet with a red cross, bearing the white-lettered words "VIGILANZA NOTTURNA."

Was it some anti-burglary association? I enquired of a serious-looking individual who happened to be passing.

His answer did not help to clear up matters.

"A pure job, *signore mio*, a pure job! There is a society in Cerignola or somewhere, a society which persuades the various town councils—*persuades* them, you understand——"

He ended abruptly, with the gesture of paying out money between his finger and thumb. Then he sadly shook his head.

I sought for more light on this cryptic utterance; in vain. What were the facts, I persisted? Did certain householders subscribe to keep a guardian on their premises at night—what had the municipalities to do with it—was there much housebreaking in Manfredonia, and, if so, had this association done anything to check it? And for how long had the institution been established?

But the mystery grew ever darker. After heaving a deep sigh, he condescended to remark:

"The usual camorra! Eat—eat; from father to son. Eat—eat! That's all they think about, the brood of assassins. . . . Just look at them!"

I glanced down the street and beheld a venerable gentleman of kindly aspect who approached slowly, leaning on the arm of a fair-haired youth—his grandson, I supposed. He wore a long white beard, and an air of apostolic detachment from the affairs of this world. They came nearer. The boy was listening, deferentially, to some remark of the elder; his lips were parted in attention and his candid, sunny face would have rejoiced the heart of della Robbia. They passed within a few feet of me, lovingly engrossed in one another.

"Well?" I queried, turning to my informant and anxious to learn what misdeeds could be laid to the charge of such godlike types of humanity.

But that person was not longer at my side. He had quietly withdrawn himself, in the interval; he had evanesced, "moved on."

An oracular and elusive citizen. . . .

III

THE ANGEL OF MANFREDONIA

WHOEVER looks at a map of the Gargano promontory will see that it is besprinkled with Greek names of persons and places—Matthew, Mark, Nikander, Onofrius, Pirgiano (Pyrgos) and so forth. Small wonder, for these eastern regions were in touch with Constantinople from early days, and the spirit of Byzance still hovers over them. It was on this mountain that the archangel Michael, during his first flight to Western Europe, deigned to appear to a Greek bishop of Sipontum, Laurentius by name; and ever since that time a certain cavern, sanctified by the presence of this winged messenger of God, has been the goal of millions of pilgrims.

The fastness of Sant' Angelo, metropolis of European angel-worship, has grown up around this "devout and honourable cave"; on sunny days its houses are clearly visible from Manfredonia. They who wish to pay their devotions at the shrine cannot do better than take with them Gregorovius, as cicerone and mystagogue.

Vainly I waited for a fine day to ascend the heights. At last I determined to have done with the trip, be the weather what it might. A coachman was summoned and negotiations entered upon for starting next morning.

Sixty-five francs, he began telling me, was the price paid by an Englishman last year for a day's visit to the sacred mountain. It may well be true—foreigners will do anything, in Italy. Or perhaps it was only said to "encourage" me. But I am rather hard to encourage, nowadays. I reminded the man that there was a diligence service there and back for a franc and a half, and even that price seemed rather extortionate. I had seen so many holy grottos in my life! And who, after all, was this Saint Michael? The Eternal Father, perchance? Nothing of the kind: just an ordinary angel! We had dozens of them, in England. Fortunately, I added, I had already received an offer to join one of the private parties who drive up, fourteen or fifteen persons behind one diminutive pony—and that, as he well knew, would be a matter of only a few pence. And even then, the threatening sky . . . Yes, on second thoughts, it was perhaps wisest to postpone the excursion altogether. Another day, if God wills! Would he accept this cigar as a recompense for his trouble in coming?

In dizzy leaps and bounds his claims fell to eight francs. It was the tobacco that worked the wonder; a gentleman who will give *something for nothing* (such was his logic)—well, you never know what you may not get out of him. Agree to his price, and chance it!

He consigned the cigar to his waistcoat pocket to smoke after dinner, and departed—vanquished, but inwardly beaming with bright anticipation.

A wretched morning was disclosed as I drew open the shutters—gusts of rain and sleet beating against the window-panes. No matter: the carriage stood below, and after that customary and hateful apology for breakfast which suffices to turn the thoughts of the sanest man towards themes of suicide and murder—when will southerners learn to eat a proper breakfast at proper hours?—we started on our journey. The sun came out in visions of tantalizing briefness, only to be swallowed up again in driving murk, and of the route we traversed I noticed only the old stony track that cuts across the twenty-one windings of the new carriage-road here and there. I tried to picture to myself the Norman princes, the emperors, popes, and other ten thousand pilgrims of celebrity crawling up these rocky slopes—barefoot—on such a day as this. It must have tried the patience even of Saint Francis of Assisi, who pilgrimaged with the rest of them and, according to Pontanus, performed a little miracle here *en passant,* as was his wont.

After about three hours' driving we reached the town of Sant' Angelo. It was bitterly cold at this elevation of 800 metres. Acting on the advice of the coachman, I at once descended into the sanctuary; it would be warm down there, he thought. The great festival of 8 May was over, but flocks of worshippers were still arriving, and picturesquely pagan they looked in grimy, tattered garments—their staves tipped with pine-branches and a scrip.

In the massive bronze doors of the chapel, that were made at Constantinople in 1076 for a rich citizen of Amalfi, metal rings are inserted; these, like a true pilgrim, you must clash furiously, to call the attention of the Powers within to your visit; and on issuing, you must once more knock as hard as you can, in order that the consummation of your act of worship may be duly reported: judging by the noise made, the deity must be very hard of hearing. Strangely deaf they are, sometimes.

The twenty-four panels of these doors are naively encrusted with representations, in enamel, of angel-apparitions of many kinds; some of them are inscribed, and the following is worthy of note: "I beg and implore the priests of Saint Michael to cleanse these gates once a year as I have now shown them, in order that they may be always bright and shining." The recommendation has plainly not been carried out for a good many years past.

Having entered the portal, you climb down a long stairway amid swarms of pious, foul clustering beggars to a vast cavern, the archangel's abode. It is a natural recess in the rock, illuminated by candles. Here divine service is proceeding to the accompaniment of cheerful operatic airs from an asthmatic organ; the water drops ceaselessly from the rocky vault on to the devout heads of kneeling worshippers that cover the floor, lighted candle in hand, rocking themselves ecstatically and droning and chanting. A weird scene, in truth. And the coachman was quite right in his surmise as to the difference in temperature. It is hot down here, damply hot, as in an orchid-house. But the aroma cannot be described as a floral emanation: it is the *bouquet*, rather, of thirteen centuries of unwashed and perspiring pilgrims. "TERRIBILIS EST LOCUS ISTE," says an inscription over the entrance of the shrine. Very true. In places like this one understands the uses, and possibly the origin, of incense.

I lingered none the less, and my thoughts went back to the East, whence these mysterious practices are derived. But an Oriental crowd of worshippers does not move me like these European masses of fanaticism; I can never bring myself to regard without a certain amount of disquietude such passionate pilgrims. Give them their new Messiah, and all our painfully accumulated art and knowledge, all that reconciles civilized man to earthly existence, is blown to the winds. Society can deal with its criminals. Not they, but fond enthusiasts such as these, are the menace to its stability. Bitter reflections; but then—the drive upward had chilled my human sympathies, and besides—that so-called breakfast. . . .

The grovelling herd was left behind. I ascended the stairs and profiting by a gleam of sunshine, climbed up to where, above the town, there stands a proud aerial ruin known as the "Castle of the Giant." On one of its stones is inscribed the date 1491—a certain Queen of Naples, they say, was murdered within those now crumbling walls.

These sovereigns were murdered in so many castles that one wonders how they ever found time to be alive at all. The structure is a wreck and its gateway closed up; nor did I feel any great inclination, in that icy blast of wind, to investigate the roofless interior. I was able to observe, however, that this "feudal absurdity" bears a number like any inhabited house of Sant' Angelo—it is No. 3.

This is the latest pastime of the Italian Government: to re-number dwellings throughout the kingdom; and not only human habitations, but walls, old ruins, stables, churches, as well as an occasional door-post and window. They are having no end of fun over the game, which promises to keep them amused for any length of time—in fact, until the next craze is invented. Meanwhile, so long as the fit lasts, half a million bright-eyed officials, burning with youthful ardour, are employed in affixing these numerals, briskly entering them into ten times as many note-books and registering them into thousands of municipal archives, all over the country, for some inscrutable but hugely important administrative purposes. "We have the employés," as a Roman deputy once told me, "and therefore: they must find some occupation."

Altogether, the weather this day sadly impaired my appetite for research and exploration. On the way to the castle I had occasion to admire the fine tower and to regret that there seemed to exist no coign of vantage from which it could fairly be viewed; I was struck, also, by the number of small figures of Saint Michael of an ultra-youthful, almost infantile, type; and lastly, by certain clean-shaven old men of the place. These venerable and decorative brigands—for such they would have been, a few years ago—now stood peacefully at their thresholds, wearing a most becoming cloak of thick brown wool, shaped like a burnous. The garment interested me; it may be a legacy from the Arabs who dominated this region for some little time, despoiling the holy sanctuary and leaving their memory to be perpetuated by the neighbouring "Monte Saraceno." The costume, on the other hand, may have come over from Greece; it is figured on Tanagra statuettes and worn by modern Greek shepherds. By Sardinians, too. . . . It may well be a primordial form of clothing with mankind.

The view from this castle must be superb on clear days. Standing there, I looked inland and remembered all the places I had intended to see—Vieste, and Lesina with its lakes, and Selva Umbra, whose very name is suggestive of dewy glades; how remote they were, under such dispiriting clouds! I shall never see them. Spring hesitates to smile upon these chill uplands; we are still in the grip of winter—

> Aut aquilonibus
> Querceti Gargani laborent
> Et foliis viduantur orni—

so sang old Horace, of Garganian winds. I scanned the horizon, seeking for his Mount Vulture, but all that region was enshrouded in a grey curtain of vapour; only the Stagno Salso—a salt mere wherein Candelaro forgets his mephitic waters—shone with a steady glow, like a sheet of polished lead.

Soon the rain fell once more and drove me to seek refuge among the houses, where I glimpsed the familiar figure of my coachman, sitting disconsolately under a porch. He looked up and remarked (for want of something better to say) that he had been searching for me all over the town, fearing that some mischief might have happened to me. I was touched by these words; touched, that is, by his child-like simplicity in imagining that he could bring me to believe a statement of such radiant improbability; so touched, that I pressed a franc into his reluctant palm and bade him buy with it something to eat. A whole franc. . . . *Aha!* he doubtless thought, *my theory of the gentleman: it begins to work.*

It was barely midday. Yet I was already surfeited with the angelic metropolis, and my thoughts began to turn in the direction of Manfredonia once more. At a corner of the street, however, certain fluent vociferations in English and Italian, which nothing would induce me to set down here, assailed my ears, coming up—apparently—out of the bowels of the earth. I stopped to listen, shocked to hear ribald language in a holy town like this; then, impelled by curiosity, descended a long flight of steps and found myself in a subterranean wine-cellar. There was drinking and card-playing going on here among a party of emigrants—merry souls; a good half of them spoke English and, despite certain irreverent phrases, they quickly won my heart with a "Here! You drink *this*, mister."

This dim recess was an instructive pendant to the archangel's cavern. A new type of pilgrim has been evolved; pilgrims who think no more of crossing to Pittsburg than a drive to Manfredonia. But their cave was permeated with an odour of spilt wine and tobacco-smoke instead of the subtle *Essence des pèlerins des Abruzzes fleuris,* and alas, the object of their worship was not the Chaldean angel, but another and equally ancient eastern shape: Mammon. They talked much of dollars; and I also heard several unorthodox allusions to the "angel-business," which was described as "played out," as well as a remark to the effect that "only damn-fools stay in this country." In short, these men were at the other end of the human scale; they were the strong, the energetic; the ruthless, perhaps; but certainly—the intelligent.

And all the while the cup circled round with genial iteration, and it was universally agreed that, whatever the other drawbacks of Sant' Angelo might be, there was nothing to be said against its native liquor.

It was, indeed, a divine product; a *vino di montagna* of noble pedigree. So I thought, as I laboriously scrambled up the stairs once more, solaced by this incident of the competition-grotto and slightly giddy, from the tobacco-smoke. And here, leaning against the door-post, stood the coachman who had divined my whereabouts by some dark masonic intuition of sympathy. His face expanded into an inept smile, and I quickly saw that instead of fortifying his constitution with sound food, he had tried alcoholic methods of defence against the inclement weather. Just a glass of wine, he explained. "But," he added, "the horse is perfectly sober."

That quadruped was equal to the emergency. Gloriously indifferent to our fates, we glided down, in a vertiginous but masterly vol-plane, from the somewhat objectionable mountain-town.

An approving burst of sunshine greeted our arrival on the plain.

IV

CAVE-WORSHIP

W HY has the exalted archangel chosen for an abode this reeking cell, rather than some well-built temple in the sunshine? "As symbolizing a ray of light that penetrates into the gloom," so they will tell you. It is more likely that he entered it as an extirpating warrior, to oust that heathen shape which Strabo describes as dwelling in its dank recesses, and to take possession of the cleft in the name of Christianity. Sant' Angelo is one of many places where Michael has performed the duty of Christian Hercules, cleanser of Augean stables.

For the rest, this cave-worship is older than any god or devil. It is the cult of the feminine principle—a relic of that aboriginal obsession of mankind to shelter in some Cloven Rock of Ages, in the sacred womb of Mother Earth who gives us food and receives us after death. Grotto-apparitions, old and new, are but the popular explanations of this dim primordial craving, and hierophants of all ages have understood the commercial value of the holy shudder which penetrates in these caverns to the heart of worshippers, attuning them to godly deeds. So here, close beside the altar, the priests are selling fragments of the so-called "Stone of Saint Michael." The trade is brisk.

The statuette of the archangel preserved in this subterranean chapel is a work of the late Renaissance. Though savouring of that mawkish elaboration which then began to taint local art and literature and is bound up with the name of the poet Marino, it is still a passably virile figure. But those countless others, in churches or over house-doors—do they indeed portray the dragon-killer, the martial prince of angels? This amiable child with girlish features—can this be the Lucifer of Christianity, the Sword of the Almighty? *Quis ut Dêus!* He could hardly hurt a fly.

The hoary winged genius of Chaldea who has absorbed the essence of so many solemn deities has now, in extreme old age, entered upon a second childhood and grown altogether too youthful for his *rôle*, undergoing a metamorphosis beyond the boundaries of legendary probability or common sense; every trace of divinity and manly strength has been boiled out of him. So young and earthly fair, he looks, rather, like some pretty boy dressed up for a game with toy sword and helmet—one wants to have a romp with him. No warrior this! *C'est beau, mais ce n'est pas la guerre.*

The gods, they say, are ever young, and a certain sensuous and fleshly note is essential to those of Italy if they are to retain the love of their worshippers. Granted. We do not need a scarred and hirsute veteran; but we need, at least, a personage capable of wielding the sword, a figure something like this:—

> His starry helm unbuckled show'd his prime
> In manhood where youth ended; by his side
> As in a glist'ring zodiac hung the sword,
> Satan's dire dread, and in his hand the spear. . . .

There! That is an archangel of the right kind.

And the great dragon, that old serpent, called the Devil, and Satan, has suffered a similar transformation. He is shrunk into a poor little reptile, the merest worm, hardly worth crushing.

But how should a sublime conception like the apocalyptic hero appeal to the common herd? These formidable shapes emerge from the dusk, offspring of momentous epochs; they stand aloof at first, but presently their luminous grandeur is dulled, their haughty contour sullied and obliterated by attrition. They are dragged down to the level of their lowest adorers, for the whole flock adapts its pace to that of the weakest lamb. No self-respecting deity will endure this treatment—to be popularized and made intelligible to a crowd. Divinity comprehended of the masses ceases to be efficacious; the Egyptians and Brahmans understood that. It is not giving gods a chance to interpret them in an incongruous and unsportsmanlike fashion. But the vulgar have no idea of propriety or fair play; they cannot keep at the proper distance; they are for ever taking liberties. And, in the end, the proudest god is forced to yield.

We see this same fatality in the very word Cherub. How different an image does this plump and futile infant evoke to the stately Minister of the Lord, girt with a sword of flame! We see it in the Italian Madonna of whom, whatever her mental acquirements may have been, a certain gravity of demeanour is to be presupposed, and who, none the less, grows more childishly smirking every day; in her Son who—hereabouts at least—has doffed all the serious attributes of manhood and dwindled into something not much better than a doll. It was the same in days of old. Apollo (whom Saint Michael has supplanted), and Eros, and Aphrodite—they all go through a process of saccharine deterioration. Our fairest creatures, once they have passed their meridian vigour, are liable to be assailed and undermined by an insidious diabetic tendency.

It is this coddling instinct of mankind which has reduced Saint Michael to his present state. And an extraneous influence has worked in the same direction—the gradual softening of manners within historical times, that demasculinization which is an inevitable concomitant of increasing social security. Divinity reflects its human creators and their environment; grandiose or warlike gods become superfluous, and finally incomprehensible, in humdrum days of peace. In order to survive, our deities (like the rest of us) must have a certain plasticity. If recalcitrant, they are quietly relieved of their functions, and forgotten. This is what has happened in Italy to God the Father and the Holy Ghost, who have vanished from the vulgar Olympus; whereas the devil, thanks to that unprincipled versatility for which he is famous, remains ever young and popular.

The art-notions of the Cinque-Cento are also to blame; indeed, so far as the angelic shapes of south Italy are concerned, the influence of the Renaissance has been wholly malefic. Aliens to the soil, they were at first quite unknown—not one is pictured in the Neapolitan catacombs. Next came the brief period of their artistic glory; then the syncretism of the Renaissance, when these winged messengers were amalgamated with pagan *amoretti* and began to flutter in foolish baroque fashion about the Queen of Heaven, after the pattern of the disreputable little genii attendant upon a Venus of a bad school. That same instinct which degraded a youthful Eros into the childish Cupid was the death-stroke to the pristine dignity and holiness of angels. Nowadays, we see the perversity of it all; we have come to our senses and can appraise the much-belauded revival at its true worth; and our modern sculptors will rear you a respectable angel, a grave adolescent, according to the best canons of taste—should you still possess the faith that once requisitioned such works of art.

We travellers acquaint ourselves with the lineage of this celestial Messenger, but it can hardly be supposed that the worshippers now swarming at his shrine know much of these things. How shall one discover their real feelings in regard to this great cave-saint and his life and deeds?

Well, some idea of this may be gathered from the literature sold on the spot. I purchased three of these modern tracts printed respectively at Bitonto, Molfetta and Naples. The "Popular Song in honour of St. Michael" contains this verse:

> Nell' ora della morte
> Ci salvi dall' inferno
> E a Regno Sempiterno
> Ci guidi per pietà.

Ci guidi per pietà.... This is the Mercury-heritage. Next, the "History and Miracles of St. Michael" opens with a rollicking dialogue in verse between the archangel and the devil concerning a soul; it ends with a goodly list, in twenty-five verses, of the miracles performed by the angel, such as helping women in childbirth, curing the blind, and other wonders that differ nothing from those wrought by humbler earthly saints. Lastly, the "Novena in Onore di S. Michele Arcangelo," printed in 1910 (third edition) with ecclesiastical approval, has the following noteworthy paragraph on the

"DEVOTION FOR THE SACRED STONES OF THE GROTTO OF ST. MICHAEL

"It is very salutary to hold in esteem the STONES which are taken from the sacred cavern, partly because from immemorial times they have always been held in veneration by the faithful and also because they have been placed as relics of sepulchres and altars. Furthermore, it is known that during the plague which afflicted the kingdom of Naples in the year 1656, Monsignor G. A. Puccini, archbishop of Manfredonia, recommended every one to carry devoutly on his person a fragment of the sacred STONE, whereby the majority were saved from the pestilence, and this augmented the devotion bestowed on them."

The cholera is on the increase, and this may account for the rapid sale of the STONES at this moment.

This pamphlet also contains a litany in which the titles of the archangel are enumerated. He is, among other things, Secretary of God, Liberator from Infernal Chains, Defender in the Hour of Death,

Custodian of the Pope, Spirit of Light, Wisest of Magistrates, Terror of Demons, Commander-in-Chief of the Armies of the Lord, Lash of Heresies, Adorer of the Word Incarnate, Guide of Pilgrims, Conductor of Mortals: Mars, Mercury, Hercules, Apollo, Mithra—what nobler ancestry can angel desire? And yet, as if these complicated and responsible functions did not suffice for his energies, he has twenty others, among them being that of "Custodian of the Holy Family"— who apparently need a protector, a Monsieur Paoli, like any mortal royalties.

"Blasphemous rubbish!" I can hear some Methodist exclaiming. And one may well be tempted to sneer at those pilgrims for the more enlightened of whom such literature is printed. For they are unquestionably a repulsive crowd: travel-stained old women, under-studies for the Witch of Endor; dishevelled, anæmic and dazed-looking girls; boys, too weak to handle a spade at home, pathetically uncouth, with mouths agape and eyes expressing every grade of uncontrolled emotion—from wildest joy to downright idiotcy. How one realizes, down in this cavern, the effect upon some cultured ancient like Rutilius Namatianus of the catacomb-worship among those early Christian converts, those *men who shun the light*, drawn as they were from the same social classes towards the same dark underground rites! One can neither love nor respect such people; and to affect pity for them would be more consonant with their religion than with my own.

But it is perfectly easy to understand them. For thirteen centuries this pilgrim-movement has been going on. Thirteen centuries? No. This site was an oracle in heathen days, and we know that such were frequented by men not a whit less barbarous and bigoted than their modern representatives—nothing is a greater mistake than to suppose that the crowds of old Rome and Athens were more refined than our own ("Demosthenes, sir, was talking to an assembly of brutes"). For thirty centuries then, let us say, a deity has attracted the faithful to his shrine—Sant' Angelo has become a vacuum, as it were, which must be periodically filled up from the surrounding country. These pilgrimages are in the blood of the people: infants, they are carried there; adults, they carry their own offspring; greybeards, their tottering steps are still supported by kindly and sturdier fellow-wanderers.

Popes and emperors no longer scramble up these slopes; the spirit of piety has abated among the great ones of the earth; so much is certain. But the rays of light that strike the topmost branches have not yet penetrated to the rank and seething undergrowth. And they—what else can one offer to these Abruzzi mountain-folk? Their life is one of miserable, revolting destitution. They have no games or sports, no local racing, clubs, cattle-shows, fox-hunting, politics, rat-catching, or any of those other joys that diversify the lives of our peasantry. No touch of humanity reaches them, no kindly dames send them jellies or blankets, no cheery doctor enquires for their children; they read no newspapers or books, and lack even the mild excitements of church *versus* chapel, or the vicar's daughter's love-affair, or the squire's latest row with his lady—nothing! Their existence is almost bestial in its blankness. I know them—I have lived among them. For four months in the year they are cooped up in damp dens, not to be called chambers, where an Englishman would deem it infamous to keep a dog—cooped up amid squalor that must be seen to be believed; for the rest of the time they struggle, in the sweat of their brow, to wrest a few blades of corn from the ungrateful limestone. Their visits to the archangel—these vernal and autumnal picnics—are their sole form of amusement.

The movement is said to have diminished since the early nineties, when thirty thousand of them used to come here annually. It may well be the case; but I imagine that this is due not so much to increasing enlightenment as to the depopulation caused by America; many villages have recently been reduced to half their former number of inhabitants.

And here they kneel, candle in hand, on the wet flags of this fœtid and malodorous cave, gazing in rapture upon the blandly beaming idol, their sensibilities tickled by resplendent priests reciting full-mouthed Latin phrases, while the organ overhead plays wheezy extracts from "La Forza del Destino" or the Waltz out of Boito's "Mefistofele". . . for sure, it must be a foretaste of Heaven! And likely enough, these are "the poor in heart" for whom that kingdom is reserved.

One may call this a debased form of Christianity. Whether it would have been distasteful to the feelings of the founder of that cult is another question, and, debased or not, it is at least alive and palpitating, which is more than can be said of certain other varieties. But the archangel, as was inevitable, has suffered a sad change. His fairest attribute of Light-bringer, of Apollo, is no longer his own; it has been claimed and appropriated by the "Light of the World," his new master. One by one, his functions have been stripped from him, all save in name, as happens to men and angels alike, when they take service under "jealous" lords.

What is now left of Saint Michael, the glittering hierarch? Can he still endure the light of sun? Or has he not shrivelled into a spectral Hermes, a grisly psychopomp, bowing his head in minished glory, and leading men's souls no longer aloft but downwards—down to the pale regions of things that have been? And will it be long ere he, too, is thrust by some flaming Demogorgon into these same realms of Minos, into that shadowy underworld where dwell Saturn, and Kronos, and other cracked and shivered ideals?

So I mused that afternoon, driving down the slopes from Sant' Angelo comfortably sheltered against the storm, while the generous mountain wine sped through my veins, warming my fancy. Then, at last, the sun came out in a sudden burst of light, opening a rift in the vapours and revealing the whole chain of the Apennines, together with the peaked crater of Mount Vulture.

The spectacle cheered me, and led me to think that such a day might worthily be rounded off by a visit to Sipontum, which lies a few miles beyond Manfredonia on the Foggia road. But I approached the subject cautiously, fearing that the coachman might demur at this extra work. Far from it. I had gained his affection, and he would conduct me whithersoever I liked. Only to Sipontum? Why not to Foggia, to Naples, to the ends of the earth? As for the horse, he was none the worse for the trip, not a bit the worse; he liked nothing better than running in front of a carriage; besides, è suo dovere—it was his duty.

Sipontum is so ancient that it was founded, they say, by that legendary Diomed who acted in the same capacity for Beneventum, Arpi, and other cities. But this record does not satisfy Monsignor Sarnelli, its historian, according to whom it was already a flourishing town when Shem, first son of Noah, became its king. He reigned about the year 1770 of the creation of the world. Two years after the deluge he was 100 years old, and at that age begat a son Arfaxad, after whose birth he lived yet another five hundred years. The second king of Sipontum was Appulus, who ruled in the year 2213. . . . Later on, Saint Peter sojourned here, and baptized a few people.

Of Sipontum nothing is left; nothing save a church, and even that built only yesterday—in the eleventh century; a far-famed church, in the Pisan style, with wrought marble columns reposing on lions, sculptured diamond ornaments, and other crafty stonework that gladdens the eye. It used to be the seat of an archbishopric, and its fine episcopal chairs are now preserved at Sant' Angelo; and you may still do homage to the authentic Byzantine Madonna painted on wood by Saint Luke, brown-complexioned, long-nosed, with staring eyes, and holding the Infant on her left arm. Earthquakes and Saracen incursions ruined the town, which became wholly abandoned when Manfredonia was built with its stones.

Of pagan antiquity there are a few capitals lying about, as well as granite columns in the curious old crypt. A pillar stands all forlorn in a field; and quite close to the church are erected two others—the larger of cipollino, beautified by a patina of golden lichen; a marble well-head, worn half through with usage of ropes, may be found buried in the rank grass. The plain whereon stood the great city of Sipus is covered, now, with bristly herbage. The sea has retired from its old beach, and half-wild cattle browse on the site of those lordly quays and palaces. Not a stone is left. Malaria and desolation reign supreme.

It is a profoundly melancholy spot. Yet I was glad of the brief vision. I shall have fond and enduring memories of that sanctuary—the travertine of its artfully carven fabric glowing orange-tawny in the sunset; of the forsaken plain beyond, full of ghostly phantoms of the past.

As for Manfredonia—it is a sad little place, when the south wind moans and mountains are veiled in mists.

V

LAND OF HORACE

VENOSA, nowadays, lies off the beaten track. There are only three trains a day from the little junction of Rocchetta, and they take over an hour to traverse the thirty odd kilometres of sparsely inhabited land. It is an uphill journey, for Venosa lies at a good elevation. They say that German professors, bent on Horatian studies, occasionally descend from those worn-out old railway carriages; but the ordinary travellers are either peasant-folk or commercial gentlemen from north Italy. Worse than malaria or brigandage, against both of which a man may protect himself, there is no escaping from the companionship of these last-named—these pathologically inquisitive, empty-headed, and altogether dreadful people. They are the terror of the south. And it stands to reason that only the most incapable and most disagreeable of their kind are sent to out-of-the-way places like Venosa.

One asks oneself whether this town has greatly changed since Roman times. To be sure it has; domestic calamities and earthquakes (such as the terrible one of 1456) have altered it beyond recognition. The amphitheatre that seated ten thousand spectators is merged into the earth, and of all the buildings of Roman date nothing is left save a pile of masonry designated as the tomb of the Marcellus who was killed here by Hannibal's soldiery, and a few reticulated walls of the second century or thereabouts know as the "House of Horace"—as genuine as that of Juliet in Verona or the Mansion of Loreto. Yet the tradition is an old one, and the builder of the house, whoever he was, certainly displayed some poetic taste in his selection of a fine view across the valley. There is an indifferent statue of Horace in the marketplace. A previous one, also described as Horace, was found to be the effigy of somebody else. Thus much I learn from Lupoli's "Iter Venusinum."

But there are ancient inscriptions galore, worked into the masonry of buildings or lying about at random. Mommsen has collected numbers of them in his *Corpus*, and since that time some sixty new ones have been discovered. And then—the stone lions of Roman days, couched forlornly at street corners, in courtyards and at fountains, in every stage of decrepitude, with broken jaws and noses, missing legs and tails! Venosa is a veritable infirmary for mutilated antiques of this species. Now the lion is doubtless a nobly decorative beast, but—*toujours perdrix!* Why not a few griffons or other ornaments? The Romans were not an imaginative race.

The country around must have looked different in olden days. Horace describes it as covered with forests, and from a manuscript of the early seventeenth century which has lately been printed one learns that the surrounding regions were full of "hares, rabbits, foxes, roe deer, wild boars, martens, porcupines, hedgehogs, tortoises and wolves"—wood-loving creatures which have now, for the most part, deserted Venosa. Still, there are left some stretches of oak at the back of the town, and the main lines of the land cannot change. Yonder lies the Horatian Forense and "Acherontia's nest"; further on, the glades of Bantia (the modern Banzi); the long-drawn Garganian Mount, on which the poet's eye must often have rested, emerges above the plain of Apulia like an island (and such it is: an island of Austrian stone, stranded upon the beach of Italy). Monte Vulture still dominates the landscape, although at this nearness the crater loses its shapely conical outline and assumes a serrated edge. On its summit I perceive a gigantic cross—one of a number of such symbols which were erected by the clericals at the time of the recent rationalist congress in Rome.

From this chronicler I learn another interesting fact: that Venosa was not malarious in the author's day. He calls it healthy, and says that the only complaint from which the inhabitants suffered was "ponture" (pleurisy). It is now within the infected zone. I dare say the deforestation of the country, which prevented the downflow of the rivers—choking up their beds with detritus and producing stagnant pools favourable to the breeding of the mosquito—has helped to spread the plague in many parts of Italy. In Horace's days Venosa was immune, although Rome and certain rural districts were already malarious. Ancient votive tablets to the fever-goddess Mephitis (malaria) have been found not far from here, in the plain below the present city of Potenza.

A good deal of old Roman blood and spirit seems to survive here. After the noise of the Neapolitan provinces, where chattering takes the place of thinking, it is a relief to find oneself in the company of these grave self-respecting folks, who really converse, like the

Scotch, in disinterested and impersonal fashion. Their attitude towards religious matters strikes me as peculiarly Horatian; it is not active scepticism, but rather a bland tolerance or what one of them described as "indifferentismo"—submission to acts of worship and all other usages (whatever they may be) consecrated by time: the *pietàs*—the conservative, law-abiding Roman spirit. And if you walk towards sunset along any of the roads leading into the country, you will meet the peasants riding home from their field labours accompanied by their dogs, pigs and goats; and among them you will recognize many types of Roman physiognomies—faces of orators and statesmen—familiar from old coins. About a third of the population are of the dark-fair complexion, with blue or green eyes. But the women are not handsome, although the town derives its name from Benoth (Venus). Some genuine Roman families have continued to exist to this day, such as that of Cenna (Cinna). One of them was the author of the chronicle above referred to; and there is an antique bas-relief worked into the walls of the Trinità abbey, depicting some earlier members of this local family.

One is astonished how large a literature has grown up around this small place—but indeed, the number of monographs dealing with every one of these little Italian towns is a ceaseless source of surprise. Look below the surface and you will find, in all of them, an undercurrent of keen spirituality—a nucleus of half a dozen widely read and thoughtful men, who foster the best traditions of the mind. You will not find them in the town council or at the café. No newspapers commend their labours, no millionaires or learned societies come to their assistance, and though typography is cheap in this country, they often stint themselves of the necessities of life in order to produce these treatises of calm research. There is a deep gulf, here, between the mundane and the intellectual life. These men are retiring in their habits; and one cannot but revere their scholarly and almost ascetic spirit that survives like a green oasis amid the desert of "politics," roguery and municipal corruption.

The City Fathers of Venosa are reputed rich beyond the dreams of avarice. Yet their town is by no means a clean place—it is twice as dirty as Lucera: a reposeful dirtiness, not vulgar or chaotic, but testifying to time-honoured neglect, to a feudal contempt of cleanliness. You crawl through narrow, ill-paved streets, looking down into subterranean family bedrooms that must be insufferably damp in winter, and filled, during the hot months, with an odour hard to conceive. There is electric lighting, of course—a paternal government having made the price of petroleum so prohibitive that the use of electricity for street-lighting became quite common in the lowliest places; but the crude glare only serves to show up the general squalor. One reason for this state of affairs is that there are no quarries for decent paving-stones in the neighbourhood. And another, that Venosa possesses no large citizen class, properly so called. The inhabitants are mostly peasant proprietors and field labourers, who leave the town in the morning and return home at night with their beasts, having learned by bitter experience to take up their domiciles in the towns rather than in the country-side, which was infested with brigandage and in an unsettled state up to a short time ago. The Cincinnatus note dominates here, and with an agricultural population no city can be kept clean.

But Venosa has one inestimable advantage over Lucera and most Italian towns: there is no octroi.

Would it be believed that Naples is surrounded by a towering Chinese wall, miles upon miles of it, crowned with a complicated apparatus of alarm-bells and patrolled night and day by a horde of *doganieri* armed to the teeth—lest some peasant should throw a bundle of onions into the sacred precincts of the town without paying the duty of half a farthing? No nation with any sense of humour would endure this sort of thing. Every one resents the airs of this army of official loafers who infest the land, and would be far better employed themselves in planting onions upon the many miles of Italy which now lie fallow; the results of the system have been shown to be inadequate, "but," as my friend the Roman deputy once asked me, "if we dismiss these fellows from their job, how are we to employ them?"

"Nothing is simpler," I replied. "Enrol them into the Town Council of Naples. It already contains more *employés* than all the government offices of London put together; a few more will surely make no difference?"

"By Bacchus," he cried, "you foreigners have ideas! We could dispose of ten of fifteen thousand of them, at least, in the way you suggest. I'll make a note of that, for our next session."

And so he did.

But the *Municipio* of Naples, though extensive, is a purely local charity, and I question whether its inmates will hear of any one save their own cousins and brothers-in-law figuring as colleagues in office.

Every attempt at innovation in agriculture, as in industry, is forthwith discouraged by new and subtle impositions, which lie in wait for the enterprising Italian and punish him for his ideas. There is, of course, a prohibitive duty on every article or implement manufactured abroad; there is the octroi, a relic of mediævalism, the most unscientific, futile, and vexatious of taxes; there are municipal dues to be paid on animals bought and animals sold, on animals kept and animals killed, on milk and vine-props and bricks, on timber for scaffolding and lead and tiles and wine—on every conceivable object which the peasant produces or requires for his existence. And one should see the faces of the municipal *employés* who extort these tributes. God alone knows from what classes of the populace they are recruited; certain it is that their physiognomy reflects their miserable calling. One can endure the militarism of Germany and the bureaucracy of Austria; but it is revolting to see decent Italian country-folk at the mercy of these uncouth savages, veritable cavemen, whose only intelligible expression is one of malice striving to break through a crust of congenital cretinism.

We hear much of the great artists and speculative philosophers of old Italy. The artists of modern Italy are her bureaucrats who design and elaborate the taxes; her philosophers, the peasants who pay them.

In point of method, at least, there is nothing to choose between the exactions of the municipal and governmental ruffians. I once saw an old woman fined fifty francs for having in her possession a pound of sea-salt. By what logic will you make it clear to ignorant people that it is wrong to take salt out of the sea, whence every one takes fish which are more valuable? The waste of time employed over red tape alone on these occasions would lead to a revolution anywhere save among men inured by long abuses to this particular form of tyranny. No wonder the women of the country-side, rather than waste three precious hours in arguments about a few cheeses, will smuggle them past the authorities under the device of being *enceintes;* no wonder their wisest old men regard the paternal government as a successfully organized swindle, which it is the citizen's bounden duty to frustrate whenever possible. Have *you* ever tried to convey—in legal fashion—a bottle of wine from one town into another; or to import, by means of a sailing boat, an old frying-pan into some village by the sea? It is a fine art, only to be learnt by years of apprenticeship. The regulations on these subjects, though ineffably childish, look simple enough on paper; they take no account of that "personal element" which is everything in the south, of the ruffled tempers of these gorgeous but inert creatures who, disturbed in their siestas or mandolin-strummings, may keep you waiting half a day while they fumble ominously over some dirty-looking scrap of paper. For on such occasions they are liable to provoking fits of conscientiousness. This is all very well, my dear sir, but—Ha! Where, where is that certificate of origin, that stamp, that *lascia-passare!*

And all for one single sou!

No wonder even Englishmen discover that law-breaking, in Italy, becomes a necessity, a rule of life.

And, soon enough, much more than a mere necessity. . . .

For even as the traveller new to Borneo, when they offer him a durian-fruit, is instantly brought to vomiting-point by its odour, but after a few mouthfuls declares it to be the very apple of Paradise, and marvels how he could have survived so long in the benighted lands where such ambrosial fare is not; even as the true connaisseur who, beholding some rare scarlet idol from the Tingo-Tango forests, at first casts it aside and then, light dawning as he ponders over those monstrous complexities, begins to realize that they, and they alone, contain the quintessential formulæ of all the fervent dreamings of Scopas and Michelangelo; even as he who first, upon a peak in Darien, gazed awestruck upon the grand Pacific slumbering at his feet, till presently his senses reeled at the blissful prospect of fresh regions unrolling themselves, boundless, past the fulfilment of his fondest hopes——

Even so, in Italy, the domesticated Englishman is amazed to find that he possesses a sense hitherto unrevealed, opening up a new horizon, a new zest in life—the sense of law-breaking. At first, being an honest man, he is shocked at the thought of such a thing; next, like a sensible person, reconciled to the inevitable; lastly, as befits his virile race, he learns to play the game so well that the horrified officials grudgingly admit (and it is their highest praise):

> Inglese italianizzato—
> Diavolo incarnato.

Yes; slowly the charm of law-breaking grows upon the Italianated Saxon; slowly, but surely. There is a neo-barbarism not only in matters of art.

VI

AT VENOSA

THERE has always, no doubt, been a castle at Venosa. Frederick Barbarossa lived here oftener than in Sicily; from these regions he could look over to his beloved East, and the security of this particular keep induced him to store his treasures therein. The indefatigable Huillard Bréholles has excavated some account of them from the Hohenstaufen records. Thus we learn that here, at Venosa, the Emperor deposited that marvel, that *tentorium*, I mean, *mirifica arte constructum, in quo imagines solis et lunæ artificialiter motæ, cursum suum certis et debitis spatiis peragrant, et horas diei et noctis infallibiliter indicant. Cuius tentorii valor viginti millium marcarum pretium dicitur transcendisse.* It was given him by the Sultan of Babylonia. Always the glowing Oriental background!

The present castle, a picturesque block with moat and corner towers, was built in 1470 by the redoubtable Pierro del Balzo. A church used to occupy the site, but the warrior, recognizing its strategic advantages, transplanted the holy edifice to some other part of the town. It is now a ruin, the inhabitable portions of which have been converted into cheap lodgings for sundry poor folk—a monetary speculation of some local magnate, who paid 30,000 francs for the whole structure. You can climb up into one of the shattered towers whereon reposes an old cannon amid a wind-sown garden of shrubs and weeds. Here the jackdaws congregate at nightfall, flying swiftly and noiselessly to their resting-place. Odd, how quiet Italian jackdaws are, compared with those of England; they have discarded their voices, which is the best thing they could have done in a land where every one persecutes them. There is also a dungeon at this castle, an underground recess with cunningly contrived projections in its walls to prevent prisoners from climbing upwards; and other horrors.

The cathedral of Venosa contains a chapel with an unusually fine portal of Renaissance work, but the chief architectural beauty of the town is the decayed Benedictine abbey of La Trinità. The building is roofless; it was never completed, and the ravages of time and of man have not spared it; earthquakes, too, have played sad tricks with its arches and columns, particularly that of 1851, which destroyed the neighbouring town of Melfi. It stands beyond the more modern settlement on what is now a grassy plain, and attached to it is a Norman chapel containing the bones of Alberada, mother of Boemund, and others of her race. Little of the original structure of this church is left, though its walls are still adorned, in patches, with frescoes of genuine angels—attractive creatures, as far removed from those bloodless Byzantine anatomies as from the plethoric and insipid females of the *settecento*. There is also a queenly portrait declared to represent Catherine of Siena. I would prefer to follow those who think it is meant for Sigilgaita.

Small as it is, this place—the church and the abbey—is not one for a casual visit. Lenormant calls the Trinità a *"Musée épigraphique"*—so many are the Latin inscriptions which the monks have worked into its masonry. They have encrusted the walls with them; and many antiquities of other kinds have been deposited here since those days. The ruin is strewn with columns and capitals of fantastic devices; the inevitable lions, too, repose upon its grassy floor, as well as a pagan altar-stone that once adorned the neighbouring amphitheatre. One thinks of the labour expended in raising those prodigious blocks and fitting them together without mortar in their present positions—they, also, came from the amphitheatre, and the sturdy letterings engraved on some of them formed, once upon a time, a sentence that ran round that building, recording the names of its founders.

Besides the Latin inscriptions, there are Hebrew funereal stones of great interest, for a colony of Jews was established here between the years 400 and 800; poor folks, for the most part; no one knows whence they came or whither they went. One is apt to forget that south Italy was swarming with Jews for centuries. The catacombs of Venosa were discovered in 1853. Their entrance lies under a hill-side not far from the modern railway station, and Professor Mueller, a lover of Venosa, has been engaged for the last twenty-five years in writing a ponderous tome on the subject. Unfortunately (so they say) there is not much chance of its ever seeing the light, for just as he is on the verge of publication, some new Jewish catacombs are discovered in another part of the world which cause the Professor to revise all his previous theories. The work must be written anew and brought up to date, and hardly is this accomplished when fresh catacombs are found elsewhere, necessitating a further revision. The Professor once more rewrites the whole. . . . You will find accounts of the Trinità in Bertaux, Schulz and other writers. Italian ones tell us what sounds rather surprising, namely that the abbey was built after a Lombard model, and not a French one. Be that as it may—and they certainly show good grounds for their contention—the ruin is a place of rare charm. Not easily can one see relics of Roman, Hebrew and Norman life crushed into so small a space, welded together by the massive yet fair architecture of the Benedictines, and interpenetrated, at the same time, with a Mephistophelian spirit of modern indifference. Of cynical *insouciance*; for although this is a "national monument," nothing whatever is done in the way of repairs. Never a month passes without some richly carven block of stonework toppling down into the weeds,* and were it not for the zeal of a private citizen, the interior of the building would long ago have become an impassable chaos of stones and shrubbery. The Trinità cannot be *restored* without enormous outlay; nobody dreams of such a thing. A yearly expenditure of ten pounds, however, would go far towards arresting its fall. But where shall the money be found? This enthusiastic nation, so enamoured of all that is exquisite in art, will spend sixty million francs on a new Ministry of Justice which, barely completed, is already showing signs of disrupture; it will cheerfully vote (*vide* daily press) the small item of eighty thousand francs to supply that institution with pens and ink—lucky contractor!—while this and a hundred other buildings of singular beauty are allowed to crumble to pieces, day by day.

Not far from the abbey there stands a church dedicated to Saint Roque. Go within, if you wish to see the difference between Benedictine dignity and the buffoonery which subsequently tainted the catholicism of the youth. On its gable sits a strange emblem: a large stone dog, gazing amiably at the landscape. The saint, during his earthly career, was always accompanied by a dog, and now likes to have him on the roof of his sanctuary.

The Norman church attached to the Trinità lies at a lower level than that building, having been constructed, says Lupoli, on the foundations of a temple to Hymenæus. It may be so; but one dis-

* The process of decay can be seen by comparing my photograph of the east front with that taken to illustrate Giuseppe de Lorenzo's monograph "Venosa e la Regione del Vulture" (Bergamo, 1906).

trusts Lupoli. A remarkable Norman capital, now wrought into a font, is preserved here, and I was interested in watching the behaviour of a procession of female pilgrims in regard to it. Trembling with emotion, they perambulated the sacred stone, kissing every one of its corners; then they dipped their hands into its basin, and kissed them devoutly. An old hag, the mistress of the ceremonies, muttered: "Tutti santi—tutti santi!" at each osculation. Next, they prostrated themselves on the floor and licked the cold stones, and after wallowing there awhile, rose up and began to kiss a small fissure in the masonry of the wall, the old woman whispering, "Santissimo!" A familiar spectacle, no doubt; but one which never fails of its effect. This anti-hygienic crack in the wall, with its suggestions of yoni-worship, attracted me so strongly that I begged a priest to explain to me its mystical signification. But he only said, with a touch of mediæval contempt:

"*Sono femine!*"

He showed me, later on, a round Roman pillar near the entrance of the church worn smooth by the bodies of females who press themselves between it and the wall, in order to become mothers. The notion caused him some amusement—he evidently thought this practice a speciality of Venosa.

In my country, I said, pillars with a contrary effect would be more popular among the fair sex.

Lear gives another account of this phallic emblem. He says that perambulating it hand in hand with another person, the two are sure to remain friends for life.

This is pre-eminently a "Victorian" version.

VII

THE BANDUSIAN FOUNT

THE traveller in these parts is everlastingly half-starved. Here, at Venosa, the wine is good—excellent, in fact; but the food monotonous and insufficient. This improper dieting is responsible for much mischief; it induces a state of chronic exacerbation. Nobody would believe how nobly I struggle, day and night, against its evil suggestions. A man's worst enemy is his own empty stomach. None knew it better than Horace.

And yet he declared that lettuces and such-like stuff sufficed him. No doubt, no doubt. "Olives nourish me." Just so! One does not grow up in the school of Mæcenas without learning the subtle delights of the simple life. But I would wager that after a week of such feeding as I have now undergone at his native place, he would quickly have remembered some urgent business to be transacted in the capital—Cæsar Augustus, methinks, would have desired his company. And even so, I have suddenly woke up to the fact that Taranto, my next resting-place, besides possessing an agreeably warm climate, has some passable restaurants. I will pack without delay. Mount Vulture must wait. The wind alone, the Vulturnus or south-easterly wind, is quite enough to make one despair of climbing hills. It has blown with objectionable persistency ever since my arrival at Venosa.

To escape from its attentions, I have been wandering about the secluded valleys that seam this region. Streamlets meander here amid rustling canes and a luxuriant growth of mares' tails and creepers; their banks are shaded by elms and poplars—Horatian trees; the thickets are loud with songs of nightingale, black-cap and oriole. These humid dells are a different country from the uplands, windswept and thriftily cultivated.

It was here, yesterday, that I came upon an unexpected sight—an army of workmen engaged in burrowing furiously into the bowels of Mother Earth. They told me that this tunnel would presently become one of the arteries of that vast system, the Apulian Aqueduct.

The discovery accorded with my Roman mood, for the conception and execution alike of this grandiose project are worthy of the Romans. Three provinces where, in years of drought, wine is cheaper than water, are being irrigated—in the teeth of great difficulties of engineering and finance. Among other things, there are 213 kilometres of subterranean tunnellings to be built; eleven thousand workmen are employed; the cost is estimated at 125 million francs. The Italian government is erecting to its glory a monument more durable than brass. This is their heritage from the Romans—this talent for dealing with rocks and waters; for bridling a destructive environment and making it subservient to purposes of human intercourse. It is a part of that practical Roman genius for "pacification." Wild nature, to the Latin, ever remains an obstacle to be overcome—an enemy.

Such was Horace's point of view. The fruitful fields and their hardy brood of tillers appealed to him; * the ocean and snowy Alps were beyond the range of his affections. His love of nature was heartfelt, but his nature was not ours; it was nature as we see it in those Roman landscapes at Pompeii; nature ancillary to human needs, in her benignant and comfortable moods. Virgil's *lachrymæ rerum* hints at mystic and extra-human yearnings; to the troubadours nature was conventionally stereotyped—a scenic decoration to set off sentiments more or less sincere; the romanticists wallow in her rugged aspects. Horace never allowed phantasy to outrun intelligence; he kept his feet on earth; man was the measure of his universe, and a sober mind his highest attribute. Nature must be kept "in her place." Her extravagances are not to be admired. This anthropocentric spirit has made him what he is—the ideal anti-sentimentalist and anti-vulgarian. For excess of sentiment, like all other intemperance, is the mark of that unsober and unsteady beast—the crowd.

Things have changed since those days; in proportion as the world has grown narrower and the element of fear and mystery diluted, our sympathies have broadened; the Goth, in particular, has learnt the knack of detecting natural charm where the Latin, to this day, beholds nothing but confusion and strife.

On the spot, I observe, one is liable to return to the antique outlook; to see the beauty of fields and rivers, yet only when subsidiary to man's personal convenience; to appreciate a fair landscape—with

* See next chapter.

a shrewd worldly sense of its potential uses. "The garden that I love," said an Italian once to me, "contains good vegetables." This utilitarian flavour of the south has become very intelligible to me during the last few days. I, too, am thinking less of calceolarias than of cauliflowers.

A pilgrimage to the Bandusian Fount (if such it be) is no great undertaking—a morning's trip. The village of San Gervasio is the next station to Venosa, lying on an eminence only thirteen kilometres from there.

Here once ran a fountain which was known as late as the twelfth century as the Fons Bandusinus, and Ughelli, in his "Italia Sacra," cites a deed of the year 1103 speaking of a church "at the Bandusian Fount near Venosa." Church and fountain have now disappeared; but the site of the former, they say, is known, and close to it there once issued a copious spring called "Fontana Grande." This is probably the Horatian one; and is also, I doubt not, that referred to in Cenna's chronicle of Venosa: "At Torre San Gervasio are the ruins of a castle and an abundant spring of water colder than all the waters of Venosa." *Frigus amabile....*

I could discover no one in the place to show me where this now vanished church stood. I rather think it occupied the site of the present church of Saint Anthony, the oldest in San Gervasio.

As to the fountain—there are now two of them, at some considerable distance from each other. Both of them are copious and both lie near the foot of the hill on which the village now stands. Capmartin de Chaupy has reasons for believing that in former times San Gervasio did not occupy its present exalted position (vol. iii, p. 538).

One of them gushes out on the plain near the railway station, and has been rebuilt within recent times. It goes by the name of "Fontana rotta." The other, the "Fontana del Fico," lies on the high road to Spinazzola; the water spouts out of seven mouths, and near at hand is a plantation of young sycamores. The basin of this fount was also rebuilt about ten years ago at no little expense, and has now a thoroughly modern and business-like aspect. But I was told that a complicated network of subterranean pipes and passages, leading to "God knows where," was unearthed during the process of reconstruction. It was magnificent masonry, said my informant, who was an eye-witness of the excavations but could tell me nothing more of interest.

The problem how far either of these fountains fulfils the conditions postulated in the last verse of Horace's ode may be solved by every one according as he pleases. In fact, there is no other way of solving it. In my professorial mood, I should cite the cavern and the "downward leaping" waters against the hypothesis that the Bandusian Fount stood on either of these modern sites; in favour of it, one might argue that the conventional rhetoric of all Roman art may have added these embellishing touches, and cite, in confirmation thereof, the last two lines of the previous verse, mentioning animals that could hardly have slaked their thirst with any convenience at a cavernous spring such as he describes. Caverns, moreover, are not always near the summits of hills; they may be at the foot of them; and water, even the Thames at London Bridge, always leaps downhill—more or less. Of more importance is old Chaupy's discovery of the northerly aspect of one of these springs—"thee the fierce season of the blazing dog-star cannot touch." There may have been a cave at the back of the "Fontana del Fico"; the "Fontana rotta" is hopelessly uncavernous.

For the rest, there is no reason why the fountain should not have changed its position since ancient days. On the contrary, several things might incline one to think that it has been forced to abandon the high grounds and seek its present lower level. To begin with, the hill on which the village stands is honeycombed by hives of caves which the inhabitants have carved out of the loose conglomerate (which, by the way, hardly corresponds with the poet's *saxum*); and it may well be that a considerable collapse of these earth-dwellings obstructed the original source of the waters and obliged them to seek a vent lower down.

Next, there are the notorious effects of deforestation. An old man told me that in his early days the hill was covered with timber—indeed, this whole land, now a stretch of rolling grassy downs, was decently wooded up to a short time ago. I observed that the roof of the oldest of the three churches, that of Saint Anthony, is formed of wooden rafters (a rare material hereabouts). Deforestation would also cause the waters to issue at a lower level.

Lastly, and chiefly—the possible shatterings of earthquakes. Catastrophes such as those which have damaged Venosa in days past may have played havoc with the water-courses of this place by choking up their old channels. My acquaintance with the habits of Apulian earthquakes, with the science of hydrodynamics and the geological formation of San Gervasio is not sufficiently extensive to allow me to express a mature opinion. I will content myself with presenting to future investigators the plausible theory—plausible because conveniently difficult to refute—that some terrestrial upheaval in past days is responsible for the present state of things.

But these are merely three hypotheses. I proceed to mention three facts which point in the same direction; i.e. that the water used to issue at a higher level. Firstly, there is that significant name "Fontana rotta"—"the broken fountain." . . . Does not this suggest that its flow may have been interrupted, or intercepted, in former times?

Next, if you climb up from this "Fontana rotta" to the village by the footpath, you will observe, on your right hand as you ascend the slope, at about a hundred yards below the Church of Saint Anthony, an old well standing in a field of corn and shaded by three walnuts and an oak. This well is still running, and was described to me as "molto antico." Therefore an underground stream—in diminished volume, no doubt—still descends from the heights.

Thirdly, in the village you will notice an alley leading out of the Corso Manfredi (one rejoices to find the name of Manfred surviving in these lands)—an alley which is entitled "Vico Sirene." The name arrests your attention, for what have the Sirens to do in these inland regions? Nothing whatever, unless they existed as ornamental statuary: statuary such as frequently gives names to streets in Italy, witness the "Street of the Faun" in Ouida's novel, or that of the "Giant" in Naples (which has now been re-christened). It strikes me as a humble but quite scholarly speculation to infer that, the chief decorative uses of Sirens being that of fountain deities, this obscure roadway keeps alive the tradition of the old "Fontana Grande"—ornamented, we may suppose, with marble Sirens—whose site is now forgotten, and whose very name has faded from the memory of the country-folk.

What, then, does my ramble of two hours at San Gervasio amount to? It shows that there is a possibility, at least, of a now vanished fountain having existed on heights where it might fulfil more accurately the conditions of Horace's ode. If Ughelli's church "at the Bandusian Fount" stood on this eminence—well, I shall be glad to corroborate, for once in the way, old Ughelli, whose book contains a deal of dire nonsense. And if the Abbé Chaupy's suggestion that the village lay at the foot of the hill should ever prove to be wrong—well, his amiable ghost may be pleased to think that even this does not necessitate the sacrifice of his Venosa theory in favour of that of the scholiast Akron; there is still a way out of the difficulty.

But whether this at San Gervasio is the actual fountain hymned by Horace—ah, that is quite another affair! Few poets to be sure, have clung more tenaciously to the memories of their childhood than did he and Virgil. And yet, the whole scene may be a figment of his imagination—the very word Bandusia may have been coined by him. Who can tell? Then there is the Digentia hypothesis. I know it, I know it! I have read some of its defenders, and consider (entre nous) that they have made out a pretty strong case. But I am not in the mood for discussing their proposition—not just now.

Here at San Gervasio I prefer to think only of the Roman singer, so sanely jovial, and of these waters as they flowed, limpid and cool, in the days when they fired his boyish fancy. Deliberately I refuse to hear the charmer Boissier. Deliberately, moreover, I shut my eyes to the present condition of affairs; to the herd of squabbling laundresses and those other incongruities that spoil the antique scene. Why not? The timid alone are scared by microscopic discords of time and place. The sage can invest this prosaic water-trough with all its pristine dignity and romance by an unfailing expedient. He closes an eye. It is an art he learns early in life; a simple art, and one that greatly conduces to happiness. The ever alert, the conscientiously wakeful—how many fine things they fail to see! Horace knew the wisdom of being genially unwise; of closing betimes an eye, or an ear; or both. *Desipere in loco. . . .*

VIII

TILLERS OF THE SOIL

I REMEMBER watching an old man stubbornly digging a field by himself. He toiled through the flaming hours, and what he lacked in strength was made up in the craftiness, *malizia*, born of long love of the soil. The ground was baked hard; but there was still a chance of rain, and the peasants were anxious not to miss it. Knowing this kind of labour, I looked on from my vine-wreathed arbour with admiration, but without envy.

I asked whether he had not children to work for him.

"All dead—and health to you!" he replied, shaking his white head dolefully.

And no grandchildren?

"All Americans (emigrants)."

He spoke in dreamy fashion of years long ago when he, too, had travelled, sailing to Africa for corals, to Holland and France; yes, and to England also. But our dockyards and cities had faded from his mind; he remembered only our men.

"*Che bella gioventù—che bella gioventù!*" ("a sturdy brood"), he kept on repeating. "And lately," he added, "America has been discovered." He toiled fourteen hours a day, and he was 83 years old.

Apart from that creature of fiction, the peasant *in fabula* whom we all know, I can find little to admire in this whole class of men, whose talk and dreams are of the things of the soil, and who knows of nothing save the regular interchange of summer and winter with their unvarying tasks and rewards. None save a Cincinnatus or Garibaldi can be ennobled by the spade. In spleenful moments, it seems to me that the most depraved of city-dwellers has flashes of enthusiasm and self-abnegation never experienced by this shifty, retrogressive and ungenerous brood, which lives like the beasts of the field and has learnt all too much of their logic. But they have a beast-virtue hereabouts which compels respect—contentment in adversity. In this point they resemble the Russian peasantry. And yet, who can pity the moujik? His cheeks are altogether too round, and his morals too superbly bestial; he has clearly been created to sing and starve by turns. But the Italian peasant who speaks in the tongue of Homer and Virgil and Boccaccio is easily invested with a halo of martyrdom; it is delightful to sympathize with men who combine the manners of Louis Quatorze with the profiles of Augustus or Plato, and who still recall, in many of their traits, the pristine life of Odyssean days. Thus, they wear to-day the identical "clouted leggings of oxhide, against the scratches of the thorns" which old Laertes bound about his legs on the upland farm in Ithaka. They call them "galandrine."

On occasions of drought or flood there is not a word of complaint. I have known these field-faring men and women for thirty years, and have yet to hear a single one of them grumble at the weather. It is not indifference; it is true philosophy—acquiescence in the inevitable. The grievances of cultivators of lemons and wholesale agriculturalists, whose speculations are often ruined by a single stroke of the human pen in the shape of new regulations or tariffs, are a different thing; *their* curses are loud and long. But the bean-growers, dependent chiefly on wind and weather, only speak of God's will. They have the same forgiveness for the shortcomings of nature as for a wayward child. And no wonder they are distrustful. Ages of oppression and misrule have passed over their heads; sun and rain, with all their caprice, have been kinder friends to them than their earthly masters. Some day, presumably, the government will wake up to the fact that Italy is not an industrial country, and that its farmers might profitably be taken into account again.

But a change is upon the land. Types like this old man are becoming extinct; for the patriarchal system of Coriolanus, the glory of southern Italy, is breaking up.

This is not the fault of conscription which, though it destroys old dialects, beliefs and customs, widens the horizon by bringing fresh ideas into the family, and generally sound ones. It does even more; it teaches the conscripts to read and write, so that it is no longer as dangerous to have dealings with a man who possesses these accomplishments as in the days when they were the prerogative of *avvocati* and other questionable characters. A countryman, nowadays, may read and write and yet be honest.

What is shattering family life is the speculative spirit born of emigration. A continual coming and going; two-thirds of the adolescent and adult male population are at this moment in Argentina or the United States—some as far afield as New Zealand. Men who formerly reckoned in sous now talk of thousands of francs; parental authority over boys is relaxed, and the girls, ever quick to grasp the advantages of money, lose all discipline and steadiness.

"My sons won't touch a spade," said a peasant to me; "and when I thrash them, they complain to the police. They simply gamble and drink, waiting their turn to sail. If I were to tell you the beatings *we* used to get, sir, you wouldn't believe me. You wouldn't believe me, not if I took my oath, you wouldn't! I can feel them still—speaking with respect—here!"

These emigrants generally stay away three or four years at a stretch, and then return, spend their money, and go out again to make more. Others remain for longer periods, coming back with huge incomes—twenty to a hundred francs a day. Such examples produce the same effect as those of the few lucky winners in the State lottery; every one talks of them, and forgets the large number of less fortunate speculators. Meanwhile the land suffers. The carob-tree is an instance. This beautiful and almost eternal growth, the "hope of the southern Apennines" as Professor Savastano calls it, whose pods constitute an important article of commerce and whose thick-clustering leaves yield a cool shelter, comparable to that of a rocky cave, in the noonday heat, used to cover large tracts of south Italy. Indifferent to the scorching rays of the sun, flourishing on the stoniest declivities, and sustaining the soil in a marvellous manner, it was planted wherever nothing else would grow—a distant but sure profit. Nowadays carobs are only cut down. Although their produce rises in value every year, not one is planted; nobody has time to wait for the fruit.*

It is nothing short of a social revolution, depopulating the country of its most laborious elements. 788,000 emigrants left in one year alone (1906); in the province of Basilicata the exodus exceeds the birthrate. I do not know the percentage of those who depart never to return, but it must be considerable; the land is full of chronic grass-widows.

Things will doubtless right themselves in due course; it stands to reason that in this acute transitional stage the demoralizing effects of the new system should be more apparent than its inevitable benefits. Already these are not unseen; houses are springing up round villages, and the emigrants return home with a disrespect for many

---

* There are a few laudable exceptions, such as Prince Belmonte, who has covered large stretches of bad land with this tree. (See Consular Reports, Italy, No. 431.) But he is not a peasant!

of their country's institutions which, under the circumstances, is neither deplorable nor unjustifiable. A large family of boy-children, once a dire calamity, is now the soundest of investments. Soon after their arrival in America they begin sending home rations of money to their parents; the old farm prospers once more, the daughters receive decent dowries. I know farmers who receive over three pounds a month from their sons in America—all under military age.

"We work, yes," they will then tell you, "but we also smoke our pipe."

Previous to this wholesale emigration, things had come to such a pass that the landed proprietor could procure a labourer at a franc a day, out of which he had to feed and clothe himself; it was little short of slavery. The rôles are now reversed, and while landlords are impoverished, the rich emigrant buys up the farms or makes his own terms for work to be done, wages being trebled. A new type of peasant is being evolved, independent of family, fatherland or traditions—with a sure haven of refuge across the water when life at home becomes intolerable.

Yes; a change is at hand.

And another of those things which emigration and the new order of affairs are surely destroying is that ancient anthropomorphic way of looking at nature, with its expressive turns of speech. A small boy, whom I watched gathering figs last year, informed me that the fig-tree was *innamorato delle pietre e cisterne*—enamoured of stones and cisterns; meaning, that its roots are searchingly destructive to masonry and display a fabulous intuition for the proximity of water. He also told me, what was news to me, that there are more than two or three varieties of figs. Will you have his list of them? Here it is:

There is the *fico arnese*, the smallest of all, and the *fico santillo*, both of which are best when dried; the *fico vollombola*,, which is never dried, because it only makes the spring fruit; the *fico molegnano*, which ripens as late as the end of October and must be eaten fresh; the *fico coretorto* ("wry-heart"—from its shape), which has the most leathery skin of all and is often destroyed by grubs after the rain; the *fico troiano*; the *fico arzano*; and the *fico vescovo*, which appears when all the others are over, and is eaten in February (this may be the kind referred to in Stamer's "Dolce Napoli" as deriving from Sorrento, where the first tree of its kind was discovered growing out of the garden wall of the bishop's palace, whence the name).

All these are *neri*—black. Now for the white kinds. The *fico parad-iso* has a tender skin, but is easily spoilt by rain and requires a ridiculous amount of sun to dry it; the *fico vottato* is also better fresh; the *fico pezzottolo* is often attacked by grubs, but grows to a large size every two or three years; the *fico pascarello* is good up till Christmas; the *fico natalino*; lastly, the *fico*——, whose name I will not record, though it would be an admirable illustration of that same anthropomorphic turn of mind. The *santillo* and *arnese*, he added, are the varieties which are cut into two and laid lengthwise upon each other and so dried (Query: Is not this the "duplex ficus" of Horace?).

"Of course there are other kinds," he said, "but I don't remember them just now." When I asked whether he could tell these different fig-trees apart by the leaves and stems alone and without the fruit, he said that each kind, even in winter, retained its peculiar "faccia" (face), but that some varieties are more easy to distinguish than others. I enquired into the mysteries of caprification, and learned that artificial ripening by means of a drop of oil is practised with some of them, chiefly the *santillo*, *vollombola*, *pascarello* and *natalino*. Then he gave me an account of the prices for the different qualities and seasons which would have astonished a grocer.

All of which proves how easy it is to misjudge of folks who, although they do not know that Paris is the capital of France, yet possess a training adapted to their present needs. They are special-ists for things of the grain-giving earth; it is a pleasure to watch them grafting vines and olives and lemons with the precision of a trained horticulturist. They talk of "governing" (*governare*) their soil; it is the word they use in respect to a child.

Now figs are neither white nor black, but such is the terminology. Stones are white or black; prepared olives are white or black; wine is white or black. Are they become colour-blind because impreg-nated, from earliest infancy, with a perennial blaze of rainbow hues—colour-blinded, in fact; or from negligence, attention to this matter not bringing with it any material advantage? Excepting that sign-language which is profoundly interesting from an artistic and ethnological point of view—why does not some scholar bring old Iorio's "Mimica degli Antichi" up to date?—few things are more worthy of investigation than the colour-sense of these people. Of blue they have not the faintest conception, probably because there are so few blue solids in nature; Max Mueller holds the idea of blue to be quite a modern acquisition on the part of the human race. So a cloudless sky is declared to be "quite white." I once asked a lad as to the colour of the sea which, at the moment, was of the most brilliant sapphire hue. He pondered awhile and then said: "Pare come fosse un colore morto" (a sort of dead colour).

Green is as little better known, but still chiefly connected with things not out of doors, as a green handkerchief. The reason may be that this tint is too common in nature to be taken note of. Or perhaps because their chain of association between green and grass is periodically broken up—our fields are always verdant, but theirs turn brown in summer. Trees they sometimes call yellow as do some ancient writers; but more generally "half-black" or "tree-colour." A beech in full leaf has been described to me as black. "*Rosso*" does not mean red, but rather dun or dingy; earth is *rosso*. When our red is to be signified, they will use the word "turco," which came in with the well-known dye-stuff of which the Turks once monoplized the secret. Thus there are "Turkish" apples and "Turkish" potatoes. But "turco" may also mean black—in accordance with the tradition that the Turks, the Saracens, were a black race. Snakes, generally greyish-brown in these parts, are described as either white or black; an eagle-owl is half-black; a kestrel *un quasi bianco*. The mixed colours of cloths or silks are either beautiful or ugly, and there's an end of it. It is curious to compare this state of affairs with that existing in the days of Homer, who was, as it were, feeling his way in a new region, and the propriety of whose colour epithets is better understood when one sees things on the spot. Of course I am only speaking of the humble peasant whose blindness, for the rest, is not incurable.

One might enlarge the argument and deduce his odd insensibility to delicate scents from the fact that he thrives in an atmosphere saturated with violent odours of all kinds; his dullness in regard to finer shades of sound—from the shrieks of squalling babies and other domestic explosions in which he lives from the cradle to the grave. That is why these people have no "nerves"; terrific bursts of din, such as the pandemonium of Piedigrotta, stimulate them in the same way that others might be stimulated by a quartette of Brahms. And if they who are so concerned about the massacre of small birds in this country would devote their energies to the invention of a noiseless and yet cheap powder, their efforts would at last have some prospects of success. For it is not so much the joy of killing, as the pleasurable noise of the gun, which creates these local sportsmen; as the sagacious "Ultramontain" observed long ago. "Le napolitain est passionné pour la chasse," he says "parce que les coups de fusil flattent son oreille."* This ingenuous love of noise may be connected, in some way, with their rapid nervous discharges.

I doubt whether intermediate convulsions have left much purity of Greek blood in south Italy, although emotional travellers, fresh from the north, are for ever discovering "classic Hellenic profiles" among the people. There is certainly a scarce type which, for want of a better hypothesis, might be called Greek: of delicate build and below the average height, small-eared and straight-nosed, with curly hair that varies from blonde to what Italians call *castagno chiaro*. It differs not only from the robuster and yet fairer northern breed, but also from the darker surrounding races. But so many contradictory theories have lately been promulgated on this head, that I prefer to stop short at the preliminary question—did a Hellenic type ever exist? No more, probably, than that charming race which the artists of Japan have invented for our delectation.

Strains of Greek blood can be traced with certainty by their track of folklore and poetry and song, such as still echoes among the vales of Sparta and along the Bosphorus. Greek words are rather rare here, and those that one hears—such as *sciusciello, caruso, crisommele, etc.*—have long ago been garnered by scholars like De Grandis, Moltedo, and Salvatore Mele. So Naples is far more Hellenic in dialect, lore, song and gesture than these regions, which are still rich in pure latinisms of speech, such as surgere (to arise); scitare (excitare—to arouse); è (est—yes); fetare (fœtare); trasete (transitus—passage of quails); titillare (to tickle); craje (cras—to-morrow); pastena (a plantation of young vines; Ulpian has "pastinum instituere"). A woman is called "muliera," a girl "figliola," and children speak of their fathers as "tata" (see Martial, epig. I, 101). Only yesterday I added a beautiful latinism to my collection, when an old woman, in whose cottage I sometimes repose, remarked to me, "Non avete virtù oggi"—you are not *up to the mark* to-day. The real, antique virtue! I ought to have embraced her. No wonder I have no "virtue" just now. This savage Vulturnian wind—did it not sap the Roman virtue at Cannæ?

All those relics of older civilizations are disappearing under the

* I have looked him up in Jos. Blanc's "Bibliographie." His name was C. Haller.

standardizing influence of conscription, emigration and national schooling.

And soon enough the *Contranome*-system will become a thing of the past. I shall be sorry to see it go, though it has often driven me nearly crazy.

What is a *contranome*?

The same as a *sopranome*. It is a nickname which, as with the Russian peasants, takes the place of Christian and surname together. A man will tell you: "My name is Luigi, but they call me, by *contranome*, O'Canzirro. I don't know my surname." Some of these nicknames are intelligible, such as O'Sborramurella, which refers to the man's profession of building those walls without mortar which are always tumbling down and being repaired again; or O'Sciacquariello (acqua—a leaking—one whose money leaks from his pocket—a spendthrift); or San Pietro, from his saintly appearance; O'Civile, who is so uncivilized, or Cristoforo Colombo, because he is so very wideawake. But eighty per cent of them are quite obscure even to their owners, going back, as they do, to some forgotten trick or incident during childhood or to some pet name which even in the beginning meant nothing. Nearly every man and boy has his contranome by which, and *by which alone*, he is known in his village; the women seldomer, unless they are conspicuous by some peculiarity, such as A'Sbirra (the spy), or A'Paponnessa (the fat one)— whose counterpart, in the male sex, would by O'Tripone.

Conceive, now, what trouble it entails to find a man in a strange village if you happen not to know his contranome (and how on earth are you to discover it?), if his surname means nothing to the inhabitants, and his Christian name is shared by a hundred others. For they have an amazing lack of inventiveness in this matter; four or five Christian names will include the whole population of the place. Ten to one you will lose a day looking for him, unless something like this takes place:

THE HAPPY HAZARDS OF THE CONTRANOME

You set forth your business to a crowd of villagers that have collected around. It is simple enough. You want to speak to Luigi So-and-so. A good-natured individual, who seems particularly anxious to help, summarizes affairs by saying:

"The gentleman wants Luigi So-and-so."

There is evidently some joke in the mere suggestion of such a thing; they all smile. Then a confused murmur of voices goes up: "Luigi—Luigi. . . . Now which Luigi does he mean?" You repeat his surname in a loud voice. It produces no effect, beyond that of increased hilarity.

"Luigi—Luigi. . . ."

"Perhaps O'Zoccolone?"

"Perhaps O'Seticchio?"

"Or the figlio d' O'Zibalocchio?"

The good-natured individual volunteers to beat the surrounding district and bring in all the Luigis he can find. After half an hour they begin to arrive, one by one. He is not among them. Dismissed with cigars, as compensation for loss of time.

Meanwhile half the village has gathered around, vastly enjoying the fun, which it hopes will last till bedtime. You are getting bewildered; new people flock in from the fields to whom the mysterious joke about Luigi must be explained.

"Luigi—Luigi," they begin again. "Now, which of them can he mean?"

"Perhaps O'Marzariello?"

"Or O'Cuccolillo?"

"I never thought of him," says the good-natured individual. "Here, boy, run and tell O'Cuccolillo that a foreign gentleman wants to give him a cigar."

By the time O'Cuccolillo appears on the scene the crowd has thickened. You explain the business for the fiftieth time; no—he is Luigi, of course, but not the right Luigi, which he regrets considerably. Then the joke is made clear to him, and he laughs again. You have lost all your nerve, but the villagers are beginning to love you.

"Can it be O'Sciabecchino?"

"Or the figlio d' O'Chiappino?"

"It might be O'Busciardiello (the liar)."

"He's dead."

"So he is. I quite forgot. Well, then it must be the husband of A'Cicivetta (the flirt)."

"He's in prison. But how about O'Caccianfierno?"

Suddenly a withered hag croaks authoritatively:

"I know! The gentleman wants O'Tentillo."

Chorus of villagers:

"Then why doesn't he say so?"

O'Tentillo lives far, far away. An hour elapses; at last he comes, full of bright expectations. No, this is not your Luigi, he is another

Luigi. You are ready to sink into the earth, but there is no escape. The crowd surges all around, the news having evidently spread to neighbouring hamlets.

"Luigi—Luigi. . . . Let me see. It might be O'Rappo."

"O'Massassillo, more likely."

"I have it! It's O'Spennatiello."

"I never thought of him," says a well-known voice. "Here, boy, run and tell——"

"Or O'Cicereniello."

"O'Vergeniello."

"O'Sciabolone. . . ."

"Never mind the G—— d—— son of b——," says a cheery person in excellent English, who has just arrived on the scene. "See here, I live fifteen years in Brooklyn; damn fine! 'Ave a glass of wine round my place. Your Luigi's in America, sure. And if he isn't, send him to Hell."

Sound advice, this.

"What's his surname, anyhow?" he goes on.

You explain once more.

"Why, there's the very man you're looking for. There standing right in front of you! He's Luigi, and that's his surname right enough. He don't know it himself, you bet."

And he points to the good-natured individual. . . .

These countryfolk can fare on strange meats. A boy consumed a snake that was lying dead by the roadside; a woman ate thirty raw eggs and then a plate of maccheroni; a man swallowed six kilograms of the uncooked fat of a freshly slaughtered pig (he was ill for a week afterwards); another one devoured two small birds alive, with beaks, claws and feathers. Such deeds are sternly reprobated as savagery; still, they occur, and nearly always as the result of wagers. I wish I could couple them with equally heroic achievements in the drinking line, but, alas! I have only heard of one old man who was wont habitually to engulph twenty-two litres of wine a day; eight are spoken of as "almost too much" in these degenerate days. . . .

Mice, says Movers, were sacrifically eaten by Babylonians. Here, as in England, they are cooked into a paste and given to children, to cure a certain complaint. To take away the dread of the sea from young boys, they mix into their food small fishes which have been devoured by larger ones and taken from their stomachs—the underlying idea being that these half-digested fry are thoroughly familiar with the storms and perils of the deep, and will communicate these virtues to the boys who eat them. It is the same principle as that of giving chamois blood to the goat-boys of the Alps, to strengthen their nerves against giddiness—pure sympathetic magic, of which there is this, at least, to be said, that "its fundamental conception is identical with that of modern science—a faith in the order or uniformity of nature."

I have also met persons who claim to have been cured of rachitic troubles in their youth by eating a puppy dog cooked in a saucepan. But only one kind of dog is good for this purpose, to be procured from those foundling hospitals whither hundreds of illegitimate infants are taken as soon as possible after birth. The mothers, to relieve the discomfort caused by this forcible separation from the newborn, buy a certain kind of puppy there, bring them home, and nourish them *in loco infantis*. These puppies cost a franc apiece, and are generally destroyed after performing their duties; it is they who are cooked for curing the scrofulous tendencies of other children. Swallows' hearts are also used for another purpose; so is the blood of tortoises—for strengthening the backs of children (the tortoise being a *hard* animal). So is that of snakes, who are held up by head and tail and pricked with needles; the greater their pain, the more beneficial their blood, which is soaked up with cotton-wool and applied as a liniment for swollen glands. In fact, nearly every animal has been discovered to possess some medicinal property.

But of the charm of such creatures the people know nothing. How different from the days of old! These legendary and gracious beasts, that inspired poets and artists and glyptic engravers—these things of beauty have now descended into the realm of mere usefulness, into the pharmacopœia.

The debasement is quite intelligible, when one remembers what accumulated miseries these provinces have undergone. Memories of refinement were starved out of the inhabitants by centuries of misrule, when nothing was of interest or of value save what helped to fill the belly. The work of bestialization was carried on by the despotism of Spanish Viceroys and Bourbons. They, the Spaniards, fostered and perhaps imported the Camorra, that monster of many heads which has established itself in nearly every town of the south. Of the deterioration in taste coincident with this period, I lately came across this little bit of evidence, curious and conclusive:—In 1558 a number of the countryfolk were captured in one of the usual Corsair raids; they were afterwards ransomed, and among the Christian names of the women I note: Livia, Fiula, Cassandra, Aurelia, Lucrezia, Verginia, Medea, Violanta, Galizia, Vittoria, Diamanta, etc. Where were these full-sounding noble names two centuries later—where are they nowadays? Do they not testify to a state of culture superior to that of the present time, when Maria, Lucia, and about four others of the most obvious catholic saints exhaust the list of all female Christian names hereabouts?

All this is changing once more; a higher standard of comfort is being evolved, though relics of this former state of insecurity may still be found; such as the absence, even in houses of good families, of clocks and watches, and convenient storage for clothes and domestic utensils; their habits of living in penury and of buying their daily food by farthings, as though one never knew what the next day might bring; their dread of going out of doors by night (they have a proverb which runs, *di notte, non parlar forte; di giorno, guardati attorno*), their lack of humour. For humour is essentially a product of ease, and nobody can be at ease in unquiet times. That is why so few poets are humorous; their restlessly querulous nature has the same effect on their outlook as an insecure environment.

But it will be long ere these superstitions are eradicated. The magic of south Italy deserves to be well studied, for the country is a cauldron of demonology wherein Oriental beliefs—imported direct from Egypt, the classic home of witchcraft—commingled with those of the West. A foreigner is at an unfortunate disadvantage; if he asks questions, he will only get answers dictated by suspicion or a deliberate desire to mislead—prudent answers; whoso accepts these explanations in good faith, might produce a wondrous contribution to ethnology.

Wise women and wizards abound, but they are not to be compared with that *santa* near Naples whom I used to visit in the nineties, and who was so successful in the magics that the Bishop of Pozzuoli, among hundreds of other clients, was wont to drive up to her door once a week for a consultation. These mostly occupy themselves with the manufacture of charms for gaining lucky lottery numbers, and for deluding fond women who wish to change their lovers.

The lore of herbs is not much studied. For bruises, a slice of the Opuntia is applied, or the cooling parietaria (known as "pareta" or "paretone"); the camomile and other common remedies are in vogue; the virtues of the male fern, the rue, sabina and (home-made) ergot of rye are well known but not employed to the extent they are in Russia, where a large progeny is a disaster. There is a certain respect for the legitimate unborn, and even in cases of illegitimacy some neighbouring foundling hospital, the house of the Madonna, is much more convenient. It is a true monk's expedient; it avoids the risk of criminal prosecution; the only difference being that the Mother of God, and not the natural mother of the infant, becomes responsible for its prompt and almost inevitable destruction. *

That the moon stands in sympathetic relations with living vegetation is a fixed article of faith among the peasantry. They will prune their plants only when the satellite is waxing—*al sottile della luna*, as they say. Altogether, the moon plays a considerable part in their lore, as might be expected in a country where she used to be worshipped under so many forms. The dusky markings on her surface are explained by saying that the moon used to be a woman and a baker of bread, her face gleaming with the reflection of the oven, but one day she annoyed her mother, who took up the brush they use for sweeping away the ashes, and smirched her face. . . .

Whoever reviews the religious observances of these people as a whole will find them a jumble of contradictions and incongruities, lightly held and as lightly dismissed. Theirs is the attitude of mind of little children—of those, I mean, who have been so saturated with Bible stories and fairy tales that they cease to care whether a thing be true or false, if it only amuses for the moment. That is what makes them an ideal prey for the quack physician. They will believe anything so long as it is strange and complicated; a straightforward doctor is not listened to; they want that mystery-making "priest-physician" concerning whom a French writer—I forget his name—has wisely discoursed. I once recommended a young woman who was bleeding at the nose to try the homely remedy of a cold key. I thought she would have died of laughing! The expedient was too absurdly simple to be efficacious.

* The scandals that occasionally arise in connection with that saintly institution, the Foundling Hospital at Naples, are enough to make humanity shudder. Of 856 children living under its motherly care during 1895, 853 "died" in the course of that one year—only three survived; a wholesale massacre. These 853 murdered children were carried forward in the books as still living, and the institution, which has a yearly revenue of over 600,000 francs, was debited with their maintenance, while 42 doctors (instead of the prescribed number of 19) continued to draw salaries for their services to these innocents that had meanwhile been starved and tortured to death. The official report on these horrors ends with the words: "There is no reason to think that these facts are peculiar to the year 1895."

The attitude of the clergy in regard to popular superstitions is the same here as elsewhere. They are too wise to believe them, and too shrewd to discourage the belief in others; these things can be turned to account for keeping the people at a conveniently low level of intelligence. For the rest, these priests are mostly good fellows of the live-and-let-live type, who would rather cultivate their own potatoes than quarrel about vestments or the Trinity. Violently acquisitive, of course, like most southerners. I know a parish priest, a son of poor parents, who by dint of sheer energy, has amassed a fortune of half a million francs. He cannot endure idleness in any shape, and a fine mediæval scene may be witnessed when he suddenly appears round the corner and catches his workmen wasting their time and his money—

"Ha, loafers, rogues, villains, vermin and sons of *bastardi cornuti!* If God had not given me these garments and thereby closed my lips to all evil-speaking (seizing his cassock and displaying half a yard of purple stocking)—wouldn't I just tell you, spawn of adulterous assassins, what I think of you!"

But under the new regime these priests are becoming mere decorative survivals, that look well enough in the landscape, but are not taken seriously save in their match-making and money-lending capacities.

The intense realism of their religion is what still keeps it alive for the poor in spirit. Their saints and devils are on the same familiar footing towards mankind as were the old gods of Greece. Children do not know the meaning of "Inferno"; they call it "casa del diavolo" (the devil's house); and if they are naughty, the mother says, "La Madonna strilla"—the Madonna will scold. Here is a legend of Saint Peter, interesting for its realism and because it has been grafted upon a very ancient *motif:*—

The apostle Peter was a dissatisfied sort of man, who was always grumbling about things in general and suggesting improvements in the world-scheme. He thought himself cleverer even than "N. S. G. C." One day they were walking together in an olive orchard, and Peter said:

"Just look at the trouble and time it takes to collect all those miserable little olives. Let's have them the size of melons."

"Very well. Have your way, friend Peter! But something awkward is bound to happen. It always does, you know, with those improvements of yours." And, sure enough, one of these enormous olives fell from the tree straight on the saint's head and ruined his new hat.

"I told you so," said N. S. G. C.

I remember a woman explaining to me that the saints in Heaven took their food exactly as we do, and at the same hours. "The same food?" I asked. "Does the Madonna really eat beans?" "Beans? Not likely! But fried fish, and beefsteaks of veal."

I tried to picture the scene, but the effort was too much for my hereditary Puritan leanings. Unable to rise to these heights of realism, I was rated a pagan for my ill-timed spirituality.

Madame est servie. . . .

IX

MOVING SOUTHWARDS

THE train conveying me to Taranto was to halt for the night at the second station beyond Venosa—at Spinazzola. Aware of this fact, I had enquired about the place and received assuring reports as to its hotel accommodation. But the fates were against me. On my arrival in the late evening I learnt that the hotels were all closed long ago, the townsfolk having gone to bed "with the chickens"; it was suggested that I had better stay at the station, where the manageress of the restaurant kept certain sleeping quarters specially provided for travellers in my predicament.

Presently the gentle dame lighted a dim lantern and led me across what seemed to be a marsh (it was raining) to the door of a hut which was to be my resting-place. At the entrance she paused, and after informing me that a band of musicians had taken all the beds save one which was at my disposal if I were good enough to pay her half a franc, she placed the lantern in my hand and stumbled back into the darkness.

I stepped into a low chamber, the beds of which were smothered under a profusion of miscellaneous wraps. The air was warm—the place exhaled an indescribable *esprit de corps.* Groping further, I reached another apartment, vaulted and still lower than the last, an old-fashioned cow-stable, possibly, converted into a bedroom. One glance sufficed me: the couch was plainly not to be trusted. Thankful to be out of the rain at least, I lit a pipe and prepared to pass the weary hours till 4 a.m.

It was not long ere I discovered that there was another bed in this den, opposite my own; and judging by certain undulatory and saltatory movements within, it was occupied. Presently the head of a youth emerged, with closed eyes and flushed features. He indulged in a series of groans and spasmodic kicks, that subsided once more, only to recommence. A flute projected from under his pillow.

"This poor young man," I thought, "is plainly in bad case. On account of illness, he has been left behind by the rest of the band, who have gone to Spinazzola to play at some marriage festival. He is feverish, or possibly subject to fits—to choriasis or who knows what disorder of the nervous system. A cruel trick, to leave a suffering youngster alone in this foul hovel." I misliked his symptoms—that anguished complexion and delirious intermittent trembling, and began to run over the scanty stock of household remedies contained in my bag, wondering which of them might apply to his complaint. There was court plaster and boot polish, quinine, corrosive sublimate and Worcester sauce (detestable stuff, but indispensable hereabouts).

Just as I had decided in favour of the last-named, he gave a more than usually vigorous jerk, sat up in bed and, opening his eyes, remarked:

"Those fleas!"

This, then, was the malady. I enquired why he had not joined his companions.

He was tired, he said; tired of life in general, and of flute-playing in particular. Tired, moreover, of certain animals; and with a tiger-like spring he leapt out of bed.

Once thoroughly awake, he proved an amiable talker, though oppressed with an incurable melancholy which no amount of tobacco and Venosa wine could dispel. In gravely boyish fashion he told me of his life and ambitions. He had passed a high standard at school, but—what would you?—every post was crowded. He liked music, and would gladly take it up as a profession, if anything could be learnt with a band such as his; he was sick, utterly sick, of everything. Above all things, he wished to travel. Visions of America floated before his mind—where was the money to come from? Besides, there was the military service looming close at hand; and then, a widowed mother at home—the inevitable mother—with a couple of little sisters; how shall a man desert his family? He was born on a farm on the Murge, the watershed between this country and the Adriatic. Thinking of the Murge, that shapeless and dismal range of limestone hills whose name suggests its sad monotony, I began to understand the origin of his pagan wistfulness.

"Happy foreigners!"—such was his constant refrain—"happy foreigners, who can always do exactly what they like! Tell me something about other countries," he said.

"Something true?"

"Anything—anything!"

To cheer him up, I replied with improbable tales of Indian life, of

rajahs and diamonds, of panthers whose eyes shine like moonbeams
in the dark jungle, of elephants huge as battleships, of sportive mon-
keys who tie knots in each others' tails and build themselves huts
among the trees, where they brew iced lemonade, which they offer
in friendliest fashion to the thirsty wayfarer, together with other
light refreshment——

"Cigarettes as well?"

"No. They are not allowed to cultivate tobacco."

"Ah, that *monopolio*, the curse of humanity!"

He was almost smiling when, at 2.30 a.m., there resounded a
furious knocking at the door, and the rest of the band appeared from
their unknown quarters in the liveliest of spirits. Altogether, a memorable night. But at four o'clock the lantern was extinguished and
the cavern, bereft of its Salvator-Rosa glamour, resolved itself into a
prosaic and infernally unclean hovel. Issuing from the door, I saw
those murky recesses invaded by the uncompromising light of dawn,
and shuddered. . . .

The railway journey soon dispelled the phantoms of the night. As
the train sped downhill, the sun rose in splendour behind the Murge
hills, devouring mists so thickly couched that, struck by the first
beams, they glistered like compact snow-fields, while their shaded
portions might have been mistaken for stretches of mysterious
swamp, from which an occasional clump of tree-tops emerged, black
and island-like. These dreamland effects lasted but a brief time, and
soon the whole face of the landscape was revealed. An arid region,
not unlike certain parts of northern Africa.

Yet the line passes through places renowned in history. Who
would not like to spend a day at Altamura, if only in memory of its
treatment by the ferocious Cardinal Ruffo and his army of cut-
throats? After a heroic but vain resistance comparable only to that
of Saguntum or Petelia, during which every available metal, and
even money, was converted into bullets to repel the assailers, there
followed a three days' slaughter of young and old; then the cardinal
blessed his army and pronounced, in the blood-drenched streets, a
general absolution. Even this man has discovered apologists. No
cause so vile, that some human being will not be found to defend it.

So much I called to mind that morning from the pages of Colletta,
and straightway formed a resolution to slip out of the carriage and
arrest my journey at Altamura for a couple of days. But I must have
been asleep while the train passed through the station, nor did I
wake up again till the blue Ionian was in sight.

At Venosa one thinks of Roman legionaries fleeing from Hannibal, of Horace, of Norman ambitions; Lucera and Manfredonia call up Saracen memories and the ephemeral gleams of Hohenstaufen; Gargano takes us back into Byzantine mysticism and monkery. And now from Altamura with its dark record of Bourbon horrors, we glide into the sunshine of Hellenic days when the wise Archytas, sage and lawgiver, friend of Plato, ruled this ancient city of Tarentum. A wide sweep of history! And if those Periclean times be not remote enough, yonder lies Oria on its hilltop, the stronghold of pre-Hellenic and almost legendary Messapians; while for such as desire more recent associations there is the Albanian colony of San Giorgio, only a few miles distant, to recall the glories of Scanderbeg and his adventurous bands.

Herein lies the charm of travel in this land of multiple civilizations—the ever-changing layers of culture one encounters, their wondrous juxtaposition.

My previous experience of Taranto hotels counselled me to take a private room overlooking the inland sea (the southern aspect is already intolerably hot), and to seek my meals at restaurants. And in such a one I have lived for the last ten days or so, reviving old memories. The place has grown in the interval; indeed, if one may believe certain persons, the population has increased from thirty to ninety thousand in—I forget how few years. The arsenal brings movement into the town; it has appropriated the lion's share of building sites in the "new" town. Is it a ripple on the surface of things, or will it truly stir the spirits of the city? So many arsenals have come and gone, at Taranto!

This arsenal quarter is a fine example of the Italian mania of *fare figura*—everything for effect. It is an agglomeration of dreary streets, haunted by legions of clamorous black swifts, and constructed on the rectangular principle dear to the Latin mind. Modern, and surpassingly monotonous. Are such interminable rows of stuccoed barracks artistic to look upon, are they really pleasant to inhabit? Is it reasonable or even sanitary, in a climate of eight months' sunshine, to build these enormous roadways and squares filled with glaring limestone dust that blows into one's eyes and almost suffocates one; these Saharas that even at the present season of the year (early June) cannot be traversed comfortably unless one wears brown spectacles and goes veiled like a Tuareg? This arsenal quarter must be a hell during the really hot season, which continues into October.

For no trees whatever are planted to shade the walking population, as in Paris or Cairo or any other sunlit city.

And who could guess the reason? An Englishman, at least, would never bring himself to believe what is nevertheless a fact, namely, that if the streets are converted into shady boulevards, the rents of the houses immediately fall. When trees are planted, the lodgers complain and finally emigrate to other quarters; the experiment has been tried, at Naples and elsewhere, and always with the same result. Up trees, down rents. The tenants refuse to be deprived of their chief pleasure in life—that of gazing at the street-passengers, who must be good enough to walk in the sunshine for their delectation. But if you are of an inquisitive turn of mind, you are quite at liberty to return the compliment and to study from the outside the most intimate details of the tenants' lives within. Take your fill of their domestic doings; stare your hardest. They don't mind in the least, not they! That feeling of privacy which the northerner fosters doggedly even in the centre of a teeming city is alien to their hearts; they like to look and be looked at; they live like fish in an aquarium. It is a result of the whole palazzo-system that every one knows his neighbour's business better than his own. What does it matter, in the end? Are we not all "Christians"?

The municipality, meanwhile, is deeply indebted for the sky-piercing ambitions which have culminated in the building of this new quarter. To meet these obligations, the octroi prices have been raised to the highest pitch by the City Fathers. This octroi is farmed out and produces (they tell me) £120 a day; there are some hundred toll-collecting posts at the outskirts of the town, and the average salary of their officials is three pounds a month. They are supposed to be respectable and honest men, but it is difficult to see how a family can be supported on that wage, when one knows how high the rents are, and how severely the most ordinary commodities of life are taxed.

I endeavoured to obtain photographs of the land as it looked ere it was covered by the arsenal quarter, but in vain. Nobody seems to have thought it worth while preserving what would surely be a notable economic document for future generations. Out of sheer curiosity I also tried to procure a plan of the old quarter, that labyrinth of thick-clustering humanity, where the streets are often so narrow that two persons can barely squeeze past each other. I was informed that no such plan had ever been drawn up; it was agreed that a map of this kind might be interesting, and suggested, furthermore, that I might undertake the task myself; the authorities would doubtless appreciate my labours. We foreigners, be it understood, have ample means and unlimited leisure, and like nothing better than doing unprofitable jobs of this kind. *

One is glad to leave the scintillating desert of this arsenal quarter, and enter the cool stone-paved streets of the other, which remind one somewhat of Malta. In the days of Salis-Marschlins this city possessed only 18,000 inhabitants, and "out-did even the customary Italian filth, being hardly passable on account of the excessive nastiness and stink." It is now scrupulously clean—so absurdly clean, that it has quite ceased to be picturesque. Not that its buildings are particularly attractive to me; none, that is, save the antique "Trinità" column of Doric gravity—sole survivor of Hellenic Taras, which looks wondrously out of place in its modern environment. One of the finest of these earlier monuments, the Orsini tower depicted in old prints of the place, has now been demolished.

Lovers of the baroque may visit the shrine of Saint Cataldo, a jovial nightmare in stone. And they who desire a literary pendant to this fantastic structure should read the life of the saint written by Morone in 1642. Like the shrine, it is the quintessence of insipid exuberance; there is something preposterous in its very title "Cataldiados," and whoever reads through those six books of Latin hexameters will arise from the perusal half-dazed. Somehow or other, it dislocates one's whole sense of terrestrial values to see a frowsy old monk† treated in the heroic style and metre, as though he were a new Achilles. As a *jeu d'esprit* the book might pass; but it is deadly serious. Single men will always be found to perpetrate monstrosities of literature; the marvel is that an entire generation of writers should have worked themselves into a state of mind which solemnly approved of such freaks.

Every one has heard of the strange position of this hoary island-citadel (a metropolis, already, in neolithic days). It is of oval shape, the broad sides washed by the Ionian Sea and an oyster-producing lagoon; bridges connect it at one extremity with the arsenal or new

---

* There is a map of old Taranto in Lasor a Varea (Savonarola) *Universus terrarum etc.*, Vol. II, p. 552, and another in J. Blaev's *Theatrum Civitatum* (1663). He talks of the "rude houses" of this town.
† This wandering Irish missionary is supposed to have died here in the seventh century, and they who are not satisfied with his printed biographies will find one in manuscript of 550 pages, compiled in 1766, in the Cuomo Library at Naples.

town, and at the other with the so-called commercial quarter. It is as if some precious gem were set, in a ring, between two others of minor worth. Or, to vary the simile, this acropolis, with its close-packed alleys, is the throbbing heart of Taranto; the arsenal quarter—its head; and that other one—well, its stomach; quite an insignificant stomach as compared with the head and corroborative, in so far, of the views of Metchnikoff, who holds that this hitherto commendable organ ought now to be reduced in size, if not abolished altogether. . . .

From out of this window I gaze upon the purple lagoon flecked with warships and sailing-boats; and beyond it, upon the venerable land of Japygia, the heel of Italy, that rises in heliotrope-tinted undulations toward the Adriatic watershed. At night-time an exquisite perfume of flowers and ripe corn comes wafted into my room over the still waters, and when the sun rises, white settlements begin to sparkle among its olives and vineyards. My eyes often rest upon one of them; it is Grottaglie, distant a few miles from Taranto on the Brindisi line. I must visit Grottaglie, for it was here that the flying monk received his education.

The flying monk!

The theme is not inappropriate at this moment, when the newspapers are ringing with the Paris-Rome aviation contest and the achievements of Beaumont, Garros and their colleagues. I have purposely brought his biography with me, to re-peruse on the spot. But let me first explain how I became acquainted with this seventeenth-century pioneer of aviation.

It was an odd coincidence.

I had arrived in Naples, and was anxious to have news of the proceedings at a certain aviation meeting in the north, where a rather inexperienced friend of mine had insisted upon taking a part; the newspaper reports of these entertainments are enough to disturb anybody. While admiring the great achievements of modern science in this direction, I wished devoutly, at that particular moment, that flying had never been invented; and it was something of a coincidence, I say, that stumbling in this frame of mind down one of the unspeakable little side-streets in the neighbourhood of the University, my glance should have fallen upon an eighteenth-century engraving in a bookseller's window which depicted a man raised above the ground without any visible means of support—flying, in short. He was a monk, floating before an altar. A companion, near at hand, was portrayed as gazing in rapturous wonder at this feat of levitation. I stepped within and demanded the volume to which this was the frontispiece.

The salesman, a hungry-looking old fellow with incredibly dirty hands and face, began to explain.

"The Flying Monk, sir, Joseph of Copertino. A mighty saint and conjuror! Or perhaps you would like some other book? I have many, many lives of *santi* here. Look at this one of the great Egidio, for instance. I can tell you all about him, for he raised my mother's grand-uncle from the dead; yes, out of the grave, as one may say. You'll find out all about it in this book; and it's only one of his thousand miracles. And here is the biography of the renowned Giangiuseppe, a mighty saint and——"

I was paying little heed; the flying monk had enthralled me. An unsuspected pioneer of aviation . . . here was a discovery!

"He flew?" I queried, my mind reverting to the much-vaunted triumphs of modern science.

"Why not? The only reason why people don't fly like that nowadays is because—well, sir, because they can't. They fly with machines, and think it something quite new and wonderful. And yet it's as old as the hills! There was Iscariot, for example—Icarus, I mean——"

"Pure legend, my good man."

"Everything becomes legend, if the gentleman will have the goodness to wait. And here is the biography of——"

"How much for Joseph of Copertino?" Cost what it may, I said to myself, that volume must be mine.

He took it up and began to turn over the pages lovingly, as though handling some priceless Book of Hours.

"A fine engraving," he observed, *sotto voce*. "And this is the best of many biographies of the flying monk. It is by Rossi, the Minister-General of the Franciscan order to which our monk belonged; the official biography, it might be called—dedicated, by permission, to His Holiness Pope Clemens XIII, and based on the documents which led to the saint's beatification. Altogether, a remarkable volume—"

And he paused awhile. Then continued:

"I possess a cheaper biography of him, also with a frontispiece, by Montanari, which has the questionable advantage of being printed as recently as 1853. And here is yet another one, by Antonio Basile— oh, he has been much written about; a most celebrated *taumaturga* (wonder-worker)! As to this *Life* of 1767, I could not, with a good conscience, appraise it at less than five francs."

"I respect your feelings. But—five francs! I have certain scruples of my own, you know, and it irks my sense of rectitude to pay five francs for the flying monk unless you can supply me with six or seven additional books to be included in that sum. Twelve *soldi* (sous) apiece—that strikes me as the proper price of such literature, for foreigners, at least. Therefore I'll have the great Egidio as well, and Montanari's life of the flying monk, and that other one by Basile, and Giangiuseppe, and——"

"By all means! Pray take your choice."

And so it came about that, relieved of a tenuous and very sticky five-franc note, and loaded down with three biographies of the flying monk, one of Egidio, two of Giangiuseppe—I had been hopelessly swindled, but there! no man can bargain in a hurry, and my eagerness to learn something of the life of this early airman had made me oblivious of the natural values of things—and with sundry smaller volumes of similar import bulging out of my pockets I turned in the direction of the hotel, promising myself some new if not exactly light reading.

But hardly had I proceeded twenty paces before the shopkeeper came running after me with another formidable bundle under his arm. More books! An ominous symptom—the clearest demonstration of my defeat; I was already a marked man, a good customer. It was humiliating, after my long years' experience of the south.

And there resounded an unmistakable note of triumph in his voice, as he said:

"Some more biographies, sir. Read them at your leisure, and pay me what you like. You cannot help being generous; I see it in your face."

"I always try to encourage polite learning, if that is what you think to decipher in my features. But it rains *santi* this morning," I added, rather sourly.

"The gentleman is pleased to joke! May it rain *soldi* tomorrow."

"A little shower, possibly. But not a cloud-burst, like today. . . ."

X

THE FLYING MONK

AS to the flying monk, there is no doubt whatever that he deserved his name.

He flew. Being a monk, these feats of his were naturally confined to convents and their immediate surroundings, but that does not alter the facts of the case.

Of the flights that he took in the little town of Copertino alone, more than seventy, says Father Rossi whom I follow throughout, are on record in the depositions which were taken on oath from eyewitnesses after his death. This is one of them, for example:

"Stupendous likewise was the *ratto* (flight or rapture) which he exhibited on a night of Holy Thursday.... He suddenly flew towards the altar in a straight line, leaving untouched all the ornaments of that structure; and after some time, being called back by his superior, returned flying to the spot whence he had set out."

And another:

"He flew similarly upon an olive tree ... and there remained in kneeling posture for the space of half an hour. A marvellous thing it was to see the branch which sustained him swaying lightly, as though a bird had alighted upon it."

But Copertino is a remote little place, already famous in the annals of miraculous occurrences. It can be urged that a kind of enthusiasm for their distinguished brother-monk may have tempted the inmates of the convent to exaggerate his rare gifts. Nothing of the kind. He performed flights not only in Copertino, but in various large towns of Italy, such as Naples, Rome, and Assisi. And the spectators were by no means an assemblage of ignorant personages, but men whose rank and credibility would have weight in any section of society.

"While the Lord High Admiral of Castille, Ambassador of Spain at the Vatican, was passing through Assisi in the year 1645, the custodian of the convent commanded Joseph to descend from the room into the church, where the Admiral's lady was waiting for him, desirous of seeing him and speaking to him; to whom Joseph replied, 'I will obey, but I do not know whether I shall be able to speak to her.' And, as a matter of fact, hardly had he entered the church and raised his eyes to a statue . . . situated above the altar, when he threw himself into a flight in order to embrace its feet at a distance of twelve paces, passing over the heads of all the congregation; then, after remaining there some time, he flew back over them with his usual cry, and immediately returned to his cell. The Admiral was amazed, his wife fainted away, and all the onlookers became piously terrified."

And if this does not suffice to win credence, the following will assuredly do so:

"And since it was God's wish to render him marvellous even in the sight of men of the highest sphere, He ordained that Joseph, having arrived in Rome, should be conducted one day by the Father-General (of the Franciscan Order) to kiss the feet of the High Pontiff, Urban the Eighth; in which act, while contemplating Jesus Christ in the person of His Vicar, he was ecstatically raised in air, and thus remained till called back by the General, to whom His Holiness, highly astonished, turned and said that 'if Joseph were to die during his pontificate, he himself would bear witness to this *successo*.' "

But his most remarkable flights took place at Fossombrone, where once "detaching himself in swiftest manner from the altar with a cry like thunder, he went, like lightning, gyrating hither and thither about the chapel, and with such an impetus that he made all the cells of the dormitory tremble, so that the monks, issuing thence in consternation, cried, 'An earthquake! An earthquake!' " Here, too, he cast a young sheep into the air, and took flight after it to the height of the trees, where he "remained in kneeling posture, ecstatic and with extended arms, for more than two hours, to the extraordinary marvel of the clergy who witnessed this." This would seem to have been his outdoor record—two hours without descent to earth.

Sometimes, furthermore, he took a passenger, if such a term can properly be applied.

So once, while the monks were at prayers, he was observed to rise up and run swiftly towards the Confessor of the convent, and "seizing him by the hand, he raised him from the ground by supernatural force, and with jubilant rapture drew him along, turning him round and round in a *violento ballo*; the Confessor moved by Joseph, and Joseph by God."

And what happened at Assisi is still more noteworthy, for here was a gentleman, a suffering invalid, whom Joseph "snatched by the hair, and, uttering his customary cry of 'oh!' raised himself from the earth, while he drew the other after him by his hair, carrying him in this fashion for a short while through the air, to the intensest admiration of the spectators." The patient, whose name was Chevalier Baldassarre, discovered, on touching earth again, that he had been cured by this flight of a severe nervous malady which had hitherto afflicted him. . . .

Searching in the biography for some other interesting traits of Saint Joseph of Copertino, I find, in marked contrast to his heaven-soaring virtues, a humility of the profoundest kind. Even as a full-grown man he retained the exhilarating, childlike nature of the pure in heart. "La Mamma mia"—thus he would speak, in playful-saintly fashion, of the Mother of God—"la Mamma mia is capricious. When I bring Her flowers, She tells me She does not want them; when I bring Her candles, She also does not want them; and when I ask Her what She wants, She says, 'I want the heart, for I feed only on hearts.' " What wonder if the "mere pronouncement of the name of Maria often sufficed to raise him from the ground into the air"?

Nevertheless, the arch-fiend was wont to creep into his cell at night and to beat and torture him; and the monks of the convent were terrified when they heard the hideous din of echoing blows and jangling chains. "We were only having a little game," he would then say. This is refreshingly boyish. He once induced a flock of sheep to enter the chapel, and while he recited to them the litany, it was observed with amazement that "they responded at the proper place to his verses—he saying Sancta Maria, and they answering, after their manner, Bah!"

I am not disguising from myself that an incident like the last-named may smack of childishness to a certain austere type of northern Puritan. Childishness! But to go into this question of the relative hilarity and moroseness of religions would take us far afield; for aught I know it may, at bottom, be a matter of climatic influences, and there we can leave it. Under the sunny sky of Italy, who would not be disposed to see the bright side of things?

Saint Joseph of Copertino performed a variety of other miracles. He multiplied bread and wine, calmed a tempest, drove out devils, caused the lame to walk and the blind to see—all of which are duly attested by eye-witnesses on oath. Though "illiterate," he had an innate knowledge of ecclesiastical dogma; he detected persons of impure life by their smell, and sinners were revealed to his eyes with faces of black colour (the Turks believe that on judgment day the damned will be thus marked); he enjoyed the company of two guardian angels, which were visible not only to himself but to other people. And, like all too many saints, he duly fell into the clutches of the Inquisition, ever on the look-out for victims pious or otherwise.

There is one little detail which it would be disingenuous to slur over. It is this. We are told that Saint Joseph was awkward and backward in his development. As a child his boy-comrades used to laugh at him for his open-mouthed staring habits; they called him "bocca-aperta" (gape-mouthed), and in the frontispiece to Montanari's life of him, which depicts him as a bearded man of forty or fifty, his mouth is still agape; he was, moreover, difficult to teach, and Rossi says he profited very little by his lessons and was of *niuna letteratura*. As a lad of seventeen he could not distinguish white bread from brown, and he used to spill water-cans, break vases and drop plates to such an extent that the monks of the convent who employed him were obliged, after eight months' probation, to dismiss him from their service. He was unable to pass his examination as priest. At the age of twenty-five he was ordained by the Bishop of Castro, without that formality.

All this points to a certain weak-mindedness or arrested development, and were this an isolated case one might be inclined to think that the church had made Saint Joseph an object of veneration on the same principles as do the Arabs, who elevate idiots, epileptics, and otherwise deficient creatures to the rank of marabouts, and credit them with supernatural powers.

But it is not an isolated case. The majority of these southern saints are distinguished from the vulgar herd by idiosyncrasies to which modern physicians give singular names such as "gynophobia," "glossolalia" and "demonomania"*; even the founder of the flying monk's order, the great Francis of Assisi, has been accused of some strange-sounding mental disorder because, with touching humility, he doffed his vestments and presented himself naked before his Creator. What are we to conclude therefrom?

The flying monk resembles Saint Francis in more than one feature. He, too, removed his clothes and even his shirt, and exposed himself thus to a crucifix, exclaiming, "Here I am, Lord, deprived of

---

* Good examples of what Max Nordau calls *Echolalie* are to be found in this biography (p. 22).

everything." He followed his prototype, further, in that charming custom of introducing the animal world into his ordinary talk ("Brother Wolf, Sister Swallow," etc.). So Joseph used to speak of himself as *l'asinello*—the little ass; and a pathetic scene was witnessed on his death-bed when he was heard to mutter: "*L'asinello* begins to climb the mountain; *l'asinello* is half-way up; *l'asinello* has reached the summit; *l'asinello* can go no further, and is about to leave his skin behind."

It is to be noted, in this connection, that Saint Joseph of Copertino was born in a stable.

This looks like more than a mere coincidence. For the divine Saint Francis was likewise born in a stable.

But why should either of these holy men be born in stables?

A reasonable explanation lies at hand. A certain Japanese statesman is credited with that shrewd remark that the manifold excellencies and diversities of Hellenic art are due to the fact that the Greeks had no "old masters" to copy from—no "schools" which supplied their imagination with ready-made models that limit and smother individual initiative. And one marvels to think into what exotic beauties these southern saints would have blossomed, had they been at liberty, like those Greeks, freely to indulge their versatile genius—had they not been bound to the wheels of inexorable precedent. If the flying monk, for example, were an ordinary mortal, there was nothing to prevent him from being born in an omnibus or some other of the thousand odd places where ordinary mortals occasionally are born. But—no! As a Franciscan saint, he was obliged to conform to the school of Bethlehem and Assisi. He was obliged to select a stable. Such is the force of tradition. . . .

Joseph of Copertino lived during the time of the Spanish viceroys, and his fame spread not only over all Italy, but to France, Germany and Poland. Among his intimates and admirers were no fewer than eight cardinals, Prince Leopold of Tuscany, the Duke of Bouillon, Isabella of Austria, the Infanta Maria of Savoy and the Duke of Brunswick, who, during a visit to various courts of Europe in 1649, purposely went to Assisi to see him, and was there converted from the Lutheran heresy by the spectacle of one of his flights. Prince Casimir, heir to the throne of Poland, was his particular friend, and kept up a correspondence with him after the death of his father and his own succession to the throne.

Towards the close of his life, the flying monk became so celebrated that his superiors were obliged to shut him up in the convent of Osimo, in close confinement, in order that his aerial voyages "should not be disturbed by the concourse of the vulgar." And here he expired, in his sixty-first year, on the 18th September, 1663. He had been suffering and infirm for some little time previous to that event, but managed to take a short flight on the very day preceding his demise.

Forthwith the evidences of his miraculous deeds were collected and submitted to the inspired examination of the Sacred Congregation of Rites in Rome. Their conscientiousness in sifting and weighing the depositions is sufficiently attested by the fact that ninety years were allowed to elapse ere Joseph of Copertino was solemnly received into the number of the blessed. This occurred in 1753; and though the date may have been accidentally chosen, some people will be inclined to detect the hand of Providence in the ordering of the event, as a challenge to Voltaire, who was just then disquieting Europe with certain doctrines of a pernicious nature.

XI

BY THE INLAND SEA

THE railway line to Grottaglie skirts the shore of the inland sea for two or three miles, and then turns away. Old Taranto glimmers in lordly fashion across the tranquil waters; a sense of immemorial culture pervades this region of russet tilth, and olives, and golden corn.

They led me, at Grottaglie, to the only convent of males now in use, San Francesco, recently acquired by the Jesuits. In the sacristy of its church, where I was told to wait, a slender young priest was praying rapturously before some image, and the clock that stood at hand recorded the flight of twenty minutes ere his devotions were ended. Then he arose slowly and turned upon me a pair of lustrous, dreamy eyes, as though awakened from another world.

This was quite a new convent, he explained; it could not possibly be the one I was seeking. But there was another one, almost a ruin, and now converted into a refuge for a flock of poor old women; he would gladly show me the way. Was I a "Germanese"?* No, I replied; I came from Scotland.

"A Calvinist," he remarked, without bitterness.

"A Presbyterian," I gently corrected.

"To be sure—a Presbyterian."

As we walked along the street under the glowing beams of midday I set forth the object of my visit. He had never heard of the flying monk—it was astonishing, he said. He would look up the subject without delay. The flying monk! That a Protestant should come all

---

* *Germanese* or *Allemanno* = a German. *Tedesco,* hereabouts, signifies an Austrian—a detested nationality, even at this distance of time. I have wondered, since writing the above, whether this is really the place of which Rossi speaks. He calls it Grottole (the difference in spelling would be of little account), and says it lies not far distant from Copertino. But there may be a place of this name still nearer; it is a common appellation in these honeycombed limestone districts. This Grottaglie is certainly the birthplace of another religious hero, the priest-brigand Ciro, who gave so much trouble to Sir R. Church.

the way from "the other end of the world" to enquire about a local Catholic saint of whose existence he himself was unaware, seemed not so much to surprise as positively to alarm him.

Among other local curiosities, he pointed out the portal of the parish church, a fine but dilapidated piece of work, with a large rosette window overhead. The town, he told me, derives its name from certain large grottoes wherein the inhabitants used to take refuge during Saracen raids. This I already knew, from the pages of Swinburne and Sanchez; and in my turn was able to inform him that a certain Frenchman, Bettaux by name, had written about the Byzantine wall-paintings within these caves. Yes, those old Greeks! he said. And that accounted for the famous ceramics of the place, which preserved the Hellenic traditions in extraordinary purity. I did not inform him that Hector Preconi, who purposely visited Grottaglie to study these potteries, was considerably disappointed.

At the door of the decayed convent my guide left me, with sundry polite expressions of esteem. I entered a spacious open courtyard; a well stood in the centre of a bare enclosure whereon, in olden days, the monks may have cultivated their fruit and vegetables; round this court there ran an arched passage, its walls adorned with frescoes, now dim and faded, depicting sacred subjects. The monastery itself was a sombre maze of stairways and cells and corridors—all the free spaces, including the very roof, encumbered with gleaming potteries of every shape and size, that are made somewhere near the premises.

I wandered about this sunless and cobwebby labyrinth, the old woman pensioners flitting round me like bats in the twilight. I peered into many dark closets; which of them was it—Joseph's famous blood-bespattered cell?

"He tormented his body so continuously and obstinately with pins, needles and blades of steel, and with such effusion of blood, that even now, after entire years, the walls of his cell and other places of retirement are discoloured and actually encrusted with blood." Which of them was it—the chamber that witnessed these atrocious macerations? It was all so gloomy and forlorn.

Then, pushing aside a door in these tenebrous regions, I suddenly found myself bathed in dazzling light. A loggia opened here, with a view over stretches of gnarled olives, shining all silvery under the immaculate sky of noonday and bounded by the sapphire belt of the Ionian. Sunshine and blue sea! Often must the monks have taken pleasure in this fair prospect; and the wiser among them, watching the labourers returning home at nightfall, the children at play, and all the happy life of a world so alien to their own, may well have heaved a sigh.

Meanwhile a crowd of citizens had assembled below, attracted by the unusual novelty of a stranger in their town. The simple creatures appeared to regard my investigations in the light of a good joke; they had heard of begging monks, and thieving monks, and monks of another variety whose peculiarities I dare not attempt to describe; but a flying monk—no, never!

"The Dark Ages," said one of them—the mayor, I dare say—with an air of grave authority. "Believe me, dear sir, the days of such fabulous monsters are over."

So they seem to be, for the present.

No picture or statue records the life of this flying wonder, this masterpiece of Spanish priestcraft; no mural table—in this land of commemorative stones—has been erected to perpetuate the glory of his signal achievements; no street is called after him. It is as if he had never existed. On the contrary, by a queer irony of fate, the roadway leading past his convent evokes the memory of a misty heathen poet, likewise native of these favoured regions, a man whose name Joseph of Copertino had assuredly never heard—Ennius, of whom I can now recall nothing save the one unforgettable line which begins "O Tite tute Tati tibi——"; Ennius, who never so much as tried to fly, but contented himself with singing, in rather bad Latin, of the things of this earth.

Via Ennio. . . .

It is the swing of the pendulum. The old pagan, at this moment, may be nearer to our ideals and aspirations than the flying monk who died only yesterday, so to speak.

But a few years hence—who can tell?

A characteristic episode. I had carefully timed myself to catch the returning train to Taranto. Great was my surprise when, half-way to the station, I perceived the train swiftly approaching. I raced it, and managed to jump into a carriage just as it drew out of the station. The guard straightway demanded my ticket and a fine for entering the train without one (return tickets, for weighty reasons of "internal administration," are not sold). I looked at my watch, which showed that we had left six minutes before the scheduled hour. He produced his; it coincided with my own. "No matter," he said. "I am not responsible for the eccentricities of the driver, who probably had some urgent private affairs to settle at Taranto. The fine must be paid." A fellow-passenger took a more charitable view of the case. He suggested that an inspector of the line had been travelling along with us, and that the driver, knowing this, was naturally ambitious to show how fast he could go.

A mile or so before reaching Taranto the railway crosses a stream that flows into the inland sea. One would be glad to believe those sages who hold it to be the far-famed Galaesus. It rises near at hand in a marsh, amid mighty tufts of reeds and odorous flowers, and the liquid bubbles up in pools of crystalline transparency—deep and perfidious cauldrons overhung by the trembling soil on which you stand. These fountains form a respectable stream some four hundred yards in length; another copious spring rises up in the sea near its mouth. But can this be the river whose virtues are extolled by: Virgil, Horace, Martial, Statius, Propertius, Strabo, Pliny, Varro and Columella? What a constellation of names around these short-lived waters! Truly, *minuit præsentia famam,* as Boccaccio says of the once-renowned Sebethus.

Often have I visited this site and tried to reconstruct its vanished glories. My enthusiasm even led me some years ago, to the town hall, in order to ascertain its true official name, and here they informed me that "it is vulgarly called Citrezze; but the correct version is 'Le Giadrezze,' which, as you are aware, sir, signifies *pleasantness."* This functionary was evidently ignorant of the fact that so long ago as 1771 the learned commentator (Carducci) of the "Delizie Tarentine" already sneered at this popular etymology; adding, what is of greater interest, that "in the time of our fathers" this region was covered with woods and rich in game. In the days of Keppel Craven, the vale was "scantily cultivated with cotton." Looking at it from above, it certainly resembles an old river-bed of about five hundred yards in breadth, and I hold it possible that the deforestation of the higher lands may have suffocated the original sources with soil carried down from thence, and forced them to seek a lower level, thus shortening the stream and reducing its volume of water.

But who shall decide? If we follow Polybius, another brook at the further end of the inland sea has more valid claims to the title of Galaesus. Virgil called it "black Galaesus"—a curious epithet, still applied to water in Italy as well as in Greece (Mavromati, etc.). "For me," says Gissing, "the Galaesus is the stream I found and tracked, whose waters I heard mingle with the little sea." There is something to be said for such an attitude, on the part of a dilettante traveller, towards these desperate antiquarian controversies.

It is an agreeable promenade from the Giadrezze rivulet to Taranto along the shore of this inland sea. Its clay banks are full of shells and potteries of every age, and the shallow waters planted with stakes indicating the places where myriads of oysters and mussels are bred—indeed, if you look at a map you will observe that the whole of this lagoon, as though to shadow forth its signification, is split up into two basins like an opened oyster.

Here and there along this beach are fishermen's huts constructed of tree-stems which are smothered under multitudinous ropes of grass, ropes of all ages and in every stage of decomposition, some fairly fresh, others dissolving once more into amorphous bundles of hay. There is a smack of the stone ages, of primeval lake-dwellings, about these shelters on the deserted shore; two or three large fetichistic stones stand near their entrance; wickerwork objects of dark meaning strew the ground; a few stakes emerge, hard by, out of the placid and oozy waters. In such a cabin, methinks, dwelt those two old fishermen of Theocritus—here they lived and slumbered side by side on a couch of sea moss, among the rude implements of their craft.

The habits of these fisherfolk are antique, because the incidents of their calling have remained unchanged. Some people have detected traces of "Greek" in the looks and language of these of Taranto. I can detect nothing of the kind.

And the same with the rest of the population. Hellenic traits have disappeared from Taranto, as well they may have done, when one remembers its history. It was completely latinized under Augustus, and though Byzantines came hither under Nicephorus Phocas—Benjamin of Tudela says the inhabitants are "Greeks"—they have long ago become merged into the Italian element. Only the barbers seem to have preserved something of the old traditions: grandiloquent and terrible talkers, like the cooks in Athenæus.

I witnessed an Aristophanic scene in one of their shops lately, when a simple-minded stranger, a north Italian—some arsenal official—brought a little boy to have his hair cut "not too short" and, on returning from a brief visit to the tobacconist next door, found it cropped much closer than he liked.

"But, damn it," he said (or words to that effect), "I told you not to cut the hair too short."

The barber, immaculate and imperturbable, gave a preliminary bow. He was collecting his thoughts, and his breath.

"I say, I told you not to cut it too short. It looks horrible——"

"Horrible? That, sir—pardon my frankness!—is a matter of opinion. I fully admit that you desired the child's hair to be cut not too short. Those, in fact, were your very words. Notwithstanding, I venture to think you will come round to my point of view, on due reflection, like most of my esteemed customers. In the first place, there is the ethnological aspect of the question. You are doubtless sufficiently versed in history to know that under the late regime it was considered improper, if not criminal, to wear a moustache. Well, nowadays we think differently. Which proves that fashions change; yes, they change, sir; and the wise man bends to them—up to a certain point, of course; up to a certain reasonable point——"

"But, damn it——"

"And in favour of my contention that hair should be worn short nowadays, I need only cite the case of His Majesty the King, whose august head, we all know, is clipped like that of a racehorse. Horrible (as you call it) or not, the system has momentarily the approval of royalty, and that alone should suffice for all loyal subjects to deem it not unworthy of imitation. Next, there are what one might describe as hygienic and climatic considerations. Summer is approaching, sir, and apart from certain unpleasant risks which I need not specify, you will surely agree with me that the solstitial heat is a needlessly severe trial for a boy with long hair. My own children are all cropped close, and I have reason to think they are grateful for it. Why not yours? Boys may differ in strength and complexion, in moral character and mental attainments, but they are remarkably unanimous as to what constitutes personal comfort. And it is obviously the duty of parents to consult the personal comfort of their offspring—within certain reasonable limits, of course——"

"But——"

"Lastly, we come to the much-debated point: I mean the æsthetic side of the matter. No doubt, to judge by some old pictures such as those of the renowned Mantegna, there must have been a time when men thought long hair in children rather beautiful than otherwise. And I am not so rigorous as to deny a certain charm to these portraits—a charm which is largely due, I fancy, to the becoming costumes of the period. At the same time——"

The stranger did not trust himself to listen any longer. He threw down a coin and walked out of the shop with his son, muttering something not very complimentary to the barber's female relations.

But the other was quite unmoved. "And after all," he continued, addressing the half-opened door through which his visitor had fled, "the true question is this: What is 'too short'? Don't cut it too short, you said. *Che vuol dire?* An ambiguous phrase! Too short for one man may be too long for another. Everything is relative. Yes, gentlemen" (turning to myself and his shop-assistant), "everything on this earth is relative."

With this sole exception, I have hitherto garnered no Hellenic traits in Taranto.

Visible even from Giadrezze, on the other side of the inland sea and beyond the arsenal, there stands a tall, solitary palm. It is the last, the very last, or almost the very last, of a race of giants that adorned the gardens which have now been converted into the "New Quarter." I imagine it is the highest existing palm in Italy, and am glad to have taken a likeness of it, ere it shall have been cut down like the rest of its fellows. Taranto was once celebrated for these queenly growths, which the Saracens brought over from their flaming Africa.

The same fate has overtaken the trees of the Villa Beaumont, which used to be a shady retreat, but was bought by the municipality and forthwith "pulizzato"—i.e. cleaned. This is in accordance with the *mutilomania* of the south: that love of torturing trees which causes them to prune pines till they look like paint-brushes that had been out all night, and which explains their infatuation for the much-enduring robinia that allows itself to be teased into any pattern suggested by their unhealthy phantasy. It is really as if there were something offensive to the Latin mind in the sight of a well-grown tree, as if man alone had the right of expanding normally. But I must not do the City Fathers an injustice. They have planted two rows of cryptomerias. Will people never learn that cryptomerias cannot flourish in south Italy? Instead of this amateurish gardening, why not consult some competent professional, who with bougain-villeas, hibiscus and fifty other such plants would soon transform this favoured spot into a miniature paradise?

The Villa Beaumont and the road along the Admiralty canal are now the citizens' chief places of disport. Before the year 1869 the Corso Vittorio Emmanuele, that skirts the sea on the south side of the old town, was their sole promenade. And even this street was built only a short time ago. Vainly one conjectures where the mediæval Tarentines took the air. It must have been like Manfredonia at the present day.

This Corso, which has a most awkward pavement and is otherwise disagreeable as looking due south, becomes interesting after sunset. Here you may see the young bloods of Taranto leaning in

rows against the railing with their backs to the sea—they are looking across the road whence, from balconies and windows, the fair
sex are displaying their charms. Never a word is spoken. They
merely gaze at each other like lovesick puppies; and after watching
the performance for several evenings, I decided in favour of robuster
methods—I decided that courtship, under conditions such as the
Corso supplies, can only be pursued by the very young or the hopelessly infatuated. But in the south, this gazing is only part of a huge
game. They are not really in love at all, these excellent young men—
not at all, at all; they know better. They are only pretending, because it looks manly.

We must revise our conceptions as to the love-passions of these
southerners; no people are more fundamentally sane in matters of
the heart; they have none of our obfuscated sentimentality; they are
seldom naively enamoured, save in early stages of life. It is then that
small girls of eight or ten may be seen furtively recording their
feelings on the white walls of their would-be lovers' houses; these
archaic scrawls go straight to the point, and are models of what
love-letters may ultimately become, in the time-saving communities of the future. But when the adolescent and perfumed-pink-paper
stage is reached, the missives relapse into barbarous ambiguity; they
grow allegorical and wilfully exuberant as a Persian carpet, the effigy
of a pierced heart at the end, with enormous blood-drops oozing
from it, alone furnishing a key to the document.

So far they are in earnest, and it is the girl who takes the lead; her
youthful *innamorato* ties these letters into bundles and returns
them conscientiously, in due course, to their respective senders.
Seldom does a boy make overtures in love; he gets more of it than he
knows what to do with; he is still torpid, and slightly bored by all
these attentions.

But presently he wakes up to the fact that he is a man among men,
and the obsession of "looking manly" becomes a part of his future
artificial and rhetorical life-scheme. From henceforth he plays to the
gallery.

Reading the city papers, one would think that south Italian youths
are the most broken-hearted creatures in the world; they are always
trying to poison themselves for love. Sometimes they succeed, of
course; but sometimes—dear me, no! Suicides look manly, that is
all. They are part of the game. The more sensible youngsters know
exactly how much corrosive sublimate to take without immediate
fatal consequences, allowing for time to reach the nearest hospital.

There, the kindly physician and his stomach-pump will perform their duty, and the patient wears a feather in his cap for the rest of his life. The majority of these suicides are on a par with French duels—a harmless institution whereby the protagonists honour themselves; they confer, as it were, a patent virility. The country people are as warm-blooded as the citizens, but they rarely indulge in suicides because—well, there are no hospitals handy, and the doctor may be out on his rounds. It is too risky by half.

And a good proportion of these suicides are only simulated. The wily victim buys some innocuous preparation which sends him into convulsions with ghastly symptoms of poisoning, and, after treatment, remains the enviable hero of a mysterious masculine passion. Ask any town apothecary. A doctor friend of mine lately analysed the results of his benevolent exertions upon a young man who had been seen to drink some dreadful liquid out of a bottle, and was carried to his surgery, writhing in most artistic agonies. He found not only no poison, but not the slightest trace of any irritant whatever.

The true courtship of these Don Giovannis of Taranto will be quite another affair—a cash transaction, and no credit allowed. They will select a life partner, upon the advice of *ma mère* and a strong committee of uncles and aunts, but not until the military service is terminated. Everything in its proper time and place.

Meanwhile they gaze and perhaps even serenade. This looks as if they were furiously in love, and has therefore been included among the rules of the game. Youth must keep up the poetic tradition of "fiery." Besides, it is an inexpensive pastime—the cinematograph costs forty centimes—and you really cannot sit in the barber's all night long.

But catch them marrying the wrong girl!

POSTSCRIPT.—Here are two samples of youthful love-letters from my collection.

I.—From a disappointed maiden, aged 13. Interesting, because intermediate between the archaic and pink-paper stages:

"IDOL OF MY HEART,

"Do not the stars call you when you look to Heaven? Does not the moon tell you, the black-cap on the willow when it says farewell to the sun? The birds of nature, the dreary country sadly covered by a few flowers that remain there? Once your look was passionate and pierced me like a sunny ray, now it seems the flame of a day. Does nothing tell you of imperishable love?

"I love you and love you as (illegible) loves its liberty, as the corn in the fields loves the sun, as the sailor loves the sea tranquil or stormy. To you I would give my felicity, my future; for one of your words I would spill my blood drop by drop.

"Of all my lovers you are the only ideal consort (*consorto*) to whom I would give my love and all the expansion of my soul and youthful enthusiasm (*intusiamo*), the greatest enthusiasm (*cotusiamo*) my heart has ever known. O cruel one who has deigned to put his sweet poison in my heart to-day, while to-morrow you will pass me with indifference. Cold, proud as ever, serious and disdainful—you understand? However that may be, I send you the unrepenting cry of my rebellious heart: I love you!

"It is late at night, and I am still awake, and at this hour my soul is sadder than ever in its great isolation (*insolamende*); I look on my past love and your dear image. Too much I love and (illegible) without your affection.

"How sadly I remember your sweet words whispered on a pathetic evening when everything around was fair and rosy. How happy I then was when life seemed radiant with felicity and brightened by your love. And now nothing more remains of it; everything is finished. How sad even to say it. My heart is shipwrecked far, far away from that happiness which I sought."

(Three further pages of this.)

2.—From a boy of 14, who takes the initiative; such letters are rare. Note the business-like brevity.

"DEAR MISS ANNE,

I write you these few lines to say that I have understood your character (*carattolo*). Therefore, if I may have the honour of being your sweetheart, you will let me know the answer at your pleasure. I salute you, and remain,

"Signing myself,

"SALVATORE.

"Prompt reply requested!"

XII

MOLLE TARENTUM

ONE looks into the faces of these Tarentines and listens to their casual conversations, trying to unravel what manner of life is theirs. But it is difficult to avoid reading into their characters what history leads one to think should be there.

The upper classes, among whom I have some acquaintance, are mellow and enlightened; it is really as if something of the honied spirit of those old Greek sages still brooded over them. Their charm lies in the fact that they are civilized without being commercialized. Their politeness is unstrained, their suaveness congenital; they remind me of that New England type which for Western self-assertion substitutes a yielding graciousness of disposition. So it is with persistent gentle upbringing, at Taranto and elsewhere. It tones the individual to reposeful sweetness; one by one, his anfractuosities are worn off; he becomes as a pebble tossed in the waters, smooth, burnished, and (to outward appearances) indistinguishable from his fellows.

But I do not care about the ordinary city folk. They have an air of elaborate superciliousness which testifies to ages of systematic half-culture. They seem to utter that hopeless word, *connu!* And what, as a matter of fact, do they know? They are only dreaming in their little backwater, like the oysters of the lagoon, distrustful of extraneous matter and oblivious of the movement in a world of men beyond their shell. You hear next to nothing of "America," that fruitful source of fresh notions; there is no emigration to speak of; the population is not sufficiently energetic—they prefer to stay at home. Nor do they care much about the politics of their own country: one sees less newspapers here than in most Italian towns. "Our middle classes," said my friend the Italian deputy of whom I have already spoken, "are like our mules: to be endurable, they must be worked thirteen hours out of the twelve." But these have no industries to keep them awake, no sports, no ambitions; and this has gone on for long centuries. In Taranto it is always afternoon. "The Tarentines," says Strabo, "have more holidays than workdays in the year."

And never was city-populatin more completely cut off from the country; never was wider gulf between peasant and townsman. There are charming walks beyond the New Quarter—a level region, with olives and figs and almonds and pomegranates standing knee-deep in ripe odorous wheat; but the citizens might be living at Timbuctu for all they know of these things. It rains little here; on the occasion of my last visit not a drop had fallen for *fourteen months*; and consequently the country roads are generally smothered in dust. Now, dusty boots are a scandal and an offence in the eyes of the gentle burghers, who accordingly never issue out of their town walls. They have forgotten the use of ordinary appliances of country life, such as thick boots and walking-sticks; you will not see them hereabouts. Unaware of this idiosyncrasy, I used to carry a stick on my way through the streets into the surroundings, but left it at home on learning that I was regarded as a kind of perambulating earthquake. The spectacle of a man clattering through the streets on horseback, such as one often sees at Venosa, would cause them to barricade their doors and prepare for the last judgment.

Altogether, essentially nice creatures, lotus-eaters, fearful of fuss or novelty, and drowsily satisfied with themselves and life in general. The breezy healthfulness of travel, the teachings of art or science, the joys of rivers and green lanes—all these things are a closed book to them. Their interests are narrowed down to the purely human: a case of partial atrophy. For the purely human needs a corrective; it is not sufficiently humbling, and that is exactly what makes them so supercilious. We must take a little account of the Cosmos nowadays—it helps to rectify our bearings. They have their history, no doubt. But save for that one gleam of Periclean sunshine the record, though long and varied, is sufficiently inglorious and does not testify to undue exertions.

A change is at hand.

Gregorovius lamented the filthy condition of the old town. It is now spotless.

He deplored that Taranto possessed no museum. This again is changed, and the provincial museum here is justly praised, though the traveller may be annoyed at finding his favourite rooms temporarily closed (is there any museum in Italy not "partially closed for alterations"?). New accessions to its store are continually pouring in; so they lately discovered, in a tomb, a Hellenistic statuette of Eros and Aphrodite, 30 centimetres high, terra-cotta work of the third century. The goddess stands, half-timidly, while Eros alights in airy fashion on her shoulders and fans her with his wings—an exquisite little thing.

He was grieved, likewise, that no public collection of books existed here. But the newly founded municipal library is all that can be desired. The stranger is cordially welcomed within its walls and may peruse, at his leisure, old Galateus, Giovan Giovene, and the rest of them.

Wandering among those shelves, I hit upon a recent volume (1910) which gave me more food for thought than any of these ancients. It is called "Cose di Puglie," and contains some dozen articles, all by writers of this province of old Calabria,* on matters of exclusively local interest—its history, meteorology, dialects, classical references to the country, extracts from old economic documents, notes on the development of Apulian printing, examples of modern local caricature, descriptions of mediæval monuments; a kind of anthology, in short, of provincial lore. The typography, paper and illustrations of this remarkable volume are beyond all praise; they would do honour to the best firm in London or Paris. What is this book? It is no commercial speculation at all; it is a wedding present to a newly married couple—a bouquet of flowers, of intellectual blossoms, culled from their native Apulian meadows. One notes with pleasure that the happy pair are neither dukes nor princes. There is no trace of snobbishness in the offering, which is simply a spontaneous expression of good wishes on the part of a few friends. But surely it testifies to most refined feelings. How immeasurably does this permanent and yet immaterial feast differ from our gross wedding banquets and ponderous gilt clocks and tea services! Such persons cannot but have the highest reverence for things of the mind; such a gift is the fairest efflorescence of civilization. And this is only another aspect of that undercurrent of spirituality in south Italy of whose existence the tourist, harassed by sordid preoccupations, remains wholly unaware.

This book was printed at Bari. Bari, not long ago, consisted of a dark and tortuous old town, exactly like the citadel of Taranto. It has now its glaring New Quarter, not a whit less disagreeable than the one here. Why should Taranto not follow suit in the matter of culture? Heraclea, Sybaris and all the Greek settlements along this coast have vanished from earth; only Taranto and Cotrone have

---

* It included the heel of Italy.

survived to carry on, if they can, the old traditions. They have survived, thanks to peculiar physical conditions that have safeguarded them from invaders. . . .

But these very conditions have entailed certain drawbacks—drawbacks which Buckle would have lovingly enumerated to prove their influence upon the habits and disposition of the Tarentines. That marine situation . . . only think of three thousand years of scirocco, summer and winter! It is alone enough to explain *molle Tarentum*—enough to drain the energy out of a Newfoundland puppy! And then, the odious dust of the country roadways—for it *is* odious. Had the soil been granitic, or even of the ordinary Apennine limestone, the population might have remained in closer contact with wild things of nature, and retained a perennial fountain of enjoyment and inspiration. A particular kind of rock, therefore, has helped to make them sluggish and incurious. The insularity of their citadel has worked in the same direction, by focussing their interests upon the purely human. That inland sea, again: were it not an ideal breeding-place for shell-fish, the Tarentines would long ago have learnt to vary their diet. Thirty centuries of mussel-eating cannot but impair the physical tone of a people.

And had the inland sea not existed, the government would not have been tempted to establish that arsenal which has led to the erection of the new town and consequent municipal exactions. "The arsenal," said a grumbling old boatman to me, "was the beginning of our purgatory." A milk diet would work wonders with the health and spirits of the citizens. But since the building of the new quarter, such a diet has become a luxury; cows and goats will soon be scarce as the megatherium. There is a tax of a franc a day on every cow, and a herd of ten goats, barely enough to keep a poor man alive, must pay annually 380 francs in octroi. These and other legalized robberies, which among a more virile populace would cause the mayor and town council to be forthwith attached to the nearest lamp-post, are patiently borne. It is *imbelle Tarentum*—a race without grit.

I would also recommend the burghers some vegetables, so desirable for their sedentary habits, but there again! it seems to be a peculiarity of the local soil to produce hardly a leaf of salad or cabbage. Potatoes are plainly regarded as an exotic—they are the size of English peas, and make me think of Ruskin's letter to those old ladies describing the asparagus somewhere in Tuscany. And all this to the waiter's undisguised astonishment.

"The gentleman is rich enough to pay for meat. Why trouble about this kind of food?" . . .

And yet—a change is at hand. These southern regions are waking up from their slumber of ages. Already some of Italy's acutest thinkers and most brilliant politicians are drawn from these long-neglected shores. For we must rid ourselves of that incubus of "immutable race characters": think only of our Anglo-Saxon race! What has the Englishman of to-day in common with that rather lovable fop, drunkard and bully who would faint with ecstasy over Byron's *Parisina* after pistolling his best friend in a duel about a wench or a lap-dog? Such differences as exist between races of men, exist only at a given moment.

And what, I sometimes ask myself—what is now the distinguishing feature between these southern men and ourselves? Briefly this, I think. In mundane matters, where the personal equation dominates, their judgment is apt to be turbid and perverse; but as one rises into questions of pure intelligence, it becomes serenely impartial. We, on the other hand, who are pre-eminently clear-sighted in worldly concerns of law and government and in all subsidiary branches of mentality, cannot bring ourselves to reason dispassionately on non-practical subjects. "L'esprit aussi a sa pudeur," says Remy de Gourmont. Well, this *pudeur de l'esprit*, discouraged among the highest classes in England, is the hall-mark of respectability hereabouts. A very real difference, at this particular moment. . . .

There is an end of philosophizing.

They have ousted me from my pleasant quarters, the landlady's son and daughter-in-law having returned unexpectedly and claiming their apartments. I have taken refuge in a hotel. My peace is gone; my days in Taranto are numbered.

Loath to depart, I linger by the beach of the Ionian Sea beyond the new town. It is littered with shells and holothurians, with antique tesseræ of blue glass and marble fragments, with white mosaic pavements and potteries of every age, from the glossy Greco-Roman ware whose delicately embossed shell devices are emblematic of this sea-girt city, down to the grosser products of yesterday. Of marbles I have found *cipollino, pavonazzetto, giallo* and *rosso antico*, but no harder materials such as porphyry or serpentine. This, and the fact that the mosaics are pure white, suggests that the houses here must have dated, at latest, from Augustan times.*

---

* Nor is there any of the fashionabole *verde antico*, and this points in the same direction. Corsi says nothing as to the date of its introduction, and I have not read the treatise of Silenziario, but my own observations lead me

Here I sit, on the tepid shingle, listening to the plash of the waves and watching the sun as it sinks over the western mountains that are veiled in mists during the full daylight, but loom up, at this sunset hour, as from a fabulous world of gold. Yonder lies the Calabrian Sila forest, the brigands' country. I will attack it by way of Rossano, and thence wander, past Longobucco, across the whole region. It may be well, after all, to come again into contact with streams and woodlands, after this drenching of classical associations and formal civic life!

Near me stands a shore-battery which used to be called "Batteria Chianca." It was here they found, some twenty years ago, a fine marble head described as a Venus, and now preserved in the local museum. I observe that this fort has lately been re-christened "Batteria Archyta." Can this be due to a burst of patriotism for the Greek warrior-sage who ruled Taranto, or is it a subtle device to mislead the foreign spy?

Here, too, are kilns where they burn the blue clay into tiles and vases. I time a small boy at work shaping the former. His average output is five tiles in four minutes, including the carrying to and fro of the moist clay; his wages about a shilling a day. But if you wish to see the manufacture of more complicated potteries, you must go to the unclean quarter beyond the railway station. Once there, you will not soon weary of that potter's wheel and the fair shapes that blossom forth under its enchanted touch. This ware of Taranto is sent by sea to many parts of south Italy, and you may see picturesque groups of it, here and there, at the street corners.

---

to think that the *lapis atracius* can hardly have been known under Tiberius. Not so those hard ones: they were imported wholesale by his predecessor Augustus, who was anxious to be known as a scorner of luxury (a favourite pose with monarchs), yet spent incalculable sums on ornamental stones both for public and private ends. One is struck by a certain waste of material; either the expense was deliberately disregarded or finer methods of working the stones were not yet in vogue. A revolution in the technique of stone-cutting must have set in soon after his death, for thenceforward we find the most intractable rocks cut into slices thin as card-board: too thin for pavements, and presumably for encrusting walls and colonnades. The Augustans, unable to produce these effects naturally, attempted imitation-stones, and with wonderful success. I have a fragment of their plaster postiche copying the close-grained Egyptian granite; the oily lustre of the quartz is so fresh and the peculiar structure of the rock, with its mica scintillations, so admirably rendered as to deceive, after two thousand years, the eye of a trained mineralogist.

Hardly has the sun disappeared before the lighthouse in the east begins to flash. The promontory on which it stands is called San Vito after one of the musty saints, now almost forgotten, whose names survive along these shores. Stoutly this venerable one defended his ancient worship against the radiant and victorious Madonna; nor did she dislodge him from a certain famous sanctuary save by the questionable expedient of adopting his name: she called herself S. M. "della Vita." That settled it. He came from Mazzara in Sicily, whither they still carry, to his lonely shrine, epileptics and others distraught in mind. And were I in a discursive mood, I would endeavour to trace some connection between his establishment here and the tarantella—between St. Vitus' dance and that other one which cured, they say, the bite of the Tarentine spider.

But I am not inclined for such matters at present. The Calabrian uplands are still visible in the gathering twilight; they draw me onwards, away from Taranto. It must be cool up there, among the firs and beeches.

And a land, moreover, of multiple memories and interests—this Calabria. A land of great men. In 1737 the learned Aceti was able to enumerate over two thousand celebrated Calabrians—athletes, generals, musicians, centenarians, inventors, martyrs, ten popes, ten kings, as well as some sixty conspicuous women. A land of thinkers. Old Zavarroni, born in 1705, gives us a list of seven hundred Calabrian writers; and I, for one, would not care to bring his catalogue up to date. The recently acquired *Biblioteca Calabra* at Naples alone contains God knows how many items, nearly all modern!

And who shall recount its natural attractions? Says another old writer:

"Here is all sorts of Corn, sundry Wines, and in great abundance, all kinds of Fruits, Oyle, Hony, Wax, Saffron, Bombace, Annis and Coriander seeds. There groweth Gum, Pitch, Turpentine and liquid Storax. In former times it was never without Mettals, but at this present it doth much abound, having in most parts divers sorts of Mines, as Gold, Silver, Iron, Marble, Alabaster, Cristal, Marchesite, three sorts of white Chaulk, Virmilion, Alume, Brimstone, and the Adamant stone, which being in the fifth degree, draweth not Iron, and is in colour black. There groweth hemp and flax of two sorts, the one called the male, the other the female: there falleth Manna from heaven, truly a thing very rare; and although there is not gathered such abundance of Silk, yet I dare say there is not had so much in all *Italy* besides. There are also bathes, both hot, luke-warm, and cold, to cure many diseases. Near the Seaside, and likewise on the Mediterrane are goodly Gardens full of Oringes, Citrons, and Lemons of divers sorts. It is watered with many Rivers. There are on the hils of the Apennine, thick Woods of high Firrs, Holms, Platanes, Oaks, where grows the white odoriferous Mushrome which shineth in the night. Here is bred the soft stone *Frigia*, which every month yields a delicate and wholesome Gum, and the stone *Aetites*, by us called the stone *Aquilina*. In this Province there is excellent hunting of divers creatures, as wild Hoggs, Staggs, Goats, Hares, Foxes, Porcupines, Marmosets. There are also ravenous beasts, as Wolves, Bears, Luzards, which are quick-sighted, and have the hinder parts spotted with divers colours. This kind of Beast was brought from *France* to *Rome* in the sports of *Pompey* the great, and Hunters affirm this Beast to be of so frail a memory, that although he eateth with hunger, if he chance to look back, remembreth no more his meat, and departing searcheth for other."

Who would not visit Calabria, if only on the chance of beholding the speckled posterior of the absent-minded Luzard?

XIII

INTO THE JUNGLE

THIS short plunge into the jungle was a relief, after the all-too-human experiences of Taranto. The forest of Policoro skirts the Ionian; the railway line cleaves it into two unequal portions, the seaward tract being the smaller. It is bounded on the west by the river Sinno, and I imagine the place has not changed much since the days when Keppel Craven explored its recesses. Twilight reigns in this maze of tall deciduous trees. There is thick undergrowth, too; and I measured an old lentiscus—a shrub, in Italy—which was three metres in circumference. But the exotic feature of the grove is its wealth of creeping vines that clamber up the trunks, swinging from one tree-top to another, and allowing the merest threads of sunlight to filter through their matted canopy. Policoro has the tangled beauty of a tropical swamp. Rank odours arise from the decaying leaves and moist earth; and once within that verdant labyrinth, you might well fancy yourself in some primeval region of the globe, where the foot of man has never penetrated.

Yet long ago it resounded with the din of battle and the trumpeting of elephants—in that furious first battle between Pyrrhus and the Romans. And here, under the very soil on which you stand, lies buried, they say, the ancient city of Siris.

They have dug canals to drain off the moisture as much as possible, but the ground is marshy in many places and often quite impassable, especially in winter. None the less, winter is the time when a little shooting is done here, chiefly wild boars and roe-deer. They are driven down towards the sea, but only as far as the railway line. Those that escape into the lower portions are safe for another year, as this is never shot over but kept as a permanent preserve. I have been told that red-deer were introduced, but that the experiment failed; probably the country was too hot and damp. In his account of Calabria, Duret de Tavel* sometimes speaks of killing

* An English translation of his book appeared in 1832.

the fallow-deer, an autochthonous Tyrrhenian beast which is now extinct on the mainland in its wild state. Nor can he be confounding it with the roe, since he mentions the two together—for instance, in the following note from Corigliano (February, 1809), which must make the modern Calabrian's mouth water:

"Game has multiplied to such an extent that the fields are ravaged, and we are rendering a real service in destroying it. I question whether there exists in Europe a country offering more varied species. . . . We return home followed by carriages and mules loaded with wild boars, roe-deer, fallow-deer, hares, pheasants, wild duck, wild geese—to say nothing of foxes and wolves, of which we have already killed an immense quantity."

The pheasants seem to have likewise died out, save in royal preserves. They were introduced into Calabria by that mighty hunter Frederick II.

The parcelling out of many of these big properties has been followed by a destruction of woodland and complete disappearance of game. It is hailed as the beginning of a new era of prosperity; and so it well may be, from a commercial point of view. But the traveller and lover of nature will be glad to leave some of these wild districts in the hands of their rich owners, who have no great interests in cultivating every inch of ground, levelling rocky spaces, draining the land and hewing down every tree that fails to bear fruit. Split into peasant proprietorships, this forest would soon become a scientifically irrigated campagna for the cultivation of tomatoes or what not, like the "Colonia Elena," near the Pontine Marshes. The national exchequer would profit, without a doubt. But I questions whether we should all take the economical point of view—whether it would be wise for humanity to do so. There is a prosperity other than material. Some solitary artist or poet, drawing inspiration from scenes like this, might have contributed more to the happiness of mankind than a legion of narrow-minded, grimy and litigious tomato-planters.

To all appearances, Italy is infected just now with a laudable mania for the "exploitation of natural resources"—at the expense, of course, of wealthy landowners, who are described as withholding from the people their due. The programme sounds reasonable enough; but one must not forget that what one reads on this subject in the daily papers is largely the campaign of a class of irresponsible pressmen and politicians, who exploit the ignorance of weak people to fill their own pockets. How one learns to loathe, in Italy and in

England, that lovely word *socialism*, when one knows a little of the inner workings of the cause and a few—just a few!—details of the private lives of these unsavoury saviours of their country! The lot of the southern serfs was bad enough before America was "discovered"; and quite unendurable in earlier times. There is a village not many hours from Naples where, in 1789, only the personal attendants of the feudal lord lived in ordinary houses; the two thousand inhabitants, the serfs, took refuge in caves and shelters of straw. Conceive the conditions in remote Calabria! Such was the anguished poverty of the country-folk that up to the eighties of last century they used to sell their children by regular contracts, duly attested before the local mayors. But nowadays I listen to their complaints with comparative indifference.

"You are badly treated, my friend? I quite believe it; indeed, I can see it. Well, go to Argentina and sell potatoes, or to the mines of Pennsylvania. There you will grow rich, like the rest of your compatriots. Then return and send your sons to the University; let them become *avvocati* and members of Parliament, who shall harass into their graves these wicked owners of the soil."

This, as a matter of fact, is the career of a considerable number of them.

For the rest, the domain of Policoro—it is spelt *Pelicaro* in older maps like those of Magini and Rizzi-Zannone—seems to be well administered, and would repay a careful study. I was not encouraged, however, to undertake this study, the manager evidently suspecting some ulterior motive to underlie my simple questions. He was not at all responsive to friendly overtures. Restive at first, he soon waxed ambiguous, and finally taciturn. Perhaps he thought I was a tax-gatherer in disguise. A large structure combining the features of palace, fortress and convent occupies an eminence, and is supposed by some to stand on the site of old Heracleia; it was erected by the Jesuits; the work-people live in humble dwellings that cluster around it. Those that are now engaged in cutting the corn receive a daily wage of two carlini (eightpence)—the Bourbon coinage still survives in name.

You walk to this building from the station along an avenue of eucalypti planted some forty years ago. Detesting, as I do, the whole tribe of gum trees, I never lose an opportunity of saying exactly what I think about this particularly odious representative of the brood, this eyesore, this grey-haired scarecrow, this reptile of a growth with which a pack of misguided enthusiasts have disfigured the entire

Mediterranean basin. They have now realized that it is useless as a protection against malaria. Soon enough they will learn that instead of preventing the disease, it actually fosters it, by harbouring clouds of mosquitoes under its scraggy so-called foliage. These abominations may look better on their native heath: I sincerely hope they do. Judging by the "Dead Heart of Australia"—a book which gave me a nightmare from which I shall never recover—I should say that a varnished hop-pole would be an artistic godsend out there.

But from here the intruder should be expelled without mercy. A single eucalyptus will ruin the fairest landscape. No plant on earth rustles in such a horribly metallic fashion when the wind blows through those everlastingly withered branches; the noise chills one to the marrow; it is like the sibilant chattering of ghosts. Its oil is called "medicinal" only because it happens to smell rather nasty; it is worthless as timber, objectionable in form and hue—objectionable, above all things, in its perverse, anti-human habits. What other tree would have the effrontery to turn the sharp edges of its leaves—as if these were not narrow enough already!—towards the sun, so as to be sure of giving at all hours of the day the minimum of shade and maximum of discomfort to mankind?

But I confess that this avenue of Policoro almost reconciled me to the existence of the anæmic Antipodeans. Almost; since for some reason or other (perhaps on account of the insufferably foul nature of the soil) their foliage is here thickly tufted; it glows like burnished bronze in the sunshine, like enamelled scales of green and gold. These eucalypti are unique in Italy. Gazing upon them, my heart softened and I almost forgave the gums their manifold iniquities, their diabolical thirst, their demoralizing aspect of precocious senility and vice, their peeling bark suggestive of unmentionable skin diseases, and that system of radication which is nothing short of a scandal on this side of the globe. . . .

In the exuberance of his joy at the prospect of getting rid of me, the manager of the estate lent me a dog-cart to convey me to the forest's edge, as well as a sleepy-looking boy for a guide, warning me, however, not to put so much as the point of my nose inside the jungle, on account of the malaria which has already begun to infect the district. One sees all too many wan faces hereabouts. Visible from the intervening plain is a large building on the summit of a hill; it is called Acinapura, and this is the place I should have gone to, had time permitted, for the sake of the fine view which it must afford over the whole Policoro region. Herds of buffaloes wallow in the mire. An old bull, reposing in solitary grandeur, allowed me so near an approach that I was able to see two or three frogs hopping about his back, and engaged in catching the mosquitoes that troubled him. How useful, if something equally efficient and inexpensive could be devised for humanity!

We entered the darksome forest. The boy, who had hitherto confined himself to monosyllables, suddenly woke up under its mysterious influence; he became alert and affable; he related thrilling tales of the outlaws who used to haunt these thickets, lamenting that those happy days were over. There were the makings of a first-class brigand in Paolo. I stimulated his brave fancy; and it was finally proposed that I should establish myself permanently with the manager of the estate, so that on Sundays we could have some brigand-sport together, on the sly.

Then out again—into the broad and sunlit bed of the Sinno. The water now ripples in bland content down a waste of shining pebbles. But its wintry convulsions are terrific, and higher up the stream, where the banks are steep, many lives are lost in those angry floods that rush down from the hill-sides, filling the riverbed with a turmoil of crested waves. At such moments, these torrents put on new faces. From placid waterways they are transformed into living monsters, Ægirs or dragons, that roll themselves seaward, out of their dark caverns, in tawny coils of destruction.

XIV

DRAGONS

AND precisely this angry aspect of the waters has been acclaimed as one of the origins of that river-dragon idea which used to be common in south Italy, before the blight of Spaniardism fell upon the land and withered up the pagan myth-making faculty. There are streams still perpetuating this name—the rivulet Dragone, for instance, which falls into the Ionian not far from Cape Colonne.

A non-angry aspect of them has also been suggested as the origin: the tortuous wanderings of rivers in the plains, like the Meander, that recall the convolutions of the serpent. For serpent and dragon are apt to be synonymous with the ancients.

Both these explanations, I think, are late developments in the evolution of the dragon-image. They leave one still puzzling as to what may be the aboriginal conception underlying this legendary beast of earth and clouds and waters. We must go further back.

What is a dragon? An animal, one might say, which looks or regards (Greek *drakon*); so called, presumably, from its terrible eyes. Homer has passages which bear out this interpretation:

$$\Sigma \mu \epsilon \rho \delta \alpha \lambda \acute{\epsilon} o \nu \ \delta \grave{\epsilon} \ \delta \acute{\epsilon} \delta o \rho \kappa \epsilon \nu, \text{ etc.}$$

Now the Greeks were certainly sensitive to the expression of animal eyes—witness "cow-eyed" Hera, or the opprobrious epithet "dog-eyed"; altogether, the more we study what is left of their zoological researches, the more we realize what close observers they were in natural history. Aristotle, for instance, points out sexual differences in the feet of the crawfish which were overlooked up to a short time ago. And Hesiod also insists upon the dragon's eyes. Yet it is significant that *ophis*, the snake, is derived, like *drakon*, from a root meaning nothing more than to perceive or regard. There is no connotation of ferocity in either of the words. Gesner long ago suspected that the dragon was so called simply from its keen or rapid perception.

One likes to search for some existing animal prototype of a fabled creature like this, seeing that to invent such things out of sheer nothing is a feat beyond human ingenuity—or, at least, beyond what the history of others of their kind leads us to expect. It may well be that the Homeric writer was acquainted with the Uromastix lizard that occurs in Asia Minor, and whoever has watched this beast, as I have done, cannot fail to have been impressed by its contemplative gestures, as if it were gazing intently (drakon) at something. It is, moreover, a "dweller in rocky places," and more than this, a vegetarian—an "eater of poisonous herbs," as Homer somewhere calls his dragon. So Aristotle says: "When the dragon has eaten much fruit, he seeks the juice of the bitter lettuce; he has been seen to do this."

Are we tracking the dragon to his lair? Is this the aboriginal beast? Not at all, I should say. On the contrary, this is a mere side-issue, to follow which would lead us astray. The reptile-dragon was invented when men had begun to forget what the arch-dragon was; it is the product of a later stage—the materializing stage; that stage when humanity sought to explain, in naturalistic fashion, the obscure traditions of the past. We must delve still deeper. . . .

My own dragon theory is far-fetched—perhaps necessarily so, dragons being somewhat remote animals. The dragon, I hold, is the personification of the life within the earth—of that life which, being unknown and uncontrollable, is *eo ipso* hostile to man. Let me explain how this point is reached.

The animal which *looks or regards*. . . . Why—why an animal? Why not *drakon* = that which looks?

Now, what looks?

The eye.

This is the key to the understanding of the problem, the key to the subterranean dragon-world.

The conceit of fountains or sources of water being things that see (drakon)—that is, eyes—or bearing some resemblance to eyes, is common to many races. In Italy, for example, two springs in the inland sea near Taranto are called "Occhi"—eyes; Arabs speak of a watery fountain as an eye; the notion exists in England too—in the "Blentarn" of Cumberland, the blind tarn (tarn = a trickling of tears), which is "blind" because dry and waterless, and therefore lacking the bright lustre of the open eye.

There is an eye, then, in the fountain: an eye which looks or regards. And inasmuch as an eye presupposes a head, and a head without body is hard to conceive, a material existence was presently imputed to that which looked upwards out of the liquid depths. This, I think, is the primordial dragon, the archetype. He is of animistic descent and survives all over the earth; and it is precisely this universality of the dragon-idea which induces me to discard all theories of local origin and to seek for some common cause. Fountains are ubiquitous, and so are dragons. There are fountain dragons in Japan, in the superstitions of Keltic races, in the Mediterranean basin. The dragon of Wantley lived in a well; the Lambton Worm began life in fresh water, and only took to dry land later on. I have elsewhere spoken of the Manfredonia legend of Saint Lorenzo and the dragon, an indigenous fable connected, I suspect, with the fountain near the harbour of that town, and quite independent of the newly-imported legend of Saint Michael. Various springs in Greece and Italy are called Dragoneria; there is a cave-fountain Dragonara on Malta, and another of the same name near Cape Misenum—all are sources of apposite lore. The water-drac. . . .

So the dragon has grown into a subterranean monster, who peers up from his dark abode wherever he can—out of fountains or caverns whence fountains issue. It stands to reason that he is sleepless; all dragons are "sleepless"; their eyes are eternally open, for the luminous sparkle of living waters never waxes dim. And bold adventurers may well be devoured by dragons when they fall into these watery rents, never to appear again.

Furthermore, since gold and other treasures dear to mankind lie hidden in the stony bowels of the earth and are hard to attain, the jealous dragon has been accredited with their guardianship—hence the plutonic element in his nature. The dragon, whose "ever-open eye" protected the garden of the Hesperides, was the *Son of Earth*.. The earth or cave-dragon. . . . Calabria has some of these dragons' caves; you can read about them in the *Campania Sotteranea* of G. Sanchez.

In volcanic regions there are fissures in the rocks exhaling pestiferous emanations; these are the *spiracula*, the breathing-holes, of the dragon within. The dragon legends of Naples and Mondragone are probably of this origin, and so is that of the Roman Campagna (1660) where the dragon-killer died from the effects of this poisonous breath. Sometimes the confined monster issues in a destructive lava-torrent—Bellerophon and the Chimæra. The fire-dragon. . . . Or floods of water suddenly stream down from the hills and fountains are released. It is the hungry dragon, rushing from his den in search of prey; the river-dragon. . . . He rages among the mountains with such swiftness and impetuosity that wings must be his portion; yes, he can cleave the heavens in the guise of lightning, or descend upon the fertile fields as a ruinous thunderstorm; the cloud-dragon. . . . Or again, he remains permanently overhead, a flaming meteor in the firmament; this is the *draco volans* of the schoolmen.

In all his protean manifestations, he represents the envious and devastating principle; the spleenful wrath of untamed (untamable) telluric forces. Everything strong and spiteful has conspired to fashion our conception of the dragon. No wonder mankind, impotent, offers sacrifices to propitiate his rage. These tributary offerings are the dragon's due—the toll exacted from the weak by the strong in all mundane affairs. They are paid until the dragon-killer appears, that rare mortal who puts an end to his depredations. For the real dragon must be exterminated; he cannot be mollified by kindness; nobody ever heard of a domesticated dragon; compromise is out of the question. Only the victim of Saint George allowed himself to be led like a "meke beest" into the city. But that was the mediæval dragon, of whom anything can be expected.

He ultimately received a concrete form from that innate craving on the part of humanity to give a poetic or pictorial image to its hopes and fears. This derivative (modern) dragon is winged or unwinged, fiery or cold, crested or smooth, of manifold hue, four-footed, two-footed, serpentine or vermiform. Such relative variety of structure is seen in all imaginings that spring up independently in different regions of the globe, and are yet due to a common belief or cause. Why has he assimilated so much of the reptilian physiognomy and framework? Well, seeing that he had to approximate his shape to some type of beast familiar to mankind, what better general model could have been found? The reptile's glassy eye; its earthward-creeping and cleft-loving habits; its blood, that recalls that chill temperature of stones and water; its hostile pose; its ferocious tenacity of life and scaly covering, as of metals? Memories of extinct reptilian monsters may have helped to colour the picture, as well as that hatred of the serpent tribe which has haunted us ever since our own arboreal days.

A prehistoric idea like this, interpretative of such diverse natural phenomena, cannot but absorb into itself all kinds of extraneous material, ridiculous and sublime. Like some avalanche rolling downhill, the dragon gathers momentum on his journey athwart the ages, and is swollen in size both by kindred beliefs that have lain in his path, and by quite incongruous accretions. This is chiefly the poets' work, though the theologians have added one or two embellishing touches. But in whatever shape he appears, whether his eyes have borrowed a more baleful fire from heathen basilisks, or traits of moral evil are instilled into his pernicious physique by amalgamation with the apocalyptic Beast, he remains the vindictive enemy of man and his ordered ways. Of late—like the Saurian tribe in general— he has somewhat degenerated. So in modern Greece, by that process of stultified anthropomorphism which results from grafting Christianity upon an alien mythopoesis, he dons human attributes, talking and acting as a man (H. F. Tozer). And here, in Calabria, he lingers in children's fables, as "sdrago," a mockery of his former self.

To follow up his wondrous metamorphoses through mediævalism would be a pastime worthy of some leisured dilettante. How many noble shapes acquired a tinge of absurdity in the Middle Ages! Switzerland alone, with its mystery of untrodden crevices, used to be crammed with dragons—particularly the calcareous (cavernous) province of Rhaetia. Secondary dragons; for the good monks saw to it that no reminiscences of the autochthonous beast survived. Modern scholars have devoted much learning to the local Tazzelwurm and Bergstutz. But dragons of our familiar kind were already well known to the chroniclers from whom old Cysat extracted his twenty-fifth chapter (wherein, by the way, you will learn something of Calabrian dragons); then came J. J. Wagner (1680); then Scheuchzer, prince of dragon-finders, who informs us that *multorum draconum historia mendax.*

But it is rather a far cry from Calabria to the asthmatic Scheuchzer, wiping the perspiration off his brow as he clambers among the Alps to record truthful dragon yarns and untruthful barometrical observations; or to China, dragon-land *par excellence;* ⃰ or even to our own Heralds' College, where these and other beasts have sought a refuge from prying professors under such queer disguises that their own mothers would hardly recognize them.

⃰ In Chinese mythology the telluric element has remained untarnished. The dragon is an earth-god, who controls the rain and thunder clouds.

XV

BYZANTINISM

EXHAUSTED with the morning's walk at Policoro, a railway journey and a long drive up nearly a thousand feet to Rossano in the heat of midday, I sought refuge, contrary to my usual custom, in the chief hotel, intending to rest awhile and then seek other quarters. The establishment was described as "ganz ordentlich" in Baedeker. But, alas! I found little peace or content. The bed on which I had hoped to repose was already occupied by several other inmates. Prompted by curiosity, I counted up to fifty-two of them; after that, my interest in the matter faded away. It became too monotonous. They were all alike, save in point of size (some were giants). A Swammerdam would have been grieved by their lack of variety.

And this, I said to myself, in a renowned city that has given birth to poets and orators, to saints like the great Nilus, to two popes and—last, but not least—one anti-pope! I will not particularize the species beyond saying that they did not hop. Nor will I return to this theme. Let the reader once and for all take *them* for granted.* Let him note that most of the inns of this region are quite uninhabitable, for this and other reasons, unless he takes the most elaborate precautions. . . .

Where, then, do I generally go for accommodation?

Well, as a rule I begin by calling for advice at the chemist's shop, where a fixed number of the older and wiser citizens congregate for a little talk. The cafés and barbers and wine-shops are also meeting-places of men; but those who gather here are not of the right type—they are the young, or empty-headed, or merely thirsty. The other is the true centre of the leisured class, the philosophers' rendezvous. Your *speciale* (apothecary) is himself an elderly and honoured man,

---

* They have their uses, to be sure. Says Kircher: *Cunices lectularii potens remedium contra quartanum est, si ab inscio aegro cum vehiculo congruo potentur; mulierum morbis medentur et uterum prolapsum solo odore in suum locum restituunt.*

full of responsibility and local knowledge; he is altogether a superior person, having been trained in a University. You enter the shop, therefore, and purchase a pennyworth of vaseline. This act entitles you to all the privileges of the club. Then is the moment to take a seat, smiling affably at the assembled company, but without proffering a syllable. If this etiquette is strictly adhered to, it will not be long ere you are politely questioned as to your plans, your present accommodation, and so forth; and soon several members will be vying with each other to procure you a clean and comfortable room at half the price charged in a hotel.

Even when this end is accomplished, my connection with the pharmacy coterie is not severed. I go there from time to time, ostensibly to talk, but in reality to listen. Here one can feel the true pulse of the place. Local questions are dispassionately discussed, with ample forms of courtesy and in a language worthy of Cicero. It is the club of the *élite*.

In olden days I used to visit south Italy armed with introductions to merchants, noblemen and landed proprietors. I have quite abandoned that system, as these people, bless their hearts, have such cordial notions of hospitality that from morning to night the traveller has not a moment he can call his own. Letters to persons in authority, such as syndics or police officers, are useless and worse than useless. Like Chinese mandarins, these officials are so puffed up with their own importance that it is sheer waste of time to call upon them. If wanted, they can always be found; if not, they are best left alone. For besides being usually the least enlightened and least amiable of the populace, they are inordinately suspicious of political or commercial designs on the part of strangers—God knows what visions are fermenting in their turbid brains—and seldom let you out of their sight, once they have known you.

Excepting at Cosenza, Cotrone and Catanzaro, an average white man will seldom find, in any Calabrian hostelry, what he is accustomed to consider as ordinary necessities of life. The thing is easily explicable. These men are not yet in the habit of "handling" civilized travellers; they fail to realize that hotel-keeping is a business to be learnt, like tailoring or politics. They are still in the patriarchal stage, wealthy proprietors of the most part, and quite independent of your custom. They have not learnt the trick of Swiss servility. You must therefore be prepared to put up with what looks like very bad treatment. On your entrance nobody moves a step to enquire after your wants; you must begin by foraging for yourself, and thank God if any notice is taken of what you say; it is as if your presence were barely tolerated. But once the stranger has learnt to pocket his pride and treat his hosts in the same offhand fashion, he will find among them an unconventional courtesy of the best kind.

The establishment being run as a rule by the proprietor's own family, gratuities with a view to exceptional treatment are refused with quiet dignity, and even when accepted will not further your interests in the least; on the contrary, you are thenceforward regarded as tactless and weak in the head. Discreet praise of their native town or village is the best way to win the hearts of the younger generation; for the parents a little knowledge of American conditions is desirable, to prove that you are a man of the world and worthy, a priori, of some respect. But if there exists a man-cook, he is generally an importation and should be periodically and liberally bribed, without knowledge of the family, from the earliest moment. Wonderful, what a cook can do!

It is customary here not to live *en pension* or to pay a fixed price for any meal, the smallest item, down to a piece of bread, being conscientiously marked against you. My system, elaborated after considerable experimentation, is to call for this bill every morning and, for the first day or two after arrival, dispute in friendly fashion every item, remorselessly cutting down some of them. Not that they overcharge; their honesty is notorious, and no difference is made in this respect between a foreigner and a native. It is a matter of principle. By this system, which must not be overdone, your position in the house gradually changes; from being a guest, you become a friend, a brother. For it is your duty to show, above all things, that you are not *scemo*—witless, soft-headed—the unforgivable sin in the south. You may be a forger or cut-throat—why not? It is a vocation like any other, a vocation for *men*. But whoever cannot take care of himself—i.e. of his money—is not to be trusted, in any walk of life; he is of no account; he is no man. I have become firm friends with some of these proprietors by the simple expedient of striking a few francs off their bills; and should I ever wish to marry one of their daughters, the surest way to predispose the whole family in my favour would be this method of amiable but unsmiling contestation.

Of course the inns are often dirty, and not only in their sleeping accommodation. The reason is that, like Turks or Jews, their owners do not see dirt (there is no word for dirt in the Hebrew language); they think it odd when you draw their attention to it. I remember complaining, in one of my fastidious moments, of a napkin, plainly

not my own, which had been laid at my seat. There was literally not
a clean spot left on its surface, and I insisted on a new one. I got it;
but not before hearing the proprietor mutter something about the
"caprices of pregnant women." . . .

The view from these my new quarters at Rossano compensates for
divers other little drawbacks. Down a many-folded gorge of glowing
red earth decked with olives and cistus the eye wanders to the Ionian Sea shining in deepest turquoise tints, and beautified by a glittering margin of white sand. To my left, the water takes a noble
sweep inland; there lies the plain of Sybaris, traversed by the Crathis
of old that has thrust a long spit of sand into the waves. On this side
the outlook is bounded by the high range of Pollino and Dolcedorme, serrated peaks that are even now (midsummer) displaying a
few patches of snow. Clear-cut in the morning light, these exquisite
mountains evaporate, towards sunset, in an amethystine haze. A
restful prospect.

But great was my amazement, on looking out of the window during the night after my arrival, to observe the Polar star placed directly over the Ionian Sea—the south, as I surely deemed it. A week
has passed since then, and in spite of he map I have not quite familiarized myself with this spectacle, nor yet with the other one of
the sun setting apparently due east, over Monte Pollino.

The glory of Rossano is the image of the Madonna Achiropita.
Bartholomaeus tells us, in his life of Saint Nilus, that in olden days
she was wont to appear, clothed in purple, and drive away with a
divine torch the Saracen invaders of this town. In more recent times,
too, she has often saved the citizens from locusts, cholera, and other
calamitous visitations. Unlike most of her kind, she was not painted
by Saint Luke. She is *acheiropœta*—not painted by any human hands
whatever, and in so far resembles a certain old image of the Magna
Mater, her prototype, which was also of divine origin. It is generally
supposed that this picture is painted on wood. Not so, says Diehl; it
is a fragment of a fresco on stone.

Hard by, in the clock-tower of the square, is a marble tablet erected
to the memory of the deputy Felice Cavalotti. We all remember
Cavalotti, the last—with Imbriani—of the republican giants, a blus-
tering rhetorician-journalist, annihilator of monarchs and popes; a
fire-eating duellist, who deserved his uncommon and unlovely fate.
He provoked a colleague to an encounter and during a frenzied attack, received into his open mouth the point of his adversary's
sword, which sealed up for ever that fountain of eloquence and
vituperation.

Cavalotti and the Virgin Achiropita—the new and the old. Really, with such extreme ideals before their eyes, the burghers of Rossano must sometimes wonder where righteousness lies.

They call themselves Calabrians. *Noi siamo calabresi!* they proudly say, meaning that they are above suspicion of unfair dealing. As a matter of fact, they are a muddled brood, and considerably given to cheating when there is any prospect of success. You must watch the peasants coming home at night from their field-work if you wish to see the true Calabrian type—whiskered, short and wiry, and of dark complexion. There is that indescribable mark of *race* in these countrymen; they are different in features and character from the Italians; it is an ascetic, a Spanish type. Your Calabrian is strangely scornful of luxury and even comfort; a creature of few but well-chosen words, straight-forward, indifferent to pain and suffering, and dwelling by preference, when religiously minded, on the harsher aspects of his faith. A note of unworldliness is discoverable in his outlook upon life. Dealing with such men, one feels that they are well disposed not from impulse, but from some dark sense of preordained obligation. Greek and other strains have infused versatility and a more smiling exterior; but the groundwork of the whole remains that old *homo ibericus* of austere gentlemanliness.

Rossano was built by the Romans, says Procopius, and during Byzantine days became a fortress of primary importance. An older settlement probably lay by the seashore, and its harbour is marked as "good" so late as the days of Edrisius. Like many of these old Calabrian ports, it is now invaded by silt and sand, though a few ships still call there. Wishful to learn something of the past glories of the town, I enquired at the municipality for the public library, but was informed by the supercilious and not over-polite secretary that this proud city possesses no such institution. A certain priest, he added, would give me all the desired information.

Canonico Rizzo was a delightful old man, with snowy hair and candid blue eyes. Nothing, it seemed, could have given him greater pleasure than my appearance at that particular moment. He discoursed awhile, and sagely, concerning England and English literature, and then we passed on, *via* Milton, to Calvin and the Puritan movement in Scotland; *via* Livingstone, to colonial enterprises in Africa; and finally, *via* Egypt, Abyssinia, and Prester John, to the early history of the eastern churches. Byzantinism—Saint Nilus; that gave me the desired opportunity, and I mentioned the object of my visit.

"The history of Rossano? Well, well! The secretary of the municipality does me too much honour. You must read the Book of Genesis and Hesiod and Berosus and the rest of them. But stay! I have something of more modern date, in which you will find these ancient authors conveniently classified."

From this book by de Rosis, printed in 1838, I gleaned two facts, firstly, that the city of Rossano is now 3663 years old—quite a respectable age, as towns go—and lastly, that in the year 1500 it had its own academy of lettered men, who called themselves "I spensierati," with the motto *Non alunt curas*—an echo, no doubt, of the Neapolitan renaissance under Alfonso the Magnificient. The popes Urban VIII and Benedict XIII belonged to this association of "thoughtless ones." The work ends with a formidable list of local personages distinguished in the past for their gentleness of birth and polite accomplishments. One wonders how all these delicately nurtured creatures can have survived at Rossano, if their sleeping accommodation——

You might live here some little time before realizing that this place, which seems to slope gently downhill against a pleasing background of wooded mountains, is capable of being strongly fortified. It lies, like other inland Calabrian (and Etruscan) cities, on ground enclosed by stream-beds, and one of these forms a deep gully above which Rossano towers on a smooth and perpendicular precipice. The upper part of this wall of rock is grey sandstone; the lower a bed of red granitic matter. From this coloured stone, which crops up everywhere, the town may have drawn its name of Rossano (rosso = red); not a very old settlement, therefore; although certain patriotic philologers insist upon deriving it from "rus sanum," healthy country. Its older names were Roscia, and Ruscianum; it is not marked in Peutinger. Countless jackdaws and kestrels nestle in this cliff, as well as clouds of swifts, both Alpine and common. These swifts are the ornithological phenomenon of Rossano, and I think the citizens have cause to be thankful for their existence; to them I attribute the fact that there are so few flies, mosquitoes, and other aerial plagues here. If only the amiable birds could be induced to extend their attentions to the bedrooms as well!

This shady glen at the back of the city, with its sparse tufts of vegetation and monstrous blocks of deep red stone cloven into rifts and ravines by the wild waters, has a charm of its own. There are undeniable suggestions of Hell about the place. A pathway runs down this vale of Hinnom, and if you follow it upwards to the junction of the streams you will reach a road that once more ascends

to the town, past the old church of Saint Mark, a most interesting
building. It has five little cupolas, but the interior, supported by
eight columns, has been whitewashed. The structure has now
rightly been declared a "national monument." It dates from the
ninth or tenth century and, according to Bertaux, has the same plan
and the same dimensions as the famous "Cattolica" at Stilo, which
the artistic Lear, though he stayed some time at that picturesque
place, does not so much as mention. They say that this chapel of
Saint Mark was built by Euprassius, protospadarius of Calabria, and
that in the days of Nilus it was dedicated to Saint Anastasius.

Here, at Rossano, we are once more *en plein Byzance*.

Rossano was not only a political bulwark, the most formidable citadel of this Byzantine province. It was a great intellectual centre,
upon which literature, theology and art converged. Among the many
perverse historical notions of which we are now ridding ourselves is
this—that Byzantinism in south Italy was a period of decay and
torpid dreamings. It needed, on the contrary, a resourceful activity
to wipe out, as did those colonists from the east, every trace of
Roman culture and language (Latin rule only revived at Rossano in
the fifteenth century). There was no lethargy in their social and
political ambitions, in their military achievements, which held the
land against overwhelming numbers of Saracens, Lombards and
other intruders. And the life of those old monks of Saint Basil, as we
now know it, represented a veritable renaissance of art and letters.

Of the ten Basilean convents that grew up in the surroundings of
Rossano the most celebrated was that of S. M. del Patir. Together
with the others, it succeeded to a period of eremitism—of solitary
anchorites whose dwellings honeycombed the warm slopes that con-
front the Ionian. . . .

The lives of some of these Greco-Calabrian hermits are valuable
documents. In the *Vitæ Sanctorum Siculorum* of O. Caietanus
(1657) the student will find a Latin translation of the biography of
one of them, Saint Elia Junior. He died in 903. It was written by a
contemporary monk, who tells us that the holy man performed
many miracles, among them that of walking over a river dryshod.
And the Bollandists (*Acta Sanctorum*, 11th September) have reprinted the biography of Saint Elia Spelaeotes—the cave-dweller—,
as composed in Greek by a disciple. It is yet more interesting. He
lived in a "honesta spelunca" which he discovered in 864 by means
of a flight of bats issuing therefrom; he suffered persecutions from a

woman, exactly after the fashion of Joseph and Potiphar's wife; he grew to be 94 years old; the Saracens vainly tried to burn his dead body, and the water in which this corpse was subsequently washed was useful for curing another holy man's toothache. Yet even these creatures were subject to gleams of common sense. "Virtues," said this one, "are better than miracles."

How are we to account for these rock-hermits and their inelegant habits? How explain this poisoning of the sources of manly self-respect?

Thus, I think: that under the influence of their creed they reverted perforce to the more bestial traits of aboriginal humanity. They were thrust back in their development. They became solitaries, animalesque and shy—such as we may imagine our hairy progenitors to have been. Hence their dirt and vermin, their horror of learning, their unkempt hair, their ferocious independence, their distrust of sunshine and ordered social life, their foul dieting, their dread of malign spirits, their cave-dwelling propensities. All bestial characteristics!

This atavistic movement, this retrogression towards primevalism, must have possessed a certain charm, for it attracted vast multitudes; it was only hemmed, at last, by a physical obstacle.

The supply of caves ran out.

Not till then were its votaries forced to congregate in those unhealthy clusters which afterwards grew to be monasteries. Where many of them were gathered together under one roof there imposed itself a certain rudimentary discipline and subordination; yet they preserved as much as they could of their savage traits, cave-like cells and hatred of cleanliness, terror of demons, matted beards.

Gradually the social habits of mundane fellow-creatures insinuated themselves into these hives of squalor and idleness. The inmates began to wash and to shave; they acquired property, they tilled the ground, they learnt to read and write, and finally became connaisseurs of books and pictures and wine and women. They were pleased to forget that the eunuch and the beggar are the true Christian or Buddhist. In other words, the allurements of rational life grew too strong for their convictions; they became reasonable beings in spite of their creed. This is how cœnobitism grew out of eremitism not only in Calabria, but in every part of the world which has been afflicted with these eccentrics. Go to Mount Athos, if you wish to see specimens of all the different stages conveniently arranged upon a small area. . . .

This convent of Patir exercised a great local influence as early as the tenth century; then, towards the end of the eleventh, it was completely rebuilt without and reorganized within. The church underwent a thorough restoration in 1672. But it was shattered, together with the rest of the edifice, by the earthquake of 1836 which, Madonna Achiropita notwithstanding, levelled to the ground one-half of the fifteen thousand houses then standing at Rossano.

These monastic establishments, as a general rule, were occupied later on by the Benedictines, who ousted the Basileans and were supplanted, in their turn, by popular orders of later days like the Theatines. Those that are conveniently situated have now been turned into post offices, municipalities, and other public buildings—such has been the common procedure. But many of them, like this of Patir, are too decayed and remote from the life of man. Fiore, who wrote in 1691, counts up 94 dilapidated Basilean monasteries in Calabria out of a former total of about two hundred; Patir and thirteen others he mentions as having, in his day, their old rites still subsisting. Batiffol has recently gone into the subject with his usual thoroughness.

Nothing is uglier than a modern ruin, and the place would assuredly not be worth the three hours' ride from Rossano were it not for the church, which has been repaired, and for the wondrous view to be obtained from its site. The journey, too, is charming, both by the ordinary track that descends from Rossano and skirts the foot of the hills through olives and pebbly stream-beds, ascending, finally, across an odorous tangle of cistus, rosemary and myrtle to the platform on which the convent stands—or by the alternative and longer route which I took on the homeward way, and which follows the old water conduit built by the monks into a forest of enormous chestnuts, oaks, hollies and Calabrian pines, emerging out of an ocean of glittering bracken.

I was pursued into the church of Patir by a bevy of country wenches who frequented this region for purposes of haymaking. There is a miraculous crucifix in this sanctuary, hidden behind a veil which, with infinite ceremony, these females withdrew for my edification. There it was, sure enough; but what, I wondered, would happen from the presence of these impure creatures in such a place? Things have changed considerably since the days of old, for such was the contamination to be expected from the mere presence of a woman within these walls that even the Mother of God, while visiting Saint Nilus—the builder, not the great saint—at work upon the foundations, often conversed with him, but never ventured to step within the area of the building itself. And later on it was a well-authenticated phenomenon recorded by Beltrano and others, that if a female entered the church, the heavens immediately became cloudy and sent down thunders and lightnings and such-like signs of celestial disapproval, which never ceased until the offending monster had left the premises.

From this ancient monastery comes, I fancy, the Achiropita image. Montorio will tell you all about it; he learnt its history in June 1712 from the local archbishop, who had extracted his information out of the espiscopal archives. Concerning another of these wonder-working idols—that of S. M. del Patirion—you may read in the ponderous tomes of Ughelli.

Whether the celebrated Purple Codex of Rossano ever formed part of the library of Patirion has not yet been determined. This wonderful parchment—now preserved at Rossano—is mentioned for the first time by Cesare Malpica, who wrote some interesting things about the Albanian and Greek colonies in Calabria, but it was only discovered, in the right sense of that word, in March 1879 by Gebhardt and Harnack. They illustrated it in their *Evangeliorum Codex Græcus*. Haseloff also described it in 1898 (*Codex Purpureus Rossanensis*), and pointed out that its iconographical value consists in the fact that it is the only Greek Testament MS. containing pictures of the life of Christ before the eighth-ninth century. These pictures are indeed marvellous—more marvellous than beautiful, like so many Byzantine productions; their value is such that the parchment has now been declared a "national monument." It is sternly guarded, and if it is moved out of Rossano—as happened lately when it was exhibited at Grottaferrata—it travels in the company of armed carbineers.

Still pursued by the flock of women, I took to examining the floor of this church, which contains tesselated marble pavements depicting centaurs, unicorns, lions, stags, and other beasts. But my contemplation of these choice relics was disturbed by irrelevant remarks on the part of the worldly females, who discovered in the head of the stag some subtle peculiarity that stirred their sense of humour.

"Look!" said one of them to her neighbour. "He has horns. Just like your Pasquale."

"Pasquale indeed! And how about Antonio?"

I enquired whether they knew what kind of animals these were.

"Beasts of the ancients. Beasts that nobody knows. Beasts that have horns—like certain Christians. . . ."

From the terrace of green sward that fronts this ruined monastery you can see the little town of Corigliano, whose coquettish white houses lie in a fold of the hills. Corigliano— ἐλαίων (land of olives): the derivation, if not correct, is at least appropriate, for it lies embowered in a forest of these trees. A gay place it was, in Bourbon times, with a ducal ruler of its own. Here, they say, the remnants of the Sybarites took refuge after the destruction of their city whose desolate plain lies at our feet, backed by the noble range of Dolcedorme. Swinburne, like a sensible man, takes the Sybarites under his protection; he defends their artificially shaded streets and those other signs of voluptuousness which, to judge by certain modern researches, seem to have been chiefly contrived for combating the demon of malaria. Earthly welfare, the cult of material health and ease—such was *their* ideal.

In sharpest contrast to these strivings stands the aim of those old monks who scorned the body as a mere encumbrance, seeking spiritual enlightenment and things not of this earth.

And now, Sybarites and Basileans—alike in ruins!

A man of to-day, asked which of the two civilizations he would wish restored, would not hesitate long in deciding for the Hellenic one. Readers of Lenormant will call to mind his glowing pages on the wonders that might be found buried on the site of Sybaris. His plan of excavation sounds feasible enough. But how remote it becomes, when one remembers the case of Herculaneum! Here, to our certain knowledge, many miracles of antique art and literature lie within a few feet of our reach; yet nothing is done. These hidden monuments, which are the heritage of all humanity, are withheld from our eyes by the dog-in-the-manger policy of a country which even without foreign assistance, could easily accomplish the work, were it to employ thereon only half the sum now spent in feeding, clothing and supervising a horde of criminals, every one of whom ought to be hanged ten times over. Meanwhile other nations are forbidden to co-operate; the fair-minded German proposals were scornfully rejected; later on, those of Sir Charles Waldstein.

"What!" says the *Giornale d' Italia*, "are we to have international excavation-committees thrust upon us? Are we to be treated like the Turks?"

That, gentle sirs, is precisely the state of the case.

The object of such committees is to do for the good of mankind what a single nation is powerless or unwilling to do. Your behaviour at Herculaneum is identical with that of the Turks at Nineveh. The system adopted should likewise be the same.

I shall never see that consummation.

But I shall not forget a certain article in an American paper—"The New York Times," I fancy—which gave me fresh food for thought, here at Patirion, in the sight of that old Hellenic colony, and with the light chatter of those women still ringing in my ears. Its writer, with whom not all of us will agree, declared that first in importance of all the antiquities buried in Italian soil come the lost poems of Sappho. The lost poems of Sappho—a singular choice! In corroboration whereof he quoted the extravagant praise of J. A. Symonds upon that amiable and ambiguous young person. And he might have added Algernon Swinburne, who calls her "the greatest poet who ever was at all."

Sappho and these two Victorians, I said to myself. . . . Why just these two? How keen is the cry of elective affinity athwart the ages! *The soul*, says Plato, *divines that which it seeks, and traces obscurely the footsteps of its obscure desire.*

The footsteps of its obscure desire——

So one stumbles, inadvertently, upon problems of the day concerning which our sages profess to know nothing. And yet I do perceive a certain Writing upon the Wall setting forth, in clearest language, that $1 + 1 = 3$; a legend which it behoves them not to expunge, but to expound. For it refuses to be expunged; and we do not need a German lady to tell us how much the "synthetic" sex, the hornless but not brainless sex, has done for the life of the spirit while those other two were reclaiming the waste places of earth, and procreating, and fighting—as befits their horned anatomy.

XVI

REPOSING AT CASTROVILLARI

I REMEMBER asking my friend the Roman deputy of whom I have already spoken, and whom I regard as a fountain of wisdom on matters Italian, how it came about that the railway stations in his country were apt to be so far distant from the towns they serve. Rocca Bernarda, I was saying, lies 33 kilometres from its station; and even some of the largest towns in the kingdom are inconveniently and unnecessarily remote from the line.

"True," he replied. "Very true! Inconveniently . . . but perhaps not unnecessarily. . . ." He nodded his head, as he often does, when revolving some deep problem in his mind.

"Well, sir?"

"Inasmuch as everything has its reasons, be they geographical, sociological, or otherwise . . ." and he mused again. "Let me tell you what I think as regards our respective English and Italian points of view," he said at last. "And to begin with—a few generalities! We may hold that success in modern life consists in correctly appreciating the principles which underlie our experiences—in what may be called the scientific attitude towards things in general. Now, do the English cultivate this attitude? Not sufficiently. They are in the stage of those mediæval scholars who contentedly alleged separate primary causes for each phenomenon, instead of seeking, by the investigation of secondary ones, for the inevitable interdependence of the whole. In other words, they do not subordinate facts; they co-ordinate them. Your politicians and all your public men are guided by impulse—by expediency, as they prefer to call it; they are empirical; they never attempt to codify their conduct; they despise it as theorizing. What happens? This old-fashioned hand-to-mouth system of theirs invariably breaks down here and there. And then? Then they trust to some divine interposition, some accident, to put things to rights again. The success of the English is largely built up on such accidents—on the mistakes of other people. Providence has favoured them so far, on the whole; but one day it may leave them in the lurch, as it did the anti-scientific Russians in their war with the Japanese. One day other people will forget to make these pleasant mistakes."

He paused, and I forbore to interrupt his eloquence.

"To come now to the practical application—to this particular instance. Tell me, does your English system testify to any constructive forethought? In London, I am assured, the railway companies have built stations at enormous expense in the very heart of the town. What will be the consequence of this hand-to-mouth policy? This, that in fifty years such structures will have become obsolete—stranded in slums at the back of new quarters yet undreamed of. New depots will have to be built. Whereas in Italy the now distant city will in fifty years have grown to reach its station and, in another half-century, will have encircled it. Thanks to our sagacity, the station will then be in its proper place, in the centre of the town. Our progeny will be grateful; and that again, you will admit, is a worthy aim for our politicians. Besides, what would happen to our coachmen if nobody needed their services on arriving at his destination? The poor men must not be allowed to starve! Cold head and warm heart, you know; humanitarian considerations cannot be thrust aside by a community that prides itself on being truly civilized. I trust I have made myself intelligible?"

"You always do. But why should I incommode myself to please your progeny, or even my own? And I don't like the kind of warm heart that subordinates my concerns to those of a cab-driver. You don't altogether convince me, dear sir."

"To speak frankly, I sometimes don't convince myself. My own country station, for example, is curiously remote from the city, and it is annoying on wintry nights to drive through six miles of level mud when you are anxious to reach home and dinner; so much so that, in my egoistical moments, I would have been glad if our administration had adopted the more specious British method. But come now! You cannot raise that objection against the terminus at Rome."

"Not that one. But I can raise two others. The platforms are inconveniently arranged, and a traveller will often find it impossible to wash his hands and face there; as to hot water——"

"Granting a certain deplorable disposition of the lines—why on earth, pray, should a man cleanse himself at the station when there are countless hotels and lodging-houses in the city? O you English originals!"

"And supposing," I urged, "he is in a hurry to catch another train going south, to Naples or Palermo?"

"There I have you, my illustrious friend! *Nobody travels south of Rome.*"

Nobody travels south of Rome. . . .

Often have I thought upon those words.

This conversation was forcibly recalled to my mind by the fact that it took our creaky old diligence two and a half hours (one of the horses had been bought the day before, for six pounds) to drive from the station of Castrovillari to the entrance of the town, where we were delayed another twenty minutes, while the octroi zealots searched through every bag and parcel on the post-wagon.

Many people have said bad things about this place. But my once unpleasant impressions of it have been effaced by my reception at its new and decent little hostelry. What a change after the sordid filth of Rossano! Castrovillari, to be sure, has no background of hoary eld to atone for such deficiencies. It was only built the other day, by the Normans; or by the Romans, who called it Aprustum; or possibly by the Greeks, who founded their Abystron on this particular site for the same reasons that commended it in yet earlier times to certain bronze and stone age primitives, whose weapons you may study in the British Museum and elsewhere. *

But what are the stone ages compared with immortal and immutable Rossano? An ecclesiastical writer has proved that Calabria was inhabited before the Noachian flood; and Rossano, we may be sure, was one of the favourite haunts of the antediluvians. None the less, it is good to rest in a clean bed, for a change; and to feed off a clean plate.

We are in the south. One sees it in sundry small ways—in the behaviour of the cats, for instance. . . .

The Tarentines, they say, imported the cat into Europe. If those of south Italy still resemble their old Nubian ancestors, the beast would assuredly not have been worth the trouble of acclimatizing. On entering these regions, one of the first things that strikes me is the difference between the appearance of cats and dogs hereabouts, and in England or any northern country; and the difference in their temperaments. Our dogs are alert in their movements and of wide-awake features; here they are drowsy and degraded mongrels, with

---

* Even so Taranto, Cumae, Paestum, Metapontum, Monteleone and other southern towns were founded by the ancients on the site of prehistoric stations.

expressionless eyes. Our cats are sleek and slumberous; here they prowl about haggard, shifty and careworn, their fur in patches and their ears a-tremble from nervous anxiety. That domestic animals such as these should be fed at home does not commend itself to the common people; they must forage for their food abroad. Dogs eat offal, while the others hunt for lizards in the fields. A lizard diet is supposed to reduce their weight (it would certainly reduce mine); but I suspect that southern cats are emaciated not only from this cause, but from systematic starvation. Many a kitten is born that never tastes a drop of cow's milk from the cradle to the grave, and little enough of its own mother's.

To say that our English *zoophilomania*—our cult of lap-dogs—smacks of degeneracy does not mean that I sympathize with the ill-treatment of beasts which annoys many visitors to these parts and has been attributed to "Saracenic" influences. Wrongly, of course; one might as well attribute it to the old Greeks.* Poor Saracens! They are a sort of whipping-boy, all over the country. The chief sinner in this respect is the Vatican, which has authorized cruelty to animals by its teaching. When Lord Odo Russell enquired of the Pope regarding the foundation of a society for the prevention of cruelty to animals in Italy, the papal answer was: "Such an association *could not be sanctioned* by the Holy See, being founded on a theological error, to wit, that Christians owed any duties to ani-

* Whose attitude towards animals, by the way, was as far removed from callousness as from sentimentalism. We know how those Hellenic oxen fared who had laboured to draw up heavy blocks for the building of a temple—how, on the completion of their task, they were led into green fields, there to pasture unmolested for the rest of their lives. We know that the Greeks were appreciative of the graces and virtues of canine nature—is not the Homeric Argo still the finest dog-type in literature? Yet to them the dog, even he of the tender Anthology, remained what he is: a tamed beast. The Greeks, sitting at dinner, resented the insolence of a creature that, watching every morsel as it disappeared into the mouth of its master, plainly discovered by its physiognomy the desire, the presumed right, to devour what he considered fit only for himself. Whence that profound word κυνώπης—dog-eyed, shameless. In contrast to this sanity, observe what an Englisman can read into a dog's eye:

> That liquid, melancholy eye,
>> From whose pathetic, soul-fed springs
> Seemed surging the Virgilian cry—
> The sense of tears in mortal things. . . .

That is how Matthew Arnold interprets the feelings of Fido, watching his master at work upon a tender beefsteak. . . .

mals." This language has the inestimable and rather unusual merit of being perspicuous. Nevertheless, Ouida's flaming letters to "The Times" inaugurated an era of truer humanity. . . .

And the lateness of the dining-hour—another symptom of the south. It was eleven o'clock when I sat down to dinner on the night of my arrival, and habitués of the hotel, engineers and so forth, were still dropping in for their evening meal. Appetite comes more slowly than ever, now that the heats have begun.

They have begun in earnest. The swoon of summer is upon the land, the grass is cut, cicadas are chirping overhead. Despite its height of a thousand feet, Castrovillari must be blazing in August, surrounded as it is by parched fields and an amphitheatre of bare limestone hills that exhale the sunny beams. You may stroll about these fields observing the construction of the line which is to pass through Cassano, a pretty place, famous for its wine and mineral springs; or studying the habits of the gigantic grasshoppers that hang in clusters to the dried thistles and start off, when scared, with the noise of a covey of partridges; or watching how the cows are shod, at this season, to thresh the corn. Old authors are unanimous in declaring that the town was embowered in oak forests; as late as 1844 it was lamented that this "ancient barbarous custom" of cutting them down had not yet been discontinued. The mischief is now done, and it would be interesting to know the difference between the present summer temperature and that of olden days.

The manna ash used to be cultivated in these parts. I cannot tell whether it purgative secretion is still in favour. The confusion between this stuff and the biblical manna gave rise to the legends about Calabria where "Manna droppeth as dew from Heaven." Sandys says it was prepared out of the mulberry. He copied assiduously, did old Sandys, and yet found room for some original blunders of his own. R. Pococke, by the way, is one of those who were dissatisfied with Castrovillari. He found no accommodation save an empty house. "A poor town." . . .

Driving through modern Castrolvillari one might think the place flat and undeserving of the name of *castrum*. But the old town is otherwise. It occupies a proud eminence—the head of a promontory which overlooks the junction of two streams; the newer settlement stands on the more level ground at its back. This acropolis, once thronged with folk but now well-nigh deserted, has all the macabre fascination of decay. A mildewy spirit haunts those tortuous and uneven roadways; plaster drops unheeded from the walls; the wild fig thrusts luxuriant arms through the windows of palaces whose balconies are rusted and painted loggias crumbling to earth . . . a mournful and malarious agglomeration of ruins.

There is a castle, of course. It was built, or rebuilt, by the Aragonese, with four corner towers, one of which became infamous for a scene that rivals the horrors of the Black Hole of Calcutta. Numbers of confined brigands, uncared-for, perished miserably of starvation within its walls. Says the historian Botta:

"The abominable taint prevented the guards from approaching; the dead bodies were not carried away. The pestilence increased; in pain and exhaustion, the dying fell shuddering on the dead; the hale on the dying; all tearing themselves like dogs with teeth and nails. The tower of Castrovillari became a foul hole of corruption, and the stench was spread abroad for a long season."

This castle is now used as a place of confinement. Sentries warned me at one point not to approach too near the walls; it was "forbidden." I had no particular desire to disobey this injunction. Judging by the number of rats that swarm about the place, it is not exactly a model prison.

One of the streets in this dilapidated stronghold bears to this day the inscription "Giudea," or Jewry. Southern Italy was well stocked with those Hebrews concerning whom Mr. H. M. Adler has sagely discoursed. They lived in separate districts, and seem to have borne a good reputation. Those of Castrovillari, on being ejected by Ferdinand the Catholic in 1511, obligingly made a donation of their school to the town. But they returned anon, and claimed it again. Persecuted as they were, they never suffered the martyrdom of the ill-starred Waldensian colonies in Calabria.

The houses of this Jewry overlook the Coscile river, the Sybaris of old, and from a spot in the quarter a steep path descends to its banks. Here you will find yourself in another climate, cool and moist. The livid waters tumble gleefully towards the plain, amid penurious plots of beans and tomatoes, and a fierce tangle of vegetation wherever the hand of man has not made clearings. Then, mounting aloft once more, you will do well to visit the far-famed chapel that sits at the apex of the promontory, Santa Maria del Castello. There is a little platform where you may repose and enjoy the view, as I have done for some evenings past—letting the eye roam up-country towards Dolcedorme and its sister peaks, and westwards over the undulating Sila lands whose highest point, Botte Donato, is unmistakable even at this distance of forty miles, from its peculiar shape.

The Madonna picture preserved within the sanctuary has performed so many miracles in ages past that I despair of giving any account of them. It is high time, none the less, for a new sign from Heaven. Shattered by earthquakes, the chapel is in a disruptured and even menacing condition. Will some returned emigrant from America come forward with the necessary funds? That would be a miracle, too, in its way. But gone, for the present, are the ages of Faith—the days when the peevishly-protestant J. H. Bartels sojourned here and groaned as he counted up the seven monasteries of Castrovillari (there used to be nearly twice that number), and viewed the 130 priests, "fat-paunched rascals, loafing about the streets and doorways." . . .

From my window in the hotel I espy a small patch of snow on the hills. I know the place; it is the so-called "Montagna del Principe" past which the track winds into the Pollino regions. Thither I am bound; but so complicated is life that even for a short three days' ramble among those forests a certain amount of food and clothing must be provided—a mule is plainly required. There seem to be none of these beasts available at Castrovillari.

"To Morano!" they tell me. "It is nearer the mountain, and there you will find mules plentiful as blackberries. To Morano!"

Morano lies a few miles higher up the valley on the great military road to Lagonegro, which was built by Murat and cuts through the interior of Basilicata, rising at Campo Tenese to a height of 1100 metres. They are now running a public motor service along this beautiful stretch of 52 kilometres, at the cheap rate of a sou per kilometre.

En route!

POSTSCRIPT.—Another symptom of the south:

Once you have reached the latitude of Naples, the word *grazie* (thank you) vanishes from the vocabulary of all save the most cultured. But to conclude therefrom that one is among a thankless race is not altogether the right inference. They have a wholly different conception of the affair. Our septentrional "thanks" is a complicated product in which gratefulness for things received and for things to come are unconsciously balanced; while their point of view differs in nothing from that of the beau-ideal of Greek courtesy, of Achilles, whose mother procured for him a suit of divine armour from Hephaistos, which he received without a word of acknowledgment either for her or for the god who had been put to some little trouble in the matter. A thing given they regard as a thing found, a hermaion, a happy hit in the lottery of life; the giver is the blind instrument of Fortune. This chill attitude repels us; and our effusive expressions of thankfulness astonish these people and the Orientals.

A further difference is that the actual gift is viewed quite extrinsically, intellectually, either in regard to what it would fetch if bartered or sold, or, if to be kept, as to how far its possession may raise the recipient in the eyes of other men. This is purely Homeric, once more—Homeric or primordial, if you prefer. Odysseus told his kind host Alkinoos, whom he was never to see again, that he would be glad to receive farewell presents from him—to cherish as a friendly memory? No, but "because they would make him look a finer fellow when he got home." The idea of a keepsake, of an emotional value attaching to some trifle, is a northern one. Here life is give and take, and lucky he who takes more than he gives; it is what Professor Mahaffy calls the "ingrained selfishness of the Greek character." Speaking of all below the upper classes, I should say that disinterested benevolence is apt to surpass their comprehension, a goodnatured person being regarded as weak in the head.

Has this man, then, no family, that he should benefit strangers? Or is he one of nature's unfortunates—soft-witted? Thus they argue. They will do acts of spontaneous kindness towards their family, far oftener than is customary with us. But outside that narrow sphere, *interesse* (Odyssean self-advantage) is the mainspring of their actions. Whence their smooth and glozing manners towards the stranger, and those protestations of undying affection which beguile the unwary—they wish to be forever in your good graces, for sooner or later you may be of use; and if perchance you do content them, they will marvel (philosophically) at your grotesque generosity, your lack of discrimination and restraint. Such *malizia* (cleverness) is none the more respectable for being childishly transparent. The profound and unscrupulous northerner quickly familiarizes himself with its technique, and turns it to his own profit. Lowering his moral notions, he soon—so one of them expressed it to me—"walks round them without getting off his chair" and, on the strength of his undeserved reputation for simplicity and fair dealing, keeps them dangling a lifetime in a tremble of obsequious amiability, cheered on by the hope of ultimately over-reaching him. Idle dream, where a pliant and sanguine southerner is pitted against the unswerving

Saxon or Teuton! This accounts for the success of foreign trading houses in the south. Business is business, and the devil take the hindmost! By all means; but they who are not rooted to the spot by commercial exigencies nor ready to adopt debased standards of conduct will find that a prolonged residence in a centre like Naples—the daily attrition of its ape-and-tiger elements—sullies their homely candour and self-respect.

For a tigerish flavour does exist in most of these southern towns. Camorra, the law of intimidation, rules the city. This is what Stendhal meant when, speaking of the "simple and inoffensive" personages in *The Vicar of Wakefield*, he remarked that "in the sombre Italy, a simple and inoffensive creature would be quickly destroyed." It is not easy to be inoffensive and yet respected in a land of teeth and claws, where a man is reverenced in proportion as he can browbeat his fellows. So much ferocity tinctures civic life, that had they not dwelt in towns while we were still shivering in bogs, one would deem them not yet ripe for herding together in large numbers; one would say that post-patriarchal conditions evoked the worst qualities of the race. And we must revise our conceptions of fat and lean men; we must pity Cassius, and dread Falstaff.

"What has happened"—you ask some enormous individual—"to your adversary at law?"

"To which one of them?"

"Oh, Signor M——, the timber merchant."

"*L'abbiamo mangiato!*" (I have eaten him.)

Beware of the fat Neapolitan. He is fat from prosperity, from dining off his leaner brothers.

Which reminds me of a supremely important subject, eating.

The feeding here is saner than ours with its all-pervading animal grease (even a boiled egg tastes of mutton fat in England), its stockpot, suet, and those other inventions of the devil whose awful effects we only survive because we are continually counteracting or eliminating them by the help of (1) pills, (2) athletics, and (3) alcohol. Saner as regards material, but hopelessly irrational in method. Your ordinary employé begins his day with a thimbleful of black coffee, nothing more. What work shall be got out of him under such antihygenic conditions? Of course it takes ten men to do the work of one; and of course all ten of them are sulky and irritable throughout the morning, thinking only of their luncheon. Then indeed—then they make up for lost time; those few favoured ones, at least, who can afford it.

I once watched a young fellow, a clerk of some kind, in a restaurant at midday. He began by informing the waiter that he had no appetite that morning—*sangue di Dio!* no appetite whatever; but at last allowed himself to be persuaded into consuming a *hors d'œuvres* of anchovies and olives. Then he was induced to try the maccheroni, because they were "particularly good that morning"; he ate, or rather drank, an immense plateful. After that came some slices of meat and a dish of green stuff sufficient to satisfy a starving bullock. A little fish? asked the waiter. Well, perhaps yes, just for form's sake—two fried mullets and some nondescript fragments. Next, he devoured a couple of raw eggs "on account of his miserably weak stomach," a bowl of salad and a goodly lump of fresh cheese. Not without a secret feeling of envy I left him at work upon his dessert, of which he had already consumed some six peaches. Add to this (quite an ordinary repast) half a bottle of heavy wine, a cup of black coffee and three glasses of water—what work shall be got out of a man after such a boa-constrictor collation? He is as exasperated and prone to take offence as in the morning—this time from another cause. . . .

That is why so many of them suffer from chronic troubles of the digestive organs. The head of a hospital at Naples tells me that stomach diseases are more prevalent there than in any other part of Europe, and the stomach, whatever sentimentalists may say to the contrary, being the true seat of the emotions, it follows that a judicious system of dieting might work wonders upon their development. Nearly all Mediterranean races have been misfed from early days; that is why they are so small. I would undertake to raise the Italian standard of height by several inches, if I had control of their nutrition for a few centuries. I would undertake to alter their whole outlook upon life, to convert them from utilitarians into romantics—were such a change desirable. For if utilitarianism be the shadow of starvation, romance is nothing by the vapour of repletion.

And yet men still talk of race-characteristics as of something fixed and immutable! The Jews, so long as they starved in Palestine, were the most acrimonious bigots on earth. Now that they live and feed sensibly, they have learnt to see things in their true perspective— they have become rationalists. Their less fortunate fellow-Semites, the Arabs, have continued to starve and to swear by the Koran— empty in body and empty in mind. No poise or balance is possible to those who live in uneasy conditions. The wisest of them can only attain to stoicism—a dumb protest against the environment. There are no stoics among well-fed people. The Romans made that discovery for themselves, when they abandoned the cheese-paring habits of the Republic.

In short, it seems to me that virtues and vices which cannot be expressed in physiological terms are not worth talking about; that when a morality refuses to derive its sanction from the laws which govern our body, it loses the right to exist. This being so, what is the most conspicuous native vice?

Envy, without a doubt.

Out of envy they pine away and die; our of envy they kill one another. To produce a more placid race,* to dilute envious thoughts and the acts to which they lead, is at bottom a question of nutrition. One would like to know for how much black brooding and for how many revengeful deeds that morning thimbleful of black coffee is responsible.

The very faces one sees in the streets would change. Envy is reflected in all too many of those of the middle classes, while the poorest citizens are often haggard and distraught from sheer hunger—hunger which has not had time to be commuted into moral poison; college-taught men, in responsible positions, being forced to live on salaries which a London lift-boy would disdain. When that other local feature, that respect for honourable poverty—the reverse of what we see in England where, since the days of the arch-snob Pope, a slender income has grown to be considered a subject of reproach.

And yet another symptom of the south——

Enough! The clock points to 6.20; it is time for an evening walk—my final one—to the terrace of S. M. del Castello.

---

* By placid I do not mean peace-loving and pitiful in the Christian sense. That doctrine of loving and forgiving one's enemies is based on sheer funk; our pity for others is dangerously akin to self-pity, most odious of vices. Catholic teaching—in practice, if not in theory—glides artfully over the desirability of these imported freak-virtues, knowing that they cannot appeal to a masculine stock. By placid I mean steady, self-contained.

XVII

OLD MORANO

THIS Morano is a very ancient city; Tufarelli, writing in 1598, proves that it was then exactly 3349 years old. Oddly enough, therefore, its foundation almost coincides with that of Rossano. . . .

There may be mules at Morano; indeed, there are. But they are illusive beasts: phantom-mules. Despite the assistance of the captain of the carbineers, the local innkeeper, the communal policeman, the secretary of the municipality, an amiable canon of the church and several non-official residents, I vainly endeavoured, for three days, to procure one—flitting about, meanwhile, between this place and Castrovillari. For Morano, notwithstanding its size (they say it is larger than the other town) offers no accommodation or food in the septentrional sense of those terms.

Its situation, as you approach from Castrovillari, is striking. The white houses stream in a cataract down one side of a steep conical hill that dominates the landscape—on the summit sits the inevitable castle, blue sky peering through its battered windows. But the interior is not at all in keeping with this imposing aspect. Morano, so far as I was able to explore it, is a labyrinth of sombre, tortuous and fetid alleys, where black pigs wallow amid heaps of miscellaneous and malodorous filth—in short, the town exemplifies that particular idea of civic liberty which consists in everybody being free to throw their own private refuse into the public street and leave it there, from generation to generation. What says Lombroso? "The street-cleaning is entrusted, in many towns, to the rains of heaven and, in their absence, to the voracity of the pigs."

None the less, while waiting for mules that never came, I took to patrolling those alleys, at first out of sheer boredom, but soon impelled by that subtle fascination which emanates from the *ne plus ultra* of anything—even of grotesque dirtiness. On the second day, however, a case of cholera was announced, which chilled my ardour for further investigations. It was on that account that I failed to inspect what was afterwards described to me as the chief marvel of the place—a carved wooden altar-piece in a certain church.

"It is prodigious and *antichissimo*," said an obliging citizen to whom I applied for information. "There is nothing like it on earth, and I have been six times to America, sir. The artist—a real artist, mind you, not a common professor—spent his whole life in carving it. It was for the church, you see, and he wanted to show what he could do in the way of a masterpiece. Then, when it was finished and in its place, the priests refused to pay for it. It was made not for them, they said, but for the glory of God; the man's reward was sufficient. And besides, he could have remission of sins for the rest of his life. He said he did not care about remission of sins; he wanted money—money! But he got nothing. Whereupon he began to brood and to grow yellow. Money—money! That was all he ever said. And at last he became quite green and died. After that, his son took up the quarrel, but he got as little out of the priests as the father. It was fixed in the church, you understand, and he could not take it away. He climbed through the window one night and tried to burn it—the marks are there to this day—but they were too sharp for him. And he took the business so much to heart that he also soon died quite young! And quite green—like his father."

The most characteristic item in the above history is that about growing green. People are apt to put on this colour in the south from disappointment or from envy. They have a proverb which runs "sfoga o schiatta"—relieve yourself or burst; our vaunted ideal of self-restraint, of dominating the reflexes, being thought not only fanciful but injurious to health. Therefore, if relief is thwarted, they either brood themselves into a green melancholy, or succumb to a sudden "colpo di sangue," like a young woman of my acquaintance who, considering herself beaten in a dispute with a tram-conductor about a penny, forthwith had a "colpo di sangue," and was dead in a few hours. A primeval assertion of the ego. . . .

Unable to perambulate the streets of Morano, I climbed to the ruined fortress along the verdant slope at its back, and enjoyed a fair view down the fertile valley, irrigated by streamlets and planted with many-hued patches of culture, with mulberries, pomegranates and poplars. Some boys were up here, engaged in fishing—fishing for young kestrels in their nest above a shattered gateway. The tackle consisted of a rod with a bent piece of wire fixed to one end, and it seemed to me a pretty unpromising form of sport. But suddenly, amid wild vociferations, they hooked one, and carried it off in triumph to supper. The mother bird, meanwhile, sailed restlessly about the æther watching every movement, as I could see by my glasses; at times she drifted quite near, then swerved again and hovered, with vibrating pinions, directly overhead. It was clear that she could not tear herself away from the scene, and hardly had the marauders departed, when she alighted on the wall and began to inspect what was left of her dwelling. It was probably rather untidy. I felt sorry for her; yet such harebrained imprudence cannot go unpunished. With so many hundred crannies in this old castle, why choose one which any boy can reach with a stick? She will know better next season.

Then an old shepherd scrambled up, and sat on the stone beside me. He was short-sighted, asthmatic, and unable to work; the doctor had recommended an evening walk up to the castle. We conversed awhile, and he extracted a carnation out of his waistcoat pocket— unusual receptacle for flowers—which he presented to me. I touched upon the all-absorbing topic of mules.

"Mules are very busy animals in Morano," he explained. "*Animali occupatissimi.*" However, he promised to exert himself on my behalf; he knew a man with a mule—two mules—he would send him round, if possible.

Quite a feature in the landscape of Morano is the costume of the women, with their home-dyed red skirts and ribbons of the same hue plaited into their hair. It is a beautiful and reposeful shade of red, between Pompeian and brick-colour, and the tint very closely resembles that of the cloth worn by the beduin (married) women of Tunisia. Maybe it was introduced by the Saracens. And it is they, I imagine, who imported that love of red peppers (a favourite dish with most Orientals) which is peculiar to these parts, where they eat them voraciously in every form, particularly in that of red sausages seasoned with these fiery condiments.

The whole country is full of Saracen memories. The name of Morano, they say, is derived from *moro,*‌* a Moor; and in its little piazza—an irregular and picturesque spot, shaded by a few grand old

---

* This is all wrong, of course. And equally wrong is the derivation from *morus,* a mulberry—abundant as these trees are. And more wrong still, if possible, is that which is drawn from a saying of the mysterious Oenotrians—that useful tribe—who, wandering in search of homesteads across these regions and observing their beauty, are supposed to have remarked: *Hic moremur*—here let us stay! Morano (strange to say) is simply the Roman Muranum.

elms amid the sound of running waters—there is a sculptured head of a Moor inserted into the wall, commemorative, I was told, of some ancient anti-Saracen exploit. It is the escutcheon of the town. This Moor wears a red fez, and his features are painted black (this is *de rigueur*, for "Saracens"); he bears the legend *Vivit sub arbore morus*. Near at hand, too, lies the prosperous village Saracena, celebrated of old for its muscatel wines. They are made from the grape which the Saracens brought over from Maskat, and planted all over Sicily.*

The men of Morano emigrate to America; two-thirds of the adult and adolescent male population are at this moment on the other side of the Atlantic. But the oldsters, with their peaked hats (capello pizzuto) shading gnarled and canny features, are well worth studying. At this summer season they leave the town at 3.30 A.M. to cultivate their fields, often far distant, returning at nightfall; and to observe these really wonderful types, which will soon be extinct, you must take up a stand on the Castrovillari road towards sunset and watch them riding home on their donkeys, or walking, after the labours of the day.

Poorly dressed, these peasants are none the less wealthy; the post office deposit of Morano is said to have two million francs to its credit, mostly the savings of these humble cultivators, who can discover an astonishing amount of money when it is a question, for example, of providing their daughters with a dowry. The bridal dress alone, a blaze of blue silk and lace and gold embroidery, costs between six hundred and a thousand francs. Altogether, Morano is a rich place, despite its sordid appearance; it is also celebrated as the birthplace of various learned men. The author of the "Calascione Scordato," a famous Neapolitan poem of the seventeenth century, certainly lived here for some time and has been acclaimed as a son of Morano, though he distinctly speaks of Naples as his home. Among its elder literary glories is that Leonardo Tufarelli, who thus apostrophizes his birthplace:

"And to proceed—how many *letterati* and *virtuosi* have issued from you in divers times? Among whom—not to name all of them—there has been in our days Leopardo de l'Osso of happy memory, physician and most excellent philosopher, singular in every science, of whom I dare say that he attained to Pythagorean heights. How many are there to-day, versed in every faculty, in theology, in the

---

* See next chapter.

two laws, and in medicine? How many historians, how many poets, grammarians, artists, actors?"

The modern writer Nicola Leoni is likewise a child of Morano; his voluminous "Della Magna Grecia e delle Tre Calabrie" appeared in 1844–1846. He, too, devotes much space to the praises of his natal city, and to lamentations regarding the sad condition of Calabrian letters during those dark years.

"Closed for ever is the academy of Amantea! Closed for ever is the academy of Rossano! Rare are the lectures in the academy of Monteleone! Rare indeed the lectures in the academy of Catanzaro! Closed for ever is the public library of Monteleone! O ancient days! O wisdom of our fathers! Where shall I find you? . . ."

To live the intellectual life amid the ferociously squalid surroundings of Morano argues an enviable philosophic calm—a detachment bordering on insensibility. But perhaps we are too easily influenced by externals, in these degenerate times. Or things may have been better in days of old—who can tell? One always likes to think so, though the evidence usually points to the contrary.

When least I expected it, a possessor of mules presented himself. He was a burly ruffian of northern extraction, with clear eyes, fair moustache, and an insidious air of cheerfulness.

Yes, he had a mule, he said; but as to climbing the mountain for three or four days on end—ha, ha!—that was rather an undertaking, you know. Was I aware that there were forests and snow up there? Had I ever been up the mountain? Indeed! Well, then I must know that there was no food——

I pointed to my store of provisions from Castrovillari. His eye wandered lovingly over the pile and reposed, finally, upon sundry odd bottles and a capacious demijohn, holding twelve litres.

"Wine of family," I urged. "None of your eating-house stuff."

He thought he could manage it, after all. Yes; the trip could be undertaken, with a little sacrifice. And he had a second mule, a lady-mule, which it struck him I might like to ride now and then; a pleasant beast and a companion, so to speak, for the other one. Two mules and two Christians—that seemed appropriate. . . . And only four francs a day more.

Done! It was really cheap. So cheap, that I straightway grew suspicious of the "lady-mule."

We sealed the bargain in a glass of the local mixture, and I thereupon demanded a *caparra*—a monetary security that he would keep his word, i.e. be round at my door with the animals at two in the morning, so as to reach the uplands before the heat became oppressive.

His face clouded—a good omen, indicating that he was beginning to respect me. Then he pulled out his purse, and reluctantly laid two francs on the table.

The evening was spent in final preparations; I retired early to bed, and tried to sleep. One o'clock came, and two o'clock, and three o'clock—no mules! At four I went to the man's house, and woke him out of ambrosial slumbers.

"You come to see me so early in the morning?" he enquired, sitting up in bed and rubbing his eyes. "Now that's really nice of you."

One of the mules, he airily explained, had lost a shoe in the afternoon. He would get it put right at once—at once.

"You might have told me so yesterday evening, instead of keeping me awake all night waiting for you."

"True," he replied. "I thought of it at the time. But then I went to bed, and slept. Ah, sir, it is good to sleep!" and he stretched himself voluptuously.

The beast was shod, and at 5 a.m. we left.

XVIII

AFRICAN INTRUDERS

THERE is a type of physiognomy here which is undeniably Semitic—with curly hair, dusky skin and hooked nose. We may take it to be of Saracenic origin, since a Phœnician descent is out of the question, while mediæval Jews never intermarried with Christians. It is the same class of face which one sees so abundantly at Palermo, the former metropolis of these Africans. The accompanying likeness is that of a native of Cosenza, a town that was frequently in their possession. Eastern traits of character, too, have lingered among the populace. So the humour of the peddling Semite who will allow himself to be called by the most offensive epithets rather than lose a chance of gaining a sou; who, eternally professing poverty, cannot bear to be twitted on his notorious riches; their ceaseless talk of hidden treasures, their secretiveness and so many other little Orientalisms that whoever has lived in the East will be inclined to echo the observation of Edward Lear's Greek servant: "These men are Arabs, but they have more clothes on."

Many Saracenic words (chiefly of marine and commercial import) have survived from this period; I could quote a hundred or more, partly in the literary language (balio, dogana, etc.), partly in dialect (cala, tavuto, etc.) and in place-names such as Tamborio (the Semitic Mount Tabor), Kalat (Calatafimi), Marsa (Marsala).

Dramatic plays with Saracen subjects are still popular with the lower classes; you can see them acted in any of the coast towns. In fact, the recollection of these intruders is very much alive to this day. The have left a deep scar.

Such being the case, it is odd to find local writers hardly referring to the Saracenic period. Even a modern like l'Occaso, who describes the Castrovillari region in a conscientious fashion, leaps directly from Greco-Roman events into those of the Normans. But this is in accordance with the time-honoured ideal of writing such works: to say nothing in dispraise of your subject (an exception may be made in favour of Spano-Bolani's History of Reggio). Malaria and earthquakes and Saracen irruptions are awkward arguments when treating of the natural attractions and historical glories of your native place. So the once renowned descriptions of this province by Grano and the rest of them are little more than rhetorical exercises; they are "Laus Calabriæ." And then—their sources of information were limited and difficult of access.

Collective works like those of Muratori and du Chesne had not appeared on the market; libraries were restricted to convents; and it was not to be expected that they should know all the chroniclers of the Byzantines, Latins, Lombards, Normans and Hohenstaufen—to say nothing of Arab writers like Nowairi, Abulfeda, Ibn Chaldun and Ibn Alathir—who throw a little light on those dark times, and are now easily accessible to scholars.

Dipping into this old-world literature of murders and prayers, we gather that in pre-Saracenic times the southern towns were denuded of their garrisons, and their fortresses fallen into disrepair. "Nec erat formido aut metus bellorum, quoniam alta pace omnes gaudebant usque ad tempora Saracenorum." In this part of Italy, as well as at Taranto and other parts of old "Calabria," the invaders had an easy task before them, at first.

In 873, on their return from Salerno, they poured into Calabria, and by 884 already held several towns, such as Tropea and Amantea, but were driven out temporarily. In 899 they ravaged, says Hepidanus, the country of the Lombards (? Calabria). In 900 they destroyed Reggio, and renewed their incursions in 919, 923, 924, 925, 927, till the Greek Emperor found it profitable to pay them an annual tribute. In 1953, this tribute not being forthcoming, they defeated the Greeks in Calabria, carrying off a large store of captives and wealth. In 981 Otto II repulsed them at Cotrone, but was beaten the following year near Squillace, and narrowly escaped capture. It was one of the most romantic incidents of these wars. During the years 986, 988, 991, 994, 998, 1002, 1003 they were continually in the country; indeed, nearly every year at the beginning of the eleventh century is marked by some fresh inroad. In 1009 they took Cosenza for the third or fourth time; in 1020 they were at Bisignano in the Crati valley, and returned frequently into those parts, defeating, in 1025, a Greek army under Orestes, and, in 1031, the assembled forces of the Byzantine Catapan——*

---

* I have not seen Moscato's "Cronaca dei Musulmani in Calabria," where these authorities might be conveniently tabulated. It must be a rare book. Martorana deals only with the Saracens of Sicily.

No bad record, from their point of view.

But they never attained their end, the subjection of the mainland. And their methods involved appalling and enduring evils.

Yet the presumable intent or ambition of these aliens must be called reasonable enough. They wished to establish a provincial government here on the same lines as in Sicily, of which island it has been said that it was never more prosperous than under their administration.

Literature, trade, industry, and all the arts of peace are described as flourishing there; in agriculture they paid especial attention to the olive; they initiated, I believe, the art of terracing and irrigating the hill-sides; they imported the date-palm, the lemon and sugar-cane (making the latter suffice not only for home consumption, but for export); their silk manufactures were unsurpassed. Older writers like Mazzella speak of the abundant growth of sugar-cane in Calabria (Capialbi, who wallowed in learning, has a treatise on the subject); John Evelyn saw it cultivated near Naples; it is now extinct from economical and possibly climatic causes. They also introduced the papyrus into Sicily, as well as the cotton-plant, which used to be common all over south Italy, where I have myself seen it growing.

All this sounds praiseworthy, no doubt. But I see no reason why they should have governed Sicily better than they did North Africa, which crumbled into dust at their touch, and will take many long centuries to recover its pre-Saracen prosperity. There is something flame-like and anti-constructive in the Arab, with his pastoral habits and contempt of forethought. In favour of their rule, much capital has been made out of Benjamin of Tudela's account of Palermo. But it must not be forgotten that his brief visit was made a hundred years after the Norman occupation had begun. Palermo, he says, has about 1500 Jews and a large number of Christians and Mohammedans; Sicily "contains all the pleasant things of this world." Well, so it did in pre-Saracen times; so it does to-day. Against the example of North Africa, no doubt, may be set their activities in Spain.

They have been accused of destroying the old temples of Magna Græcia from religious or other motives. I do not believe it; this was against their usual practice. They sacked monasteries, because these were fortresses defended by political enemies and full of gold which they coveted; but in their African possessions, during all this period, the ruins of ancient civilizations were left untouched, while Byzantine cults lingered peacefully side by side with Moslemism; why not here? Their fanaticism has been much exaggerated. Weighing the balance between conflicting writers, it would appear that Christian rites were tolerated in Sicily during all their rule, though some governors were more bigoted than others; the proof is this, that the Normans found resident fellow-believers there, after 255 years of Arab domination.* It was the Christians rather, who with the best intentions set the example of fanaticism during their crusades; these early Saracen raids had no more religious colouring than our own raids into the Transvaal or elsewhere. The Saracens were out for plunder and fresh lands, exactly like the English.

Nor were they tempted to destroy these monuments for decorative purposes, since they possessed no palaces on the mainland like the Palermitan Cuba or Zisa; and that sheer love of destructiveness with which they have been credited certainly spared the marbles of Paestum which lay within a short distance of their strongholds, Agropoli and Cetara. No. What earthquakes had left intact of these classic relics was filched by the Christians, who ransacked every corner of Italy for such treasures to adorn their own temples in Pisa, Rome and Venice—displaying small veneration for antiquity, but considerable taste. In Calabria, for instance, the twenty granite pillars of the cathedral of Gerace were drawn from the ruins of old Locri; those of Melito came from the ancient Hipponium (Monteleone). So Paestum, after the Saracens, became a regular quarry for the Lombards and the rich citizens of Amalfi when they built their cathedral; and above all, for the shrewdly pious Robert Guiscard. Altogether, these Normans, dreaming through the solstitial heats in pleasaunces like Ravello, developed a nice taste in the matter of marbles, and were not particular where they came from, so long as they came from somewhere. The antiquities remained intact, at least, which was better than the subsequent system of Colonna and Frangipani, who burnt them into lime.

Whatever one may think of the condition of Sicily under Arab rule, the proceedings of these strangers was wholly deplorable so far as the mainland of Italy was concerned. They sacked and burnt wherever they went; the sea-board of the Tyrrhenian, Ionian and Adriatic was depopulated of its inhabitants, who fled inland; towns and villages vanished from the face of the earth, and the richly cultivated land became a desert; they took 17,000 prisoners from

* The behaviour of the Normans was wholly different from that of the Arabs. Immediately on their occupation of the country they razed to the ground thousands of Arab temples and sanctuaries. Of several hundred in Palermo alone, not a single one was left standing.

Reggio on a single occasion—13,00 from Termula; they reduced
Matera to such distress, that a mother is said to have slaughtered
and devoured her own child. Such was their system on the mainland, where they swarmed. Their numbers can be inferred from a
letter written in 871 by the Emperor Ludwig II to the Byzantine
monarch, in which he complains that "Naples has become a second
Palermo, a second Africa," while three hundred years later, in 1196,
the Chancellor Konrad von Hildesheim makes a noteworthy observation, which begins: "In Naples I saw the Saracens, who with their
spittle destroy venomous beasts, and will briefly set forth how they
came by this virtue. . . ."*

It is therefore no exaggeration to say that the coastal regions of
south Italy were practically in Arab possession for centuries, and
one is tempted to dwell on their long semi-domination here because
it has affected to this day the vocabulary of the people, their lore,
their architecture, their very faces—and to a far greater extent than
a visitor unacquainted with Moslem countries and habits would
believe. Saracenism explains many anomalies in their mode of life
and social conduct.

From these troublous times dates, I should say, that use of the
word *cristiano* applied to natives of the country—as opposed to Mo-
hammedan enemies.

"Saraceno" is still a common term of abuse.

The fall of Luceria may be taken as a convenient time-boundary to
mark the end of the Saracenic period. A lull, but no complete repose
from attacks, occurs between that event and the fall of Granada.
Then begins the activity of the corsairs. There is this difference

---

* He goes on to say, "Paulus Apostolus naufragium passus, apud Cpream
insulam applicuit [sic] quae in Actibus Apostolorum Mitylene nuncupatur,
et cum multis aliis evadens, ab indigenis terrae benigne acceptatus est."
Then follows the episode of the fire and of the serpent which Paul casts
from him; whereupon the Saracens, naturally enough, begin to adore him as
a saint. In recompense for this kind treatment Paul grants to them and their
descendants the power of killing poisonous animals in the manner afore-
said—i.e. with their spittle—a superstition which is alive in south Italy to
this day. These gifted mortals are called Sanpaulari, or by the Greek word
Cerauli; they are men who are born either on St. Paul's night (24-25 Janu-
ary) or on 29 June.

Saint Paul, the "doctor of the Gentiles," is a great wizard hereabouts, and
an invocation to him runs as follows: "Saint Paul, thou wonder-worker, kill
this beast, which is hostile to God; and save me, for I am a son of Maria."

between them, that the corsairs merely paid flying visits; a change of wind, the appearance of an Italian sail, an unexpected resistance on the part of the inhabitants, sufficed to unsettle their ephemeral plans. The coast-lands were never in their possession; they only harried the natives. The system of the Saracens on the mainland, though it seldom attained the form of a provincial or even military government, was different. They had the *animus manendi.* Where they dined, they slept.

In point of destructiveness, I should think there was little to choose between them. One thinks of the hundreds of villages the corsairs devastated; the convents and precious archives they destroyed, * the thousands of captives they carried off—sometimes in such numbers that the ships threatened to sink till the more unsaleable portion of the human freight had been cast overboard. And it went on for centuries. Pirates and slave-hunters they were; but not a whit more so than their Christian adversaries, on whose national rivalries they thrived. African slaves, when not chained to the galleys, were utilized on land; so the traveller Moore records that the palace of Caserta was built by gangs of slaves, half of them Italian, half Turkish. We have not much testimony as to whether these Arab slaves enjoyed their lot in European countries; but many of the Christians in Algiers certainly enjoyed theirs. A considerable number of them refused to profit by Lord Exmouth's arrangement for their ransom. I myself knew the descendant of a man who had been thus sent back to his relations from captivity, and who soon enough returned to Africa declaring that the climate and religion of Europe were alike insupportable.

In Saracen times the Venetians actually sold Christian slaves to the Turks. Parrino cites the severe enactments which were issued in the sixteenth century against Christian sailors who decoyed children on board their boats and sold them as slaves to the Moslem. I

* In this particular branch again, the Christians surpassed the unbeliever. More archives were destroyed in the so-called "Age of Lead"—the closing period of Bourbonism—than under Saracens and Corsairs combined. It was quite the regular thing to sell them as waste-paper to the shopkeepers. Some of them escaped this fate by the veriest miracle—so those of the celebrated Certoza of San Lorenzo in Padula. The historian Marincola, walking in the market of Salerno, noticed a piece of cheese wrapped up in an old parchment. He elicited the fact that it came from this Certosa, intercepted the records on their way for sale in Salerno, and contrived by a small present to the driver that next night two cartloads of parchments were deposited in the library of La Cava.

question whether the Turks were ever guilty of a corresponding infamy.

This Parrino, by the way, is useful as showing the trouble to which the Spanish viceroys were put by the perpetual inroads of these Oriental pests. Local militia were organized, heavy contributions levied, towers of refuge sprang up all along the coast—every respectable house had its private tower as well (for the dates, see G. del Giudice, *Del Grande Archivio di Napoli*, 1871, p. 108). The daring of the pirates knew no bounds; they actually landed a fleet at Naples itself, and carried off a number of prisoners. The entire kingdom, save the inland parts, was terrorized by their lightning-like descents.

A particular literature grew up about this time—those "Lamenti" in rime, which set forth the distress of the various places they afflicted.

The saints had work to do. Each divine protector fought for his own town or village, and sometimes we see the pleasing spectacle of two patrons of different localities joining their forces to ward off a piratical attack upon some threatened district by means of fiery hail, tempests, apparitions and other celestial devices. A bellicose type of Madonna emerges, such as S. M. della Libera and S. M. di Constantinpoli, who distinguishes herself by a fierce martial courage in the face of the enemy. There is no doubt that these inroads acted as a stimulus to the Christian faith; that they helped to seat the numberless patron saints of south Italy more firmly on their thrones. The Saracens as saint-makers. . . .

But despite occasional successes, the marine population suffered increasingly. Historians like Summonte have left us descriptions of the prodigious exodus of the country people from Calabria and elsewhere into the safer capital, and how the polished citizens detested these new arrivals.

The ominous name "Torre di Guardia" (tower of outlook)—a cliff whence the sea was scanned for the appearance of Turkish vessels—survives all over the south. Barbarossa, too, has left his mark; many a hill, fountain or castle has been named after him. In the two Barbarossas were summed up the highest qualities of the pirates, and it is curious to think that the names of those scourges of Christendom, Uruj and Kheir-eddin, should have been contracted into the classical forms of Horace and Ariadne. The picturesque Uruj was painted by Velasquez; the other entertained a polite epistolary correspondence with Aretino, and died, to his regret, "like a coward" in bed. I never visit Constantinople without paying my respects to that calm tomb at Beshiktah, where, after life's fitful fever, sleeps the *Chief of the Sea.*

And so things went on till recently. K. Ph. Moritz writes that King Ferdinand of Naples, during his sporting excursions to the islands of his dominions, was always accompanied by two cruisers, to forestall the chance of his being carried off by these *Turchi.* But his loyal subjects had no cruisers at their disposal; they lived *Turcarum prædonibus semper obnoxii.* Who shall calculate the effects of this long reign of terror on the national mind?

For a thousand years—from 830 to 1830—from the days when the Amalfitans won the proud title of "Defenders of the Faith" up to those of the sentimental poet Waiblinger (1826), these shores were infested by Oriental ruffians, whose activities were an unmitigated evil. It is all very well for Admiral de la Gravière to speak of "Gallia Victrix"—the Americans, too, might have something to say on that point. The fact is that neither European nor American arms crushed the pest. But for the invention of steam, the Barbary corsairs might still be with us.

XIX

UPLANDS OF POLLINO

IT has a pleasant signification, that word "dolcedorme": it means *Sweet slumber*. But no one could tell me how the mountain group came by this name; they gave me a number of explanations, all fanciful and unconvincing.

Pollino, we are told, is derived from Apollo, and authors of olden days sometimes write of it as "Monte Apollino." But Barrius suggests an alternative etymology, equally absurd, and connected with the medicinal herbs which are found there. *Pollino, he says, a polleo dictus, quod nobilibus herbis medelæ commodis polleat. Provenit enim ibi, ut ab herbariis accepi, tragium dictamnum Cretense, chamæleon bigenum, draucus, meum, nardus, celtica, anonides, anemone, peucedamum, turbit, reubarbarum, pyrethrum, juniperus ubertim, stellaria, imperatoria, cardus masticem fundens, dracagas, cythisus*—whence likewise the magnificent cheeses; gold and the Phrygian stone, he adds, are also found here.

Unhappily Barrius—we all have a fling at this "Strabo and Pliny of Calabria"! So jealous was he of his work that he procured a prohibition from the Pope against all who might reprint it, and furthermore invoked the curses of heaven and earth upon whoever should have the audacity to translate it into Italian. Yet his shade ought to be appeased with the monumental edition of 1737, and, as regards his infallibility, one must not forget that among his contemporaries the more discerning had already censured his *philopatria*, his immoderate love of Calabria. And that is the right way to judge of men who were not so much ignorant as unduly zealous for the fair name of their natal land. To sneer at them is to misjudge their period. It was the very spirit of the Renaissance to press rhetorical learning into the service of patriotism. They made some happy guesses and not a few mistakes; and when they lied deliberately, it was done in what they held a just cause—as scholars and gentlemen.

The *Calabria Illustrata* of Fiore also fares badly at the hands of critics. But I shall not repeat what they say; I confess to a sneaking fondness for Father Fiore.

Marafioti, a Calabrian monk, likewise dwells on these same herbs of Pollino, and gives a long account of a medical secret which he learnt on the spot from two Armenian botanists. Alas for Marafioti! Despite his excellent index and seductively chaste Paduan type and paper, the impartial Soria is driven to say that "to make his shop appear more rich in foreign merchandise, he did not scruple to adorn it with books and authors apocryphal, imaginary, and unknown to the whole human race." In short, he belonged to the school of Pratilli, who wrote a wise and edifying history of Capua on the basis of inscriptions which he himself had previously forged; of Ligorio Pirro, prince of his tribe, who manufactured thousands of coins, texts and marbles out of sheer exuberance of creative artistry!

Gone are those happy days of authorship, when the constructive imagination was not yet blighted and withered. . . .

Marching comfortably, it will take you nearly twelve hours to go from Morano to the village of Terranova di Pollino, which I selected as my first night-quarter. This includes a scramble up the peak of Pollino, locally termed "telegrafo," from a pile of stones—? an old signal-station—erected on the summit. But since decent accommodation can only be obtained at Castrovillari, a start should be made from there, and this adds another hour to the trip. Moreover, as the peak of Pollino lies below that of Dolcedorme, which shuts off a good deal of its view seaward, this second mountain ought rather to be ascended, and that will probably add yet another hour—fourteen altogether. The natives, ever ready to say what they think will please you, call it a six hours' excursion. As a matter of fact, although I spoke to numbers of the population of Morano, I only met two men who had ever been to Terranova, one of them being my muleteer; the majority had not so much as heard its name. They dislike mountains and torrents and forests, not only as an offence to the eye, but as hindrances to agriculture and enemies of man and his ordered ways. "La montagna" is considerably abused, all over Italy.

It takes an hour to cross the valley and reach the slopes of the opposite hills. Here, on the plain, lie the now faded blossoms of the monstrous arum, the botanical glory of these regions. To see it in flower, in early June, is alone almost worth the trouble of a journey to Calabria.

On a shady eminence at the foot of these mountains, in a most picturesque site, there stands a large castellated building, a monastery. It is called Colorito, and is now a ruin; the French, they say, shelled it for harbouring the brigand-allies of Bourbonism. Nearly all convents in the south, and even in Naples, were at one time or another refuges of bandits, and this association of monks and robbers used to give much trouble to conscientious politicians. It is a solitary building, against the dark hill-side; a sombre and romantic pile such as would have charmed Anne Radcliffe; one longs to explore its recesses. But I dreaded the coming heats of midday. Leone da Morano, who died in 1645, belonged to this congregation, and was reputed an erudite ecclesiastic. The life of one of its greatest luminaries, Fra Bernardo da Rogliano, was described by Tufarelli in a volume which I have never been able to catch sight of. It must be very rare, yet it certainly was printed. *

The path ascends now through a long and wearisome limestone gap called valle di Gaudolino, only the last half-hour of the march being shaded by trees. It was in this gully that an accidental encounter took place between a detachment of French soldiers and part of the band of the celebrated brigand Scarolla, whom they had been pursuing for months all over the country. The brigands were sleeping when the others fell upon them, killing numbers and carrying off a large booty; so rich it was, that the soldiers were seen playing at "petis palets"—whatever that may be—with quadruples of Spain—whatever *that* may be. Scarolla escaped wounded, but was afterwards handed over to justice, for a consideration of a thousand ducats, by some shepherds with whom he had taken refuge; and duly hanged. His band consisted of four thousand ruffians; it was one of several that infested south Italy. This gives some idea of the magnitude of the evil.

It was my misfortune that after weeks of serene weather this particular morning should be cloudy. There was sunshine in the valley below, but wreaths of mist were skidding over the summit of Pollino; the view, I felt sure, would be spoilt. And so it was. Through swiftly-careering cloud-drifts I caught glimpses of the plain and the blue Ionian; of the Sila range confronting me; of the peak of Dolcedorme to the left, and the "Montagna del Principe" on the right; of the large forest region at my back. Tantalizing visions!

Viewed from below, this Pollino is shaped like a pyramid, and promises rather a steep climb over bare limestone; but the ascent is quite easy. No trees grow on the pyramid. The rock is covered with

* Haym has no mention of this work. But it is fully quoted in old Toppi's "Biblioteca" (p. 317), and also referred to in Savonarola's "Universus Terrarum," etc. (1713. Vol I, p. 216). Both say it was printed at Cosenza; the first, in 1650; the second, in 1630.

a profusion of forget-me-nots and gay pansies; some mezereon and a few dwarfed junipers—earthward-creeping—nearly reach the summit. When I passed here on a former trip, on the 6th of June, this peak was shrouded in snow. There are some patches of snow even now, one of them descending in glacier fashion down the slope on the other side; they call it "eternal," but I question whether it will survive the heats of autumn. Beyond a brace of red-legged partridges, I saw no birds whatever. This group of Pollino, descending its seven thousand feet in a precipitous flight of terraces to the plain of Sibari, is an imposing *finale* to the Apennines that have run hitherward, without a break, from Genoa and Bologna. Westward of this spot there are mountains galore; but no more Apennines; no more limestone precipices. The boundary of the old provinces of Calabria and Basilicata ran over this spot. . . .

I was glad to descend once more, and to reach the *Altipiano di Polino*—meadow with a little lake (the merest puddle), bright with rare and beautiful flowers. It lies 1780 metres above sea-level, and no one who visits these regions should omit to see this exquisite tract encircled by mountain peaks, though it lies a little off the usual paths. Strawberries, which I had eaten at Rossano, had not yet opened their flowers here; the flora, boreal in parts, has been studied by Terracciano and other Italian botanists.

It was on this verdant, flower-enamelled mead that, fatigued with the climb, I thought to try the powers of my riding mule. But the beast proved vicious; there was no staying on her back. A piece of string attached to her nose by way of guiding-rope was useless as a rein; she had no mane wherewith I might have steadied myself in moments of danger, and as to seizing her ears for that purpose, it was out of the question, for hardly was I in the saddle before her head descended to the ground and there remained, while her hinder feet essayed to touch the stars. After a succession of ignominious and painful flights to earth, I complained to her owner, who had been watching the proceedings with quiet interest.

"That lady-mule," he said, "is good at carrying loads. But she has never had a Christian on her back till now. I was rather curious to see how she would behave."

"*Santo Dio!* And do you expect me to pay four francs a day for having my bones broken in this fashion?"

"What would you, sir? She is still young—barely four years old. Only wait! Wait till she is ten or twelve."

To do him justice, however, he tried to make amends in other ways. And he certainly knew the tracks. But he was a returned emigrant, and when an Italian has once crossed the ocean he is useless for my purposes, he has lost his savour—the virtue has gone out of him. True Italians will soon be rare as the dodo in these parts. These *americani* cast off their ancient animistic traits and patriarchal disposition with the ease of a serpent; a new creature emerges, of a wholly different character—sophisticated, extortionate at times, often practical and in so far useful; scorner of every tradition, infernally wideawake and curiously deficient in what the Germans call "Gemüt" (one of those words which we sadly need in our own language). Instead of being regaled with tales of Saint Venus and fairies and the Evil Eye, I learnt a good deal about the price of food in the Brazilian highlands.

The only piece of local information I was able to draw from him concerned a mysterious plant in the forest that "shines by night." I dare say he meant the *dictamnus fraxinella*, which is sometimes luminous.

The finest part of the forest was traversed in the afternoon. It is called Janace, and composed of firs and beeches. The botanist Tenore says that firs 150 feet in height are "not difficult to find" here, and some of the beeches, a forestal inspector assured me, attain the height of 35 metres. They shoot up in straight silvery trunks; their roots are often intertwined with those of the firs. The track is not level by any means. There are torrents to be crossed; rocky ravines with splashing waters where the sunshine pours down through a dense network of branches upon a carpet of russet leaves and grey boulders—the envious beeches allowing of no vegetation at their feet; occasional meadows too, bright with buttercups and orchids. No pines whatever grow in this forest. Yet a few stunted ones are seen clinging to the precipices that descend into the Coscile valley; their seeds may have been wafted across from the Sila mountains.

In olden days all this country was full of game; bears, stags and fallow-deer are mentioned. Only wolves and a few roe-deer are now left. The forest is sombre, but not gloomy, and one would like to spend some time in these wooded regions, so rare in Italy, and to study their life and character—but how set about it? The distances are great; there are no houses, not even a shepherd's hut or a cave; the cold at night is severe, and even in the height of midsummer one must be prepared for spells of mist and rain. I shall be tempted, on another occasion, to provide myself with a tent such as is supplied to military officers. They are light and handy and perhaps camping out with a man-cook of the kind that one finds in the Abruzzi provinces would be altogether the best way of seeing the remoter parts of south and central Italy. For decent food-supplies can generally be obtained in the smallest places; the drawback is that nobody can cook them. Dirty food by day and dirty beds by night will daunt the most enterprising natures in the long run.

These tracks are only traversed in summer. When I last walked through this region—in the reverse direction, from Lagonegro over Latronico and San Severino to Castrovillari—the ground was still covered with stretches of snow, and many brooks were difficult to cross from the swollen waters. This was in June. It was odd to see the beeches rising, in full leaf, out of the deep snow.

During this afternoon ramble I often wondered what the burghers of Taranto would think of these sylvan solitudes. Doubtless they would share the opinion of a genteel photographer of Morano who showed me some coloured pictures of local brides in their appropriate costumes, such as are sent to relatives in America after weddings. He possessed a good camera, and I asked whether he had never made any pictures of this fine forest scenery. No, he said; he had only once been to the festival of the Madonna di Pollino, but he went alone—his companion, an *avvocato*, got frightened and failed to appear at the last moment.

"So I went alone," he said, "and those forests, it must be confessed, are too savage to be photographed. Now, if my friend had come, he might have posed for me, sitting comically at the foot of a tree, with crossed legs, and smoking a cigar, like this. . . . Or he might have pretended to be a wood-cutter, bending forwards and felling a tree . . . tac, tac, tac . . . without his jacket, of course. That would have made a picture. But those woods and mountains, all by themselves—no! The camera revolts. In photography, as in all good art, the human element must predominate."

It is sad to think that in a few years' time nearly all these forests will have ceased to exist; another generation will hardly recognize the site of them. A society from Morbegno (Valtellina) has acquired rights over the timber, and is hewing down as fast as it can. They import their own workmen from north Italy, and have built at a cost of two million francs (say the newspapers) a special funicular railway, 23 kilometres long, to carry the trunks from the mountain to Francavilla at its foot, where they are sawn up and conveyed to the railway station of Cerchiara, near Sibari. This concession, I am told, extends to twenty-five years—they have now been at work for two, and the results are already apparent in some almost bare slopes once clothed with these huge primeval trees. There are inspectors, some of them conscientious, to see that a due proportion of the timber is left standing; but we all know what the average Italian official is, and must be, considering his salary. One could hardly blame them greatly if, as I have been assured is the case, they often sell the wood which they are paid to protect.

The same fate is about to overtake the extensive hill forests which lie on the watershed between Morano and the Tyrrhenian. These, according to a Castrovillari local paper, have lately been sold to a German firm for exploitation.

It is useless to lament the inevitable—this modern obsession of "industrialism" which has infected a country purely agricultural. Nor is it any great compensation to observe that certain small tracts of the hill-side behind Morano are being carefully reafforested by the Government at this moment. Whoever wishes to see these beautiful stretches of woodland ere their disappearance from earth—let him hasten!

After leaving the forest region it is a downhill walk of nearly three hours to reach Terranova di Pollino, which lies, only 910 metres above sea-level, against the slope of a wide and golden amphitheatre of hills, at whose entrance the river Sarmento has carved itself a prodigious gateway through the rock. A dirty little place; the male inhabitants are nearly all in America; the old women nearly all afflicted with goitre. I was pleased to observe the Calabrian system of the house-doors, which life in civilized places had made me forget. These doors are divided into two portions, not vertically like ours, but horizontally. The upper portion is generally open, in order that the housewife sitting within may have light and air in her room, and an opportunity of gossiping with her neighbours across the street; the lower part is closed, to prevent the pigs in the daytime from entering the house (where they sleep at night). The system testifies to social instincts and a certain sense of refinement.

The sights of Terranova are soon exhausted. They had spoken to me of a house near the woods, about four hours distant, inhabited just now by shepherds. Thither we started, next day, at 3 p.m.

The road climbs upwards through bare country till it reaches a dusky pinnacle of rock, a conspicuous landmark, which looks volcanic but is nothing of the kind. It bears the name of Pietra-Sasso—

the explanation of this odd pleonasm being, I suppose, that here the whole mass of rock, generally decked with grass or shrubs, is as bare as any single stone.

There followed a pleasant march through pastoral country of streamlets and lush grass, with noble views downwards on our right, over many-folded hills into the distant valley of the Sinno. To the left is the forest region. But the fir trees are generally mutilated— their lower branches lopped off; and the tree resents this treatment and often dies, remaining a melancholy stump among the beeches. They take these branches not for fuel, but as fodder for the cows. A curious kind of fodder, one thinks; but Calabrian cows will eat anything, and their milk tastes accordingly. No wonder the natives prefer even the greasy fluid of their goats to that of cows. "How?" they will ask. "You Englishmen, with all your money— you drink the milk of cows?"

Goats are over-plentiful here, and the hollies, oaks and thorns along the path have been gnawed by them into quaint patterns like the topiarian work in old-fashioned gardens. If they find nothing to their taste on the ground, they actually climb trees; I have seen them browsing thus, at six feet above the ground. These miserable beasts are the ruin of south Italy, as they are of the whole Mediterranean basin. What malaria and the Barbary pirates have done to the sea-board, the goats have accomplished for the regions further inland; and it is really time that sterner legislation were introduced to limit their grazing-places and incidentally reduce their numbers, as has been done in parts of the Abruzzi, to the great credit of the authorities. But the subject is a well-worn one.

The solitary little house which now appeared before us is called "Vitiello," presumably from its owner or builder, a proprietor of the village of Noepoli. It stands in a charming site, with a background of woodland whence rivulets trickle down—the immediate surroundings are covered with pasture and bracken and wild pear trees smothered in flowering dog-roses. I strolled about in the sunset amid tinkling herds of sheep and goats that were presently milked and driven into their enclosure of thorns for the night, guarded by four or five of those savage white dogs of the Campagna breed. Despite these protectors, the wolf carried off two sheep yesterday, in broad daylight. The flocks come to these heights in the middle of June, and descend again in October.

The shepherds offered us the only fare they possessed—the much belauded Pollino cheeses, the same that were made, long ago, by

Polyphemus himself. You can get them down at a pinch, on the principle of the German proverb, "When the devil is hungry, he eats flies." Fortunately our bags still contained a varied assortment, though my man had developed an appetite and a thirst that did credit to his Berserker ancestry.

We retired early. But long after the rest of them were snoring hard I continued awake, shivering under my blanket and choking with the acrid smoke of a fire of green timber. The door had been left ajar to allow it to escape, but the only result of this arrangement was that a glacial blast of wind swept into the chamber from outside. The night was bitterly cold, and the wooden floor on which I was reposing seemed to be harder than the majority of its kind. I thought with regret of the tepid nights of Taranto and Castrovillari, and cursed my folly for climbing into these Arctic regions; wondering, as I have often done, what demon of restlessness or perversity drives one to undertake such insane excursions.

XX

A MOUNTAIN FESTIVAL

LEAVING the hospitable shepherds in the morning, we arrived after midday, by devious woodland paths, at the Madonna di Pollino. This solitary fane is perched, like an eagle's nest, on the edge of a cliff overhanging the Frida torrent. Owning to this fact, and to its great elevation, the views inland are wonderful; especially towards evening, when crude daylight tints fade away and range after range of mountains reveal themselves, their crests outlined against each other in tender gradations of mauve and grey. The prospect is closed, at last, by the lofty groups of Sirino and Alburno, many long leagues away. On all other sides are forests, interspersed with rock. But near at hand lies a spacious green meadow, at the foot of a precipice. This is now covered with encampments in anticipation of to-morrow's festival, and the bacchanal is already in full swing.

Very few foreigners, they say, have attended this annual feast, which takes place on the first Saturday and Sunday of July, and is worth coming a long way to see. Here the old types, uncontaminated by modernism and emigration, are still gathered together. The whole country-side is represented; the peasants have climbed up with their entire households from thirty or forty villages of this thinly popu-lated land, some of them marching a two days' journey; the greater the distance, the greater the "divozione" to the Mother of God. *Piety conquers rough tracks,* as old Bishop Paulinus sang, nearly fifteen hundred years ago.

It is a vast picnic in honour of the Virgin. Two thousand persons are encamped about the chapel, amid a formidable army of donkeys and mules whose braying mingles with the pastoral music of reeds and bagpipes—bagpipes of two kinds, the common Calabrian variety and that of Basilicata, much larger and with a resounding base key, which will soon cease to exit. A heaving ebb and flow of humanity fills the eye; fires are flickering before extempore shelters, and an ungodly amount of food is being consumed, as traditionally prescribed for such occasions—"si mangia per divozione." On all sides picturesque groups of dancers indulge in the old peasants' measure, the *pecorara*, to the droning of bagpipes—a demure kind of tarantella, the male capering about with faun-like attitudes of invitation and snappings of fingers, his partner evading the advances with downcast eyes. And the church meanwhile, is filled to overflowing; orations and services follow one another without interruption; the priests are having a busy time of it.

The rocky pathway between this chapel and the meadow is obstructed by folk and lined on either side with temporary booths of green branches, whose owners vociferously extol the merits of their wares—cloths, woollens, umbrellas, hot coffee, wine, fresh meat, fruit, vegetables (the spectre of cholera is abroad, but no one heeds)—as well as gold watches, rings and brooches, many of which will be bought ere to-morrow morning, in memory of to-night's tender meetings. The most interesting shops are those which display ex-votos, waxen reproductions of various ailing parts of the body which have been miraculously cured by the Virgin's intercession: arms, legs, fingers, breasts, eyes. There are also entire infants of wax. Strangest of all of them is a many-tinted and puzzling waxen symbol which sums up all the internal organs of the abdomen in one bold effort of artistic condensation; a kind of heraldic, materialized stomache-ache. I would have carried one away with me, had there been the slightest chance of its remaining unbroken. *

These are the votive offerings which catch the visitor's eye in southern churches, and were beloved not only of heathendom, but of the neolithic gentry; a large deposit has been excavated at Taranto; the British Museum has some of marble, from Athens; others were of silver, but the majority terra-cotta. The custom must have entered Christianity in early ages, for already Theodoret, who died in 427, says, "some bring images of eyes, others of feet, others of hands; and sometimes they are made of gold, sometimes of silver. These votive gifts testify to cure of maladies." Nowadays, when they become too numerous, they are melted down for candles; so Pericles, in some speech, talks of selling them for the benefit of the commonwealth.

One is struck with the feast of costumes here, by far the brightest being those of the women who have come up from the seven or eight

* A good part of these, I dare say are intended to represent the enlarged spleen of malaria. In old Greece, says Dr. W. H. D. Rouse, votives of the trunk are commonest, after the eyes—malaria, again.

Albanian villages that surround these hills. In their variegated array of chocolate-brown and white, of emerald-green and gold and flashing violet, these dames move about the sward like animated tropical flowers. But the Albanian girls of Cività stand out for aristocratic elegance—pleated black silk gowns, discreetly trimmed with gold and white lace, and open at the breast. The women of Morano, too, make a brave show.

Night brings no respite; on the contrary, the din grows livelier than ever; fires gleam brightly on the meadow and under the trees; the dancers are unwearied, the bagpipers with their brazen lungs show no signs of exhaustion. And presently the municipal music of Castrovillari, specially hired for the occasion, ascends an improvised bandstand and pours brisk strains into the night. Then the fireworks begin, sensational fireworks, that have cost a mint of money; flaring wheels and fiery devices that send forth a pungent odour; rockets of many hues, lighting up the leafy recesses, and scaring the owls and wolves for miles around.

Certain persons have told me that if you are of a prying disposition, now is the time to observe amorous couples walking hand in hand into the gloom—passionate young lovers from different villages, who have looked forward to this night of all the year on the chance of meeting, at last, in a fervent embrace under the friendly beeches. These same stern men (they are always men) declare that such nocturnal festivals are a disgrace to civilization; that the Greek Comedy, long ago, reprobated them as disastrous to the morals of females—that they were condemned by the Council of Elvira, by Vigilantius of Marseilles and by the great Saint Jerome, who wrote that on such occasions no virgin should wander a hand's-breadth from her mother. They wish you to believe that on these warm summer nights, when the pulses of nature are felt and senses stirred with music and wine and dance, the *Gran Madre di Dio* is adored in a manner less becoming Christian youths and maidens, than heathens celebrating mad orgies to *Magna Mater* in Daphne, or the Babylonian groves (where she was not worshipped at all—though she might have been).

In fact, they insinuate that——

It may well be true. What were the moralists doing there?

Festivals like this are relics of paganism, and have my cordial approval. We English ought to have learnt by this time that the repression of pleasure is a dangerous error. In these days when even Italy, the grey-haired *cocotte*, has become tainted with Anglo-

Pecksniffian principles, there is nothing like a little time-honoured bestiality for restoring the circulation and putting things to rights generally. On ethical grounds alone—as safety-valves—such nocturnal feasts ought to be kept up in regions such as these, where the country-folk have not our "facilities." Who would grudge them these primordial joys, conducted under the indulgent motherly eye of Madonna, and hallowed by antiquity and the starlit heavens above? Every one is so happy and well-behaved. No bawling, no quarrelsomeness, no staggering tipplers; a spirit of universal good cheer broods over the assembly. Involuntarily, one thinks of the drunkard-strewn field of battle at the close of our Highland games; one thinks of God-fearing Glasgow on a Saturday evening, and of certain other aspects of Glasgow life. . . .

I accepted the kindly proffered invitation of the priests to share their dinner; they held out hopes of some sort of sleeping accommodation as well. It was a patriarchal hospitality before that fire of logs (the night had grown chilly), and several other guests partook of it, forestal inspectors and such-like notabilities—one lady among them who, true to feudal traditions, hardly spoke a word the whole evening. I was struck, as I have sometimes been, at the attainments of these country priests; they certainly knew our Gargantuan novelists of the Victorian epoch uncommonly well. Can it be that these authors are more readable in Italian translations than in the original? One of them took to relating, in a strain of autumnal humour, experiences of his life in the wilds of Bolivia, where he had spent many years among the Indians; my neighbour, meanwhile, proved to be steeped in Horatian lore. It was his pet theory, supported by a wealth of aptly cited lines, that Horace was a "typical Italian countryman," and great was his delight on discovering that I shared his view and could even add another—somewhat improper—utterance of the poet's to his store of illustrative quotations.

They belonged to the old school, these sable philosophers; to the days when the priest was arbiter of life and death, and his mere word sufficient to send a man to the galleys; when the cleverest boys of wealthy and influential families were chosen for the secular career and carefully, one might say liberally, trained to fulfil those responsible functions. The type is becoming extinct, the responsibility is gone, the profession has lost its glamour; and only the clever sons of pauper families, or the dull ones of the rich, are now tempted to forsake the worldly path.

Regarding the origin of this festival, I learned that it was "tradition." It had been suggested to me that the Virgin had appeared to a shepherd in some cave near at hand—the usual Virgin, in the usual cave; a cave which, in the present instance, no one was able to point out to me. *Est traditio, ne quæras amplius.* My hosts answered questions on this subject with benignant ambiguity, and did not trouble to defend the divine apparition on the sophistical lines laid down in Riccardi's "Santuari." The truth, I imagine, is that they have very sensibly not concerned themselves with inventing an original legend. The custom of congregating here on these fixed days seems to be recent, and I am inclined to think that it has been called into being by the zeal of some local men of standing. On the other hand, a shrine may well have stood for many years on this spot, for it marks the half-way house in the arduous two days' journey between San Severino and Castrovillari, a summer *trek* that must date from hoary antiquity.

Our bedroom contained two rough couches which were to be shared between four priests and myself. Despite the fact that I occupied the place of honour between the two oldest and wisest of my ghostly entertainers, sleep refused to come; the din outside had grown to a pandemonium. I lay awake till, at 2.30 a.m., one of them arose and touched the others with a whispered and half-jocular *oremus!* They retired on tiptoe to the next room, noiselessly closing the door, to prepare themselves for early service. I could hear them splashing vigorously at their ablutions in the icy water, and wondered dreamily how many Neapolitan priests would indulge at that chill hour of the morning in such a lustral rite, prescribed as it is by the rules of decency and of their church.

After that, I stretched forth at my ease and endeavoured to repose seriously. There were occasional lulls, now, in the carnival, but explosions of sound still broke the stillness, and phantoms of the restless throng began to chase each other through my brain. The exotic costumes of the Albanian girls in their green and gold wove themselves into dreams and called up colours seen in Northern Africa during still wilder festivals—negro festivals such as Fromentin loved to depict. In spectral dance there flitted before my vision nightmarish throngs of dusky women bedizened in that same green and gold; Arabs I saw, riding tumultuously hither and thither with burnous flying in the wind; beggars crawling about the hot sand and howling for alms; ribbons and flags flying—a blaze of sunshine overhead, and on earth a seething orgy of colour and sound; methought I heard the guttural yells of the fruit-vendors, musketry firing, braying of asses, the demoniacal groans of the camels——

Was it really a camel? No. It was something infinitely worse, and within a few feet of my ears. I sprang out of bed. There, at the very window, stood a youth extracting unearthly noises out of the Basilicata bagpipe. To be sure! I remembered expressing an interest in this rare instrument to one of my hosts who, with subtle delicacy, must have ordered the boy to give me a taste of his quality—to perform a matutinal serenade, for my especial benefit. How thoughtful these people are. It was not quite 4 a.m. With some regret, I said farewell to sleep and stumbled out of doors, where my friends of yesterday evening were already up and doing. The eating, the dancing, the bagpipes—they were all in violent activity, under the sober and passionless eye of morning.

A gorgeous procession took place about midday. Like a many-coloured serpent it wound out of the chapel, writhed through the intricacies of the pathway, and then unrolled itself freely, in splendid convolutions, about the sunlit meadow, saluted by the crash of mortars, bursts of military music from the band, chanting priests and women, and all the bagpipers congregated in a mass, each playing his own favourite tune. The figure of the Madonna—a modern and unprepossessing image—was carried aloft, surrounded by resplendent ecclesiastics and followed by a picturesque string of women bearing their votive offerings of candles, great and small. Several hundredweight of wax must have been brought up on the heads of pious female pilgrims. These multi-coloured candles are arranged in charming designs; they are fixed upright in a framework of wood, to resemble baskets or bird-cages, and decked with bright ribbons and paper flowers.

Who settles the expenses of such a festival? The priests, in the first place, have paid a good deal to make it attractive; they have improved the chapel, constructed a number of permanent wooden shelters (rain sometimes spoils the proceedings), as well as a capacious reservoir for holding drinking water, which has to be transported in barrels from a considerable distance. Then—as to the immediate outlay for music, fireworks, and so forth—the Madonna-statue is "put up to auction": *fanno l'incanto della Madonna*, as they say; that is, the privilege of helping to carry the idol from the church and back in the procession is sold to the highest bidders. Inasmuch as She is put up for auction several times during this short perambulation, fresh enthusiasts coming forward gaily with bank-notes and shoulders—whole villages competing against each other—a good deal of money is realized in this way. There are also spontaneous gifts of money. Goats and sheep, too, decorated with coloured rags, are led up by peasants who have "devoted" them to the Mother of God; the butchers on the spot buy these beasts for slaughter, and their price goes to swell the funds.

This year's expenditure may have been a thousand francs or so, and the proceeds are calculated at about two-thirds of that sum. No matter. If the priests do not make good the deficiency, some one else will be kind enough to step forward. Better luck next year! The festival, they hope, is to become more popular as time goes on, despite the chilling prophecy of one of our friends: "It will finish, this comedy!" The money, by the way, does not pass through the hands of the clerics, but of two individuals called "Regolatore" and "Priore," who mutually control each other. They are men of reputable families, who burden themselves with the troublesome task for the honour of the thing, and make up any deficiencies in the accounts out of their own pockets. Cases of malversation are legendary.

This procession marked the close of the religious gathering. Hardly was it over before there began a frenzied scrimmage of departure. And soon the woodlands echoed with the laughter and farewellings of pilgrims returning homewards by divergent paths; the whole way through the forest, we formed part of a jostling caravan along the Castrovillari-Morano track—how different from the last time I had traversed this route, when nothing broke the silence save a chaffinch piping among the branches or the distant tap of some woodpecker!

So ended the *festa*. Once in the year this mountain chapel is rudely disquieted in its slumbers by a boisterous riot; then it sinks again into tranquil oblivion, while autumn dyes the beeches to gold. And very soon the long winter comes; chill tempests shake the trees and leaves are scattered to earth; towards Yuletide some woodman of Viggianello adventuring into these solitudes, and mindful of their green summer revels, discovers his familiar sanctuary entombed up to the door-lintel under a glittering sheet of snow. . . .

There was a little episode in the late afternoon. We had reached the foot of the Gaudolino valley and begun the crossing of the plain, when there met us a woman with dishevelled hair, weeping bitterly and showing other signs of distress; one would have thought she had been robbed or badly hurt. Not at all! Like the rest of us, she had attended the feast and, arriving home with the first party, had been stopped at the entrance of the town, where they had insisted upon fumigating her clothes as a precaution against cholera, and those of her companions. That was all. But the indignity choked her—she had run back to warn the rest of us, all of whom were to be treated to the same outrage. Every approach to Morano, she declared, was watched by doctors, to prevent wary pilgrims from entering by unsuspected paths.

During her recital my muleteer had grown thoughtful.

"What's to be done?" he asked.

"I don't much mind fumigation," I replied.

"Oh, but I do! I mind it very much. And these doctors are so dreadfully distrustful. How shall we cheat them? . . . I have it, I have it!"

And he elaborated the following stratagem:

"I go on ahead of you, alone, leading the two mules. You follow, out of sight, behind. And what happens? When I reach the doctor, he asks slyly: 'Well, and how did you enjoy he festival this year?' Then I say: 'Not this year, doctor; alas, no festival for me! I've been with an Englishman collecting beetles in the forest, and see? here's his riding mule. He walks on behind—oh, quite harmless, doctor! a nice gentleman, indeed—only, he prefers walking; he really *likes* it, ha, ha, ha!——' "

"Why mention about my walking?" I interrupted. The lady-mule was still a sore subject.

"I mention about your not riding," he explained graciously, "because it will seem to the doctor a sure sign that you are a little"—here he touched his forehead with a significant gesture—"a little like some other foreigners, you know. And that, in its turn, will account for your collecting beetles. And that, in its turn, will acount for your not visiting the Madonna. You comprehend the argument: how it all hangs together?"

"I see. What next?"

"Then you come up, holding one beetle in each hand, and pretend not to know a word of Italian—not a word! You must smile at the doctor, in friendly fashion; he'll like that. And besides, it will prove what I said about—" (touching his forehead once more). "In fact, the truth will be manifest. And there will be no fumigation for us."

It seemed a needlessly circuitous method of avoiding such a slight inconvenience. I would have put more faith in a truthful narrative by myself, suffused with that ingratiating amiability which I would perforce employ on such occasions. But the stronger mind, as usual, had its way.

"I'll smile," I agreed. "But you shall carry my beetles; it looks more natural, somehow. Go ahead, and find them."

He moved forward with the beasts and, after destroying a considerable tract of stone wall, procured a few specimens of native coleoptera, which he carefully wrapped up in a piece of paper. I followed slowly.

Unfortunately for him, that particular doctor happened to be an *americano*, a snappy little fellow, lately returned form the States. "Glad to make your acquaintance, sir," he began, as I came up to where the two were arguing together. "I've heard of your passing through the other day. So you don't talk Italian? Well, then, see here: this man of yours, this God-damn son of Satan, has been showing me a couple of bugs and telling me a couple of hundred lies about them. Better move on right away; lucky you struck *me!* As for this son of a ——, you bet I'll sulphur him, bugs and all, to hell!"

I paid the crestfallen muleteer then and there; took down my bags, greatly lightened, and departed with them. Glancing round near the little bridge, I saw that the pair were still engaged in heated discussion, my man clinging despairingly, as it seemed, to the beetle-hypothesis; he looked at me with reproachful eyes, as though I had deserted him in his hour of need.

But what could I do, not knowing Italian?

Moreover, I remembered the "lady-mule."

Fifteen minutes later a light carriage took me to Castrovillari, whence, after a bath and dinner that compensated for past hardships, I sped down to the station and managed, by a miracle to catch the night-train to Cosenza.

XXI

MILTON IN CALABRIA

YOU may spend pleasant days in this city of Cosenza, doing nothing whatever. But I go there for a set purpose, and bristling with energy. I go there to hunt for a book by a certain Salandra, which was printed on the spot, and which I have not yet been able to find, although I once discovered it in an old catalogue, priced at 80 *grani*. Gladly would I give 8000 for it!

The author was a contemporary of that Flying Monk of whom I spoke in Chapter X, and he belonged to the same religious order. If, in what I then said about the flying monk, there appears to be some trace of light fooling in regard to this order and its methods, let amends be made by what I have to tell about old Salandra, the discovery of whose book is one of primary importance for the history of English letters. Thus I thought at the time; and thus I still think, with all due deference to certain grave and discerning gentlemen, the editors of various English monthlies to whom I submitted a paper on this subject—a paper which they promptly returned with thanks. No; that is not quite correct. One of them has kept it; and as six years have passed over our heads, I presume he has now acquired a title by "adverse possession." Much good may it do him!

Had the discovery been mine, I should have endeavoured to hide my light under the proverbial bushel. But it is not mine, and therefore I make bold to say that Mr. Bliss Perry, of the "Atlantic Monthly," knew better than his English colleagues when he published the article from which I take what follows.

Charles Dunster ("Considerations on Milton's Early Reading," etc., 1810) traces the *prima stamina* of "Paradise Lost" to Sylvester's "Du Bartas." Masenius, Cedmon, Vondel, and other older writers have also been named in this connection, while the majority of Milton's English commentators—and among foreigners Voltaire and Tiraboschi—are inclined to regard the "Adamus Exul" of Grotius or Andreini's sacred drama of "Adamo" as the prototype. This latter can be consulted in the third volume of Cowper's "Milton" (1810). The matter is still unsettled, and in view of the number of recent scholars who have interested themselves in it, one is really surprised that no notice has yet been taken of an Italian article which goes far towards deciding this question and proving that the chief source of "Paradise Lost" is the "Adamo Caduto," a sacred tragedy by Serafino della Salandra. The merit of this discovery belongs to Francesco Zicari, whose paper, "Sulla scoverta dell' originale italiano da cui Milton trasse il suo poema del paradiso perduto," is printed on pages 245 to 276 in the 1845 volume of the Naples "Album scientifico-aristico-letterario" now lying before me. It is in the form of a letter addressed to his friend Francesco Ruffa, a native of Tropea in Calabria.*

Salandra, it is true, is named among the writers of sacred tragedies in Todd's "Milton" (1809, vol. ii, p. 244), and also by Hayley, but neither of them had the curiosity, or the opportunity, to examine his "Adamo Caduto"; Hayley expressly says that he has not seen it. More recent works, such as that of Moers ("De fontibus Paradisi Amissi Miltoniani," Bonn, 1860), do not mention Salandra at all. Byse ("Milton on the Continent," 1903) merely hints at some possible motives for the Allegro and the Penseroso.

As to dates, there can be no doubt to whom the priority belongs. The "Adamo" of Salandra was printed at Cosenza in 1647. Richardson thinks that Milton entered upon his "Paradise Lost" in 1654, and that it was shown, as done, in 1665; D. Masson agrees with this, adding that "it was not published till two years afterwards." The date 1665 is fixed, I presume, by the Quaker Elwood's account of his visit to Milton in the autumn of that year, when the poet gave him the manuscript to read; the two years' delay in publication may possibly have been due to the confusion occasioned by the great plague and fire of London.

* Zicari contemplated another paper on this subject, but I am unaware whether this was ever published. The Neapolitan Minieri-Riccio, who wrote his "Memorie Storiche" in 1844, speaks of this article as having been already printed in 1832, but does not say where. This is corroborated by N. Falcone ("Biblioteca storica-topografica della Calabria," 2nd ed., Naples, 1846, pp. 152-154), who gives the same date, and adds that Zicari was the author of a work on the district of Fuscaldo. He was born at Paola in Calabria, of which he wrote a (manuscript) history, and died in 1846. In this Milton article, he speaks of his name being "unknown in the republic of letters." He is mentined by Nicola Leoni ("Della Magna Grecia," vol. ii, p. 153).

The castigation bestowed upon Lauder by Bishop Douglas, followed, as it was, by a terrific "back-hander" from the brawny arm of Samuel Johnson, induces me to say that Salandra's "Adamo Caduto," though extremely rare—so rare that neither the British Museum not the Paris Bibliothèque Nationale possesses a copy—is *not* an imaginary book; I have had it in my hands, and examined it at the Naples Biblioteca Nazionale; it is a small octavo of 251 pages (not including twenty unnumbered ones, and another one at the end for correction of misprints); badly printed and bearing all the marks of genuineness, with the author's name and the year and place of publication clearly set forth on the title-page. I have carefully compared Zicari's references to it, and quotations from it, with the original. They are correct, save for a few insignificant verbal discrepancies which, so far as I can judge, betray no indication of an attempt on his part to mislead the reader, such as using the word *tromba* (trumpet) instead of Salandra's term *sambuca* (sackbut).

And if further proof of authenticity be required, I may note that the "Adamo Caduto" of Salandra is already cited in old bibliographies like Toppi's "Biblioteca Napoletana" (1678), or that of Joannes a S. Antonio ("Bilioteca universa Franciscana, etc.," Madrid, 1732–1733, vol. iii, p. 88). It appears to have been the only literary production of its author, who was a Franciscan monk and is described as "Preacher, Lector and Definitor of the Reformed Province of Basilicata."

We may take it, then, that Salandra was a real person, who published a mystery called "Adamo Caduto" in 1647; and I will now, without further preamble, extract from Zicari's article as much as may be sufficient to show ground for his contention that Milton's "Paradise Lost" is a transfusion, in general and in particular, of this same mystery.

Salandra's central theme is the Universe shattered by the disobedience of the First Man, the origin of our unhappiness and sins. The same with Milton.

Salandra's chief personages are God and His angels; the first man and woman; the serpent; Satan and his angels. The same with Milton.

Salandra, at the opening of his poem (the prologue), sets forth his argument, and dwells upon the Creative Omnipotence and his works. The same with Milton.

Salandra then describes the council of the rebel angels, their fall from heaven into a desert and sulphurous region, their discourses.

Man is enviously spoken of, and his fall by means of stratagem decided upon; it is resolved to reunite in council in Pandemonium or the Abyss, where measures may be adopted to the end that man may become the enemy of God and the prey of hell. The same with Milton.

Salandra personifies Sin and Death, the latter being the child of the former. The same with Milton.

Salandra describes Omnipotence foreseeing the effects of the temptation and fall of man, and preparing his redemption. The same with Milton.

Salandra depicts the site of Paradise and the happy life there. The same with Milton.

Salandra sets forth the miraculous creation of the universe and of man, and the virtues of the forbidden fruit. The same with Milton.

Salandra reports the conversation between Eve and the Serpent; the eating of the forbidden fruit and the despair of our first parents. The same with Milton.

Salandra describes the joy of Death at the discomfiture of Eve; the rejoicings in hell; the grief of Adam; the flight of our first parents, their shame and repentance. The same with Milton.

Salandra anticipates the intercession of the Redeemer, and the overthrow of Sin and Death; he dwells upon the wonders of the Creation, the murder of Abel by his brother Cain, and other human ills; the vices of the Antediluvians, due to the fall of Adam; the infernal gift of war. The same with Milton.

Salandra describes the passion of Jesus Christ, and the comforts which Adam and Eve receive from the angel who announces the coming of the Messiah; lastly, their departure from the earthly paradise. The same with Milton.

So much for the general scheme of both poems. And now for a few particular points of resemblance, verbal and otherwise.

The character of Milton's Satan, with the various facets of pride, envy, vindictiveness, despair, and impenitence which go to form that harmonious whole, are already clearly mapped out in the Lucifero of Salandra. For this statement, which I find correct, Zicari gives chapter and verse, but it would take far too long to set forth the matter in this place. The speeches of Lucifero, to be sure, read rather like a caricature—it must not be forgotten that Salandra was writing for lower-class theatrical spectators, and not for refined readers—but the elements which Milton has utilized are already there.

Here is a coincidence:

> Here we may reign secure. . .
> Better to reign in Hell than serve in Heaven.
> > MILTON (i, 258).

> . . . Quì propria voglia,
> Son capo, son quì duce, son lor Prence.
> > SALANDRA (p. 49).

And another:

> . . . Whom shall we find
> Sufficient? . . . This enterprise
> None shall partake with me.
> > MILTON (ii, 403, 465).

> A chi basterà l'anima di voi?
> . . . certo che quest' affare
> A la mia man s' aspetta.
> > SALANDRA (p.64).

Milton's Terror is partially taken from the Megera of the Italian poet. The "grisly Terror" threatens Satan (ii, 699), and the office of Megera, in Salandra's drama, is exactly the same—that is, to threaten and chastise the rebellious spirit, which she does very effectually (pages 123–131). The identical monsters—Cerberus, Hydras, and Chimæras—are found in their respective abodes, but Salandra does not content himself with these three; his list includes such a mixed assemblage of creatures as owls, basilisks, dragons, tigers, bears, crocodiles, sphynxes, harpies, and panthers. Terror moves with dread rapidity:

> . . . and from his seat
> The monster moving onward came as fast
> With horrid strides.
> > MILTON (ii, 675).

and so does Megera:

> In atterir, in spaventar son . . .
> Rapido sì ch' ogni ripar è vano.
> > SALANDRA (p. 590).

Both Milton and Salandra use the names of the gods of antiquity for their demons, but the narrative epic of the English poet naturally permitted of far greater prolixity and variety in this respect. A most curious parallelism exists between Milton's Belial and that of Salandra. Both are described as luxurious, timorous, slothful, and scoffing, and there is not the slightest doubt that Milton has taken over these mixed attributes from the Italian.*

The words of Milton's Beelzebub (ii, 368):

> Seduce them our party, that their god
> May prove their foe . . .

are copied from those of the Italian Lucifero (p. 52):

> . . .Facciam
> Acciò, che l'huom divenga
> A Dio nemico . . .

Regarding the creation of the world, Salandra asks (p. 11):

> Qual lingua può di Dio,
> Benchè da Dio formato
> Lodar di Dio le meraviglie estreme?

which is thus echoed by Milton (vii, 112):

> . . . to recount almighty works
> What words or tongue of Seraph can suffice?

There is a considerable resemblance between the two poets in their descriptions of Paradise and of its joys. In both poems, too, Adam warns his spouse of her frailty, and in the episode of Eve's meeting with the serpent there are no less than four verbal coincidences. Thus Salandra writes (p. 68):

> Ravviso gli animal, ch' a schiera a schiera
> Già fanno humil e *reverente* inclino . . .

* This is one of the occasions in which Zicari appears, at first sight, to have stretched a point in order to improve his case, because, in the reference he gives, it is Behemoth, and not Belial, who speaks of himself as cowardly (*imbelle*). But in another place Lucifer applies this designation to Belial as well.

> Ravveggio il bel serpente *avvolto* in giri;
> O sei bello
> Con tanta varietà che certo sembri
> Altro stellato ciel, *smaltata* terra.
> O che sento, *tu parli?*

and Milton transcribes it as follows (ix, 517-554):

> . . . She minded not, as used
> To such disport before her through the field
> From every beast, more *duteous* at her call . . .
> Curled many a wanton *wreath* in sight of Eve.
> His turret crest and sleek *enamelled* neck . . .
> What may this mean? Language of man *pronounced*
> By tongue of brute?

Altogether, Zicari has observed that Rolli, although unacquainted with the "Adamo Caduto," has sometimes inadvertently hit upon the same words in his Italian translation of Milton which Salandra used before him.

Eve's altered complexion after the eating of the forbidden fruit is noted by both poets:

> Torbata ne la faccia? Non sei quella
> Qual ti lasciai contenta . .
> SALANDRA (p.89).

> Thus Eve with countenance blithe her story told;
> But in her cheek distemper flushing glowed.
> MILTON (ix, 886).

only with this difference, that the Italian Eve adds a half-lie by way of explaining the change:

> . . . Forse cangiata (del che non mi avveggio)
> Sono nel volto per la tua partenza.—(p. 89).

In both poems Sin and Death reappear on the scene after the transgression.

The flight of Innocence from earth; the distempered lust which dominates over Adam and Eve after the Fall; the league of Sin and Death to rule henceforward over the world; the pathetic lament of Adam regarding his misfortune and the evils in store for his progeny; his noble sentiment, that none can withdraw himself from the all-seeing eye of God—all these are images which Milton has copied from Salandra.

Adam's state of mind, after the fall, is compared by Salandra to a boat tossed by impetuous winds (p. 228):

> Qual agitato legno d'Austro, e Noto,
> Instabile incostante, non hai pace,
> Ta vivi pur . . .

which is thus paraphrased in Milton (ix, 1122):

> . . . High winds worse within
> Began to rise . . . and shook sore
> Their inward state of mind, calm region once
> And full of peace, now tossed and turbulent.

Here is a still more palpable adaptation:

> . . . So God ordains:
> God is thy law, thou mine.
> MILTON (iv, 636).

> . . . Un voler sia d' entrambi,
> E quel' uno di noi, di Dio sia tutto.
> SALANDRA (p. 42).

After the Fall, according to Salandra, *vacillò la terra* (1), *gemè* (2), *e pianse* (3). *rumoreggiano i tuoni* (4), *accompagnti da grandini* (5), *e dense nevi* (6) (pp. 138, 142, 218). Milton translates this as follows: Earth trembled from her entrails (1), and nature gave a second groan (2); sky loured and, muttering thunders (4), some sad drops wept (3), the winds, armed with ice and snow (6) and hail (5). ("Paradise Lost," ix, 1000; x, 697).

Here is another translation:

> . . . inclino il cielo
> Giù ne la terra, e questa al Ciel innalza.
> SALANDRA (p. 242).

> And Earth be changed to Heaven, and Heaven to Earth.
> MILTON (vii, 160).

It is not to my purpose to do Zicari's work over again, as this would entail a complete translation of his long article (it contains nearly ten thousand words), to which, if the thing is to be done properly, must be appended Salandra's "Adamo," in order that his quotations from it can be tested. I will therefore refer to the originals those who wish to go into the subject more fully, warning them, *en passant*, that they may find the task of verification more troublesome than it seems owing to a stupid mistake on Zicari's part. For in his references to Milton, he claims (p. 252) to use an 1818 Venice translation of the "Paradise Lost" by Rolli. Now Rolli's "Paradiso Perduto" is a well-known work which was issued in many editions in London, Paris, and Italy throughout the eighteenth century. But I cannot trace this particular one of Venice, and application to many of the chief libraries of Italy has convinced me that it does not exist, and that 1818 must be a misprint for some other year. The error would be of no significance if Zicari had referred to Rolli's "Paradiso" by the usual system of cantos and lines, but he refers to it by pages, and the pagination differs in every one of the editions of Rolli which have passed through my hands. Despite every effort, I have not been able to hit upon the precise one which Zicari had in mind, and if future students are equally unfortunate, I wish them joy of their labours.*

These few extracts, however, will suffice to show that, without Salandra's "Adamo," the "Paradise Lost," as we know it, would not be in existence; and that Zicari's discovery is therefore one of primary importance for English letters, although it would be easy to point out divergencies between the two works—divergencies often due to the varying tastes and feelings of a republican Englishman and an Italian Catholic, and to the different conditions imposed by an epic and a dramatic poem. Thus, in regard to this last point,

---

* Let me take this opportunity of expressing my best thanks to Baron E. Tortora Brayda, of the Naples Biblioteca Nazionale, who has taken an infinity of trouble in this matter.

Zicari has already noted (p. 270) that Salandra's scenic acts were necessarily reproduced in the form of *visions* by Milton, who could not avail himself of the mechanism of the drama for this purpose.

Milton was a man of the world, traveller, scholar, and politician; but it will not do for us to insist too vehemently upon the probable mental inferiority of the Calabrian monk, in view of the high opinion which Milton seems to have had of his talents. Imitation is the sincerest form of flattery. The "Adamo Caduto," of course, is only one of a series of similar works concerning which a large literature has now grown up, and it might not be difficult to prove that Salandra was indebted to some previous writer for those words and phrases which he passed on to the English poet.

But where did Milton become acquainted with this tragedy? It was at Naples, according to Cowper ("Milton," vol. iii, p, 206), that the English poet may first have entertained the idea of "the loss of paradise as a subject peculiarly fit for poetry." He may well have discussed sacred tragedies, like those of Andreini, with the Marquis Manso. But Milton had returned to England long before Salandra's poem was printed; nor can Manso have sent him a copy of it, for he died in 1645—two years before its publication—and Zicari is thus mistaken in assuming (p. 245) that Milton became acquainted with it in the house of the Neapolitan nobleman. Unless, therefore, we take for granted that Manso was intimate with the author Salandra—he knew most of his literary countrymen—and sent or gave to Milton a copy of the manuscript of "Adamo" before it was printed, or that Milton was personally familiar with Salandra, we may conclude that the poem was forwarded to him from Italy by some other friend, perhaps by some member of the *Accademia degli Oziosi* which Manso had founded.

A chance therefore seems to have decided Milton; Salandra's tragedy fell into his hands, and was welded into the epic form which he had designed for Arthur the Great, even as, in later years, a chance question on the part of Elwood led to his writing "Paradise Regained."* For this poem there were not so many models handy as for the other, but Milton has written too little to enable us to decide how far its inferiority to the earlier epic is due to this fact, and how far to the inherent inertia of its subject-matter. Little movement can be contrived in a mere dialogue such as "Paradise Regained"; it

---

* *Thou hast said much of Paradise Lost, but what hast thou to say of Paradise Found?* He made no answer, but sat some time in a muse. . . .

lacks the grandiose *mise-en-scène* and the shifting splendours of the greater epic; the stupendous figure of the rebellious archangel, the true hero of "Paradise Lost," is here dwarfed into a puny, malignant sophist; nor is the final issue in the later poem even *for a moment* in doubt—a serious defect from an artistic point of view. Jortin holds its peculiar excellence to be "artful sophistry, false reasoning, set off in the most specious manner and refuted by the Son of God with strong unaffected eloquence"; merits for which Milton needed no original of any kind, as his own lofty religious sentiments, his argumentative talents and long experience of political pamphleteering, stood him in good stead. Most of us must have wondered how it came about that Milton could not endure to hear "Paradise Lost" preferred to "Paradise Regained," in view of the very apparent inferiority of the latter. If we had known what Milton knew, namely, to how large an extent "Paradise Lost" was not the child of his own imagination, and therefore not so precious in his eyes as "Paradise Regained," we might have understood his prejudice.

Certain parts of "Paradise Lost" are drawn, as we all know, from other Italian sources, from Sannazario, Ariosto, Guarini, Bojardo, and others. Zicari who, it must be said, has made the best of his case, will have it that the musterings and battles of the good and evil angels are copied from the "Angeleide" of Valvasone published at Milan in 1590. But G. Polidori, who has reprinted the "Angeleide" in his Italian version of Milton (London, 1840), has gone into this matter and thinks otherwise. These devil-and-angel combats were a popular theme at the time, and there is no reason why the English poet should copy continental writers in such descriptions, which necessarily have a common resemblance. The Marquis Manso was very friendly with the poets Tasso and Marino, and it is also to be remarked that entire passages in "Paradise Lost" are copies, *totidem verbis*, from the writings of these two, Manso having no doubt drawn Milton's attention to their beauties. In fact, I am inclined to think that Manso's notorious enthusiasm for the *warlike* epic of Tasso may first of all have diverted Milton from purely pastoral ideals and inflamed him with the desire of accomplishing a similar feat, whence the well-known lines in Milton's Latin verses to this friend, which contain the first indication of such a design on his part. Even the familiar invocation, "Hail, wedded Love," is bodily drawn from one of Tasso's letters (see Newton's "Milton," 1773, vol. i, pp. 312, 313).

It has been customary to speak of these literary appropriations as "imitations"; but whoever compares them with the originals will find that many of them are more correctly termed translations. The case, from a literary-moral point of view, is different as regards ancient writers, and it is surely idle to accuse Milton, as has been done, of pilferings from Æschylus or Ovid. There is no such thing as robbing the classics. They are our literary fathers, and what they have left behind them is our common heritage; we may adapt, borrow, or steal from them as much as will suit our purpose; to acknowledge such "thefts" is sheer pedantry and ostentation. But Salandra and the rest of them were Milton's contemporaries. It is certainly an astonishing fact that no scholar of the stamp of Thyer was acquainted with the "Adamo Caduto"; and it says much for the isolation of England that, at a period when poems on the subject of paradise lost were being scattered broadcast in Italy and elsewhere—when, in short, all Europe was ringing with the doleful history of Adam and Eve—Milton could have ventured to speak of his work as "Things unattempted yet in prose or rhyme"—an amazing verse which, by the way, is literally transcribed out of Ariosto ("Cosa, non detta in prosa mai, nè in rima"). But even now the acquaintance of the British public with the productions of continental writers is superficial and spasmodic, and such was the ignorance of English scholars of this earlier period, that Birch maintained that Milton's drafts, to be referred to presently, indicated his intention of writing an *opera* (!); while as late as 1776 the poet Mickle, notwithstanding Voltaire's authority, questioned the very existence of Andreini, who has written thirty different pieces.

Some idea of the time when Salandra's tragedy reached Milton might be gained if we knew the date of his manuscript projects for "Paradise Lost" and other writings which are preserved at Cambridge. R. Garnett ("Life of Milton," 1890, p. 129) supposes these drafts to date from about 1640 to 1642, and I am not sufficiently learned in Miltonian lore to controvert or corroborate in a general way this assertion. But the date must presumably be pushed further forward in the case of the skeletons for "Paradise Lost," which are modelled to a great extent upon Salandra's "Adamo" of 1647, though other compositions may also have been present before Milton's mind, such as that mentioned on page 234 of the second volume of Todd's "Milton," from which he seems to have drawn the hint of a "prologue spoken by Moses."

Without going into the matter exhaustively, I will only say that from these pieces it is clear that Milton's primary idea was to write, like Salandra, a sacred tragedy upon this theme, and not an epic. These drafts also contain a chorus, such as Salandra has placed in his drama, and a great number of mutes, who do not figure in the English epic, but who reappear in the "Adamo Caduto" and all similar works. Even Satan is here designated as Lucifer, in accordance with the Italian Lucifero; and at the end of one of Milton's drafts we read "at last appears Mercy, comforts him, promises the Messiah, etc.," which is exactly what Salandra's Misericordia (Mercy) does in the same place.

Milton no doubt kept on hand many loose passages of poetry, both original and borrowed, ready to be worked up into larger pieces; all poets are smothered in odd scraps of verse and lore which they "fit in" as occasion requires; and it is therefore quite possible that some fragments now included in "Paradise Lost" may have been complete before the "Adamo Caduto" was printed. I am referring, more especially, to Satan's address to the sun, which Philips says was written before the commencement of the epic. Admitting Philips to be correct, I still question whether this invocation was composed before Milton's visit to Naples; and if it was, the poet may well have intended it for some other of the multitudinous works which these drafts show him to have been revolving in his mind, or for none of them in particular.

De Quincey rightly says that Addison gave the initial bias in favour of "Paradise Lost" to the English national mind, which has thenceforward shrunk, as Addison himself did, from a dispassionate contemplation of its defects; the idea being, I presume, that a "divine poem" in a manner disarmed rational criticism. And strange to say, even the few faults which earlier scholars did venture to point out in Milton's poem will be found in that of Salandra. There is the same superabundance of allegory; the same confusion of spirit and matter among the supernatural persons; the same lengthy astronomical treatise; the same personification of Sin and Death; the same medley of Christian and pagan mythology; the same tedious historico-theological disquisition at the end of both poems.

For the rest, it is to be hoped that we have outgrown our fastidiousness on some of these points. Theological fervour has abated, and in a work of the pure imagination, as "Paradise Lost" is now—is it not?—considered to be, there is nothing incongruous or offensive in an amiable commingling of Semitic and Hellenic deities after the approved Italian recipe; nor do a few long words about geography or science disquiet us any more. Milton was not writing for an uncivilized mob, and his occasional displays of erudition will represent to a cultured person only those breathing spaces so refreshing in all epic poetry. That Milton's language is saturated with Latinisms and Italianisms is perfectly true. His English may not have been good enough for his contemporaries. But it is quite good enough for us.

That "grand manner" which Matthew Arnold claimed for Milton, that sustained pitch of kingly elaboration and fullness, is not wholly an affair of high moral tone; it results in part from the humbler ministrations of words happily chosen—from a felicitous alloy of Mediterranean grace and Saxon mettle. For, whether consciously or not, we cannot but be influenced by the *colour-effects* of mere words, that arouse in us definite but indefinable moods of mind. To complain of the foreign phraseology and turns of thought in "Paradise Lost" would be the blackest ingratitude nowadays, seeing that our language has become enriched by steady gleams of pomp and splendour due, in large part, to the peculiar *lustre* of Milton's comely importations.

XXII

THE "GREEK" SILA

I T was to be the Sila in earnest, this time. I would traverse the whole country, from the Coscile valley to Catanzaro, at the other end.

Arriving from Cosenza the train deposited me, once more, at the unlovely station of Castrovillari. I looked around the dusty square, half-dazed by the sunlight—it was a glittering noon-day in July—but the postal waggon to Spezzano Albanese, my first resting point, had not yet arrived. Then a withered old man, sitting on a vehicle behind the sorry skeleton of a horse, volunteered to take me there at once; we quickly came to terms; it was too hot, we both agreed, to waste breath in bargaining. With the end of his whip he pointed out the church of Spezzano on its hilltop; a proud structure it looked at this distance, though nearer acquaintance reduced it to extremely humble proportions.

The Albanian Spezzano (Spezzano Grande is another place) lies on the main road from Castrovillari to Cosenza, on the summit of a long-stretched tongue of limestone which separates the Crati river from the Esaro; this latter, after flowing into the Coscile, joins its waters with the Crati, and so closes the promontory. An odd geographical feature, this low stretch, viewed from the greater heights of Sila or Pollino; one feels inclined to take a broom and sweep it into the sea, so that the waters may mingle sooner.

Our road ascended the thousand feet in a sinuous ribbon of white dust, and an eternity seemed to pass as we crawled drowsily upwards to the music of the cicadas, under the simmering blue sky. There was not a soul in sight; a hush had fallen upon all things; great Pan was brooding over the earth. At last we entered the village, and here, once more, deathlike stillness reigned; it was the hour of post-prandial slumber.

At our knocking the proprietor of the inn, situated in a side-street, descended. But he was in bad humour, and held out no hopes of refreshment. Certain doctors and government officials, he said, were gathered together in his house, telegraphically summoned to consult about a local case of cholera. As to edibles, the gentlemen had lunched, and nothing was left, absolutely nothing; it had been *uno sterminio*—an extermination—of all he possessed. The prospect of walking about the burning streets till evening did not appeal to me, and as this was the only inn at Spezzano I insisted, first gently, then forcibly—in vain. There was not so much as a chair to sit upon, he avowed; and therewith retired into his cool twilight.

Despairing, I entered a small shop wherein I had observed the only signs of life so far—an Albanian woman spinning in patriarchal fashion. It was a low-ceilinged room, stocked with candles, seeds, and other commodities which a humble householder might desire to purchase, including certain of those water-gugglets of Corigliano ware in whose shapely contours something of the artistic dreamings of old Sybaris still seems to linger. The proprietress, clothed in gaudily picturesque costume, greeted me with a smile and the easy familiarity which I have since discovered to be natural to all these women. She had a room, she said, where I could rest; there was also food, such as it was, cheese, and wine, and——

"Fruit?" I queried.

"Ah, you like fruit? Well, we may not so much as speak about it just now—the cholera, the doctors, the policeman, the prison! I was going to say *salami*."

Salami? I thanked her. I know Calabrian pigs and what they feed on, though it would be hard to describe in the language of polite society.

Despite the heat and the swarms of flies in that chamber, I felt little desire for repose after her simple repast; the dame was so affable and entertaining that we soon became great friends. I caused her some amusement by my efforts to understand and pronounce her language—these folk speak Albanian and Italian with equal facility—which seemed to my unpractised ears as hopeless as Finnish. Very patiently, she gave me a long lesson during which I thought to pick up a few words and phrases, but the upshot of it all was:

"You'll never learn it. You have begun a hundred years too late."

I tried her with modern Greek, but among such fragments as remained on my tongue after a lapse of over twenty years, only hit upon one word that she could understand.

"Quite right!" she said encouragingly. "Why don't you always speak properly? And now, let me hear a little of your own language."

I gave utterance to a few verses of Shakespeare, which caused considerable merriment.

"Do you mean to tell me," she asked, "that people really talk like that?"

"Of course they do."

"And pretend to understand what it means?"

"Why, naturally."

"Maybe they do," she agreed. "But only when they want to be thought funny by their friends."

The afternoon drew on apace, and at last the pitiless sun sank to rest. I perambulated Spezzano in the gathering twilight; it was now fairly alive with people. An unclean place; an epidemic of cholera would work wonders here. . . .

At 9.30 p.m. the venerable coachman presented himself, by appointment; he was to drive me slowly (out of respect for his horse) through the cool hours of the night as far as Vaccarizza, on the slopes of the Greek Sila, where he expected to arrive early in the morning. (And so he did; at half-past five.) Not without more mirth was my leave-taking from the good shopwoman; something, apparently, was hopelessly wrong with the Albanian words of farewell which I had carefully memorized from our preceding lesson. She then pressed a paper parcel into my hand.

"For the love of God," she whispered, "silence! Or we shall all be in jail to-morrow."

It contained a dozen pears.

Driving along, I tried to enter into conversation with the coachman who, judging by his face, was a mine of local lore. But I had come too late; the poor old man was so weakened by age and infirmities that he cared little for talk, his thoughts dwelling, as I charitably imagined, on his wife and children, all dead and buried (so he said) many long years ago. He mentioned, however, the *diluvio*, the deluge, which I have heard spoken of by older people, among whom it is a fixed article of faith. This deluge is supposed to have affected the whole Crati valley, submerging towns and villages. In proof, they say that if you dig near Tarsia below the present river-level, you will pass through beds of silt and ooze to traces of old walls and cultivated land. Tarsia used to lie by the river-side, and was a flourishing place, according to the descriptions of Leandro Alberti and other early writers; floods and malaria have now forced it to climb the hills.

The current of the Crati is more spasmodic and destructive than in classical times when the river was "navigable"; and to one of its inundations may be due this legend of the deluge; to the same one, maybe, that affected the courses of this river and the Coscile, mingling their waters which used to flow separately into the Ionian. Or it may be a hazy memory of the artificial changing of the riverbed when the town of Sybaris, lying between these two rivers, was destroyed. Yet the streams are depicted as entering the sea apart in old maps such as those of Magini, Fiore, Coronelli, and Cluver; and the latter writes that "near the mouth of the Crati there flows into the same sea a river vulgarly called Cochile."* This is important. It remains to be seen whether this statement is the result of a personal visit, or whether he simply repeated the old geography. His text in many places indicates a personal acquaintance with southern Italy—*Italiam,* says Heinsius, *non semel peragravit*—and he may well have been tempted to investigate a site like that of Sybaris. If so, the change in the river courses and possibly this "deluge" has taken place since his day.

Deprived of converse, I relapsed into a doze, but soon woke up with a start. The carriage had stopped; it was nearly midnight; we were at Terranova di Sibari, whose houses were lit up by the silvery beams of the moon.

Thurii—death-place of Herodotus! How one would like to see this place by daylight. On the ancient site, which lies at a considerable distance, they have excavated antiquities, a large number of which are in the possession of the Marchese Galli at Castrovillari. I endeavoured to see his museum, but found it inaccessible for "family reasons." The same answer was given me in regard to a valuable private library at Rossano, and annoying as it may be, one cannot severely blame such local gentlemen for keeping their collections to themselves. What have they to gain from the visits of inquisitive travellers?

During these meditations on my part, the old man hobbled busily to and fro with a bucket, bearing water from a fountain near at hand wherewith to splash the carriage-wheels. He persisted in this singular occupation for an unreasonably long time. Water was good for the wheels, he explained; it kept them cool.

At last we started, and I began to slumber once more. The carriage seemed to be going down a steep incline; endlessly it descended, with a pleasant swaying motion. . . . Then an icy shiver roused me from my dreams. It was the Crati whose rapid waves, fraught with

---

* In the earlier part of Rathgeber's astonishing "Grossgriechenland und Pythagoras" (1866) will be found a good list of old maps of the country.

unhealthy chills, rippled brightly in the moonlight. We crossed the malarious valley, and once more touched the hills.

From those treeless slopes there streamed forth deliciously warm emanations stored up during the scorching hours of noon; the short scrub that clothed them was redolent of the peculiar Calabrian odour which haunts one like a melody—an odour of dried cistus and other aromatic plants, balsamic by day, almost overpowering at this hour. To aid and diversify the symphony of perfume, I lit a cigar, and then gave myself up to contemplation of the heavenly bodies. We passed a solitary man, walking swiftly with bowed head. What was he doing there?

"Lupomanaro," said the driver.

A werewolf. . . .

I had always hoped to meet with a werewolf on his nocturnal rambles, and now my wish was gratified. But it was disappointing to see him in human garb—even werewolves, it seems, must march with the times. This enigmatical growth of the human mind flourishes in Calabria, but is not popular as a subject of conversation. The more old-fashioned werewolves cling to the true *versipellis* habits, and in that case only the pigs, the inane Calabrian pigs, are dowered with the faculty of distinguishing them in daytime, when they look like any other "Christian." There is a record, in Fiore's book, of an epidemic of lycanthropy that attacked the boys of Cassano. (Why only the boys?) It began on 31 July, 1210; and the season of the year strikes me as significant.

After that I fell asleep in good earnest, nor did I wake up again till the sun was peering over the eastern hills. We were climbing up a long slope; the Albanian settlements of Vaccarizza and San Giorgio lay before us and, looking back, I still saw Spezzano on its ridge; it seemed so close that a gunshot could have reached it.

These non-Italian villages date from the centuries that followed the death of Scanderbeg, when the Grand Signior consolidated his power. The refugees arrived in flocks from over the sea, and were granted tracts of wild land whereon to settle—some of them on this incline of the Sila, which was accordingly called "Greek" Sila, the native confusing these foreigners with the Byzantines whose dwellings, as regards Calabria, are now almost exclusively confined to the distant region of Aspromonte. Colonies of Albanians are scattered all over South Italy, chiefly in Apulia, Calabria, Basilicata, and Sicily; a few are in the north and centre—there is one on the Po, for instance, now reduced to 200 inhabitants; most of these latter have become absorbed into the surrounding Italian element. Angelo Masci (reprinted 1846) says there are 59 villages of them, containing altogether 83,000 inhabitants—exclusive of Sicily; Morelli (1842) gives their total population for Italy and Sicily as 103,466. If these figures are correct, the race must have multiplied latterly, for I am told there are now some 200,000 Albanians in the kingdom, living in about 80 villages. This gives approximately 2500 for each settlement—a likely number, if it includes those who are at present emigrants in America. There is a voluminous literature on the subject of these strangers, the authors of which are nearly all Albanians themselves. The fullest account of older conditions may well be that contained in the third volume of Rodotà's learned work (1758); the ponderous Francesco Tajani (1886) brings affairs up to date, or nearly so. If only he had provided his book with an index!

There were troubles at first. Arriving, as they did, solely "with their shirts and rhapsodies" (so one of them described it to me)—that is, despoiled of everything, they indulged in robberies and depredations somewhat too freely even for those free days, with the result that ferocious edicts were issued against them, and whole clans wiped out. It was a case of necessity knowing no law. But in proportion as the forests were hewn down and crops sown, they became as respectable as their hosts. They are bilingual from birth, one might almost say, and numbers of the men also express themselves correctly in English, which they pick up in the United States.

These islands of alien culture have been hotbeds of Liberalism throughout history. The Bourbons persecuted them savagely on that account, exiling and hanging the people by scores. At this moment there is a good deal of excitement going on in favour of the Albanian revolt beyond the Adriatic, and it was proposed, among other things, to organize a demonstration in Rome, where certain Roman ladies were to dress themselves in Albanian costumes and thus work upon the sentiments of the nation; but "the authorities" forbade this and every other movement. None the less, there has been a good deal of clandestine recruiting, and bitter recriminations against this turcophile attitude on the part of Italy—this "reactionary rigorism against every manifestation of sympathy for the Albanian cause." Patriotic pamphleteers ask, rightly enough, why difficulties should be placed in the way of recruiting for Albania, when, in the recent cases of Cuba and Greece, the despatch of volunteers was actually encouraged by the government? "Legality has ceased to exist here; we

Albanians are watched and suspected exactly as our compatriots now are by the Turks. . . . They sequestrate our manifestos, they forbid meetings and conferences, they pry into our postal correspondence. . . . Civil and military authorities have conspired to prevent a single voice of help and comfort reaching our brothers, who call to us from over the sea." A hard case, indeed. But Vienna and Cettinje might be able to throw some light upon it.*

The Albanian women, here as elsewhere, are the veriest beasts of burden; unlike the Italians, they carry everything (babies, and wood, and water) on their backs. Their crudely tinted costumes would be called more strange than beautiful under any but a bright sunshiny sky. The fine native dresses of the men have disappeared long ago; they even adopted, in days past, the high-peaked Calabrian hat which is now only worn by the older generation. Genuine Calabrians often settle in these foreign villages, in order to profit by their anti-feudal institutions. For even now the Italian cultivator is supposed to make, and actually does make, "voluntary" presents to his landlord at certain seasons; gifts which are always a source of irritation and, in bad years, a real hardship. The Albanians opposed themselves from the very beginning against these mediæval practices. "They do not build houses," says an old writer, "so as not to be subject to barons, dukes, princes, or other lords. And if the owner of the land they inhabit ill-treats them, they set fire to their huts and go elsewhere." An admirable system, even nowadays.

One would like to be here at Easter time to see the *rusalet*—those Pyrrhic dances where the young men group themselves in martial array, and pass through the streets with song and chorus, since, soon enough, America will have put an end to such customs. The old Albanian guitar of nine strings has already died out, and the double tibia—*biforem dat tibia cantum*—will presently follow suit. This instrument, familiar from classical sculpture and lore, and still used in Sicily and Sardinia, was once a favourite with the Sila shepherds, who called it "fischietto a pariglia." But some years ago I vainly sought it in the central Sila; the answer to my enquiries was everywhere the same: they knew it quite well; so and so used to play it; certain persons in certain villages still made it—they described it accurately enough, but could not produce a specimen. Single pipes, yes; and bagpipes galore; but the *tibiæ pares* were "out of fashion" wherever I asked for them.

---

* This was written before the outbreak of the Balkan war.

Here, in the Greek Sila, I was more fortunate. A boy at the village of Macchia possessed a pair which he obligingly gave me, after first playing a song—a farewell song—a plaintive ditty that required, none the less, an excellent pair of lungs, on account of the two mouthpieces. Melodies on this double flageolet are played principally at Christmas time. The two reeds are about twenty-five centimetres in length, and made of hollow cane; in my specimen, the left hand controls four, the other six holes; the Albanian name of the instrument is "fiscarol."

From a gentleman at Vaccarizza I received a still more valuable present—two neolithic celts (aenolithic, I should be inclined to call them) wrought in close-grained quartzite, and found not far from that village. These implements must be rare in the uplands of Calabria, as I have never come across them before, though they have been found, to my knowledge, at Savelli in the central Sila. At Vaccarizza they call such relics "pic"—they are supposed, as usual, to be thunderbolts, and I am also told that a piece of string tied to one of them cannot be burnt in fire. The experiment might be worth trying.

Meanwhile, the day passed pleasantly at Vaccarizza. I became the guest of a prosperous resident, and was treated to genuine Albanian hospitality and excellent cheer. I only wish that all his compatriots might enjoy one meal of this kind in their lifetime. For they are poor, and their homes of miserable aspect. Like all too many villages in South Italy, this one is depopulated of its male inhabitants, and otherwise dirty and neglected. The impression one gains on first seeing one of these places is more than that of Oriental decay; they are not merely ragged at the edges. It is a deliberate and sinister chaos, a note of downright anarchy—a contempt for those simple forms of refinement which even the poorest can afford. Such persons, one thinks, cannot have much sense of home and its hallowed associations; they seem to be everlastingly ready to break with the existing state of things. How different from England, where the humblest cottages, the roadways, the very stones testify to immemorial love of order, to neighbourly feelings and usages sanctioned by time!

They lack the sense of home as a fixed and old-established topographical point; as do the Arabs and Russians, neither of whom have a word expressing our "home" or "Heimat." Here, the nearest equivalent is *la famiglia*. We think of a particular house or village where we were born and where we spent our impressionable days of childhood; these others regard home not as a geographical but as a social centre, liable to shift from place to place; they are at home everywhere, so long as their clan is about them. That acquisitive sense which affectionately adorns our meanest dwelling, slowly saturating it with memories, has been crushed out of them—if it ever existed—by hard blows of fortune; it is safer, they think, to transform the labour of their hands into gold, which can be moved from place to place or hidden from the tyrant's eye. They have none of our sentimentality in regard to inanimate objects. Eliza Cook's feelings towards her "old arm-chair" would strike them as savouring of childishness. Hence the unfinished look of their houses, within and without. Why expend thought and wealth upon that which may be abandoned to-morrow?

The two churches of Vaccarizza, dark and unclean structures, stand side by side, and I was shown through them by their respective priests, Greek and Catholic, who walked arm in arm in friendly wise, and meekly smiled at a running fire of sarcastic observations on the part of another citizen directed against the "bottega" in general—the *shop*, as the church is sometimes irreverently called. The Greco-Catholic cult to which these Albanians belong is a compromise between the Orthodox and Roman; their priests may wear beards and marry wives, they use bread instead of the wafer for sacramental purposes, and there are one or two other little differences of grave import.

Six Albanian settlements lie on these northern slopes of the Sila—San Giorgio, Vaccarizza, San Cosimo, Macchia, San Demetrio Corone, and Santa Sofia d' Epiro. San Demetrio is the largest of them, and thither, after an undisturbed night's rest at the house of my kind host—the last, I fear, for many days to come—I drove in the sunlit hours of next morning. Along the road one can see how thoroughly the Albanians have done their work; the land is all under cultivation, save for a dark belt of trees overhead, to remind one of what once it was. Perhaps they have eradicated the forest over-zealously, for I observe in San Demetrio that the best drinking water has now to be fetched from a spring at a considerable distance from the village; it is unlikely that this should have been the original condition of affairs; deforestation has probably diminished the water-supply.

It was exhilarating to traverse these middle heights with their aerial views over the Ionian and down olive-covered hill-sides towards the wide valley of the Crati and the lofty Pollino range, now swimming in midsummer haze. The road winds in and out of gullies where rivulets descend from the mountains; they are clothed in cork-oak, ilex, and other trees; golden orioles, jays, hoopoes and rollers flash among the foliage. In winter these hills are swept by boreal blasts from the Apennines, but at this season it is a delightful tract of land.

XXIII

ALBANIANS AND THEIR COLLEGE

SAN Demetrio, famous for its Italo-Albanian College, lies on a fertile incline sprinkled with olives and mulberries and chestnuts, fifteen hundred feet above sea-level. They tell me that within the memory of living man no Englishman has ever entered the town. This is quite possible; I have not yet encountered a single English traveller, during my frequent wanderings over South Italy. Gone are the days of Keppel Craven and Swinburne, of Eustace and Brydone and Hoare! You will come across sporadic Germans immersed in Hohenstaufen records, or searching after Roman antiquities, butterflies, minerals, or landscapes to paint—you will meet them in the most unexpected places; but never an Englishman. The adventurous type of Anglo-Saxon probably thinks the country too tame; scholars, too trite; ordinary tourists, too dirty.

The accommodation and food in San Demetrio leave much to be desired; its streets are irregular lanes, ill-paved with cobbles of gneiss and smothered under dust and refuse. None the less, what noble names have been given to these alleys—names calculated to fire the ardent imagination of young Albanian students, and prompt them to valorous and patriotic deeds! Here are the streets of "Odysseus," of "Salamis" and "Marathon" and "Thermopylae," telling of the glory that was Greece; "Via Skanderbeg" and "Hypsilanti" awaken memories of more immediate renown; "Corso Dante Alighieri" reminds them that their Italian hosts, too, have done something in their day; the "Piazza Francesco Ferrer" causes their ultra-liberal breasts to swell with mingled pride and indignation; while the "Via dell' Industria" hints, not obscurely, at the great truth that genius, without a capacity for taking pains, is an idle phrase. Such appellations, without a doubt, are stimulating and glamorous. But if the streets themselves have seen a scavenger's broom within the last half-century, I am much mistaken. The goddess "Hygeia" dost not figure among their names, nor yet that Byzantine Monarch whose infantile exploit might be re-enacted in ripest maturity without attracting any attention in San Demetrio. To the pure all things are pure.

The town is exclusively Albanian; the Roman Catholic church has fallen into disrepair, and is now used as a shed for timber. But at the door of the Albanian sanctuary I was fortunate enough to intercept a native wedding, just as the procession was about to enter the portal. Despite the fact that the bride was considered the ugliest girl in the place, she had been duly "robbed" by her bold or possibly blind lover—her features were providentially veiled beneath her nuptial *flammeum*, and of her squat figure little could be discerned under the gorgeous accoutrements of the occasion. She was ablaze with ornaments and embroidery of gold, on neck and shoulders and wrist; a wide lace collar fell over a bodice of purple silk; silken too, and of brightest green, was her pleated skirt. The priest seemed ineffably bored with his task, and mumbled through one or two pages of holy books in record time; there were holdings of candles, interchange of rings, sacraments of bread and wine and other solemn ceremonies—the most quaint being the *stephanoma*, or crowning, of the happy pair, and the moving of their respective crowns from the head of one to that of the other. It ended with a chanting perlustration of the church, led by the priest: this is the so-called "pesatura."

I endeavoured to attune my mind to the gravity of this marriage, to the deep historico-ethnologico-poetical significance of its smallest detail. Such rites, I said to myself, must be understood to be appreciated, and had I not been reading certain native commentators on the subject that very morning? Nevertheless, my attention was diverted from the main issue—the bridegroom's face had fascinated me. The self-conscious male is always at a disadvantage during grotesquely splendid buffooneries of this kind; and never, in all my life, have I seen a man looking such a sorry fool as this individual, never; especially during the perambulation, when his absurd crown was supported on his head, from behind, by the hand of his best man.

Meanwhile a handful of boys, who seemed to share my private feelings in regard to the performance, had entered the sacred precincts, their pockets stuffed with living cicadas. These Albanian youngsters, like all true connaisseurs, are aware of the idiosyncrasy of the classical insect which, when pinched or tickled on a certain spot, emits its characteristic and ear-piercing note—the "lily-soft voice" of the Greek bard. The cicadas, therefore, were duly pinched and then let loose; like squibs and rockets they careered among the congregation, dashing in our faces and clinging to our garments; the church resounded like an olive-copse at noon. A hot little hand conveyed one of these tremulously throbbing creatures into my own, and obeying a whispered injunction of "Let it fly, sir!" I had the joy of seeing the beast alight with a violent buzz on the head of the bride—doubtless the happiest of auguries. Such conduct, on the part of English boys, would be deemed very naughty and almost irreverent; but here, one hopes, it may have its origin in some obscure but pious credence such as that which prompts the populace to liberate birds in churches, at Easter time. These escaping cicadas, it may be, are symbolical of matrimony—the individual man and woman freed, at last, from the dungeon-like horrors of celibate existence; or, if that parallel be far-fetched, we may conjecture that their liberation represents the afflatus of the human soul, aspiring upwards to merge its essence into the Divine All. . . .

The pride of San Demetrio is its college. You may read about it in Professor Mazziotti's monograph; but whoever wishes to go to the fountain-head must peruse the *Historia Erectionis Pontifici Collegi Corsini Ullanensis, etc.,* of old Zavarroni—an all-too-solid piece of work. Founded under the auspices of Pope Clement XII in 1733 (or 1735) at San Benedetto Ullano, it was moved hither in 1794, and between that time and now has passed through fierce vicissitudes. Its president, Bishop Bugliari, was murdered by the brigands in 1806; much of its lands and revenues have been dissipated by maladministration; it was persecuted for its Liberalism by the Bourbons, who called it a "workshop of the devil." It distinguished itself during the anti-dynastic revolts of 1799 and 1848 and, in 1860, was presented with twelve thousand ducats by Garibaldi, "in consideration of the signal services rendered to the national cause by the brave and generous Albanians."* Even now the institution is honeycombed with Freemasonry—the surest path to advancement in any career, in modern Italy. Times indeed have changed since the "Inviolable Constitutions" laid it down that *nullus omnino Alumnus in Collegio detineatur, cuius futuræ Christianæ pietatis significatio non extet.* But only since 1900 has it been placed on a really sound and prosperous footing. An agricultural school has lately been added, under the supervision of a trained expert. They who are qualified to judge speak of the college as a beacon of learning—an institution whose aims and results are alike deserving of high respect. And certainly it can boast of a fine list of prominent men who have issued from its walls.

This little island of stern mental culture contains, besides twenty-

---

* There used to be regiments of these Albanians at Naples. In Pilati de Tassulo's sane study (1777) they are spoken of as highly prized.

five teachers and as many servants, some three hundred scholars preparing for a variety of secular professions. About fifty of them are Italo-Albanians, ten or thereabouts are genuine Albanians from over the water, the rest Italians, among them two dozen of those unhappy orphans from Reggio and Messina who flooded the country after the earthquake, and were "dumped down" in colleges and private houses all over Italy. Some of the boys come of wealthy families in distant parts, their parents surmising that San Demetrio offers no temptations to youthful folly and extravagance. In this, so far as I can judge, they are perfectly correct.

The heat of summer and the fact that the boys were in the throes of their examinations may have helped to make the majority of them seem pale and thin; they certainly complained of their food, and the cook was the only prosperous-looking person whom I could discover in the establishment—his percentages, one suspects, being considerable. The average yearly payment of each scholar for board and tuition is only twenty pounds (it used to be twenty ducats); how shall superfluities be included in the bill of fare for such a sum?

The class-rooms are modernized; the dormitories neither clean nor very dirty; there is a rather scanty gymnasium as well as a physical laboratory and museum of natural history. Among the recent acquisitions of the latter is a vulture (*Gyps fulvus*) which was shot here in the spring of this year. The bird, they told me, has never been seen in these regions before; it may have come over from the east, or from Sardinia, where it still breeds. I ventured to suggest that they should lose no time in securing a native porcupine, an interesting beast concerning which I never fail to enquire on my rambles. They used to be encountered in the Crati valley; two were shot near Corigliano a few years ago, and another not far from Cotronei on the Neto; they still occur in the forests near the "Pagliarelle" above Petilia Policastro; but, judging by all indications, I should say that this animal is rapidly approaching extinction not only here, but all over Italy. Another very rare creature, the otter, was killed lately at Vaccarizza, but unfortunately not preserved.

Fencing and music are taught, but those athletic exercises which led to the victories of Marathon and Salamis are not much in vogue—*mens sana in corpore sano* is clearly not the ideal of the place; fighting among the boys is reprobated as "savagery," and corporal punishment forbidden. There is no playground or workshop, and their sole exercise consists in dull promenades along the high road under the supervision of one or more teachers, during which the youngsters indulge in attempts at games by the wayside which are truly pathetic. So the old "Inviolable Constitutions" ordain that "the scholars must not play outside the college, and if they meet any one, they should lower their voices." A rule of recent introduction is that in this warm weather they must all lie down to sleep for two hours after the midday meal; it may suit the managers, but the boys consider it a great hardship and would prefer being allowed to play. Altogether, whatever the intellectual results may be, the moral tendency of such an upbringing is damaging to the spirit of youth and must make for precocious frivolity and brutality. But the pædagogues of Italy are like her legislators: theorists. They close their eyes to the cardinal principles of all education—that the waste products and toxins of the imagination are best eliminated by motor activities, and that the immature stage of human development, far from being artificially shortened, should be prolonged by every possible means.

If the internal arrangement of this institution is not all it might be as regards the healthy development of youth, the situation of the college resembles the venerable structures of Oxford in that it is too good, far too good, for mere youngsters. This building, in its seclusion from the world, its pastoral surroundings and soul-inspiring panorama, is an abode not for boys but for philosophers; a place to fill with a wave of deep content the sage who has outgrown earthly ambitions. Your eye embraces the snow-clad heights of Dolcedorme and the Ionian Sea, wandering over forests, and villages, and rivers, and long reaches of fertile country; but it is not the variety of the scene, nor yet the historical memories of old Sybaris which kindle the imagination so much as the spacious amplitude of the whole prospect. In England we think something of a view of ten miles. Conceive, here, a grandiose valley wider than from Dover to Calais, filled with an atmosphere of such impeccable clarity that there are moments when one thinks to see every stone and every bush on the mountains yonder, thirty miles distant. And the cloud-effects, towards sunset, are such as would inspire the brush of Turner or Claude Lorraine. . . .

For the college, as befits its grave academic character, stands by itself among fruitful fields and backed by a chestnut wood, at ten minutes' walk from the crowded streets. It is an imposing edifice— the Basilean convent of St. Adrian, with copious modern additions; the founders may well have selected this particular site on account of its fountain of fresh water, which flows on as in days of yore. One thinks of those communities of monks in the Middle Ages, scattered over this wild region and holding rare converse with one another by gloomy forest paths—how remote their life and ideals! In the days of Fiore (1691) the inmates of this convent still practised their old rites. The nucleus of the building is the old chapel, containing a remarkable font; two antique columns sawn up (apparently for purposes of transportation from some pagan temple by the shore)—one of them being of African marble and the other of grey granite; there is also a tessellated pavement with beast-patterns of leopards and serpents akin to those of Patir. Bertaux gives a reproduction of this serpent; he assimilates it, as regards technique and age, to that which lies before the altar of Monte Cassino and was wrought by Greek artisans of the abbot Desiderius. The church itself is held to be two centuries older than that of Patir.

The library, once celebrated, contains musty folios of classics and their commentators, but nothing of value. It has been ransacked of its treasures like that of Patir, whose *disjecta membra* have been tracked down by the patience and acumen of Monsignor Batiffol.

Batiffol, Bertaux—Charles Diehl, Jules Gay (who has also written on San Demetrio)—Huillard-Bréholles—Luynes—Lenormant . . . here are a few French scholars who have recently studied these regions and their history. What have we English done in this direction?

Nothing. Absolutely nothing.

Such thoughts occur inevitably.

It may be insinuated that researches of this kind are gleanings; that our English genius lies rather in the spade-work of pioneers like Leake or Layard. Granted. But a hard fact remains; the fact, namely, that could any of our scholars have been capable of writing in the large and profound manner of Bertaux or Gay, not one of our publishers would have undertaken to print his work. Not one. They know their business; they know that such a book would have been a dead loss. Therefore let us frankly confess the truth: for things of the mind there is a smaller market in England than in France. *How much smaller* only they can tell, who have familiarized themselves with other departments of French thought.

Here, then, I have lived for the past few days, strolling among the fields, and attempting to shape some picture of these Albanians from their habits and such of their literature as has been placed at my disposal. So far, my impression of them has not changed since the days when I used to rest at their villages, in Greece. They remind me of the Irish. Both races are scattered over the earth and seem to prosper best outside their native country; they have the same songs and bards, the same hero-chieftains, the same combativeness and frank hospitality;

both are sunk in bigotry and broils; they resemble one another in their love of dirt, disorder and display, in their enthusiastic and adventurous spirit, their versatile brilliance of mind, their incapacity for self-government and general (Keltic) note of inspired inefficiency. And both profess a frenzied allegiance to an obsolete tongue which, were it really cultivated as they wish, would put a barrier of triple brass between themselves and the rest of humanity.

Even as the Irish despise the English as their worldly and effete relatives, so the Albanians look down upon the Greeks—even those of Pericles—with profoundest contempt. The Albanians, so says one of their writers, are "the oldest people upon earth," and their language is the "divine Pelasgic mother-tongue." I grew interested awhile in Stanislao Marchianò's plausibly entrancing study on this language, as well as in a pamphlet of de Rada's on the same subject; but my ardour has cooled since learning, from another native grammarian, that these writers are hopelessly in the wrong on nearly every point. So much is certain, that the Albanian language already possesses more than *thirty different alphabets* (each of them with nearly fifty letters). Nevertheless they have not yet, in these last four (or forty) thousand years, made up their minds which of them to adopt, or whether it would not be wisest, after all, to elaborate yet another one—a thirty-first. And so difficult is their language with any of these alphabets that even after a five days' residence on the spot I still find myself puzzled by such simple passages as this:

> ... Zilji,
> mosse vet, ce asso mbremie
> te ngcriret me iljiζ, praa
> gjiθ e miegculem, mhi ζiaarr
> rriij i sgjuat. Nje voogh e keljbur
> ζorrevet te ljosta
> ndjej se i oχtenej
> e pisseroghej. Zuu shiu
> menes; ne mee se ljinaar
> chish ljeen pa-shuatur
> sκiotta, e i ducheje per moon.

I will only add that the translation of such a passage—it contains twenty-eight accents which I have omitted—is mere child's play to its pronunciation.

XXIV

AN ALBANIAN SEER

SOMETIMES I find my way to the village of Macchia, distant about three miles from San Demetrio. It is a dilapidated but picturesque cluster of houses, situate on a projecting tongue of land which is terminated by a little chapel to Saint Elias, the old sun-god Helios, lover of peaks and promontories, whom in his Christian shape the rude Albanian colonists brought hither from their fatherland, even as, centuries before, he had accompanied the Byzantines on the same voyage and, fifteen centuries yet earlier, the Greeks.

At Macchia was born, in 1814, of an old and relatively wealthy family, Girolamo de Rada,* a flame-like patriot in whom the tempestuous aspirations of modern Albania took shape. The ideal pursued during his long life was the regeneration of his country; and if the attention of international congresses and linguists and folklorists is now drawn to this little corner of the earth—if, in 1902, twenty-one newspapers were devoted to the Albanian cause (eighteen in Italy alone, and one even in London)—it was wholly his merit.

He was the son of a Greco-Catholic priest. After a stern religious upbringing under the paternal roof at Macchia and in the college of San Demetrio, he was sent to Naples to complete his education. It is characteristic of the man that even in the heyday of youth he cared little for modern literature and speculations and all that makes for exact knowledge, and that he fled from his Latin teacher, the celebrated Puoti, on account of his somewhat exclusive love of

---

* Thus his friend and compatriot, Dr. Michele Marchianò, spells the name in a biography which I recommend to those who think there is no intellectual movement in South Italy. But he himself, at the very close of his life, in 1902, signs himself Ger. de Rhada. So this village of Macchia is spelt indifferently by Albanians as Maki or Makji. They have a fine Elizabethan contempt for orthography—as well they may have, with their thirty alphabets.

grammatical rules. None the less, though congenitally averse to the materialistic and subversive theories that were then seething in Naples, he became entangled in the anti-Bourbon movements of the late thirties, and narrowly avoided the death-penalty which struck down some of his comrades. At other times his natural piety laid him open to the accusation of reactionary monarchical leanings.

He attributed his escape from this and every other peril to the hand of God. Throughout life he was a zealous reader of the Bible, a firm and even ascetic believer, forever preoccupied, in childlike simplicity of soul, with first causes. His spirit moved majestically in a world of fervent platitudes. The whole Cosmos lay serenely distended before his mental vision; a benevolent God overhead, devising plans for the prosperity of Albania; a malignant, ubiquitous and very real devil, thwarting these His good intentions whenever possible; mankind on earth, sowing and reaping in the sweat of their brow, as was ordained of old. Like many poets, he never disabused his mind of this comfortable form of anthropomorphism. He was a firm believer, too, in dreams. But his guiding motive, his sun by day and star by night, was a belief in the "mission" of the Pelasgian race now scattered about the shores of the Inland Sea—in Italy, Sicily, Greece, Dalmatia, Romania, Asia Minor, Egypt—a belief as ardent and irresponsible as that which animates the *Lost Tribe* enthusiasts of England. He considered that the world hardly realized how much it owed to his country-folk; according to his views, Achilles, Philip of Macedon, Alexander the Great, Aristotle, Pyrrhus, Diocletian, Julian the Apostate—they were all Albanians. Yet even towards the end of his life he is obliged to confess:—

"But the evil demon who for over four thousand years has been hindering the Pelasgian race from collecting itself into one state, is still endeavouring by insidious means to thwart the work which would lead it to that union."

Disgusted with the clamorous and intriguing bustle of Naples, he retired, at the early age of 34, to his natal village of Macchia, throwing over one or two offers of lucrative worldly appointments. He describes himself as wholly disenchanted with the "facile fatuity" of Liberalism, the fact being, that he lacked what a French psychologist has called the *function of the real*; his temperament was not of the kind to cope with actualities. This retirement is an epoch in his life—it is the Grand Renunciation. Henceforward he loses personal touch with thinking humanity. At Macchia he remained, brooding on Albanian wrongs, devising remedies, corresponding with foreigners and writing—ever writing; consuming his patrimony in the cause of Albania, till the direst poverty dogged his footsteps.

I have read some of his Italian works. They are curiously oracular, like the whisperings of those fabled Dodonian oaks of his fatherland; they heave with a darkly-virile mysticism. He shares Blake's ruggedness, his torrential and confused utterance, his benevolence, his flashes of luminous inspiration, his moral background. He resembles that visionary in another aspect: he was a consistent and passionate adorer of the *Ewig-weibliche*. Some of the female characters in his poems retain their dewy freshness, their exquisite originality, even after passing through the translator's crucible.

At the age of 19 he wrote a poem on "Odysseus," which was published under a pseudonym. Then, three years later, there appeared a collection of rhapsodies entitled "Milosao," which he had garnered from the lips of Albanian village maidens. It is his best-known work, and has been translated into Italian more than once. After his return to Macchia followed some years of apparent sterility, but later on, and especially during the last twenty years of his life, his literary activity became prodigious. Journalism, folklore, poetry, history, grammar, philology, ethnology, æsthetics, politics, morals—nothing came amiss to his gifted pen, and he was fruitful, say his admirers, even in his errors. Like other men inflamed with one single idea, he boldly ventured into domains of thought where specialists fear to tread. His biographer enumerates forty-three different works from his pen. They all throb with a resonant note of patriotism; they are "fragments of a heart," and indeed, it has been said of him that he utilized even the grave science of grammar as a battlefield whereon to defy the enemies of Albania. But perhaps he worked most successfully as a journalist. His "Fiamuri Arberit" (the Banner of Albania) became the rallying cry of his countrymen in every corner of the earth.

These multifarious writings—and doubtless the novelty of his central theme—attracted the notice of German philologers and linguists, of all lovers of freedom, folklore and verse. Leading Italian writers like Cantù praised him highly; Lamartine, in 1844, wrote to him: "Je suis bien-heureux de ce signe de fraternité poétique et politique entre vous et moi. La poésie est venue de vos rivages et doit y retourner. . . ." Hermann Buchholtz discovers scenic changes worthy of Shakespeare, and passages of Æschylean grandeur, in his tragedy "Sofonisba." Camet compares him with Dante, and the omniscient Mr. Gladstone wrote in 1880—a post card, presumably—

belauding his disinterested efforts on behalf of his country. He was made the subject of many articles and pamphlets, and with reason. Up to his time, Albania had been a myth. He it was who divined the relationship between the Albanian and Pelasgian tongues; who created the literary language of his country, and formulated its political ambitions.

Whereas the hazy "Autobiologia" records complicated political intrigues at Naples that are not connected with his chief strivings, the little "Testamento politico," printed towards the end of his life, is more interesting. It enunciates his favourite and rather surprising theory that the Albanians cannot look for help and sympathy save only to their *brothers*, the Turks. Unlike many Albanians on either side of the Adriatic, he was a pronounced Turcophile, detesting the "stolid perfidy" and "arrogant disloyalty" of the Greeks. Of Austria, the most insidious enemy of his country's freedom, he seems to have thought well. A year before his death he wrote to an Italian translator of "Milosao" (I will leave the passage in the original, to show his cloudy language):

"Ed un tempo propizio la accompagna: la ricostituzione dell' Epiro nei suoi quattro vilayet autonomi quale è nei propri consigli e nei propri desideri; recostituzione, che pel suo Giornale, quello dell' ottimo A. Lorecchio—cui precede il principe Nazionale Kastriota, Chini—si annuncia fatale, e quasi fulcro della stabilità dello impero Ottomano, a della pace Europea; preludio di quella diffusione del regno di Dio sulla terra, che sarà la Pace tra gli Uomini."

Truly a remarkable utterance, and one that illustrates the disadvantages of living at a distance from the centres of thought. Had he travelled less with the spirit and more with the body, his opinions might have been modified and corrected. But he did not even visit the Albanian colonies in Italy and Sicily. Hence that vast confidence in his mission—a confidence born of solitude, intellectual and geographical. Hence the ultra-terrestrial yearning which tinges his apparently practical aspirations.

He remained at home, ever poor and industrious; wrapped in bland exaltation and oblivious to contemporary movements of the human mind. Not that his existence was without external activities. A chair of Albanian literature at San Demetrio, instituted in 1849 but suppressed after three years, was conferred on him in 1892 by the historian and minister Pasquale Villari; for a considerable time, too, he was director of the communal school at Corigliano, where, with characteristic energy, he set up a printing press; violent journalistic campaigns succeeded one another; in 1896 he arranged for the first congress of Albanian language in that town, which brought together delegates from every part of Italy and elicited a warm telegram of felicitation from the minister Francesco Crispi, himself an Albanian. Again, in 1899, we find him reading a paper before the twelfth international congress of Orientalists at Rome.

But best of all, he loved the seclusion of Macchia.

Griefs clustered thickly about the closing years of this unworldly dreamer. Blow succeeded blow. One by one, his friends dropped off; his brothers, his beloved wife, his four sons—he survived them all; he stood alone at last, a stricken figure, in tragic and sublime isolation. Over eighty years old, he crawled thrice a week to deliver his lectures at San Demetrio; he still cultivated a small patch of ground with enfeebled arm, composing, for relaxation, poems and rhapsodies at the patriarchal age of 88! They will show you the trees under which he was wont to rest, the sunny views he loved, the very stones on which he sat; they will tell you anecdotes of his poverty—of an indigence such as we can scarcely credit. During the last months he was often thankful for a crust of bread, in exchange for which he would bring a sack of acorns, self-collected, to feed the giver's pigs. Destitution of this kind, brought about by unswerving loyalty to an ideal, ceases to exist in its sordid manifestations: it exalts the sufferer. And his life's work is there. Hitherto there had been no "Albanian Question" to perplex the chanceries of Europe. He applied the match to the tinder; he conjured up that phantom which refuses to be laid.

He died, in 1903, at San Demetrio; and there lies entombed in the cemetery on the hill-side, among the oaks.

But you will not easily find his grave.

His biographer indulges a poetic fancy in sketching the fair monument which a grateful country will presently rear to his memory on the snowy Acroceraunian heights. It might be well, meanwhile, if some simple commemorative stone were placed on the spot where he lies buried. Had he succumbed at his natal Macchia, this would have been done; but death overtook him in the alien parish of San Demetrio, and his remains were mingled with those of its poorest citizens. A microcosmic illustration of the clannish spirit of Albania which he had spent a lifetime in endeavouring to direct to nobler ends!

He was the Mazzini of his nation.

A Garibaldi, when the crisis comes, may possibly emerge from that tumultuous horde.

Where is the Cavour?

XXV

SCRAMBLING TO LONGOBUCCO

A DRIVING road to connect San Demetrio with Acri whither I was now bound was begun, they say, about twenty years ago; one can follow it for a considerable distance beyond the Albanian College. Then, suddenly, it ends. Walking to Acri, however, by the old track, one picks up, here and there, conscientiously-engineered little stretches of it, already overgrown with weeds; these, too, break off as abruptly as they began, in the wild waste. For purposes of wheeled traffic these picturesque but disconnected fragments are quite useless.

Perhaps the whole undertaking will be completed some day—*speriamo!* as the natives say, when speaking of something rather beyond reasonable expectation. But possibly not; and in that case—*pazienza!* meaning, that all hope may now be abandoned. There is seldom any great hurry, with non-governmental works of this kind.

It would be interesting if one could learn the inner history of these abortive transactions. I have often tried, in vain. It is impossible for an outsider to pierce the jungle of sordid mystery and intrigue which surrounds them. So much I gathered: that the original contract was based on the wages then current and that, the price of labour having more than doubled in consequence of the "discovery" of America, no one will undertake the job on the old terms. That is sufficiently intelligible. But why operations proceeded so slowly at first, and why a new contract cannot now be drawn up—who can tell! The persons interested blame the contractor, who blames the engineer, who blames the dilatory and corrupt administration of Cosenza. My private opinion, is that the last three parties have agreed to share the swag between them. Meanwhile everybody has just grounds of complaint against everybody else; the six or seven inevitable lawsuits have sprung up and promise to last any length of time, seeing that important documents have been lost of stolen and that half the original contracting parties have died in the interval: nobody knows what is going to happen in the end. It all depends upon whether some patriotic person will step forward and grease the wheels in the proper quarter.

And even then, if he hails from Acri, they of San Demetrio will probably work against the project, and vice versa. For no love is lost between neighbouring communities—wonderful, with what venomous feudal animosity they regard each other! United Italy means nothing to these people, whose conceptions of national and public life are those of the cock on his dung-hill. You will find in the smallest places intelligent and broad-minded men, tradespeople or professionals or landed proprietors, but they are seldom members of the *municipio;* the municipal career is also a money-making business, yes; but of another kind, and requiring other qualifications.

Foot-passengers like myself suffer no inconvenience by being obliged to follow the shorter and time-honoured mule-track that joins the two places. It rises steeply at first, then begins to wind in and out among shady vales of chestnut and oak, affording unexpected glimpses now towards distant Tarsia and now, through a glade on the right, on to the ancient citadel of Bisignano, perched on its rock.

I reached Acri after about two and a half hours' walking. It lies in a theatrical situation and has a hotel; but the proprietor of that establishment having been described to me as "the greatest brigand of the Sila" I preferred to refresh myself at a small wineshop, whose manageress cooked me an uncommonly good luncheon and served some of the best wine I had tasted for long. Altogether, the better-class women here are far more wideawake and civilized than those of the Neapolitan province; a result of their stern patriarchal upbringing and of their possessing more or less sensible husbands.

Thus fortified, I strolled about the streets. One would like to spend a week or two in a place like this, so little known even to Italians, but the hot weather and bad feeding had begun to affect me disagreeably and I determined to push on without delay into cooler regions. It would never do to be laid up at Acri with heat-stroke, and to have one's last drops of life drained away by copious bloodlettings, relic of Hispano-Arabic practices and the favourite remedy for every complaint. Acri is a large place, and its air of prosperity contrasts with the slumberous decay of San Demetrio; there is silk-rearing, and so much emigration into America that nearly every man I addressed replied in English. New houses are rising up in all directions, and the place is celebrated for its rich citizens.

But these same wealthy men are in rather a dilemma. Some local authority, I forget who, has deduced from the fact that there are so many forges and smiths' shops here that this must be the spot to which the over-sensitive inhabitants of Sybaris banished their workers in metal and other noisy professions. Now the millionaires would like to be thought Sybarites by descent, but it is hardly respectable to draw a pedigree from these outcasts.

They need not alarm themselves. For Acri, as Forbiger has shown, is the old Acherontia; the river Acheron, the Mocone or Mucone of to-day, flows at its foot, and from one point of the town I had a fine view into its raging torrent.

A wearisome climb of two hours brought me to the *Croce Greca*, the Greek Cross, which stands 1185 metres above sea-level. How hot it was, in that blazing sun! I should be sorry to repeat the trip, under the same conditions. A structure of stone may have stood here in olden days; at present it is a diminutive wooden crucifix by the roadside. It marks, none the less, an important geographical point: the boundary between the "Greek" Sila which I was now leaving and the Sila Grande, the central and largest region. Beyond this last-named lies the lesser Sila, or "Sila Piccola"; and if you draw a line from Rogliano (near Cosenza) to Cotrone you will approximately strike the watershed which divides the Sila Grande from this last and most westerly of the three Sila divisions. After that comes Catanzaro and the valley of the Corace, the narrowest point of the Italian continent, and then the heights of Serra and Aspromonte, the true "Italy" of old, that continue as far as Reggio.

Though I passed through some noble groves of chestnut on the way up, the country here was a treeless waste. Yet it must have been forest up to a short time ago, for one could see the beautiful vegetable mould which has not yet had time to be washed down the hill-sides. A driving road passes the Croce Greca; it joins Acri with San Giovanni, the capital of Sila Grande, and with Cosenza.

It was another long hour's march, always uphill, before I reached a spacious green meadow or upland with a few little buildings. The place is called Verace and lies on the watershed between the upper Crati valley and the Ionian; thenceforward my walk would be a descent along the Trionto river, the Traeis of old, as far as Longobucco which overlooks its flood. It was cool here at last, from the altitude and the decline of day; and hay-making was going on, amid the pastoral din of cow-bells and a good deal of blithe lovemaking and chattering.

After some talk with these amiable folks, I passed on to where the young Traeis bubbles up from the cavernous reservoirs of the earth. Of those chill and roguish wavelets I took a draught, mindful of the day when long ago, by these same waters, an irreparable catastrophe overwhelmed our European civilization. For it was the Traeis near whose estuary was fought the battle between 300,000 Sybarites (I refuse to believe these figures) and the men of Croton conducted by their champion Milo—a battle which led to the destruction of Sybaris and, incidentally, of Hellenic culture throughout the mainland of Italy. This was in the same fateful year 510 that witnessed the expulsion of the Tarquins from Rome and the Pisistratidae from Athens.

Pines, the characteristic tree of the Sila, now begin to appear. Passing through Verace I had already observed, on the left, a high mountain entirely decked with them. It is the ridge marked Paleparto on the map; the Trionto laves its foot. But the local pronunciation of this name is Palépite, and I cannot help thinking that here we have a genuine old Greek name perpetuated by the people and referring to this covering of hoary pines—a name which the cartographers, arbitrary and ignorant as they often are, have unconsciously disguised. (It occurs in some old charts, however, as Paleparto.) An instructive map of Italy could be drawn up, showing the sites and cities wrongly named from corrupt etymology or falsified inscriptions, and those deliberately miscalled out of principles of local patriotism. The whole country is full of these inventions of *litterati* which date, for the most part, from the enthusiastic but undisciplined Cinque-Cento.

The minute geographical triangle comprised between Cosenza, Longobucco and San Demetrio which I was now traversing is one of the least known corners of Italy, and full of dim Hellenic memories. The streamlet "Calamo" flows through the valley I ascended from Acri, and at its side, a little way out of the town, stands the fountain "Pompeio" where the brigands, not long ago, used to lie in wait for women and children coming to fetch water, and snatch them away for ransom. On the way up, I had glimpses down a thousand feet or more into the Mucone or Acheron, raging and foaming in its narrow valley. It rises among the mountains called "Fallistro" and "Li Tartari"—unquestionably Greek names.

On this river and somewhere above Acri stood, according to the scholarly researches of Lenormant, the ancient city of Pandosia. I do not know if its site has been determined since his day. It was "very strong" and rich and at its highest prosperity in the fourth century

B. C.; after the fall of Sybaris it passed under the supremacy of Croton. The god Pan was figured on some of its coins, and appropriately enough, considering its sylvan surroundings; others bear the head of the nymph Pandosia with her name and that of the river Crates, under the guise of a young shepherd: they who wish to learn his improper legend will find it in the pages of Ælian, or in chapter xxxii of the twenty-fifth book of Rhodiginus, beginning *Quæ sit brutorum affectio*, etc.* We have here not the Greece of mediæval Byzantine times, much less that of the Albanians, but the sunny Hellas of the days when the world was young, when these ardent colonists sailed westwards to perpetuate their names and legends in the alien soil of Italy.

The Mucone has always been known as a ferocious and pitiless torrent, and maintains to this day its Tartarean reputation. Twenty persons a year, they tell me, are devoured by its angry waters: *mangia venti cristiani all'anno!* This is as bad as the Amendolea near Reggio. But none of its victims have attained the celebrity of Alexander of Molossus, King of Epirus, who perished under the walls of Pandosia in 326 B. C. during an excursion against the Lucanians. He had been warned by the oracle of Dodona to avoid the waters of Acheron and the town of Pandosia; once in Italy, however, he paid small heed to these words, thinking they referred to the river and town of the same name in Thesprotia. But the gods willed otherwise, and you may read of his death in the waters, and the laceration of his body by the Lucanians, in Livy's history.

It is a strange caprice that we should now possess what is in every probability the very breastplate worn by the heroic monarch on that occasion. It was found in 1820, and thereafter sold—some fragments of it, at least—to the British Museum, where under the name of "Bronze of Siris" it may still be admired: a marvellous piece of repoussée work, in the style of Lysippus, depicting the combat of Ajax and the Amazons. . . .

The streamlet Trionto, my companion to Longobucco, glides

---

* *Brutii a brutis moribus*: so say certain spiteful writers, an accusation which Strabo and Horace extend to all Calabrians. As to the site of Pandosia, a good number of scholars, such as old Prosper Parisius and Luigi Maria Greco, locate it at the village of Mendicino on the river Merenzata, which was called Arconte (?Acheron) in the Middle Ages. So the Trionto is not unquestionably the Traeis, and in Marincola Pistoia's good little "Cose di Sibari" (1845) the distinction is claimed for one of four rivers—the Lipuda, Colognati, Trionto, or Fiuminicà.

along between stretches of flowery meadow-land—fit emblem of placid rural contentment. But soon this lyric mood is spent. It enters a winding gorge that shuts out the sunlight and the landscape abruptly assumes an epic note; the water tumbles wildly downward, hemmed in by mountains whose slopes are shrouded in dusky pines wherever a particle of soil affords them foothold. The scenery in this valley is as romantic as any in the Sila. Affluents descend on either side, while the swollen rivulet writhes and screeches in its narrow bed, churning the boulders with hideous din. The track, meanwhile, continues to run beside the water till the passage becomes too difficult; it must perforce attack the hill-side. Up it climbs, therefore, in never-ending ascension, and then meanders at a great height above the valley, in and out of its tributary glens.

I was vastly enjoying this promenade—the shady pines, whose fragrance mingled with that of a legion of tall aromatic plants in full blossom—the views upon the river, shining far below me like the thread of silver—when I observed with surprise that the whole mountain-side which the track must manifestly cross had lately slipped down into the abyss. A cloud-burst two or three days ago, as I afterwards learned, had done the mischief. On arrival at the spot, the path was seen to be interrupted—clean gone, in fact, and not a shred of earth or trees left; there confronted me a bare scar, a wall of naked rock which not even a chamois could negotiate. Here was a dilemma. I must either retrace my steps along the weary road to Verace and there seek a night's shelter with the gentle hay-makers, or clamber down into the ravine, follow the river and—chance it! After anxious deliberation, the latter alternative was chosen.

But the Trionto was now grown into a formidable torrent of surging waves and eddies, with a perverse inclination to dash from one side to the other of its prison, so as to necessitate frequent fordings on my part. These watery passages, which I shall long remember, were not without a certain danger. The stream was still swollen with the recent rains, and its bed, invisible under the discoloured element, sufficiently deep to inspire respect and studded, furthermore, with slippery boulders of every size, concealing insidious gulfs. Having only a short walking-stick to support me through this raging flood, I could not but picture to myself the surprise of the village maidens of Cropolati, lower down, on returning to their laundry work by the river-side next morning and discovering the battered anatomy of an Englishman—a rare fish, in these waters—stranded upon their familiar beach. Murdered, of course. What a galaxy of brigand legends would have clustered round my memory! Evening was closing in, and I had traversed the stream so often and stumbled so long amid this chaos of roaring waters and weirdly-tinted rocks, that I began to wonder whether the existence of Longobucco was not a myth. But suddenly, at a bend of the river, the whole town, still distant, was revealed, upraised on high and framed in the yawning mouth of the valley. After the solitary ramble of that afternoon, my eyes familiarized to nothing save the wild things of nature, this unexpected glimpse of complicated civilized structures had all the improbability of a mirage. Longobucco, at that moment, arose before me like those dream-cities in the Arabian tale, conjured by enchantment out of the desert waste.

The vision, though it swiftly vanished again, cheered me on till after a good deal more scrambling and wading, with boots torn to rags, lame, famished and drenched to the skin, I reached the bridge of the Rossano highway and limped upwards, in the twilight, to the far-famed "Hotel Vittoria."

Soon enough, be sure, I was enquiring as to supper. But the manageress met my suggestions about eatables with a look of blank astonishment.

Was there nothing in the house, then? No cheese, or meat, or maccheroni, or eggs—no wine to drink?

"Nothing!" she replied. "Why should you eat things at this hour? You must find them yourself, if you really want them. I might perhaps procure you some bread."

Avis aux voyageurs, as the French say.

Undaunted, I went forth and threw myself upon the mercy of a citizen of promising exterior, who listened attentively to my case. Though far too polite to contradict, I could see that nothing in the world would induce him to credit the tale of my walking from San Demetrio that day—it was tacitly relegated to the regions of fable. With considerable tact, so as not to wound my feelings, he avoided expressing any opinion on so frivolous a topic; nor did the reason of his reluctance to discuss my exploit dawn upon me till I realized, later on, that like many of the inhabitants he had never heard of the track over Acri, and consequently disbelieved its existence. They reach San Demetrio by a two or even three days' drive over Rossano, Corigliano, and Vaccarizza. He became convinced, however, that for some reason or other I was hungry, and thereupon good-naturedly conducted me to various places where wine and other necessities of life were procured.

The landlady watched me devouring this fare, more astonished than ever—indeed, astonishment seemed to be her chronic condition so long as I was under her roof. But the promised bread was not forthcoming, for the simple reason that there was none in the house. She had said that she could procure it for me, not that she possessed it; now, since I had given no orders to that effect, she had not troubled about it.

Nobody travels south of Rome. . . .

Strengthened beyond expectation by this repast, I sallied into the night once more, and first of all attended an excellent performance at the local cinematograph. After that, I was invited to a cup of coffee by certain burghers, and we strolled about the piazza awhile, taking our pleasure in the cool air of evening (the town lies 794 metres above sea-level). Its streets are orderly and clean; there are no Albanians, and no costumes of any kind. Here, firm-planted on the square, and jutting at an angle from the body of the church, stands a massive bell-tower overgrown from head to foot with pendent weeds and grasses whose roots have found a home in the interstices of its masonry; a grimly venerable pile, full of character.

Weary but not yet satiated, I took leave of the citizens and perambulated the more ignoble quarters, all of which are decently lighted with electricity. Everywhere in these stiller regions was the sound of running waters, and I soon discerned that Longobucco is an improvement on the usual site affected by Calabrian hill-towns— the Y-shaped enclosure, namely, at the junction of two rivers— inasmuch as it has contrived to perch itself on a lofty platform protected by no less than three streams that rush impetuously under its walls: the Trionto and two of its affluents. On the flank inclined towards the Ionian there is a veritable chasm; the Trionto side is equally difficult of approach—the rear, of course, inaccessible. No wonder the brigands chose it for their chief citadel.

I am always on the look-out for modern epigraphical curiosities; regarding the subject as one of profound social significance (postage stamps, indeed!) I have assiduously formed a collection, the envy of connaisseurs, about one-third of whose material, they tell me, might possibly be printed at Brussels or Geneva. Well, here is a mural *graffito* secured in the course of this evening's walk:

Albaso [sic] *questo paese sporco incivile:* down with this dirty savage country!

There is food for thought in this inscription. For if some bilious hyper-civilized stranger were its author, the sentiments might pass. But coming from a native, to what depths of morbid discontent do they testify! Considering the recent progress of these regions that has led to a security and prosperity formerly undreamed of, one is driven to the conjecture that these words can only have been penned by some cantankerous churl of an emigrant returning to his native land after an easeful life in New York and compelled—"for his sins," as he would put it—to reside at the "Hotel Vittoria."

Towards that delectable hostelry I now turned, somewhat regretfully, to face a bedroom whose appearance had already inspired me with anything but confidence. But hardly were the preliminary investigations begun, when a furious noise in the street below drew me to the window once more. Half the town was passing underneath in thronged procession, with lighted torches and flags, headed by the municipal band discoursing martial strains of music.

Whither wending, at this midnight hour?

To honour a young student, native of the place, now returning up the Rossano road from Naples, where he had distinguished himself prominently in some examination. I joined the crowd, and presently we were met by a small carriage whence there emerged a pallid and frail adolescent with burning eyes, who was borne aloft in triumph and cheered with that vociferous, masculine heartiness which we Englishmen reserve for our popular prize-fighters. And this in the classic land of brigandage and bloodshed!

The intellectual under-current. . . .

It was an apt commentary on my *graffito*. And another, more personally poignant, not to say piquant, was soon to follow: the bed. But no. I will say nothing about the bed, nothing whatever; nothing beyond this, that it yielded an entomological harvest which surpassed my wildest expectations.

XXVI

AMONG THE BRUTTIANS

CONSPICUOUS among the wise men of Longobucco in olden days was the physician Bruno, who "flourished" about the end of the thirteenth century. He called himself *Longobur-gensis Calaber*, and his great treatise on anatomical dissection, embodying much Greek and Arabic lore, was printed many years after his death. Another was Francesco Maria Labonia; he wrote, in 1664, "De vera loci urbis Timesinæ situatione, etc.," to prove, presumably, that his birthplace occupied the site whence the Homeric ore of Temese was derived. There are modern writers who support this view.

The local silver mines were exploited in antiquity; first by Sybaris, then by Croton. They are now abandoned, but a good deal has been written about them. In the year 1200 a thousand miners were employed, and the Anjous extracted a great deal of precious metal thence; the goldsmiths of Longobucco were celebrated throughout Italy during the Middle Ages. The industrious H. W. Schulz has unearthed a Royal rescript of 1274 charging a certain goldsmith Johannes of Longobucco with researches into the metal and salt resources of the whole kingdom of Naples.

Writing from Longobucco in 1808 during a brigand-hunt, Duret de Tavel says:

"The high wooded mountains which surround this horrible place spread over it a sombre and savage tint which saddens the imagination. This borough contains a hideous population of three thousand souls, composed of nail-makers, of blacksmiths and charcoal-burners. The former government employed them in working the silver mines situated in the neighbourhood which are now abandoned."

He tells a good deal about the brigandage that was then rife here, and the atrocities which the repression of this pest entailed. Soon after his arrival, for instance, four hundred soldiers were sent to a village where the chiefs of the brigand "insurrection" were supposed to be sheltered. The soldiers, he says, "poured into the streets like a torrent in flood, and there began a horrible massacre, rendered inevitable by the obstinacy of the insurgents, who fired from all the houses. This unhappy village was sacked and burnt, suffering all the horrors inseparable from a capture by assault." Two hundred dead were found in the streets. But the brigand chiefs, the sole pretext of this bloodshed, managed to escape. Perhaps they were not within fifty miles of the place.

Be that as it may, they were captured later on by their own compatriots, after the French had waited a month at Longobucco. Their heads were brought in, still bleeding, and "l'identité ayant été suffisamment constatée, la mort des principaux acteurs a terminé cette sanglante tragédie, et nous sommes sortis de ces catacombes apénnines pour revoir le plus brillant soleil."

Wonderful tales are still told of the brigands in these forests. They will show you notches on the trees, cut by such and such a brigand for some particular purpose of communication with his friends; buried treasure has been found, and even nowadays shepherds sometimes discover rude shelters of bark and tree trunks built by them in the thickest part of the woods. There are legends, too, of caverns wherein they hived their booty—caverns with cleverly concealed entrances—caverns which (many of them, at least) I regard as a pure invention modelled after the authentic brigand caves of Salerno and Abuzzi, where the limestone rock is of the kind to produce them. Bourbonism fostered the brood, and there was a fierce recrudescence in the troubled sixties. They lived in bands, *squadrigli*, burning and plundering with impunity. Whoever refused to comply with their demands for food or money was sure to repent of it. All this is over, for the time being; the brigands are extirpated, to the intense relief of the country people, who were entirely at their mercy, and whose boast it is that their district is now as safe as the streets of Naples. Qualified praise, this. . . . *

It is an easy march of eight hours or less, through pleasing scenery and by a good track, from Longobucco to San Giovanni in Fiore, the capital of the Sila. The path leaves Longobucco at the rear of the town and, climbing upward, enters a valley which it follows to its head. The peasants have cultivated patches of ground along the stream; the slopes are covered, first with chestnuts and then with

---

* See next chapter.

hoary firs—a rare growth, in these parts—from whose branches hangs the golden bough of the mistletoe. And now the stream is ended and a dark ridge blocks the way; it is overgrown with beeches, under whose shade you ascend in steep curves. At the summit the vegetation changes once more, and you find yourself among magnificent stretches of pines that continue as far as the governmental domain of Galoppano, a forestal station, two hours' walk from Longobucco.

This pine is a particular variety (*Pinus laricio*, var. *Calabra*), known as the "Pino della Sila"—it is found over this whole country, and grows to a height of forty metres with a silvery-grey trunk, exhaling a delicious aromatic fragrance. In youth, especially where the soil is deep, it shoots up prim and demure as a Nuremberg toy; but in old age grows monstrous. High-perched upon some lonely granite boulder, with roots writhing over the bare stone like the arms of an octopus, it sits firm and unmoved, deriding the tempest and flinging fantastic limbs into the air—emblem of tenacity in desolation. From these trees, which in former times must have covered the Sila region, was made the Bruttian pitch mentioned by Strabo and other ancient writers; from them the Athenians, the Syracusans, Tarentines and finally the Romans built their fleets. Their timber was used in the construction of Caserta palace.

A house stands here, inhabited by government officials the whole year round—one may well puzzle how they pass the long winter, when snow lies from October to May. So early did I arrive at this establishment that the more civilized of its inhabitants were still asleep; by waiting, I might have learnt something of the management of the estate, but gross material preoccupations—the prospect of a passable luncheon at San Giovanni after the "Hotel Vittoria" fare—tempted me to press forwards. A boorish and unreliable-looking individual volunteered three pieces of information—that the house was built thirty years ago, that a large nursery for plants lies about ten kilometres distant, and that this particular domain covers "two or four thousand hectares." A young plantation of larches and silver birches—aliens to this region—seemed to be doing well.

Not far from here, along my track, lies Santa Barbara, two or three huts, with corn still green—like Verace (above Acri) on the watershed between the Ionian and upper Crati. Then follows a steep climb up the slopes of Mount Pettinascura, whose summit lies 1708 metres above sea-level. This is the typical landscape of the Sila Grande.

There is not a human habitation in sight; forests all around, with views down many-folded vales into the sea and towards the distant and fairy-like Apennines, a serrated edge, whose limestone precipices gleam like crystals of amethyst between the blue sky and the dusky woodlands of the foreground.

Here I reposed awhile, watching the crossbills, wondrously tame, at work among the branches overhead, and the emerald lizard peering out of the bracken at my side. This *lucertone*, as they call it, is a local beast, very abundant in some spots (at Venosa and Patirion, for example); it is elsewhere conspicuous by its absence. The natives are rather afraid of it, and still more so of the harmless gecko, the "salamide," which is reputed highly poisonous.

Then up again, through dells and over uplands, past bubbling streams, sometimes across sunlit meadows, but oftener in the leafy shelter of maples and pines—a long but delightful track, winding always high above the valleys of the Neto and Lese. At last, towards midday, I struck the driving road that connects San Giovanni with Savelli, crossed a bridge over the foaming Neto, and climbed into the populous and dirty streets of the town—the "Siberia of Calabria," as it may well be, for seven months of the year.

At this season, thanks to its elevation of 1050 metres, the temperature is all that could be desired, and the hotel, such as it is, compares favourably indeed with the den at Longobucco. Instantly I felt at home among these good people, who recognized me, and welcomed me with the cordiality of old friends.

"Well," they asked, "and have you found it at last?"

They remembered my looking for the double flute, the *tibiæ pares*, some years ago.

It will not take you long to discover that the chief objects of interest in San Giovanni are the women. Many Calabrian villages still possess their distinctive costumes—Marcellinara and Cimigliano are celebrated in this respect—but it would be difficult to find anywhere an equal number of handsome women on such a restricted space. In olden days it was dangerous to approach these attractive and mirthful creatures; they were jealously guarded by brothers and husbands. But the brothers and husbands, thank God, are now in America, and you may be as friendly with them as ever you please, provided you confine your serious attentions to not more than two or three. Secrecy in such matters is out of the question, as with the Arabs; there is too much gossip, and too little coyness about what is natural;

your friendships are openly recognized, and tacitly approved. The priests do not interfere; their hands are full.

To see these women at their best one must choose a Sunday or a feast-day; one must go, moreover, to the favourite fountain of Santa Lucia, which lies on the hill-side and irrigates some patches of corn and vegetables. Their natural charms are enhanced by elaborate and tasteful golden ornaments, and by a pretty mode of dressing the hair, two curls of which are worn hanging down before their ears with an irresistibly seductive air. Their features are regular; eyes black or deep gentian blue; complexion pale; movements and attitudes impressed with a stamp of rare distinction. Even the great-grandmothers have a certain austere dignity—sinewy, indestructible old witches, with tawny hide and eyes that glow like lamps.

And yet San Giovanni is as dirty as can well be; it has the accumulated filth of an Eastern town, while lacking all its glowing tints or harmonious outlines. We are disposed to associate squalor with certain artistic effects, but it may be said of this and many other Calabrian places that they have solved the problem how to be ineffably squalid without becoming in the least picturesque. Much of this sordid look is due to the smoke which issues out of all the windows and blackens the house walls, inside and out—the Calabrians persisting in a prehistoric fashion of cooking on the floor. The buildings themselves look crude and gaunt from their lack of plaster and their eyeless windows; black pigs wallowing at every doorstep contribute to this slovenly *ensemble*. The City Fathers have turned their backs upon civilization; I dare say the magnitude of the task before them has paralysed their initiative.

Nothing is done in the way of public hygiene, and one sees women washing linen in water which is nothing more or less than an open drain. There is no street-lighting whatever; a proposal on the part of a North Italian firm to draw electric power from the Neto was scornfully rejected; one single tawdry lamp, which was bought some years ago "as a sample" in a moment of municipal recklessness, was lighted three times in as many years, and on the very day when it was least necessary—to wit, on midsummer eve, which happens to be the festival of their patron saint (St. John). "It now hangs"—so I wrote some years ago—"at a dangerous angle, and I doubt whether it will survive till its services are requisitioned next June." Prophetic utterance! It was blown down that same winter, and has not yet been replaced. This in a town of 20,000 (?) inhabitants—and in Italy, where the evening life of the populace plays such an important rôle. No wonder North Italians, judging by such external indications, regards all Calabrians as savages.

Some trees have been planted in the piazza since my last stay here; a newspaper has also been started—it is called "Co-operation: Organ of the Interests of San Giovanni in Fiore," and its first and possibly unique number contains a striking article on the public health, as revealed in the report of two doctors who had been despatched by the provincial sanitary authorities to take note of local conditions of hygiene. "The illustrious scientists" (thus it runs) "were horrified at the filth, mud and garbage which encumbered, and still encumbers, our streets, sending forth in the warm weather a pestilential odour. . . . They were likewise amazed at the vigorously expressed protest of our mayor, who said: '*My people cannot live without their pigs wallowing in the streets. San Giovanni in Fiore is exempt from earthquakes and epidemics because it is under the protection of Saint John the Baptist, and because its provincial councillor is a saintly man.*' " Such journalistic plain speaking, such lack of sweet reasonableness, cannot expect to survive in a world governed by compromise, and if the gift of prophecy had not deserted me, I should say that "Co-operation" has by this time ended its useful mission upon earth.

This place is unhealthy; its water-supply is not what it should be, and such commodities as eggs and milk are rather dear, because "the invalids eat everything" of that kind. Who are the invalids? Typhoid patients and, above all, malarious subjects who descend to the plains as agricultural labourers and return infected to the hills, where they become partially cured, only to repeat the folly next year. It is the same at Longobucco and other Sila towns. Altogether, San Giovanni has grave drawbacks. The streets are too steep for comfort, and despite its height, the prospect towards the Ionian is intercepted by a ridge; in point of situation it cannot compare with Savelli or the neighbouring Casino, which have impressive views both inland, and southward down undulating slopes that descend in a stately procession of four thousand feet to the sea, where sparkles the gleaming horn of Cotrone. And the surroundings of the place are nowise representative of the Sila in a good sense. The land has been so ruthlessly deforested that it has become a desert of naked granite rocks; even now, in midsummer, the citizens are already collecting fuel for their long winter from enormous distances. As one crawls and skips among these unsavoury tenements, one cannot help regretting that Saint John the Baptist, or the piety of a provincial councillor, should have hindered the earthquakes from doing their obvious duty.

Were I sultan of San Giovanni, I would certainly begin by a general bombardment. Little in the town is worth preserving from a cataclysm save the women, and perhaps the old convent on the summit of the hill where the French lodged during their brigand-wars, and that other one, famous in the ecclesiastical annals of Calabria—the monastery of Floriacense, founded at the end of the twelfth century, round which the town gradually grew up. Its ponderous portal is much injured, having been burnt, I was told, by the brigands in 1860. But the notary, who kindly looked up the archives for me, has come to the conclusion that the French are responsible for the damage. It contains, or contained, a fabulous collection of pious lumber—teeth and thigh-bones and other relics, the catalogue of which is one of my favourite sections of Father Fiore's work. I would make an exception, also, in favour of the doorway of the church, a finely proportioned structure of the Renaissance in black stone, which looks ill at ease among its ignoble environment. A priest, to whom I applied for information as to its history, told me with the usual Calabrian frankness that he never bothered his head about such things.

San Giovanni was practically unknown to the outside world up to a few years ago. I question whether Lenormant or any of them came here. Pacicchelli did, however, in the seventeenth century, though he has left us no description of the place. He crossed the whole Sila from the Ionian to the other sea. I like this amiable and loquacious creature, restlessly gadding about Europe, gloriously complacent, hopelessly absorbed in trivialities, and credulous beyond belief. In fact (as the reader may have observed), I like all these old travellers, not so much for what they actually say, as for their implicit outlook upon life. This Pacicchelli was a fellow of our Royal Society, and his accounts of England are worth reading; here, in Calabria (being a non-southerner) his "Familiar Letters" and "Memoirs of Travel" act as a wholesome corrective. Which of the local historians would have dared to speak of Cosenza as "città aperta, scomposta, e disordinata di fabbriche"?

That these inhabitants of the Sila are Bruttians may be inferred from the superior position occupied by their women-folk, who are quite differently treated to those of the lowlands. There—all along the coasts of South Italy—the cow-woman is still found, unkempt and uncivilized; there, the male is the exclusive bearer of culture. Such things are not seen among the Bruttians of the Sila, any more than among the grave Latins or Samnites. These non-Hellenic races are, generally speaking, honest, dignified and incurious; they are bigoted, not to say fanatical; and their women are not exclusively beasts of burden, being better dressed, better looking, and often as intelligent as the men. They are the fruits of a female selection.

But wherever the mocking Ionic spirit has penetrated—and the Ionian women occupied even a lower position than those of the Dorians and Æolians—it has resulted in a glorification of masculinity. Hand in hand with this depreciation of the female sex go other characteristics which point to Hellenic influences: lack of commercial morality, of veracity, of seriousness in religious matters; a persistent, light-hearted inquisitiveness; a levity (or sprightliness, if you prefer it) of mind. The people are fetichistic, amulet-loving, rather than devout. We may certainly suspect Greek or Saracen strains wherever women are held in low estimation; wherever, as the god Apollo himself said, "the mother is but the nurse." In the uplands of Calabria the mother is a good deal more than the nurse.

For the rest, it stands to reason that in proportion as the agricultural stage supplants that of pasturage, the superior strength and utility of boys over girls should become more apparent, and this in South Italy is universally proclaimed by the fact that everything large and fine is laughingly described as "maschio" (male), and by some odd superstitions in disparagement of the female sex, such as these: that in giving presents to women, uneven numbers should be selected, lest even ones "do them more good than they deserve"; that to touch the hump of a female hunchback brings no luck whatever; that if a woman be the first to drink out of a new earthenware pitcher, the vessel may as well be thrown away at once—it is tainted for ever.* Yet the birth of a daughter is no Chinese calamity; even girls are "Christians" and welcomed as such, the populace having never sunk to the level of our theologians, who were wont to discuss *an fæmina sint monstra.*

All over the Sila there is a large preponderance of women over men, nearly the whole male section of the community, save the

* In Japan, says Hearn, the first bucketful of water to be drawn out of a cleaned well must be drawn by a man; for if a woman first draw water, the well will always thereafter remain muddy. Some of these prejudices seem to be based on primorial misreadings of physiology. There is also a strong feeling in favour of dark hair. No mother would entrust her infant to a fair wet-nurse; the milk even of white cows is considered "lymphatic" and not strengthening; perhaps the eggs of white hens are equally devoid of the fortifying principle. There is something to be said for this since, in proportion as we go south, the risk of irritation, photophobia, and other complaints incidental to the xanthous complexion becomes greater.

quite young and the decrepit, being in America. This emigration brings much money into the country and many new ideas; but the inhabitants have yet to learn the proper use of their wealth, and to acquire a modern standard of comfort. Together with the Sardinians, these Calabrians are the hardiest of native races, and this is what makes them prefer the strenuous but lucrative life in North American mines to the easier career in Argentina, which Neapolitans favour. There they learn English. They remember their families and the village that gave them birth, but their patriotism towards Casa Savoia is of the slenderest. How could it be otherwise? I have spoken to numbers of them, and this is what they say:

"This country has done nothing for us; why should we fight its battles? Not long ago we were almost devouring each other in our hunger; what did they do to help us? If we have emerged from misery, it is due to our own initiative and the work of our own hands; if we have decent clothes and decent houses, it is because they drove us from our old homes with their infamous misgovernment to seek work abroad."

Perfectly true! They have redeemed themselves, though the new régime has hardly had a fair trial. And the drawbacks of emigration (such as a slight increase of tuberculosis and alcoholism) are nothing compared with the unprecedented material prosperity and enlightenment. There has also been—in these parts, at all events—a marked diminution of crime. No wonder, seeing that three-quarters of the most energetic and turbulent elements are at present in America, where they recruit the Black Hand. That the Bruttian is not yet ripe for town life, that his virtues are pastoral rather than civic, might have been expected; but the Arab domination of much of his territory, one suspects, may have infused fiercer strains into his character and helped to deserve for him that epithet of *sanguinario* by which he is proud to be known.

XXVII

CALABRIAN BRIGANDAGE

THE last genuine bandit of the Sila was Gaetano Ricca. On account of some trivial misunderstanding with the authorities, this man was compelled in the early eighties to take to the woods, where he lived a wild life (*alla campagna; alla macchia*) for some three years. A price was set on his head, but his daring and knowledge of the country intimidated every one. I should be sorry to believe in the number of carbineers he is supposed to have killed during that period; no doubt the truth came out during his subsequent trial. On one occasion he was surrounded, and while the officer in command of his pursuers, who had taken refuge behind a tree, ordered him to yield, Ricca waited patiently till the point of his enemy's foot became visible, when he pierced his ankle-bone with his last bullet and escaped. He afterwards surrendered and was imprisoned for twenty years or so; then returned to the Sila, where up to a short time ago he was enjoying a green old age in his home at Parenti—Parenti, already celebrated in the annals of brigandage by the exploit of the perfidious Francatripa (Giacomo Pisani), who, under pretence of hospitality, enticed a French company into his clutches and murdered its three officers and all the men, save seven. The memoirs of such men might be as interesting as those of the Sardinian Giovanni Tolù which have been printed. I would certainly have paid my respects to Ricca had I been aware of his existence when, some years back, I passed through Parenti on my way—a long day's march!—from Rogliano to San Giovanni. He has died in the interval.

But the case of Ricca is a sporadic one, such as may crop up anywhere and at any time. It is like that of Musolino—the case of an isolated outlaw, who finds the perplexed geographical configuration of the country convenient for offensive and defensive purposes. Calabrian brigandage, as a whole, has always worn a political character.

The men who gave the French so much trouble were political brigands, allies of Bourbonism. They were commanded by creatures like Mammone, an anthropophagous monster whose boast it was that he had personally killed 455 persons with the greatest refinements of cruelty, and who wore at his belt the skull of one of them, out of which he used to drink human blood at mealtime; he drank his own blood as well; indeed, he "never dined without having a bleeding human heart on the table." This was the man whom King Ferdinand and his spouse loaded with gifts and decorations, and addressed as "Our good Friend and General—the faithful Support of the Throne." The numbers of these savages were increased by shiploads of professional cut-throats sent over from Sicily by the English to help their Bourbon friends. Some of these actually wore the British uniform; one of the most ferocious was known as "L'Inglese"— the Englishman.

One must go to the fountain-head, to the archives, in order to gain some idea of the sanguinary anarchy that desolated South Italy in those days. The horrors of feudalism, aided by the earthquake of 1784 and by the effects of Cardinal Ruffo's Holy Crusade, had converted the country into a pandemonium. In a single year (1809) thirty-three thousand crimes were recorded against the brigands of the Kingdom of Naples; in a single month they are said to have committed 1200 murders in Calabria alone. These were the bands who were described by British officers as "our chivalrous brigand-allies."

It is good to bear these facts in mind when judging of the present state of this province, for the traces of such a reign of terror are not easily expunged. Good, also, to remember that this was the period of the highest spiritual eminence to which South Italy has ever attained. Its population of four million inhabitants were then consoled by the presence of no less than 120,000 holy persons—to wit, 22 archbishops, 116 bishops, 65,500 ordained priests, 31,800 monks, and 23,600 nuns. Some of these ecclesiastics, like the Bishop of Capaccio, were notable brigand-chiefs.

It must be confessed that the French were sufficiently cold-blooded in their reprisals. Colletta himself saw, at Lagonegro, a man impaled by order of a French colonel; and some account of their excesses may be gleaned from Duret de Tavel, from Rivarol (rather a disappointing author), and from the flamboyant epistles of P. L. Courier, a soldier-scribe of rare charm, who lost everything in this campaign. "J'ai perdu huit chevaux, mes habits, mon linge, mon manteau, mes pistolets, mon argent (12,247 francs). . . . Je ne regrette que mon Homère [a gift from the Abbé Barthélemy], et pour le ravoir, je donnerais la seule chemise qui me reste."

But even that did not destroy the plague. The situation called for a genial and ruthless annihilator, a man like Sixtus V, who asked for brigands' heads and got them so plentifully that they lay "thick as melons in the market" under the walls of Rome, while the Castel Sant' Angelo was tricked out like a Christmas tree with quartered corpses—a man who told the authorities, when they complained of the insufferable stench of the dead, that the smell of living iniquity was far worse. Such a man was wanted. Therefore, in 1810, Murat gave *carte blanche* to General Manhes, the greatest brigand-catcher of modern times, to extirpate the ruffians, root and branch. He had just distinguished himself during a similar errand in the Abruzzi and, on arriving in Calabria, issued proclamations of such inhuman severity that the inhabitants looked upon them as a joke. They were quickly undeceived. The general seems to have considered that the end justified the means, and that the peace and happiness of a province was not to be disturbed year after year by the malignity of a few thousand rascals; his threats were carried out to the letter, and whatever may be said against his methods, he certainly succeeded. At the end of a few months' campaign, every single brigand, and all their friends and relations, were wiped off the face of the earth—together with a very considerable number of innocent persons. The high roads were lined with decapitated bandits, the town walls decked with their heads; some villages had to be abandoned, on account of the stench; the Crati river was swollen with corpses, and its banks whitened with bones. God alone knows the cruelties which were enacted; Colletta confesses that he "lacks courage to relate them." Here is his account of the fate of the brigand chief Benincasa:

"Betrayed and bound by his followers as he slept in the forest of Cassano, Benincasa was brought to Cosenza, and General Manhes ordered that both his hands be lopped off and that he be led, thus mutilated, to his home in San Giovanni, and there hanged; a cruel sentence, which the wretch received with a bitter smile. His right hand was first cut off and the stump bound, not out of compassion or regard for his life, but in order that all his blood might not flow out of the opened veins, seeing that he was reserved for a more miserable death. Not a cry escaped him, and when he saw that the first operation was over, he voluntarily laid his left hand upon the block and coldly watched the second mutilation, and saw his two amputated hands lying on the ground, which were then tied together by the thumbs and hung round his neck; an awful and piteous spectacle. This happened at Cosenza. On the same day he began his march to San Giovanni in Fiore, the escort resting at intervals; one of them offered the man food, which he accepted; he ate and drank what was placed in his mouth, and not so much in order to sustain life, as with real pleasure. He arrived at his home, and slept through the following night; on the next day, as the hour of execution approached, he refused the comforts of religion, ascended the gallows neither swiftly nor slowly, and died admired for brutal intrepidity."*

For the first time since long Calabria was purged. Ever since the Bruttians, irreclaimable plunderers, had established themselves at Cosenza, disquieting their old Hellenic neighbours, the recesses of this country had been a favourite retreat of political malcontents. Here Spartacus drew recruits for his band of rebels; here "King Marcone" defied the oppressive Spanish Viceroys, and I blame neither him nor his imitators, since the career of bandit was one of the very few that still commended itself to decent folks, under that régime.

During the interregnum of Bourbonism between Murat and Garibaldi the mischief revived—again in a political form. Brigands drew pensions from kings and popes, and the system gave rise to the most comical incidents; the story of the pensioned malefactors living together at Monticello reads like an extravaganza. It was the spirit of Offenbach, brooding over Europe. One of the funniest episodes was a visit paid in 1865 by the disconsolate Mrs. Moens to the ex-brigand Talarico, who was then living in grand style on a government pension. Her husband had been captured by the band of Manzi (another brigand), and expected to be murdered every day, and the lady succeeded in procuring from the chivalrous monster—"an extremely handsome man, very tall, with the smallest and most delicate hands"—an exquisite letter to his colleague, recommending him to be merciful to the Englishman and to emulate his own conduct in that respect. The letter had no effect, apparently; but Moens escaped at last, and wrote his memoirs, while Manzi was caught and executed in 1868 after a trial occupying nearly a month, during which the jury had to answer 311 questions.

His villainies were manifold. But they were put in the shade by

* This particular incident was flatly denied by Manhes in a letter dated 1835, which is quoted in the "Notizia storica del Conte C. A. Manhes" (Naples, 1846)—one of a considerable number of pro-Bourbon books that cropped up about this time. One is apt to have quite a wrong impression of Manhes, that inexorable but incorruptible scourge of evildoers. One pictures him a grey-haired veteran, scarred and gloomy; and learns, on the contrary, that he was only thirty-two years old at this time, gracious in manner and of surprising personal beauty.

those of others of his calling—of Caruso, for example, who was known to have massacred in one month (September, 1863) two hundred persons with his own hands. Then, as formerly, the Church favoured the malefactors, and I am personally acquainted with priests who fought on the side of the brigands. Francis II endeavoured to retrieve his kingdom by the help of an army of scoundrels like those of Ruffo, but the troops shot them down. Brigandage, as a governmental institution, came to an end. Unquestionably the noblest figure in this reactionary movement was that of José Borjès, a brave man engaged in an unworthy cause. You can read his tragic journal in the pages of M. Monnier or Maffei. It has been calculated that during these last years of Bourbonism the brigands committed seven thousand homicides a year in the kingdom of Naples.

Schools and emigration have now brought sounder ideas among the people, and the secularization of convents with the abolition of ecclesiastical right of asylum (Sixtus V had wisely done away with it) has broken up the prosperous old bond between monks and malefactors. What the government has done towards establishing decent communications in this once lawless and pathless country ranks, in its small way, beside the achievement of the French who, in Algeria, have built nearly ten thousand miles of road. But it is well to note that even as the mechanical appliance of steam destroyed the corsairs, the external plague, so this hoary form of internal disorder could have been permanently eradicated neither by humanity nor by severity. A scientific invention, the electric telegraph, is the guarantee of peace against the rascals.

These brigand chiefs were often loaded with gold. On killing them, the first thing the French used to do was to strip them. "On le dépouilla." Francatripa, for instance, possessed "a plume of white ostrich feathers, clasped by a golden band and diamond Madonna" (a gift from Queen Caroline)—Cerino and Manzi had "bunches of gold chains as thick as an arm suspended across the breasts of their waistcoats, with gorgeous brooches at each fastening." Some of their wealth now survives in certain families who gave them shelter in the towns in winter time, or when they were hard pressed. These *favoreggiatori* or *manutengoli* (the terms are interconvertible, but the first is the legal one) were sometimes benevolently inclined. But occasionally they conceived the happy idea of being paid for their silence and services. The brigand, then, was hoist with his own petard and forced to disgorge his ill-gotten summer gains to these blood-suckers, who extorted heavy blackmail under menaces of disclosure to the police, thriving on their double infamy to such an extent that they acquired immense riches. One of the wealthiest men in Italy descends from this class; his two hundred million (?) francs are invested, mostly, in England; every one knows his name, but the origin of his fortune is no longer mentioned, since (thanks to this money) the family has been able to acquire not only respectability but distinction.

XXVIII

THE GREATER SILA

A GREAT project is afoot.

As I understand it, a reservoir is being created by damming up the valley of the Ampollina; the artificial lake thus formed will be enlarged by the additional waters of the Arvo, which are to be led into it by means of a tunnel, about three miles long, passing underneath Monte Nero. The basin, they tell me, will be some ten kilometres in length; the work will cost forty million francs, and will be completed in a couple of years; it will supply the Ionian lowlands with pure water and with power for electric and other industries.

And more than that. The lake is to revolutionize the Sila; to convert these wildernesses into a fashionable watering-place. Enthusiasts already see towns growing upon its shores—there are visions of gorgeous hotels and flocks of summer visitors in elegant toilettes, villa-residences, funicular railways up all the mountains, sailing regattas, and motor-boat services. In the place of the desert there will arise a "Lucerna di Calabria."

A Calabrian Lucerne. H'm. . . .

It remains to be seen whether, by the time the lake is completed, there will be any water left to flow into it. For the catchment basins are being so conscientiously cleared of their timber that the two rivers cannot but suffer a great diminution in volume. By 1896 already, says Marincola San Floro, the destruction of woodlands in the Sila had resulted in a notable lack of moisture. Ever since then the vandalism has been pursued with a zeal worthy of a better cause. One trembles to think what these regions will be like in fifty years; a treeless and waterless tableland—worse than the glaring limestone deserts of the Apennines in so far as they, at least, are diversified in contour.

So the healthfulness, beauty, and exchequer value of enormous tracts in this country are being systematically impaired, day by day. Italy is ready, said D'Azeglio, but where are the Italians?

Let us give the government credit for any number of good ideas. It actually plants bare spaces; it has instituted a "Festa degli alberi" akin to the American Arbour Day, whereby it is hoped, though scarcely believed, that the whole of Italy will ultimately be replenished with trees; it encourages schools of forestry, supplies plants free of cost to all who ask for them, despatches commissions and prints reports. Above all, it talks prodigiously and very much to the purpose.

But it omits to administer its own laws with becoming severity. A few exemplary fines and imprisonments would have a more salutary effect than the commissioning of a thousand inspectors whom nobody takes seriously, and the printing of ten thousand reports which nobody reads.

With a single stroke of the pen the municipalities could put an end to the worst form of forest extirpation—that on the hillsides—by forbidding access to such tracts and placing them under the "vincolo forestale." To denude slopes in the moist climate and deep soil of England entails no risk; in this country it is the beginning of the end. And herein lies the ineptitude of the Italian regulations, which entrust the collective wisdom of rapacious farmers with measures of this kind, taking no account of the destructively utilitarian character of the native mind, of that canniness which overlooks a distant profit in its eagerness to grasp the present—that beast avarice which Horace recognized as the root of all evil. As if provisions like this of the "vincolo forestale" were ever carried out! Peasants naturally prefer to burn the wood in their own chimneys or to sell it; and if a landslide then crashes down, wrecking houses and vineyards—let the government compensate the victims!

An ounce of fact—

In one year alone (1903), and in the sole province of Cosenza wherein San Giovanni lies, there were 156 landslides; they destroyed 1940 hectares of land, and their damage amounted to 432,738 francs. The two other Calabrian provinces—Reggio and Catanzaro—doubtless also had their full quota of these catastrophes, all due to mischievous deforestation. So the bare rock is exposed, and every hope of planting at an end.

Vox clamantis! The Normans, Anjou and Aragonese concerned themselves with the proper administration of woodlands. Even the Spanish Viceroys, that ineffable brood, issued rigorous enactments on the subject; while the Bourbons (to give the devil his due) actually distinguished themselves as conservators of forests. As to Napoleon—he was busy enough, one would think, on this side of the Alps. Yet he found time to frame wise regulations concerning trees which the present patriotic parliament, during half a century of frenzied confabulation, has not yet taken to heart. How a great man will leave his mark on minutiæ!

I passed through the basin of this future lake when, in accordance with my project, I left San Giovanni to cross the remaining Sila in the direction of Catanzaro. This getting up at 3.30 a.m., by the way, rather upsets one's daily routine; at breakfast time I already find myself enquiring anxiously for dinner.

The Ampollina valley lies high; here, in the dewy grass, I enjoyed what I well knew would be my last shiver for some time to come; then moved for a few miles on the further bank of the rivulet along that driving road which will soon be submerged under the waters of the lake, and struck up a wooded glen called Barbarano. At its head lies the upland Circilla.

There is no rock scenery worth mentioning in all this Sila country; no waterfalls or other Alpine features. It is a venerable granitic tableland, that has stood here while the proud Apennines were still slumbering in the oozy bed of ocean*—a region of gentle undulations, the hill-tops covered with forest-growth, the valleys partly arable and partly pasture. Were it not for the absence of heather with its peculiar mauve tints, the traveller might well imagine himself in Scotland. There is the same smiling alternation of woodland and meadow, the same huge boulders of gneiss and granite which give a distinctive tone to the landscape, the same exuberance of living waters. Water, indeed, is one of the glories of the Sila—everywhere it bubbles forth in chill rivulets among the stones and trickles down the hill-sides to join the larger streams that wend their way to the forlorn and fever-stricken coastlands of Magna Graecia. Often, as I refreshed myself at these icy fountains, did I thank Providence for making the Sila of primitive rock, and not of the thirsty Apennine limestone.

"Much water in the Sila," an old shepherd once observed to me, "much water! And little tobacco."

One of the largest of these rivers is the Neto, the classic Neaithos sung by Theocritus, which falls into the sea north of Cotrone; San

* Nissen says that "no landscape of Italy has lost so little of its original appearance in the course of history as Calabria." This may apply to the mountains; but the lowlands have suffered hideous changes.

Giovanni overlooks its raging flood, and, with the help of a little imagination here and there, its whole course can be traced from eminences like that of Pettinascura. The very name of these streams—Neto, Arvo, Lese, Ampolina—are redolent of pastoral life. All of them are stocked with trout; they meander in their upper reaches through valleys grazed by far-tinkling flocks of sheep and goats and grey cattle—the experiment of acclimatizing Swiss cattle has proved a failure, I know not why—and their banks are brilliant with blossoms. Later on, in the autumn, the thistles begin to predominate—the finest of them being a noble ground thistle of pale gold, of which they eat the unopened bud; it is the counterpart of the silvery one of the Alps. The air in these upper regions is keen. I remember, some years ago, that during the last week of August a lump of snow, which a goat-boy produced as his contribution to our luncheon, did not melt in the bright sunshine on the summit of Monte Nero.

From whichever side one climbs out of the surrounding lowlands into the Sila plateau, the same succession of trees is encountered. To the warmest zone of olives, lemons and carobs succeeds that of the chestnuts, some of them of gigantic dimensions and yielding a sure though moderate return in fruit, others cut down periodically as coppice for vine-props and scaffoldings. Large tracts of these old chestnut groves are now doomed; a French society in Cosenza, so they tell me, is buying them up for the extraction out of their bark of some chemical or medicine. The vine still flourishes at this height, though dwarfed in size; soon the oaks begin to dominate, and after that we enter into the third and highest region of the pines and beeches. Those accustomed to the stony deserts of nearly all South European mountain districts will find these woodlands intensely refreshing. Their inaccessibility has proved their salvation—up to a short time ago.

Nearly all the cattle on the Sila, like the land itself, belongs to large proprietors. These gentlemen are for the most part invisible; they inhabit their palaces in the cities, and the very name of the Sila sends a cold shudder through their bones; their revenues are collected from the shepherds by agents who seem to do their work very conscientiously. I once observed, in a hut, a small fragment of the skin of a newly killed kid; the wolf had devoured the beast, and the shepherd was keeping this *corpus delicti* to prove to his superior, the agent, that he was innocent of the murder. There was something naive in his honesty—as if a shepherd could not eat a kid as well as any wolf, and keep a portion of its skin! The agent, no doubt, would hand it on to his lord, by way of *confirmation and verification*. Another time I saw the debris of a goat hanging from a tree; it was the wolf again; the boy had attached these remains to the tree in order that all who passed that way might be his witnesses, if necessary, that the animal had not been sold underhand.

You may still find the legendary shepherds here—curly-haired striplings, reclining *sub tegmine fagi* in the best Theocritean style, and piping wondrous melodies to their flocks. These have generally come up for the summer season from the Ionian lowlands. Or you may encounter yet more primitive creatures, forest boys, clad in leather, with wild eyes and matted locks, that take an elvish delight in misdirecting you. These are the Lucanians of old. "They bring them up from childhood in the woods among the shepherds," says Justinus, "without servants, and even without any clothes to cover them, or to lie upon, that from their early years they may become inured to hardiness and frugality, and have no intercourse with the city. They live upon game, and drink nothing but water or milk." But the majority of modern Sila shepherds are shrewd fellows of middle age (many of them have been to America), who keep strict business accounts for their masters of every ounce of cheese and butter produced. The local cheese, which Cassiodorus praises in one of his letters, is the *cacciacavallo* common all over South Italy; the butter is of the kind which has been humorously, but quite wrongly, described by various travellers.

Although the old wolves are shot and killed by spring guns and dynamite while the young ones are caught alive in steel traps and other appliances, their numbers are still formidable enough to per-turb the pastoral folks. One is therefore surprised to see what a poor breed of dogs they keep; scraggy mongrels that run for their lives at the mere sight of a wolf who can, and often does, bite them into two pieces with one snap of his jaws. They tell me that there is a gov-ernment reward for every wolf killed, but it is seldom paid; whoever has the good fortune to slay one of these beasts, carries the skin as proof of his prowess from door to door, and receives a small present everywhere—half a franc, or a cheese, or a glass of wine.

The goats show fight, and therefore the wolf prefers sheep. Shep-herds have told me that he comes up to them *delicatamente*, and then, fixing his teeth in the wool of their necks, pulls them onward, caressing their sides with his tail. The sheep are fascinated with his gentle manners, and generally allow themselves to be led up to the spot he has selected for their execution; the truth being that he is too lazy to carry them, if he can possibly avoid it. He will promptly kill his quarry and carry its carcase downhill on the rare occasions when the flocks are grazing above his haunt; but if it is an uphill walk, they must be good enough to use their own legs. Incredible stories of his destructiveness are related.

Fortunately, human beings are seldom attacked, a dog or a pig being generally forthcoming when the usual prey is not to be found. Yet not long ago a sad affair occurred; a she-wolf attacked a small boy before the eyes of his parents, who pursued him, powerless to help—the head and arms had already been torn off before a shot from a neighbour despatched the monster. Truly, "a great family displeasure," as my informant styled it. Milo of Croton, the famous athlete, is the most renowned victim of these Sila wolves. Tradition has it that, relying on his great strength, he tried to rend asunder a mighty log of wood which closed, however, and caught his arms in its grip; thus helpless, he was devoured alive by them.

By keeping to the left of Circilla, I might have skirted the forest of Gariglione. This tract lies at about four and a half hours' distance from San Giovanni; I found it, some years ago, to be a region of real "Urwald" or primary jungle; there was nothing like it, to my knowledge, on this side of the Alps, nor yet in the Alps themselves; nothing of the kind nearer than Russia. But the Russian jungles, apart from their monotony of timber, foster feelings of sadness and gloom, whereas these southern ones, as Hehn has well observed, are full of a luminous beauty—their darkest recesses being enlivened by a sense of benignant mystery. Gariglione was at that time a virgin forest, untouched by the hand of man; a dusky ridge, visible from afar; an impenetrable tangle of forest trees, chiefest among them being the "garigli" (*Quercus cerris*) whence it derives its name, as well as thousands of pines and bearded firs and all that hoary indigenous vegetation struggling out of the moist soil wherein their progenitors had lain decaying time out of mind. In these solitudes, if anywhere, one might still have found the absent-minded luzard (lynx) of the veracious historian; or the squirrel whose "calabrere" fur, I strongly suspect, came from Russia; or, at any rate, the Mushroom-stone *which shineth in the night.**

---

* As a matter of fact, the mushroom-stone is a well-known commodity, being still collected and eaten, for example, at Santo Stefano in Aspromonte. Older travellers tell us that it used to be exported to Naples and kept in the cellars of the best houses for the enjoyment of its fruit—sometimes in lumps measuring two feet in diameter which, being soaked in water, pro-

Well, I am glad my path to-day did not lead me to Gariglione, and so destroy old memories of the place. For the domain, they tell me, has been sold for 350,000 francs to a German company; its primeval silence is now invaded by an army of 260 workmen, who have been cutting down the timber as fast as they can. So vanishes another fair spot from earth! And what is left of the Sila, once these forests are gone? Not even the charm, such as it is, of Caithness. . . .

After Circilla comes the watershed that separates the Sila Grande from the westerly regions of Sila Piccola. Thenceforward it was downhill walking, at first through forest lands, then across verdant stretches, bereft of timber and simmering in the sunshine. The peculiar character of this country is soon revealed—ferociously cloven ravines, utterly different from the Sila Grande.

With the improvidence of the true traveller I had consumed my stock of provisions ere reaching the town of Taverna after a march of nine hours or thereabouts. A place of this size and renown, I had argued, would surely be able to provide a meal. But Taverna belies its name. The only tavern discoverable was a composite hovel, half wine-shop, half hen-house, whose proprietor, disturbed in his noonday nap, stoutly refused to produce anything eatable. And there I stood in the blazing sunshine, famished and unbefriended. Forthwith the strength melted out of my bones; the prospect of walking to Catanzaro, so alluring with a full stomach, faded out of the realm of possibility; and it seemed a special dispensation of Providence when, at my lowest ebb of vitality, a small carriage suddenly hove in sight.

"How much to Catanzaro?"

The owner eyed me critically, and then replied in English:

"You can pay twenty dollars."

Twenty dollars—a hundred francs! But it is useless trying to bargain with an *americano* (their time is too valuable).

"A dollar a mile?" I protested.

"That's so."

"You be damned."

"Same to you, mister." And he drove off.

---

duced these edible fungi. A stone yielding food—a miracle! It is a porous tufa adapted, presumably, for sheltering and fecundating vegetable spores. A little pamphlet by Professor A. Trotter ("Flora Montana della Calabria") gives some idea of the local plants and contains a useful bibliography. A curious feature is the relative abundance of boreal and Balkan-Oriental forms; another, the rapid spread of *Genista anglica*, which is probably an importation.

Such bold defiance of fate never goes unrewarded. A two-wheeled cart conveying some timber overtook me shortly afterwards on my way from the inhospitable Taverna. For a small consideration I was enabled to pass the burning hours of the afternoon in an improvised couch among its load of boards, admiring the scenery and the engineering feats that have carried a road through such difficult country, and thinking out some further polite remarks to be addressed to my twenty-dollar friend, in the event of our meeting at Catanzaro. . . .

One must have traversed the Sila in order to appreciate the manifold charms of the mountain town—I have revelled in them since my arrival. But it has one irremediable drawback: the sea lies at an inconvenient distance. It takes forty-five minutes to reach the shore by means of two railways in whose carriages the citizens descend after wild scrambles for places, packed tight as sardines in the sweltering heat. Only a genuine enthusiast will undertake the trip more than once. For the Marina itself—at this season, at least—is an unappetizing spot; a sordid agglomeration of houses, a few dirty fruit-stalls, ankle-deep dust, swarms of flies. I prefer to sleep through the warm hours of the day, and then take the air in that delightful public garden which, by the way, has already become too small for the increasing population.

At its entrance stands the civic museum, entrusted, just now, to the care of a quite remarkably ignorant and slatternly woman. It contains two rooms, whose exhibits are smothered in dust and cobwebs; as neglected, in short, as her own brats that sprawl about its floor. I enquired whether she possessed no catalogue to show where the objects, bearing no labels, had been found. A catalogue was unnecessary, she said; she knew everything—everything!

And everything, apparently, hailed from "Stromboli." The Tiriolo helmet, the Greek vases, all the rest of the real and sham treasures of this establishment: they were all discovered at Stromboli.

"Those coins—whence?"

"Stromboli!"

Noticing some neolithic celts similar to those I obtained at Vaccarizza, I would gladly have learnt their place of origin. Promptly came the answer:

"Stromboli!"

"Nonsense, my good woman. I've been three times to Stromboli; it is an island of black stones where the devil has a house, and such things are not found there." (Of course she meant Strongoli, the ancient Petelia.)

This vigorous assertion made her more circumspect. Thenceforward everything was declared to come from the province—*dalla provincia*; it was safer.

"That bad picture—whence?"

"Dalla provincia!"

"Have you really no catalogue?"

"I know everything."

"And this broken statue—whence?"

"Dalla provincia!"

"But the province is large," I objected.

"So it is. Large, and old."

I have also revisited Tiriolo, once celebrated for the "Sepulchres of the Giants" (Greek tombs) that were unearthed here, and latterly for a certain more valuable antiquarian discovery. Not long ago it was a considerable undertaking to reach this little place, but nowadays a public motor-car whirls you up and down the ravines at an alarming pace and will deposit you, within a few hours, at remote Cosenza, once an enormous drive. It is the same all over modern Calabria. The diligence service, for instance, that used to take fourteen hours from San Giovanni to Cosenza has been replaced by motors that cover the distance in four or five. One is glad to save time, but this new element of mechanical hurry has produced a corresponding kind of traveller—a machine-made creature, devoid of the humanity of the old; it has done away with the personal note of conviviality that reigned in the post-carriages. What jocund friendships were made, what songs and tales applauded, during those interminable hours in the lumbering chaise!

You must choose Sunday for Tiriolo, on account of the girls, whose pretty faces and costumes are worth coming any distance to see. A good proportion of them have the fair hair which seems to have been eliminated, in other parts of the country, through the action of malaria.

Viewed from Catanzaro, one of the hills of Tiriolo looks like a broken volcanic crater. It is a limestone ridge, decked with those characteristic flowers like *Campanula fragilis* which you will vainly seek on the Sila. Out of the ruins of some massive old building they have constructed, on the summit, a lonely weather-beaten fabric that would touch the heart of Maeterlinck. They call it a seismological station. I pity the people that have to depend for their warnings of earthquakes upon the outfit of a place like this. I could see no signs of life here; the windows were broken, the shutters decaying, an old lightening-rod dangled disconsolately from the roof; it looked as abandoned as any old tower in a tale. There is a noble view from this point over both seas and into the riven complexities of Aspromonte, when the peak is not veiled in mists, as it frequently is. For Tiriolo lies on the watershed; there (to quote from a "Person of Quality") "where the Apennine is drawn into so narrow a point, that the rain-water which descendeth from the ridge of some one house, falleth on the left in the Terrene Sea, and on the right into the Adriatick...."

My visits to the provincial museum have become scandalously frequent during the last few days. I cannot keep away from the place. I go there not to study the specimens but to converse with their keeper, the woman who, in her quiet way, has cast a sort of charm over me. Our relations are the whispered talk of the town; I am suspected of matrimonial designs upon a poor widow with the ulterior object of appropriating the cream of the relics under her care. Regardless of the perils of the situation, I persevere; for the sake of her company I forswear the manifold seductions of Catanzaro. She is a noteworthy person, neither vicious nor vulgar, but simply the *dernier mot* of incompetence. Her dress, her looks, her children, her manners—they are all on an even plane with her spiritual accomplishments; at no point does she sink, or rise, beyond that level. They are not as common as they seem to be, these harmoniously inefficient females.

Why has she got this job in a progressive town containing so many folks who could do it creditably? Oh, that is simple enough! She needs it. On the platform of the Reggio station (long before the earthquake) I once counted five station-masters and forty-eight other railway officials, swaggering about with a magnificent air of incapacity. What were they doing? Nothing whatever. They were like this woman: they needed a job.

We are in a patriarchal country; work is pooled; it is given not to those who can do it best, but to those who need it most—given, too, on pretexts which sometimes strike one as inadequate, not to say recondite. So the street-scavengering in a certain village has been entrusted to a one-armed cripple, utterly unfit for the business— why? Because his maternal grand-uncle is serving a long sentence in gaol. The poor family must be helped! A brawny young fellow will be removed from a landing-stage boat, and his place taken by some tottering old peasant who has never handled an oar—why? The old man's nephew has married again; the family must be helped. A secretarial appointment was specially created for an acquaintance of mine who could barely sign his own name, for the obvious reason that his cousin's sister was rheumatic. One must help that family. A postman whom I knew delivered the letters only once every three days, alleging, as unanswerable argument in his defence, that his brother's wife had fifteen children.

One must help that family!

Somebody seems to have thought so, at all events.

XXIX

CHAOS

I HAVE never beheld the enchantment of the Straits of Messina, that Fata Morgana, when, under certain conditions of weather, phantasmagoric palaces of wondrous shape are cast upon the waters—not mirrored, but standing upright; tangible, as it were; yet diaphanous as a veil of gauze.

A Dominican monk and correspondent of the Naples Academy, Minasi by name, friend of Sir W. Hamilton, wrote a dissertation upon this atmospheric mockery. Many have seen and described it, among them Pilati de Tassulo; Nicola Leoni reproduces the narrative of an eye-witness of 1643; another account appears in the book of A. Fortis ("Mineralogische Reisen, 1788"). The apparition is coy. Yet there are pictures of it—in an article in "La Lettura" by Dr. Vittorio Boccara, who therein refers to a scientific treatise by himself on the subject, as well as in the little volume "Da Reggio a Metaponto" by Lupi-Crisafi, which was printed at Gerace some years ago. I mention these writers for the sake of any one who, luckier than myself, may be able to observe this phenomenon and become interested in its history and origin. . . .

The chronicles of Messina record the scarcely human feats of the diver Cola Pesce (Nicholas the Fish). The dim submarine landscapes of the Straits with their caves and tangled forests held no secrets from him; his eyes were as familiar with sea-mysteries as those of any fish. Some think that the legend dates from Frederick II, to whom he brought up from the foaming gulf that golden goblet which has been immortalized in Schiller's ballad. But Schneegans says there are Norman documents that speak of him. And that other tale, according to which he took to his watery life in pursuit of some beloved maiden who had been swallowed by the waves, makes one think of old Glaucus as his prototype.

Many are the fables connected with his name, but the most portentous is this: One day, during his subaqueous wanderings, he discovered the foundations of Messina. They were insecure! The city rested upon three columns, one of them intact, another quite decayed away, the third partially corroded and soon to crumble into ruin. He peered up from his blue depths, and in a fateful couplet of verses warned the townsmen of their impending doom. In this prophetic utterance ascribed to the fabulous Cola Pesce is echoed a popular apprehension that was only too justified.

F. Münter—one of a band of travellers who explored these regions after the earthquake of 1783—also gave voice to his fears that Messina had not yet experienced the full measure of her calamities. . . .

I remember a night in September of 1908, a Sunday night, fragrant with the odours of withered rosemary and cistus and fennel that streamed in aromatic showers from the scorched heights overhead—a starlit night, tranquil and calm. Never had Messina appeared so attractive to me. Arriving there generally in the daytime and from larger and sprightlier centres of civilization, one is prone to notice only its defects. But night, especially a southern night, has a wizard touch. It transforms into objects of mysterious beauty all unsightly things, or hides them clean away; while the nobler works of man, those façades and cornices and full-bellied balconies of cunningly wrought iron rise up, under its enchantment, ethereal as the palace of fairies. And coming, as I then did, from the sun-baked river-beds of Calabria, this place, with its broad and well-paved streets, its glittering cafés and demure throng of evening idlers, seemed a veritable metropolis, a world-city.

With deliberate slowness, *ritardando con molto sentimento*, I worked my way to the familiar restaurant.

At last! At last, after an interminable diet of hard bread, onions and goat's cheese, I was to enjoy the complicated menu mapped out weeks beforehand, after elaborate consideration and balancing of merits; so complicated, that its details have long ago lapsed from my memory. I recollect only the sword-fish, a local speciality, and (as crowning glory) the *cassata alla siciliana*, a glacial symphony, a multicoloured ice of commingling flavours, which requires far more time to describe than to devour. Under the influence of this Sybaritic fare, helped down with a crusted bottle of Calabrian wine—your Sicilian stuff is too strong for me, too straightforward, uncompromising; I prefer to be wheedled out of my faculties by inches, like a gentleman—under this genial stimulus my extenuated frame was definitely restored; I became mellow and companionable; the traveller's lot, I finally concluded, is not the worst on earth.

Everything was as it should be. As for Messina—Messina was unquestionably a pleasant city. But why were all the shops shut so early in the evening?

"These Sicilians," said the waiter, an old Neapolitan acquaintance, in reply to my enquiries, "are always playing some game. They are pretending to be Englishmen at this moment; they have the Sunday-closing obsession on the brain. Their attacks generally last a fortnight; it's like the measles. Poor people."

Playing at being Englishmen!

They have invented a new game now, those that are left of them. They are living in dolls' houses, and the fit is likely to last for some little time.

An engineer remarked to me, not long ago, among the ruins:

"This *baracca*, this wooden shelter, has an interior surface area of less than thirty square metres. Thirty-three persons—men, women, and children—have been living and sleeping in it for the last five months."

"A little overcrowded?" I suggested.

"Yes. Some of them are beginning to talk of overcrowding. It was all very well in the winter months, but when August comes. . . . Well, we shall see."

No prophetic visions of the Messina of to-day, with its minute sheds perched among a wilderness of ruins and haunted by scared shadows in sable vestment of mourning, arose in my mind that evening as I sat at the little marble table, sipping my coffee—over-roasted, like all Italian coffee, by exactly two minutes—and puffing contentedly at my cigar, while the sober crowd floated hither and thither before my eyes. Yes, everything was as it should be. And yet, what a chance!

What a chance for some God, in this age of unbelief, to establish his rule over mankind on the firm foundations of faith! We are always complaining, nowadays, of an abatement of religious feeling. How easy for such a one to send down an Isaiah to foretell the hour of the coming catastrophe, and thus save those of its victims who were disposed to hearken to the warning voice; to reanimate the flagging zeal of worshippers, to straighten doubts and segregate the sheep from the goats! Truly, He moves in a mysterious way, for no divine message came; the just were entombed with the unjust amid a considerable deal of telegraphing and heart-breaking.

A few days after the disaster the Catholic papers explained matters by saying that the people of Messina had not loved their Madonna sufficiently well. But she loved them none the less, and sent the earthquake as an admonishment. Rather a robust method of conciliating their affection; not exactly the *suaviter in modo*. . . . .

But if genuine prophets can only flourish among the malarious willow swamps of old Babylon and such-like improbable spots, we might at least have expected better things of our modern spiritualists. Why should their apparitions content themselves with announcing the decease, at the Antipodes, of profoundly uninteresting relatives? Alas! I begin to perceive that spirits of the right kind, of the useful kind, have yet to be discovered. Our present-day ghosts are like seismographs; they chronicle the event after it has happened. Now, what we want is——

"The Signore smokes, and smokes, and smokes. Why not take the tram and listen to the municipal music in the gardens?"

"Music? Gardens? An excellent suggestion, Gennarino."

Even as a small Italian town would be incomplete without its piazza where streets converge and commercial pulses beat their liveliest measure, so every larger one contrives to possess a public garden for the evening disport of its citizens; night-life being the true life of the south. Charming they are, most of them; none more delectable than that of old Messina—a spacious pleasaunce, decked out with trim palms and flower-beds and labyrinthine walks freshly watered, and cooled, that evening, by stealthy breezes from the sea. The grounds were festively illuminated, and as I sat down near the bandstand and watched the folk meandering to and fro, I calculated that no fewer than thirty thousand persons were abroad, taking their pleasure under the trees, in the bland air of evening. An orderly, well-dressed crowd. We may smile when they tell us that these people will stint themselves of the necessities of life in order to wear fine clothes, but the effect, for an outsider, is all that it should be. For the rest, the very urchins, gambolling about, had an air of happy prosperity, different from the squalor of the north with its pinched white faces, its over-breeding and under-feeding.

And how well the sensuous Italian strains accord with such an hour and scene! They were playing, if I remember rightly, the ever-popular Aïda; other items followed later—more ambitious ones; a Hungarian rhapsody, Berlioz, a selection from Wagner.

"*Musica filosofica*," said my neighbour, alluding to the German composer. He was a spare man of about sixty; a sunburnt, military countenance, seamed by lines of suffering. "*Non và in Sicilia*—it won't do in this country. Not that we fail to appreciate your great thinkers," he added. "We read and admire your Schopenhauer, your Spencer. They give passable representations of Wagner in Naples. But——"

"The climate?"

"Precisely. I have travelled, sir; and knowing your Berlin, and London, and Boston, have been able to observe how ill our Italian architecture looks under your grey skies, how ill our music sounds among the complex appliances of your artificial life. It has made you earnest, this climate of yours, and prone to take earnestly your very pastimes. Music, for us, has remained what it was in the Golden Age—an unburdening of the soul on a summer's night. They play well, these fellows. Palermo, too, has a respectable band—Oh! a little too fast, that *recitativo!*"

"The Signore is a musician?"

"A *proprietario*. But I delight in music, and I beguiled myself with the fiddle as a youngster. Nowadays—look here!" And he extended his hand; it was crippled. "Rheumatism. I have it here, and here"—pointing to various regions of his body—"*and* here! Ah, these doctors! The baths I have taken! The medicines—the ointments—the embrocations: a perfect pharmacopœia! I can hardly crawl now, and without the help of these two devoted boys even this harmless little diversion would have been denied me. My nephews—orphans," he added, observing the direction of my glance.

They sat on his other side, handsome lads, who spoke neither too much nor too little. Every now and then they rose with one accord and strolled among the surging crowd to stretch their legs, returning after five minutes to their uncle's side. His eyes always followed their movements.

"My young brother, had he lived, would have made men of them," he once observed.

The images revive, curiously pertinacious, with dim lapses and gulfs. I can see them still, the two boys, their grave demeanour belied by mobile lips and mischievous fair curls of Northern ancestry; the other, leaning forward intent upon the music, and caressing his moustache with bent fingers upon which glittered a jewel set in massive gold—some scarab or intaglio, the spoil of old Magna Graecia. His conversation, during the intervals, moved among the accepted formulas of cosmopolitanism with easy flow, quickened at times by the individual emphasis of a man who can forsake conventional tracks and think for himself. Among other things, he had contrived an original project for reviving the lemon industry of his country, which, though it involved a few tariff modifications—"a mere detail"—struck me as amazingly effective and ingenious. The local deputy, it seems, shared my view, for he had undertaken to bring it before the notice of Parliament.

What was it?

I have forgotten!

So we discussed the world, while the music played under the starlit southern night.

It must have been midnight ere a final frenzied galop on the part of the indefatigable band announced the close of the entertainment. I walked a few paces beside the lame "proprietor" who, supported on the arms of his nephews, made his way to the spot where the cabs were waiting—his rheumatism, he explained, obliging him to drive. How he had enjoyed walking as a youth, and what pleasure it would now have given him to protract, during a promenade to my hotel, our delightful conversation! But infirmities teach us to curtail our pleasures, and many things that seem natural to man's bodily configuration are found to be unattainable. He seldom left his rooms; the stairs—the diabolical stairs! Would I at least accept his card and rest assured how gladly he would receive me and do all in his power to make my stay agreeable?

That card has gone the way of numberless others which the traveller in Southern Europe gathers about him. I have also forgotten the old man's name. But the *palazzo* in which he lived bore a certain historical title which happened to be very familiar to me. I remember wondering how it came to reach Messina.

In the olden days, of course, the days of splendour.

Will they ever return?

It struck me that the sufferings of the survivors would be alleviated if all the sheds in which they are living could be painted white or pearl-grey in order to protect them, as far as possible, from the burning rays of the sun. I mentioned the idea to an overseer.

"We are painting as fast as we can," he replied. "An expensive matter, however. The Villagio Elena alone has cost us, in this respect, twenty thousand francs—with the greatest economy."

This will give some notion of the scale on which things have to be done. The settlement in question contains some two hundred sheds—two hundred out of over ten thousand.

But I was alluding not to these groups of hygienic bungalows erected by public munificence and supplied with schools, laboratories, orphanages, hospitals, and all that can make life endurable, but to the others—those which the refugees built for themselves—ill-contrived hovels, patched together with ropes, potato-sacks, petroleum cans and miscellaneous odds and ends. A coat of white-wash, at least, inside and out. . . . I was thinking, too, of those still stranger dwellings, the disused railway trucks which the government has placed at the disposal of homeless families. At many stations along the line may be seen strings of these picturesque wigwams crowded with poor folk who have installed themselves within, apparently for ever. They are cultivating their favourite flowers and herbs in gaudy rows along the wooden platforms of the carriages; the little children all dressed in black, play about in the shade underneath. The people will suffer in these narrow tenements under the fierce southern sun, after their cool courtyards and high-vaulted chambers! There will be diseases, too; typhoids from the disturbed drainage and insufficient water-supply; eye troubles, caused by the swarms of flies and tons of accumulated dust. The ruins are also overrun with hordes of mangy cats and dogs which ought to be exterminated without delay.

If, as seems likely, those rudely improvised sheds are to be inhabited indefinitely, we may look forward to an interesting phenomenon, a reversion to a corresponding type of man. The lack of the most ordinary appliances of civilization, such as linen, washing-basins and cooking utensils, will reduce them to the condition of savages who view these things with indifference or simple curiosity; they will forget that they ever had any use for them. And life in these huts where human beings are herded together after the manner of beasts—one might almost say *fitted in*, like the fragments of a mosaic pavement—cannot but be harmful to the development of growing children.

The Calabrians, I was told, distinguished themselves by unearthly ferocity; Reggio was given over to a legion of fiends that descended from the heights during the week of confusion. "They tore the rings and brooches off the dead," said a young official to me. "They strangled the wounded and dying, in order to despoil them more comfortably. Here, and at Messina, the mutilated corpses were past computation; but the Calabrians were the worst."

Vampires, offspring of Night and Chaos.

So Dolomieu, speaking of the *dépravation incroyable des mœurs* which accompanied the earthquake of 1783, recounts the case of a householder of Polistena who was pinned down under some masonry, his legs emerging out of the ruins; his servant came and took the silver buckles off his shoes and then fled, without attempting to free him. We have seen something of this kind more recently at San Francisco.

"After despoiling the corpses, they ransacked the dwellings. Five thousand beds, sir, were carried up from Reggio into the mountains."

"Five thousand beds! *Per Dio!* It seems a considerable number."

A young fellow, one of the survivors, attached himself to me in the capacity of guide through the ruins of Reggio. He wore the characteristic earthquake look, a dazed and bewildered expression of countenance; he spoke in a singularly deliberate manner. Knowing the country, I was soon bending my steps in the direction of the cemetery, chiefly for the sake of the exquisite view from those windswept heights, and to breathe more freely after the dust and desolation of the lower parts. This burial-ground is in the same state as that of Messina, once the pride of its citizens; the insane frolic of nature has not respected the slumber of the dead or their commemorative shrines; it has made a mockery of the place, twisting the solemn monuments into repulsive and irreverential shapes.

But who can recount the freaks of stone and iron during those moments—the hair-breadth escapes? My companion's case was miraculous enough. Awakened from sleep with the first shock, he saw, by the dim light of the lamp which burns in all their bedrooms, the wall at his bedside weirdly gaping asunder. He darted to reach the opening, but it closed again and caught his arm in a stony grip. Hours seemed to pass—the pain was past enduring; then the kindly cleft yawned once more, allowing him to jump into the garden below. Simultaneously he heard a crash as the inner rooms of the house fell; then climbed aloft, and for four days wandered among the bleak, wet hills. Thousands were in the same plight.

I asked what he found to eat.

"*Erba, Signore.* We all did. You could not touch property; a single orange, and they would have killed you."

Grass!

He bore a name renowned in the past, but his home being turned into a dust-heap under which his money, papers and furniture, his two parents and brothers, are still lying, he now gains a livelihood by carrying vegetables and fruit from the harbour to the collection of sheds honoured by the name of the market. Later in the day we happened to walk past the very mansion, which lies near the quay. "Here is my house and my family," he remarked, indicating, with a gesture of antique resignation, a pile of wreckage.

Hard by, among the ruins, there sat a young woman with dishevelled hair, singing rapturously. "Her husband was crushed to death," he said, "and it unhinged her wits. Strange, is it not, sir? They used to fight like fiends, and now—she sings to him night and day to come back."

Love—so the Greeks fabled—was the child of Chaos.

In this part of the town stands the civic museum, which all readers of Gissing's "Ionian Sea" will remember as the closing note of those harmonious pages. It is shattered, like everything else that he visited in Reggio; like the hotel where he lodged; like the cathedral whose proud superscription *Circumlegentes devenimus Rhegium* impressed him so deeply; like that "singular bit of advanced civilization, which gave me an odd sense of having strayed into the world of those romancers who forecast the future—a public slaughter-house of tasteful architecture, set in a grove of lemon trees and palms, suggesting the dreamy ideal of some reformer whose palate shrinks from vegetarianism." We went the round of all these places, not forgetting the house which bears the tablet commemorating the death of a young soldier who fell fighting against the Bourbons. From its contorted iron balcony there hangs a rope by which the inmates may have tried to let themselves down.

A friend of mine, Baron C—— of Stilo, is a member of that same patriotic family, and gave me the following strange account. He was absent from Reggio at the time of the catastrophe, but three others of them were staying there. On the first shock they rushed together, panic-stricken, into one room; the floor gave way, and they suddenly found themselves sitting in their motor-car which happened to be placed exactly below them. They escaped with a few cuts and bruises.

An inscription on a neighbouring ruin runs to the effect that the *mansion having been severely damaged in the earthquake of* 1783, *its owner had rebuilt it on lines calculated to defy future shatterings.* Whether he would rebuild it yet again?

Nevertheless, there seems to be some chance for the revival of Reggio; its prognosis is not utterly hopeless.

But Messina is in desperate case.

That haughty sea-front, with its long line of imposing edifices—imagine a painted theatre decoration of cardboard through which some sportive behemoth has been jumping with frantic glee; there you have it. And within, all is desolation; the wreckage reaches to the windows; you must clamber over it as best you can. What an all-absorbing post-tertiary deposit for future generations, for the crafty antiquarian who deciphers the history of mankind out of kitchen-middens and deformed heaps of forgotten trash! The whole social life of the citizens, their arts, domestic economy, and pastimes, lies embedded in that rubbish. "A musical race," he will conclude, observing the number of decayed pianofortes, guitars, and mandolines. The climate of Messina, he will further argue, must have been a wet one, inasmuch as there are umbrellas everywhere, standing upright among the debris, leaning all forlorn against the ruins, or peering dismally from under them. It rained much during those awful days, and umbrellas were at a premium. Yet fifty of them would not have purchased a loaf of bread.

It was Goethe who, speaking of Pompeii, said that of the many catastrophes which have afflicted mankind few have given greater pleasure to posterity. The same will never be said of Messina, whose relics, for the most part, are squalid and mean. The German poet, by the way, visited this town shortly after the disaster of 1783, and describes its *zackige Ruinenwüste*—words whose very sound is suggestive of shatterings and dislocations. Nevertheless, the place revived again.

But what was 1783?

A mere rehearsal, an amateur performance.

Wandering about in this world of ghosts, I passed the old restaurant where the sword-fish had once tasted so good—an accumulation of stones and mortar—and reached the cathedral. It is laid low, all save the Gargantuan mosaic figures that stare down from behind the altar in futile benediction of Chaos; inane, terrific. This, then, is the house of that feudal lady of the *fortiter in re*, who sent an earthquake and called it love. Womanlike, she doted on gold and precious stones, and they recovered her fabulous hoard, together with a copy of a Latin letter she sent to the Christians of Messina by the hand of Saint Paul.

And not long afterwards—how came it to pass?—my steps were guided amid that wilderness towards a narrow street containing the ruins of a *palazzo* that bore, on a tablet over the ample doorway, an inscription which arrested my attention. It was an historical title familiar to me; and forthwith a train of memories, slumbering in the caverns of my mind, was ignited. Yes; there was no doubt about it: the old "proprietor" and his nephews, he of the municipal gardens. . . .

I wondered how they had met their fate, on the chill wintry morning. For assuredly, in that restricted space, not a soul can have escaped alive; the wreckage, hitherto undisturbed, still covered their remains.

And, remembering the old man and his humane converse that evening under the trees, the true meaning of the catastrophe began to disentangle itself from accidental and superficial aspects. For I confess that the massacre of a myriad Chinamen leaves me cool and self-possessed; between such creatures and ourselves there is hardly more than the frail bond of a common descent from the ape; they are altogether too remote for our narrow world-sympathies. I would as soon shed tears over the lost Pleiad. But these others are our spiritual cousins; we have deep roots in this warm soil of Italy, which brought forth a goodly tithe of what is best in our own lives, in our arts and aspirations.

And I thought of the two nephews, their decent limbs all distorted and mangled under a heap of foul rubbish, waiting for a brutal disinterment and a nameless grave. This is no legitimate death, this murderous violation of life. How inconceivably hateful is such a leave-taking, and all that follows after! To picture a fair young body, that divine instrument of joy, crushed into an unsightly heap; once loved, now loathed of all men, and thrust at last, with abhorrence, into some common festering pit of abominations. . . . The Northern type—a mighty bond, again; a tie of blood, this time, between our race and those rulers of the South, whose exploits in this land of orange and myrtle surpassed the dreamings of romance.

Strange to reflect that, without the ephemeral friendship of that evening, Messina of to-day might have represented to my mind a mere spectacle, the hecatomb of its inhabitants extorting little more than a conventional sigh. So it is. The human heart has been constructed on somewhat ungenerous lines. Moralists, if any still exist on earth, may generalize with eloquence from the masses, but our poets have long ago succumbed to the pathos of single happenings; the very angels of Heaven, they say, take more joy in one sinner that repenteth than in a hundred righteous, which, duly apprehended, is only an application of the same illiberal principle.

A rope of bed-sheets knotted together dangled from one of the upper windows, its end swaying in mid-air at the height of the second floor. Many of them do, at Messina: a desperate expedient adorned the other windows, whose glass panes were unbroken. But for the ominous sunlight pouring through them from *within*, the building looked fairly intact on this outer side. Its ponderous gateway, however, through which I had hoped to enter, was choked up by internal debris, and I was obliged to climb, with some little trouble, to the rear of the house.

If a titanic blade had sheared through the *palazzo* lengthwise, the thing could not have been done more neatly. The whole interior had gone down, save a portion of the rooms abutting on the street-front; these were literally cut in half, so as to display an ideal section of domestic architecture. The house with its inmates and all it contained was lying among the high-piled wreckage within, under my feet; masonry mostly—entire fragments of wall interspersed with crumbling mortar and convulsed iron girders that writhed over the surface or plunged sullenly into the depths; fetid rents and gullies in between, their flanks affording glimpses of broken vases, candelabras, hats, bottles, birdcages, writing-books, brass pipes, sofas, picture-frames, tablecloths, and all the paltry paraphernalia of everyday life. No attempt at stratification, horizontal, vertical, or inclined; it was as if the objects had been thrown up by some playful volcano and allowed to settle where they pleased. Two immense chiselled blocks of stone—one lying prone at the bottom of a miniature ravine, the other proudly erect, like a Druidical monument, in the upper regions—reminded me of the existence of a staircase, a *diabolical* staircase.

Looking upwards, I endeavoured to reconstruct the habits of the inmates, but found it impossible, the section that remained being too shallow. Sky-blue seems to have been their favourite colour. The kitchen was easily discernible, the hearth with its store of charcoal underneath, copper vessels hanging in a neat row overhead, and an open cupboard full of household goods; a neighbouring room (the communicating doors were all gone), with lace window-curtains, a table, lamp, and book, and a bedstead toppling over the abyss; another one, carpeted and hung with pictures and a large faded mirror, below which ran a row of shelves that groaned under a multitudinous collection of phials and bottles.

The old man's embrocations. . . .

XXX

THE SKIRTS OF MONTALTO

AFTER such sights of suffering humanity—back to the fields and mountains!

Aspromonte, the wild region behind Reggio, was famous, not long ago, for Garibaldi's battle. But the exploits of this warrior have lately been eclipsed by those of the brigand Musolino, who infested the country up to a few years ago, defying the soldiery and police of all Italy. He would still be safe and unharmed had he remained in these fastnesses. But he wandered away, wishful to leave Italy for good and all, and was captured far from his home by some policemen who were looking for another man, and who nearly fainted when he pronounced his name. After a sensational trial, they sentenced him to thirty odd years' imprisonment; he is now languishing in the fortress of Porto Longone on Elba. Whoever has looked into this Spanish citadel will not envy him. Of the lovely little bay, of the loadstone mountain, of the romantic pathway to the hermitage of Monserrato or the glittering beach at Rio—of all the charms of Porto Longone he knows nothing, despite a lengthy residence on the spot.

They say he has grown consumptive and witless during the long solitary confinement which preceded his present punishment—an eternal night in a narrow cell. No wonder. I have seen the condemned on their release from these boxes of masonry at the island of Santo Stefano: dazed shadows, tottering, with complexions the colour of parchment. These are the survivors. But no one asks after the many who die in these dungeons frenzied, or from battering their heads against the wall; no one knows their number save the doctor and the governor, whose lips are sealed. . . .

I decided upon a rear attack of Aspromonte. I would go by rail as far as Bagnara on the Tyrrhenian, the station beyond Scylla of old renown; and thence afoot via Sant' Eufemia* to Sinopoli, pushing

---

* Not to be confounded with the railway station on the gulf of that name, near Maida.

on, if day permitted, as far as Delianuova, at the foot of the mountain. Early next morning I would climb the summit and descend to the shores of the Ionian, to Bova. It seemed a reasonable programme. All this Tyrrhenian coast-line is badly shattered; far more so than the southern shore. But the scenery is finer. There is nothing on that side to compare with the views from Nicastro, or Monteleone, or Sant' Elia near Palmi. It is also more smiling, more fertile, and far less malarious. Not that cultivation of the land implies absence of malaria—nothing is a commoner mistake! The Ionian shore is not malarious because it is desert—it is desert because malarious. The richest tracts in Greece are known to be very dangerous, and it is the same in Italy. Malaria and intensive agriculture go uncommonly well together. The miserable anopheles-mosquito loves the wells that are sunk for the watering of the immense orange and lemon plantations in the Reggio district; it displays a perverse predilection for the minute puddles left by the artificial irrigation of the fields that are covered with fruit and vegetables. This artificial watering, in fact, seems to be partly responsible for the spread of the disease. It is doubtful whether the custom goes back into remote antiquity, for the climate used to be moister and could dispense with these practices. Certain products, once grown in Calabria, no longer thrive there, on account of the increased dryness and lack of rainfall.

But there are some deadly regions, even along this Tyrrhenian shore. Such is the plain of Maida, for instance, where stood not long ago the forest of Sant' Eufemia, safe retreat of Parafante and other brigand heroes. The level lands of Rosarno and Gioia are equally ill-reputed. A French battalion stationed here in the summer of 1807 lost over sixty men in fourteen days, besides leaving two hundred invalids in the hospital at Monteleone. Gioia is so malarious that in summer every one of the inhabitants who can afford the price of a ticket goes by the evening train to Palmi, to sleep there. You will do well, by the way, to see something of the oil industry of Palmi, if time permits. In good years, 200,000 quintals of olive oil are manufactured in the regions of which it is the commercial centre. Not long ago, before modern methods of refining were introduced, most of this oil was exported to Russia, to be burned in holy lamps; nowadays it goes for the most part to Lucca, to be adulterated for foreign markets (the celebrated Lucca oil, which the simple Englishman regards as pure); only the finest quality is sent elsewhere, to Nice. From Gioia there runs a postal diligence once a day to Delianuova of which I might have availed myself, had I not preferred to traverse the country on foot.

The journey from Reggio to Banara on this fair summer morning, along the rippling Mediterranean, was short enough, but sufficiently long to let me overhear the following conversation:

A.—What a lovely sea! It is good, after all, to take three or four baths a year. What think you?

B.—I? No. For thirteen years I have taken no baths. But they are considered good for children.

The calamities that Bagnara has suffered in the past have been so numerous, so fierce and so varied that, properly speaking, the town has no right to exist any longer. It has enjoyed more than its full share of earthquakes, having been shaken to the ground over and over again. Sir William Hamilton reports that 3017 persons were killed in that of 1783. The horrors of war, too, have not spared it, and a certain modern exploit of the British arms here strikes me as so instructive that I would gladly extract it from Grant's "Adventures of an Aide-de-Camp," were it not too long to transcribe, and far too good to abbreviate.

A characteristic story, further, is told of the methods of General Manhes at Bagnara. It may well be an exaggeration when they say that the entire road from Reggio to Naples was lined with the heads of decapitated brigands; be that as it may, it stands to reason that Bagnara, as befits an important place, was to be provided with an appropriate display of these trophies. The heads were exhibited in baskets, with strict injunctions to the authorities that they were not to be touched, seeing that they served not only for decorative but also moral purposes—as examples. Imagine, therefore, the General's feelings on being told that one of these heads had been stolen; stolen, probably, by some pious relative of the deceased rascal, who wished to give the relic a decent Christian burial.

"That's rather awkward," he said, quietly musing. "But of course the specimen must be replaced. Let me see. . . . Suppose we put the head of the mayor of Bagnara into the vacant basket? Shall we? Yes, we'll have the mayor. It will make him more careful in future." And within half an hour the basket was filled once more.

There was a little hitch in starting from Bagnara. From the windings of the carriage-road as portrayed by the map, I guessed that there must be a number of short cuts into the uplands at the back of the town, undiscoverable to myself, which would greatly shorten the journey. Besides, there was my small bag to be carried. A porter familiar with the tracks was plainly required, and soon enough I found a number of lusty youths leaning against a wall and doing nothing in particular. Yes, they would accompany me, they said, the whole lot of them, just for the fun of the thing.

"And my bag?" I asked.

"A bag to be carried? Then we must get a woman."

They unearthed a nondescript female who undertook to bear the burden as far as Sinopoli for a reasonable consideration. So far good. But as we proceeded, the boys began to drop off, till only a single one was left. And then the woman suddenly vanished down a side street, declaring that she must change her clothes. We waited for three-quarters of an hour, in the glaring dust of the turnpike; she never emerged again, and the remaining boy stoutly refused to handle her load.

"No," he declared. "She must carry the bag. And I will keep you company."

The precious morning hours were wearing away, and here we stood idly by the side of the road. It never struck me that the time might have been profitably employed in paying a flying visit to one of the most sacred objects in Calabria and possibly in the whole world, one which Signor N. Marcone describes as reposing at Bagnara in a rich reliquary—the authentic Hat of the Mother of God. A lady tourist would not have missed this chance of studying the fashions of those days.*

Finally, in desperation, I snatched up the wretched luggage and poured my griefs with unwonted eloquence into the ears of a man driving a bullock-cart down the road. So much was he moved, that he peremptorily ordered his son to conduct me then and there to Sinopoli, to carry the bag, and claim one franc by way of payment. The little man tumbled off the cart, rather reluctantly.

"Away with you!" cried the stern parent, and we began the long march, climbing uphill in the blazing sunshine; winding, later on, through shady chestnut woods and across broad tracts of cultivated land. It was plain that the task was beyond his powers, and when we had reached spot where the strange-looking new village of Sant' Eufemia was visible—it is built entirely of wooden shelters; the stone town was greatly shaken in the late earthquake—he was obliged to halt, and thenceforward stumbled slowly into the place. There he deposited the bag on the ground, and faced me squarely.

---

* See next chapter.

"No more of this!" he said, concentrating every ounce of his virility into a look of uncompromising defiance.

"Then I shall not pay you a single farthing, my son. And, moreover, I will tell your father. You know what he commanded: to Sinopoli. This is only Sant' Eufemia. Unless——"

"You will tell my father? Unless——?"

"Unless you discover some one who will carry the bag not only to Sinopoli, but as far as Delianuova." I was not in the mood for repeating the experiences of the morning.

"It is difficult. But we will try."

He went in search and returned anon with a slender lad of unusual comeliness—an earthquake orphan. "This big one," he explained, "walks wherever you please and carries whatever you give him. And you will pay him nothing at all, unless he deserves it. Such is the arrangement. Are you content?"

"You have acted like a man."

The earthquake survivor set off at a swinging pace, and we soon reached Sinopoli—new Sinopoli; the older settlement lies at a considerable distance. Midday was past, and the long main street of the town—a former fief of the terrible Ruffo family—stood deserted in the trembling heat. None the less there was sufficient liveliness within the houses; the whole place seemed in a state of jollification. It was Sunday, the orphan explained; the country was duller than usual, however, because of the high price of wine. There had been no murders to speak of—no, not for a long time past. But the vintage of this year, he added, promises well, and life will soon become normal again.

The mule track from here to Delianuova traverses some pretty scenery, both wild and pastoral. But the personal graces of my companion made me take small heed of the landscape. He was aglow with animal spirits, and his conversation naively brilliant and of uncommon import. Understanding at a glance that he belonged to a type which is rather rare in Calabria, that he was a classic (of a kind), I made every effort to be pleasant to him; and I must have succeeded, for he was soon relating anecdotes which would have been neither instructive, nor even intelligible, to the *jeune fille*; all this, with angelic serenity of conscience.

This radiantly-vicious child was the embodiment of the joy of life, the perfect immoralist. There was no cynicism in his nature, no cruelty, no obliquity, no remorse; nothing but sunshine with a few clouds sailing across the fathomless blue spaces—the sky of Hellas.

Nihil humani alienum; and as I listened to those glad tales, I marvelled at the many-tinted experiences that could be crammed into seventeen short years; what a document the adventures of such a frolicsome demon would be, what a feast for the initiated, could some one be induced to make them known! But such things are hopelessly out of the question. And that is why so many of our wise people go into their graves without ever learning what happens in this world.

Among minor matters, he mentioned that he had already been three times to prison for "certain little affairs of blood," while defending "certain friends." Was it not dull, I asked, in prison? "The time passes pleasantly anywhere," he answered, "when you are young. I always make friends, even in prison." I could well believe it. His affinities were with the blithe crew of the Liber Stratonis. He had a roving eye and the mouth of Antinous; and his morals were those of a condescending tiger-cub.

Arriving at Delianuova after sunset, he conceived the project of accompanying me next morning up Montalto. I hesitated. In the first place, I was going not only up that mountain, but to Bova on the distant Ionian littoral——

"For my part," he broke in, "*ho pigliato confidenza.* If you mistrust me, here! take my knife," an ugly blade, pointed, and two inches in excess of the police regulation length. This act of quasifilial submission touched me; but it was not his knife I feared so much as that of "certain friends." Some little difference of opinion might arise, some question of money or other argument, and lo! the friends would be at hand (they always are), and one more stranger might disappear among the clefts and gullies of Montalto. Aspromonte, the roughest corner of Italy, is no place for misunderstandings; the knife decides promptly who is right or wrong, and only two weeks ago I was warned not to cross the district without a carbineer on either side of me.

But to have clothed my thoughts in words during his gracious mood would have been supremely unethical. I contented myself with the trite but pregnant remark that things sometimes looked different in the morning, which provoked a pagan fit of laughter; farewelled him "with the Madonna!" and watched as he withdrew under the trees, lithe and buoyant, like a flame that is swallowed up in the night.

Only then did the real business begin. I should be sorry to say into how many houses and wine-shops the obliging owner of the local inn conducted me, in search of a guide. We traversed all the lanes of this straggling and fairly prosperous place, and even those of its suburb Paracorio, evidently of Byzantine origin; the answer was everywhere the same: To Montalto, yes; to Bova, no! Night drew on apace and, as a last resource, he led the way to the dwelling of a gentleman of the old school—a retired brigand, to wit, who, as I afterwards learned, had some ten or twelve homicides to his account. Delianuova, and indeed the whole of Aspromonte, has a bad reputation for crime.

It was our last remaining chance.

We found the patriarch sitting in a simple but tidy chamber, smoking his pipe and playing with a baby; his daughter-in-law rose as we entered, and discreetly moved into an adjoining room. The cheery cut-throat put the baby down to crawl on the floor, and his eyes sparkled when he heard of Bova.

"Ah, one speaks of Bova!" he said. "A fine walk over the mountain!" He much regretted that he was too old for the trip, but so-and-so, he thought, might know something of the country. It pained him, too, that he could not offer me a glass of wine. There was none in the house. In his day, he added, it was not thought right to drink in the modern fashion; this wine-bibbing was responsible for considerable mischief; it troubled the brain, driving men to do things they afterwards repented. He drank only milk, having become accustomed to it during a long life among the hills. Milk cools the blood, he said, and steadies the hand, and keeps a man's judgment undisturbed.

The person he had named was found after some further search. He was a bronzed, clean-shaven type of about fifty, who began by refusing his services point-blank, but soon relented, on hearing the ex-brigand's recommendation of his qualities.

XXXI

SOUTHERN SAINTLINESS

SOUTHERN saints, like their worshippers, put on new faces and vestments in the course of ages. Old ones die away; new ones take their place. Several hundred of the older class of saint have clean faded from the popular memory, and are now so forgotten that the wisest priest can tell you nothing about them save, perhaps, that "he's in the church"—meaning, that some fragment of his holy anatomy survives as a relic amid a collection of similar antiques. But you can find their histories in early literature, and their names linger on old maps where they are given to promontories and other natural features which are gradually being rechristened.

Such saints were chiefly non-Italian: Byzantines or Africans who, by miraculous intervention, protected the village or district of which they were patrons from the manifold scourges of mediævalism; they took the place of the classic tutelar deities. They were men; they could fight; and in those troublous times that is exactly what saints were made for.

With the softening of manners a new element appears. Male saints lost their chief *raison d'être*, and these virile creatures were superseded by pacific women. So, to give only one instance, Saint Rosalia in Palermo displaced the former protector Saint Mark. Her sacred bones were miraculously discovered in a cave; and have since been identified as those of a goat. But it was not till the twelfth century that the cult of female saints began to assume imposing dimensions.

Of the Madonna no mentions occurs in the songs of Bishop Paulinus (fourth century); no monument exists in the Neapolitan catacombs. Thereafter her cult begins to dominate.

She supplied the natives with what orthodox Christianity did not give them, but what they had possessed from early times—a female element in religion. Those Greek settlers had their nymphs, their Venus, and so forth; the Mother of God absorbed and continued their functions. There is indeed only one of these female pagan divinities whose rôle she has not endeavoured to usurp—Athene. Herein she reflects the minds of her creators, the priests and common people, whose ideal woman contents herself with the duties of motherhood. I doubt whether an Athene-Madonna, an intellectual goddess, could ever have been evolved; their attitude towards gods in general is too childlike and positive.

South Italians, famous for abstractions in philosophy, cannot endure them in religion. Unlike ourselves, they do not desire to learn anything from their deities or to argue about them. They only wish to love and be loved in return, reserving to themselves the right to punish them, when they deserve it. Countless cases are on record where (pictures or statues of) Madonnas and saints have been thrown into a ditch for not doing what they were told, or for not keeping their share of a bargain. During the Vesuvius eruption of 1906 a good number were subjected to this "punishment," because they neglected to protect their worshippers from the calamity according to contract (so many candles and festivals—so much protection).

For the same reason the adult Jesus—the teacher, the God—is practically unknown. He is too remote from themselves and the ordinary activities of their daily lives; he is not married, like his mother; he has no trade, like his father (Mark calls him a carpenter); moreover, the maxims of the Sermon on the Mount are so repugnant to the South Italian as to be almost incomprehensible. In effigy, this period of Christ's life is portrayed most frequently in the primitive monuments of the catacombs, erected when tradition was purer.

Three tangibly-human aspects of Christ's life figure here: the *bambino*-cult, which not only appeals to the people's love of babyhood but also carries on the old traditions of the Lar Familiaris and of Horus; next, the youthful Jesus, beloved of local female mystics; and lastly the Crucified—that grim and gloomy image of suffering which was imported, or at least furiously fostered, by the Spaniards.

The engulfing of the saints by the Mother of God is due also to political reasons. The Vatican, once centralized in its policy, began to be disquieted by the persistent survival of Byzantinism (Greek cults and language lingered up to the twelfth century); with the Tacitean *odium fratrum* she exercised more severity towards the sister-faith than towards actual paganism.* The Madonna was a fit

---

* Greek and Egyptian anchorites were established in south Italy by the fourth century. But paganism was still flourishing, locally, in the sixth. There is some evidence that Christians used to take part in pagan festivals.

instrument for sweeping away the particularist tendencies of the past; she attacked relic-worship and other outworn superstitions; like a benignant whirlwind she careered over the land, and these now enigmatical shapes and customs fell faster than leaves of Vallombrosa. No sanctuary or cave so remote that she did not endeavour to expel its male saint—its old presiding genius, whether Byzantine or Roman. But saints have tough lives, and do not yield without a struggle; they fought for their time-honoured privileges like the "dæmons" they were, and sometimes came off victorious. Those sanctuaries that proved too strong to be taken by storm were sapped by an artful and determined siege. The combat goes on to this day. This is what is happening to the thrice-deposed and still triumphant Saint Januarius, who is hard pressed by sheer force of numbers. Like those phagocytes which congregate from all sides to assail some weakened cell in the body physical, even so Madonna-cults—in frenzied competition with each other—cluster thickest round some imperilled venerable of ancient lineage, bent on his destruction. The Madonna dell' Arco, del Soccorso, and at least fifty others (not forgetting the newly-invented Madonna di Pompei)— they have all established themselves in the particular domain of St. Januarius; they are all undermining his reputation, and claiming to possess his special gifts.*

Early monastic movements of the Roman Church also played their part in obliterating old religious landmarks. Settling down in some remote place with the Madonna as their leader or as their "second Mother," these companies of holy men soon acquired such temporal and spiritual influence as enabled them successfully to oppose their divinity to the local saint, whose once bright glories began to pale before her effulgence. Their labours in favour of the Mother of God were part of that work of consolidating Papal power which was afterwards carried on by the Jesuits.

Perhaps what chiefly accounts for the spread of Madonna-worship is the human craving for novelty. You can invent most easily where no fixed legends are established. Now the saints have fixed legendary attributes and histories, and as culture advances it becomes increasingly difficult to manufacture new saints with fresh and original characters and yet passable pedigrees (the experiment is tried,

---

* He is known to have quelled an outbreak of Vesuvius in the fifth century, though his earliest church, I believe, only dates from the ninth. His blood, famous for liquefaction, is not mentioned till 1337.

now and again); while the old saints have been exploited and are now inefficient—worn out, like old toys. Madonna, on the other hand, can subdivide with the ease of an amœba, and yet never lose her identity or credibility; moreover, thanks to her divine character, anything can be accredited to her—anything good, however wonderful; lastly, the traditions concerning her are so conveniently vague that they actually foster the mythopoetic faculty. Hence her success. Again: the man-saints were separatists; they fought for their own towns against African intruders, and in those frequent and bloody inter-communal battles which are a feature of Italian mediævalism. Nowadays it is hardly proper that neighbouring townsmen, aided and abetted by their respective saints, should sally forth to cut each others' throats. The Madonna, as cosmopolitan Niké, is a fitter patroness for settled society.

She also found a ready welcome in consequence of the pastoral institutions of the country in which the mother plays such a conspicuous rôle. So deeply are they ingrained here that if the Mother of God had not existed, the group would have been deemed incomplete; a family without a mother is to them like a tree without roots—a thing which cannot be. This accounts for the fact that their Trinity is not ours; it consists of the Mother, the Father (Saint Joseph), and the Child—with Saint Anne looming in the background (the grandmother is an important personage in the patriarchal family). The Creator of all things and the Holy Ghost have evaporated; they are too intangible and non-human.

But She never became a true cosmopolitan Niké, save in literature. The decentralizing spirit of South Italy was too strong for her. She had to conform to the old custom of geographical specialization. In all save in name she doffed her essential character of Mother of God, and became a local demi-god; an accessible wonder-worker attached to some particular district. An inhabitant of village A would stand a poor chance of his prayers being heard by the Madonna of village B; if you have a headache, it is no use applying to the *Madonna of the Hens*, who deals with diseases of women; you will find yourself in a pretty fix if you expect financial assistance from the Madonna of village C: she is a weather-specialist. In short, these hundreds of Madonnas have taken up the qualities of the saints they supplanted.

They can often outdo them; and this is yet another reason for their success. It is a well-ascertained fact, for example, that many holy men have been nourished by the Milk of the Mother of God, "not," as a Catholic writer says, "in a mystic or spiritual sense, but with their actual lips"; Saint Bernard "among a hundred, a thousand, others." Nor is this all, for in the year 1690, a painted image of the Madonna, not far from the city of Carinola, was observed to "diffuse abundant milk" for the edification of a great concourse of spectators—a miracle which was recognized as such by the bishop of that diocese, Monsignor Paolo Ayrola, who wrote a report on the subject. Some more of this authentic milk is kept in a bottle in the convent of Mater Domini on Vesuvius, and the chronicle of that establishment, printed in 1834, says:

"Since Mary is the Mother and Co-redeemer of the Church, may she not have left some drops of her precious milk as a gift to this Church, even as we still possess some of the blood of Christ? In various churches there exists some of this milk, by means of which many graces and benefits are obtained. We find such relics, for example, in the church of Saint Luigi in Naples, namely, two bottles full of the milk of the Blessed Virgin; and this milk becomes fluid on feast-days of the Madonna, as everybody can see. Also in this convent of Mater Domini the milk sometimes liquefies." During eruptions of Vesuvius this bottle is carried abroad in procession, and always dispels the danger. Saint Januarius must indeed look to his laurels! Meanwhile it is interesting to observe that the Mother of God has condescended to employ the method of holy relics which she once combated so strenuously, her milk competing with the blood of Saint John, the fat of Saint Laurence, and those other physiological curios which are still preserved for the edification of believers.

All of which would pass if a subtle poison had not been creeping in to taint religious institutions. Taken by themselves, these infantile observances do not necessarily harm family life, the support of the state; for a man can believe a considerable deal of nonsense, and yet go about his daily work in a natural and cheerful manner. But when the body is despised and tormented the mind loses its equilibrium, and when that happens nonsense may assume a sinister shape. We have seen it in England, where, during the ascetic movement of Puritanism, more witches were burnt than in the whole period before and after.

The virus of asceticism entered South Italy from three principal sources. From early ages the country had stood in commercial relations with the valley of the Nile; and even as its black magic is largely tinged with Egyptian practices, so its magic of the white kind—its saintly legends—bear the impress of the self-macerations and perverted life-theories of those desert-lunatics who called themselves Christians.* But this Orientalism fell at first upon unfruitful soil; the Vatican was yet wavering, and Hellenic notions of conduct still survived. It received a further rebuff at the hands of men like Benedict, who set up sounder ideals of holiness, introducing a gleam of sanity even in that insanest of institutions—the herding together of idle men to the glory of God. But things became more centralized as the Papacy gained ground. The strong Christian, the independent ruler or warrior or builder saint, was tolerated only if he conformed to its precepts; and the inauspicious rise of subservient ascetic orders like the Franciscans and Dominicans, who quickly invaded the fair regions of the south, gave an evil tone to their Christianity.

There has always been a contrary tendency at work: the Ionic spirit, heritage of the past. Monkish ideals of chastity and poverty have never appealed to the hearts of people, priests or prelates of the south; they will endure much fondness in their religion, but not those phenomena of cruelty and pruriency which are inseparably connected with asceticism; their notions have ever been akin to those of the sage Xenocrates, who held that "happiness consists not only in the possession of human virtues, but *in the accomplishment of natural acts.*" Among the latter they include the acquisition of wealth and the satisfaction of carnal needs. At this time, too, the old Hellenic curiosity was not wholly dimmed; they took an intelligent interest in imported creeds like that of Luther, which, if not convincing, at least satisfied their desire for novelty. Theirs was exactly the attitude of the Athenians towards Paul's "New God"; and Protestantism might have spread far in the south, had it not been ferociously repressed.

But after the brilliant humanistic period of the Aragons there followed the third and fiercest reaction—that of the Spanish viceroys, whose misrule struck at every one of the roots of national prosperity. It is that "seicentismo" which a modern writer (A. Niceforo, "L'Italia barbara," 1898) has recognized as the blight, the evil genius, of south Italy. The Ionic spirit did not help the people much

* These ascetics were here before Christianity (see Philo Judæus); in fact, there is not a single element in the new faith which had not been independently developed by the pagans, many of whom, like Seneca, Epictetus, and Marcus Aurelius, were ripe for the most abject self-abasement.

at this time. The greatest of these viceroys, Don Pietro di Toledo, hanged 18,000 of them in eight years, and then confessed, with a sigh, that "he did not know what more he could do." What more *could* he do? As a pious Spaniard he was incapable of understanding that quarterings and breakings on the rack were of less avail than the education of the populace in certain secular notions of good conduct—notions which it was the business of his Church not to teach. Reading through the legislation of the viceregal period, one is astonished to find how little was done for the common people, who lived like the veriest beasts of earth. Their civil rulers—scholars and gentlemen, most of them—really believed that the example of half a million illiterate and vicious monks was all the education they needed. And yet one notes with surprise that the Government was perpetually at loggerheads with the ecclesiastical authorities. True; but it is wonderful with what intuitive alacrity they joined forces when it was a question of repelling their common antagonist, enlightenment.

From this rank soil there sprang up an exotic efflorescence of holiness. If south Italy swarmed with sinners, as the experiences of Don Pietro seemed to show, it also swarmed with saints. And hardly one of them escaped the influence of the period, the love of futile ornamentation. Their piety is overloaded with embellishing touches and needless excrescences of virtue. It was the baroque period of saintliness, as of architecture.

I have already given some account of one of them, the Flying Monk (Chapter X), and have perused the biographies of at least fifty others. One cannot help observing a great uniformity in their lives—a kind of family resemblance. This parallelism is due to the simple reason that there is only one right for a thousand wrongs. One may well look in vain, here, for those many-tinted perversions and aberrations which disfigure the histories of average mankind. These saints are all alike—monotonously alike, if one cares to say so—in their chastity and other official virtues. But a little acquaintance with the subject will soon show you that, so far as the range of their particular Christianity allowed of it, there is a praiseworthy and even astonishing diversity among them. Nearly all of them could fly, more or less; nearly all of them could cure diseases and cause the clouds to rain; nearly all of them were illiterate; and every one of them died in the odour of sanctity—with roseate complexion, sweetly smelling corpse, and flexible limbs. Yet each one has his particular gifts, his strong point. Joseph of Copertino specialized in flying; others were conspicuous for their heroism in sitting in hot baths, devouring ordure, tormenting themselves with pins, and so forth.

Here, for instance, is a good representative biography—the Life of Saint Giangiuseppe della Croce (born 1654), reprinted for the occasion of his solemn sanctification.*

He resembled other saints in many points. He never allowed the "vermin which generated in his bed" to be disturbed; he wore the same clothes for sixty-four years on end; with women his behaviour was that of an "animated statue," and during his long life he never looked any one in the face (even his brother-monks were known to him only by their voices); he could raise the dead, relieve a duchess of a devil in the shape of a black dog, change chestnuts into apricots, and bad wine into good; his flesh was encrusted with sores, the result of his fierce scarifications; he was always half starved, and when delicate viands were brought to him, he used to say to his body: "Have you seen them? Have you smelt them? Then let that suffice for you."

He, too, could fly a little. So once, when he was nowhere to be found, the monks of the convent at last discovered him in the church, "raised so high above the ground that his head touched the ceiling." This is not a bad performance for a mere lad, as he then was. And how useful this gift became in old age was seen when, being almost incapable of moving his legs, and with body half paralysed, he was nevertheless enabled to accompany a procession for the length of two miles on foot, walking, to the stupefaction of thousands of spectators, at about a cubit's height above the street, on air; after the fashion of those Hindu gods whose feet—so the pagans fable—are too pure to touch mortal earth.

His love of poverty, moreover, was so intense that even after his death a picture of him, which his relatives had tried to attach to the wall in loving remembrance, repeatedly fell down again, although nailed very securely; nor did it remain fixed until they realized that its costly gilt frame was objectionable to the saint in heaven, and accordingly removed it. No wonder the infant Jesus was pleased to descend from the breast of Mary and take rest for several hours in the arms of Saint Giangiuseppe, who, on being disturbed by some

---

* "Vita di S. Giangiuseppe della Croce ... Scritta dal P. Fr. Diodato dell' Assunta per la Beatificazione ed ora ristampata dal postulatore della causa P. Fr. Giuseppe Rostoll in occasione della solenne Santificazione." Roma, 1839.

priestly visitor, exclaimed, "O how I have enjoyed holding the Holy Babe in my arms!" This is an old and favourite motif; it occurs, for example, in the Fioretti of Saint Francis; there are precedents, in fact, for all these divine favours.

But his distinguishing feature, his "dominating gift," was that of prophecy, especially in foretelling the deaths of children, "which he almost always accompanied with jocular words (scherzi) on his lips." He would enter a house and genially remark: "O, what an odour of Paradise"; sooner or later one or more of the children of the family would perish. To a boy of twelve he said, "Be good, Natale, for the angels are coming to take you." These playful words seem to have weighed considerably on the boy's mind and, sure enough, after a few years he died. But even more charming—più grazioso, the biographer calls it—was the incident when he once asked a father whether he would give his son to Saint Pasquale. The fond parent agreed, thinking that the words referred to the boy's future career in the Church. But the saint meant something quite different—he meant a career in heaven! And in less than a month the child died. To a little girl who was crying in the street he said: "I don't want to hear you any more. Go and sing in Paradise." And meeting her a short time after, he said, "What, are you still here?" In a few days she was dead.

The biography gives many instances of this pretty gift which would hardly have contributed to the saint's popularity in England or any other country save this, where—although the surviving youngsters are described as "struck with terror at the mere name of the Servant of God"—the parents were naturally glad to have one or two angels in the family, to act as avvocati (pleaders) for those that remained on earth.

And the mention of the legal profession brings me to one really instructive miracle. It is usually to be observed, after a saint has been canonized, that heaven, by some further sign or signs, signifies approval of this solemn act of the Vicar of God; indeed, to judge by these biographies, such a course is not only customary but, to use a worldly expression, de rigueur. And so it happened after the decree relative to Saint Giangiuseppe had been pronounced in the Vatican basilica by His Holiness Pius VI, in the presence of the assembled cardinals. Innumerable celestial portents (their enumeration fills eleven pages of the "Life") confirmed and ratified the great event, and among them this: the notary, who had drawn up both the ordinary and the apostolic processi, was cured of a grievous apoplexy, survived for four years, and finally died on the very anniversary of the death of the saint. Involuntarily one contrasts this heavenly largesse with the sordid guineas which would have contented an English lawyer. . . .

Or glance into the biography of the Venerable Sister Orsola Benincasa. She, too, could fly a little and raise men from the dead. She cured diseases, foretold her own death and that of others, lived for a month on the sole nourishment of a consecrated wafer; she could speak Latin and Polish, although she had been taught nothing at all; wrought miracles after death, and possessed to a heroic degree the virtues of patience, humility, temperance, justice, etc., etc. So inflamed was she with divine love, that almost every day thick steam issued out of her mouth, which was observed to be destructive to articles of clothing; her heated body, when ice was applied, used to hiss like a red-hot iron under similar conditions. As a child, she already cried for other people's sins; she was always hunting for her own and would gladly, at the end of her long and blameless career, have exchanged her sins for those of the youthful Duchess of Aquaro. An interesting phenomenon, by the way, the theory of sinfulness which crops up at this particular period of history. For our conception of sin is alien to the Latin mind. There is no "sin" in Italy (and this is not the least of her many attractions); it is an article manufactured exclusively for export.*

Orsola's speciality, however, were those frequent trance-like conditions by reason of which, during her lifetime, she was created "Protectress of the City of Naples." I cannot tell whether she was the first woman-saint to obtain this honour. Certainly the "Seven Holy Protectors" concerning whom Paolo Regio writes were all musty old males. . . .

And here is quite another biography, that of Alfonso di Liguori

---

* "Vita della Venerabile Serva di Dio Suor Orsola Benincasa, Scritta da un cherico regolare," Rome, 1796. There are, of course, much earlier biographies of all these saints; concerning Sister Orsola we possess, for instance, the remarkable pamphlet by Cesare d'Eboli ("Caesaris Aevoli Neapolitani Apologia pro Ursula Neapolitana quæ ad urbem acessit MDLXXXIII," Venice, 1589), which achieves the distinction of never mentioning Orsola by name: she is only once referred to as "mulier de qua agitur." But I prefer to quote from the more recent ones because they are authoritative, in so far as they have been written on the basis or miracles attested by eye-witnesses and accepted as veracious by the Vatican tribunal. Sister Orsola, though born in 1547, was only declared Venerable by Pontifical decree of 1793. Biographies prior to that date are therefore ex-parte statements and might conceivably contain errors of fact. This is out of the question here, as is clearly shown by the author on p. 178.

(born 1696), the founder of the Redemptorist order and canonized saint. He, too, could fly a little and raise the dead to life; he suffered devil-temptations, caused the clouds to rain, calmed an eruption of Vesuvius, multiplied food, and so forth. Such was his bashfulness, that even as an aged bishop he refused to be unrobed by his attendants; such his instinct for moral cleanliness that once, when a messenger had alighted at his convent accompanied by a soldier, he instantly detected, under the military disguise, the lineaments of a young woman-friend. Despite these divine gifts, he always needed a confessor. An enormous batch of miracles accompanied his sanctification.

But he only employed these divine graces by the way; he was by profession not a *taumaturgo*, but a clerical instructor, organizer, and writer. The Vatican has conferred on him the rare title of "Doctor Ecclesiæ," which he shares with Saint Augustine and some others.

The biography from which I have drawn these details was printed in Rome in 1839. It is valuable because it is modern and so far authentic; and for two other reasons. In the first place, curiously enough, it barely mentions the saint's life-work—his writings. Secondly, it is a good example of what I call the pious palimpsest. It is over-scored with contradictory matter. The author, for example, while accidentally informing us that Alfonso kept a carriage, imputes to him a degrading, Oriental love of dirt and tattered garments, in order (I presume) to make his character conform to the grosser ideals of the mendicant friars. I do not believe in these traits—in his hatred of soap and clean apparel. From his works I deduce a different original. He was refined and urbane; of a casuistical and prying disposition; like many sensitive men, unduly preoccupied with the sexual life of youth; like a true feudal aristocrat, ever ready to apply force where verbal admonition proved unavailing. . . .

In wonder-working capacities these saints were all put in the shade by the Calabrian Francesco di Paola, who raised fifteen persons from the dead in his boyhood. He used to perform a hundred miracles a day, and "it was a miracle, when a day passed without a miracle." The index alone of any one of his numerous biographies is enough to make one's head swim.

The vast majority of saints of this period do not belong to that third sex after which, according to some, the human race has ever striven—the constructive and purposeful third sex. They are wholly sexless, unsocial and futile beings, the negation of every masculine

or feminine virtue. Their independence fettered by the iron rules of the Vatican and of their particular order, these creatures had *nothing to do*; and like the rest of us under such conditions, became vacuously introspective. Those honourable saintly combats of the past with external enemies and plagues and stormy seasons were transplanted from without into the microcosm within, taking the shape of hallucinations and demon-temptations. They were no longer actors, but sufferers; automata, who attained a degree of inanity which would have made their old Byzantine prototypes burst with envy. Yet they vary in their gifts; each one, as I have said, has his or her strong point. Why? The reason of this diversity lies in the furious competition between the various monastic orders of the time—in those unedifying squabbles which led to never-ending litigation and complaints to head-quarters in Rome. Every one of these saints, from the first dawning of his divine talents, was surrounded by an atmosphere of jealous hatred on the part of his co-religionists. If one order came out with a flying wonder, another, in frantic emulation, would introduce some new speciality to eclipse his fame—something in the fasting line, it may be; or a female mystic whose palpitating letters to Jesus Christ would melt all readers to pity. The Franciscans, for instance, dissected the body of a certain holy Margaret and discovered in her heart the symbols of the Trinity and of the Passion. This bold and original idea would have gained them much credit, but for the rival Dominicans, who promptly discovered, and dissected, another saintly Margaret, whose heart contained three stones on which were engraven portraits of the Virgin Mary. *
So they ceaselessly unearthed fresh saints with a view to disparaging each other—all of them waiting for a favourable moment when the Vatican could be successfully approached to consider their particular claims. For it stands to reason that a Carmelite Pope would prefer a Carmelite saint to one of the Jesuits, and so forth.

And over all throned the Inquisition in Rome, alert, ever-suspicious; testing the "irregularities" of the various orders and harassing their respective saints with Olympic impartiality.

I know that mystics such as Orsola Benincasa are supposed to have another side to their character, an eminently practical side. It is perfectly true—and we need not go out of England to learn it—that

---

* These and other details will be found in the four volumes "Das Heidentum in der römischen Kirche" (Gotha, 1889-91), by Theodor Trede, a late Protestant parson in Naples, strongly tinged with anti-Catholicism, but whose facts may be relied upon. Indeed, he gives chapter and verse for them.

piety is not necessarily inconsistent with nimbleness in worldly affairs. But the mundane achievements, the monasteries and churches, of nine-tenths of these southern ecstatics are the work of the confessor and not of the saint. Trainers of performing animals are aware how these differ in plasticity of disposition and amenability to discipline; the spiritual adviser, who knows his business, must be quick to detect these various qualities in the minds of his penitents and to utilize them to the best advantage. It is inconceivable, for instance, that the convent-foundress Orsola was other than a neuropathic nonentity—a blind instrument in the hands of what we should call her backers, chiefest of whom (in Naples) were two Spanish priests, Borli and Navarro, whose local efforts were supported, at head-quarters, by the saintly Filippo Neri and the learned Cardinal Baronius.

This is noticeable. The earlier of these godly biographies are written in Latin, and these are more restrained in their language; they were composed, one imagines, for the priests and educated classes who could dispense to a certain degree with prodigies. But the later ones, from the viceregal period onwards, are in the vernacular and display a marked deterioration; one must suppose that they were printed for such of the common people as could still read (up to a few years ago, sixty-five per cent of the populace were analphabetic). They are pervaded by the characteristic of all contemporary literature and art: that deliberate intention to *astound* which originated with the poet Marino, who declared such to have been his object and ideal. The miracles certainly do astound; they are as *strepitosi* (clamour-arousing) as the writers claim them to be; how they ever came to occur must be left to the consciences of those who swore on oath to the truth of them.

During this period the Mother of God as a local saint increased in popularity. There was a ceaseless flow of monographs dealing with particular Madonnas, as well as a small a library on what the Germans would doubtless call the "Madonna as a Whole." Here is Serafino Montorio's "Zodiaco di Maria," printed in 1715 on the lines of that monster of a book by Gumppenberg. It treats of over two hundred subspecies of Madonna worshipped in different parts of south Italy which is divided, for these celestial purposes, into twelve regions, according to the signs of the Zodiac. The book is dedicated by the author to his "Sovereign Lady the *Gran Madre di dio*," and might, in truth, have been written to the glory of that protean old Magna Mater by one of Juvenal's "tonsured herd" possessed of much industry but little discrimination.* Such as it is, it reflects the crude mental status of the Dominican order to which the author belonged. I warmly recommend this book to all Englishmen desirous of understanding the south. It is pure, undiluted paganism—paganism of a bad school; one would think it marked the lowest possible ebb of Christian spirituality. But this is by no means the case, as I shall presently show.

How different, from such straightforward unreason, are the etherealized, saccharine effusions of the "Glories of Mary," by Alfonso di Liguori! They represent the other pole of Mariolatry—the gentlemanly pole. And under the influence of Mary-worship a new kind of saintly physiognomy was elaborated, as we can see from contemporary prints and pictures. The bearded men-saints were extinct; in the place of them this mawkish, sub-sexual love for the Virgin developed a corresponding type of adorer—clean-shaven, emasculate youths, posing in ecstatic attitudes with a nauseous feminine smirk. Rather an unpleasant sort of saint.

The unwholesome chastity-ideal, without which no holy man of the period was "complete," naturally left its mark upon literature, notably on that of certain Spanish theologians. But good specimens of what I mean may also be found in the Theologia Moralis of Liguori; the kind of stuff, that is, which would be classed as "curious" in catalogues and kept in a locked cupboard by the most broadminded paterfamilias. Reading these elucubrations of Alfonso's, one feels that the saint has pondered long and lovingly upon themes like *an et quando peccata sint oscula* or *de tactu et adspectu corporis*; he writes with all the authority of an expert whose richly-varied experiences in the confessional have been amplified and irradiated by divine inspiration. I hesitate what to call this literature, seeing that it was obviously written to the glory of God and His Virgin Mother. The congregation of the Index, which was severe in the matter of indecent publications and prohibited Boccaccio's Decameron on these grounds, hailed with approval the appearance of such treatises composed, as they were, for the guidance of young priests.

Cruelty (in the shape of the Inquisition) and lasciviousness (as exemplified by such pious filth)—these are the prime fruits of that cult of asceticism which for centuries the Government strove to

---

* The Mater Dei was officially installed in the place of Magna Mater at the Synod of Ephesus in 431.

impose upon south Italy. If the people were saved, it was due to that substratum of sanity, of Greek σωφροσύνη, which resisted the one and derided the other. Whoever has saturated himself with the records will marvel not so much that the inhabitants preserved some shreds of common sense and decent feeling, as that they survived at all—he will marvel that the once fair kingdom was not converted into a wilderness, saintly but uninhabited, like Spain itself.

For the movement continued in a vertiginous crescendo. Spaniardism culminated in Bourbonism, and this, again, reached its climax in the closing years of the eighteenth century, when the conditions of south Italy baffled description. I have already (p. 213) given the formidable number of its ecclesiastics; the number of saints was commensurate, but—as often happens when the quantity is excessive—the quality declined. This lazzaroni-period was the debâcle of holiness. So true it is that our gods reflect the hearts that make them.

The Venerable Fra Egidio, a native of Taranto, is a good example of contemporary godliness. My biography of him was printed in Naples in 1876, * and contains a dedicatory epistle addressed to the Blessed Virgin by her "servant, subject, and most loving son Rosario Frungillo"—a canon of the church and the author of the book.

This "taumaturgo" could perform all the ordinary feats; I will not linger over them. What has made him popular to this day are those wonders which appealed to the taste of the poorer people, such as, for example, that miracle of the eels. A fisherman had brought fourteen hundredweight of these for sale in the market. Judge of his disappointment when he discovered that they had all died during the journey (southerners will not pay for dead eels). Fortunately, he saw the saint arriving in a little boat, who informed him that the eels were "not dead, but only asleep," and who woke them up again by means of a relic of Saint Pasquale which he always carried about with him, after a quarter of an hour's devout praying, during which the perspiration oozed from his forehead. The eels, says the writer, had been dead and slimy, but now turned their bellies downwards once more and twisted about in their usual spirals; there began a general weeping among the onlookers, and the fame of the miracle immediately spread abroad. He could do the same with lobsters, cows, and human beings.

---

* "Vita del Venerabile servo di Dio Fra Egidio da S. Giuseppe laico professo alcantarino." Napoli, 1876.

Thus a cow belonging to Fra Egidio's monastery was once stolen by an impious butcher, and cut up into the usual joints with a view to a clandestine sale of the meat. The saint discovered the beast's remains, ordered that they should be laid together on the floor in the shape of a living cow, with the entrails, head and so forth in their natural positions; then, having made the sign of the cross with his cord upon the slaughtered beast, and rousing up all his faith, he said: "In the name of God and of Saint Pasquale, arise, Catherine!" (Catherine was the cow's name.) "At these words the animal lowed, shook itself, and stood up on its feet alive, whole and strong, even as it had been before it was killed."

In the case of one of the dead men whom he brought to life, the undertakers were already about their sad task; but Fra Egidio, viewing the corpse, remarked in his usual manner that the man was "not dead, but only asleep," and after a few saintly manipulations, roused him from his slumber. The most portentous of his wonders, however, are those which he wrought *after his own death* by means of his relics and otherwise; they have been sworn to by many persons. Nor did his hand lose its old cunning, in these posthumous manifestations, with the finny tribe. A certain woman, Maria Scuotto, was enabled to resuscitate a number of dead eels by means of an image of the deceased saint which she cast among them.

Every one of the statements in this biography is drawn from the *processi* to which I will presently refer; there were 202 witnesses who deposed "under the rigour and sanctity of oath" to the truth of these miracles; and among those who were personally convinced of the Venerable's rare gifts was the Royal Family of Naples, the archbishop of that town, as well as innumerable dukes and princes. An embittered rationalist would note that the reading of Voltaire, at this period, was punished with three years' galley-slavery and that several thousand citizens were hanged for expressing liberal opinions; he will suggest that belief in the supernatural, rejected by the thinking classes, finds an abiding shelter among royalty and the proletariat.

It occurs to me, a propos of Fra Egidio, to make the obvious statement that an account of an occurrence is not necessarily true, because it happened long ago. Credibility does not improve, like violins and port wine, with lapse of years. This being the case, it will not be considered objectionable to say that there are certain deeds attributed to holy men of olden days which, to speak frankly, are open to doubt; or at least not susceptible of proof. Who were these men, if they ever existed? and who vouches for their prodigies? This makes me think that Pope Gelasius showed no small penetration in excluding, as early as the fifth century, some few *acta sanctorum* from the use of the churches; another step in the same direction was taken in the twelfth century when the power of canonizing saints, which had hitherto been claimed by all bishops, became vested in the Pope alone; and yet another, when Urban VIII forbade the nomination of local patron saints by popular vote. Pious legends are supposed to have their uses as an educative agency. So be it. But such relations of imperfectly ascertained and therefore questionable wonders suffer from one grave drawback: they tend to shake our faith in the evidence of well-authenticated ones. Thus Saint Patrick is also reported to have raised a cow from the dead—five cows, to be quite accurate; but who will come forward and vouch for the fact? No one. That is because Saint Patrick belongs to the legendary stage; he died, it is presumed, about 490.

Here, with Saint Egidio, we are on other ground; on the ground of bald actuality. He expired in 1812, and the contemporaries who have attested his miraculous deeds are not misty phantoms of the Thebais; they were creatures of flesh and blood, human, historical personages, who were dressed and nourished and educated after the fashion of our own grandfathers. Yet it was meet and proper that the documentary evidence as to his divine graces should be conscientiously examined. And only in 1888 was the crowning work accomplished. In that year His Holiness Leo XIII and the Sacred Congregation of Cardinals solemnly approved the evidence and inscribed the name of Egidio in the book of the Blessed.

To touch upon a few minor matters—I observe that Fra Egidio, like the Flying Monk, was "illiterate," and similarly preserved up to a decrepit age "the odorous lily of purity, which made him appear in words and deeds as a most innocent child." He was accustomed to worship before a favourite picture of the Mother of God which he kept adorned with candles; and whenever the supply of these ran out, he was wont to address Her with infantile simplicity of heart and in the local dialect: "Now there's no wax for You; so think about it Yourself; if not, You'll have to go without." The playful-saintly note. . . .

But there is this difference between him and earlier saints that whereas they, all too often, suffered in solitude, misunderstood and rejected of men, he enjoyed the highest popularity during his whole long life. Wherever he went, his footsteps were pursued by crowds of admirers, eager to touch his wonder-working body or to cut off shreds of his clothing as amulets; hardly a day passed that he did not return home with garments so lacerated that only half of them was left; every evening they had to be patched up anew, although they were purposely stitched full of wires and small chains of iron as a protection. The same passionate sympathy continued after death, for while his body was lying in state a certain Luigi Ascione, a surgeon, pushed through the crowd and endeavoured to cut off one of his toe-nails with the flesh attached to it; he admitted being driven to this act of pious depredation by the pleading request of the Spanish Ambassador and a Neapolitan princess, who held Fra Egidio in great veneration.

This is not an isolated instance. Southerners love their saints, and do not content themselves with chill verbal expressions of esteem. So the biographer of Saint Giangiuseppe records that "one of the deceased saint's toes was bitten off with most regretable devotion by the teeth of a man in the crowd, who wished to preserve it as a relic. And the blood from the wound flowed so copiously and so freely that many pieces of cloth were saturated with it; nor did it cease to flow till the precious corpse was interred." It is hard to picture such proofs of fervid popularity falling to the lot of English deans and bishops.

He was modern, too, in this sense, that he did not torment himself with penitences (decay of Spanish austerity); on the contrary, he even kept chocolate, honey and suchlike delicacies in his cell. In short, he was an up-to-date saint, who despised mediæval practices and lived in a manner befitting the age which gave him birth. In this respect he resembles our English men of holiness, who exercise a laudable self-denial in resisting the seductions of the ascetic life.

Meanwhile, the cult of the Mother of God continued to wax in favour, and those who are interested in its development should read the really remarkable book by Antonio Cuomó, "Saggio apologetico della belezza celeste e divina di Maria S.S. Madre di Dio" (Castellamare, 1863). It is a diatribe against modernism by a champion of lost causes, an exacerbated lover of the "Singular Virgin and fecund Mother of the Verb." His argument, as I understand it, is the *consensus gentium* theory applied to the Virgin Mary. In defence of this thesis, the book has been made to bristle with quotations; they stand out like quills upon the porcupine, ready to impale the adventurous sceptic. Pliny and Virgil and the Druids and Balaam's Ass are invoked as foretelling Her birth; the Old Testament—that venerable sufferer, as Huxley called it—is twisted into dire convulsions for the same purpose; much evidence is also drawn from Hebrew observances and from the Church Fathers. But the New Testamentary record is seldom invoked; the Saviour, on the rare occasions when He is mentioned, being dismissed as "G. C." The volume ends with a pyrotechnical display of invective against non-Catholic heretics; a medley of threats and abuse worthy of those breezy days of Erasmus, when theologians really said what they thought of each other. The frank polytheism of Montorio is more to my taste. This outpouring of papistical rhetoric gives me unwarrantable sensations—it makes me feel positively Protestant.

Another sign of increasing popularity is that the sacred bacchanals connected with the "crowning" of various Madonnas were twice as numerous, in Naples, in the nineteenth as in the eighteenth century. Why an image of the Mother of God should be decked with this worldly symbol, as a reward for services rendered, will be obscure only to those who fail to appreciate the earthly-tangible complexion of southern religion. Puerility is its key-note. The Italian is either puerile or adult; the Englishman remains everlastingly adolescent. . . .

Now of course it is open to any one to say that the pious records from which I have quoted are a desolation of the spirit; that they possess all the improbability of the "Arabian Nights," and none of their charm; that all the distempered dreamings to which our poor humanity is subject have given themselves a rendezvous in their pages. I am not for disputing the point, and I can understand how one man may be saddened by their perusal, while another extracts therefrom some gleams of mirth. For my part, I merely verify this fact: the native has been fed with this stuff for centuries, and if we desire to enter into his feelings, we must feed ourselves likewise—up to a point. The past is the key to the present. That is why I have dwelt at such length on the subject—in the hope of clearing up the enigma in the national character: the unpassable gulf, I mean, between the believing and the unbelieving sections of the community.

An Anglo-Saxon arriving at Bagnara and witnessing a procession in honour of that Sacred Hat of the Mother of God which has led me into this disquisition, would be shocked at the degree of bigotry implied. "The Hat of the Virgin Mary," he would say—"what next?" Then, accosting some ordinary citizen not in the procession—any butcher or baker—he would receive a shock of another kind; he would be appalled at the man's language of contemptuous derision towards everything which he, the Anglo-Saxon, holds sacred in biblical tradition. There is no attempt, here, at "reconciliation." The classes calling themselves enlightened are making a clean sweep of the old gods in a fashion that bewilders us who have accustomed ourselves to see a providential design in everything that exists (possibly because our acquaintance with a providentially-designed Holy Office is limited to an obsolete statute, the genial: *de hæretico comburendo*). The others, the fetishists, have remained on the spiritual level of their own saints. And there we stand today. That section so numerous in England, the pseudo-pagans, crypto-Christians, or whatever obscurantists like Messrs. A. J. Balfour and Mallock like to call themselves (the men who, with disastrous effects, transport into realms of pure intelligence the spirit of compromise which should be restricted to practical concerns)—that section has no representatives hereabouts.

Fully to appreciate their attitude as opposed to ours, we must also remember that the south Italian does not trouble himself about the objective truth of any miracle whatever; his senses may be perverted, but his intelligence remains outside the sphere of infection. This is his saving grace. To the people here, the affair of Moses and the Burning Bush, the raising of Lazarus, and Egidio's cow-revival, are on the identical plane of authenticity; the Bible is one of a thousand saints' books; its stories may be as true as theirs, or just as untrue; in any case, what has that to do with his own worldly conduct? But the Englishman with ingenuous ardour thinks to believe in the Burning Bush wonder, and in so far his intelligence is infected; with equal ardour he excludes the cow-performance from the range of possibility; and to him it matters considerably which of the miracles are true and which are false, seeing that his conduct is supposed to take colour from such supernatural events. Ultracredulous as to one set of narratives, he has no credulity left for other sets; he concentrates his believing energies upon a small space, whereas the Italian's are diffused, thinly, over a wide area. It is the old story: Gothic intensity and Latin spaciousness. So the Gothic believer takes his big dose of irrationalism on one fixed day; the Latin, by attending Mass every morning, spreads it over the whole week. And the sombre strenuousness of our northern character expects a remuneration for this outlay of faith, while the other contents himself with such sensuous enjoyment as he can momentarily extract from his ceremonials. That is why our English religion has a *democratic* tinge distasteful to the Latin who, at bottom, is always a philosopher; democratic because it relies for its success, like democratic politicians, upon promises—promises that may or may not be kept—promises that form no part (they are only an official appendage) of the childlike paganism of the south. . . .

Fifteen francs will buy you a reliable witness for a south Italian lawsuit; you must pay a good deal more in England. Thence one might argue that the cult of credulity implied by these saintly biographies is responsible for this laxness, for the general disregard of veracity. I doubt it. I am not inclined to blame the monkish saint-makers for this particular trait; I suspect that for fifteen francs you could have bought a first-class witness under Pericles. Southerners are not yet pressed for time; and when people are not pressed for time, they do not learn the time-saving value of honesty. Our respect for truth and fair dealing, such as it is, derives from modern commerce; in the Middle Ages nobody was concerned about honesty save a few trading companies like the Hanseatic League, and the poor mediæval devil (the only gentleman of his age) who was generally pressed for time and could be relied upon to keep his word. Even God, of whom they talked so much, was systematically swindled. Where time counts for nothing, expeditious practices between man and man are a drug in the market. Besides, it must be noted that this churchly misteaching was only a fraction of that general shattering which has disintegrated all the finer fibres of public life. It stands to reason that the fragile tissues of culture are dislocated, and its delicate edges defaced, by such persistive governmental brutalization as the inhabitants have undergone. None but the grossest elements in a people can withstand enduring misrule; none but a mendacious and servile nature will survive its wear and tear. So it comes about that up to a few years ago the nobler qualities which we associate with those old Hellenic colonists—their intellectual curiostiy, their candid outlook upon life, their passionate sense of beauty, their love of nature—all these things had been abraded, leaving, as residue, nothing save what the Greeks shared with ruder races. There are indications that this state of affairs is now ending.

The position is this. The records show that the common people never took their saints to heart in the northern fashion—as moral exemplars; from beginning to end, they have only utilized them as a pretext for fun and festivals, a means of brightening the catacombic, the essentially sunless, character of Christianity. So much for the popular saints, the patrons and heroes. The others, the ecclesiastical ones, are an artificial product of monkish institutions. These monkeries were established in the land by virtue of civil authority. Their continued existence, however, was contingent upon the goodwill of the Vatican. One of the surest and cheapest methods of obtaining this goodwill was to produce a satisfactory crop of saints whose beatification swelled the Vatican treasury with the millions collected from a deluded populace for that end. The monks paid nothing; they only furnished the saint and, in due course, the people's money. Can we wonder that they discovered saints galore? Can we wonder that the Popes were gratified by their pious zeal?

So things went on till yesterday. But now a large proportion of the ten thousand (?) churches and monasteries of Naples are closed or actually in ruins; wayside sanctuaries crumble to dust in picturesque fashion; the price of holy books has fallen to zero, and the godly brethren have emigrated to establish their saint-manufactories elsewhere. Not without hope of success; for they will find purchasers of their wares wherever mankind can be interested in that queer disrespect of the body which is taught by the metaphysical ascetics of the East.

It was Lewes, I believe, who compared metaphysics to ghosts by saying that there was no killing either of them; one could only dissipate them by throwing light into the dark places they love to inhabit—to show that nothing is there. Spectres, likewise, are these saintly caricatures of humanity, perambulating metaphysics, the application *in corpore vili* of Oriental fakirism. Nightmare-literature is the crazy recital of their deeds and sufferings. Pathological phantoms! The state of mind which engenders and cherishes such illusions is a disease, and it has been well said that "you cannot refute a disease." You cannot nail ghosts to the counter.

But a ray of light. . . .

XXXII

ASPROMONTE, THE CLOUD-GATHERER

DAY was barely dawning when we left Delianuova and began the long and weary climb up Montalto. Chestnuts gave way to beeches, but the summit receded ever further from us. And even before reaching the uplands, the so-called Piano di Carmelia, we encountered a bank of bad weather. A glance at the map will show that Montalto must be a cloud-gatherer, drawing to its flanks every wreath of vapour that rises from Ionian and Tyrrhenian; a west wind was blowing that morning, and thick fogs clung to the skirts of the peak. We reached the summit (1956 metres) at last, drenched in an icy bath of rain and sleet, and with fingers so numbed that we could hardly hold our sticks.

Of the superb view—for such it must be—nothing whatever was to be seen; we were wrapped in a glacial mist. On the highest point stands a figure of the Redeemer. It was dragged up in pieces from Delianuova some seven years ago, but soon injured by frosts; it has lately been refashioned. The original structure may be due to the same pious stimulus as that which placed the crosses on Monte Vulture and other peaks throughout the country—a counterblast to the rationalistic congress at Rome in 1904, when Giordano Bruno became, for a while, the hero of the country. This statue does not lack dignity. The Saviour's regard turns towards Reggio, the capital of the province; and one hand is upraised in calm and godlike benediction.

Passing through magnificent groves of fir, we descended rapidly into another climate, into realms of golden sunshine. Among these trees I espied what has become quite a rare bird in Italy—the common wood-pigeon. The few that remain have been driven into the most secluded recesses of the mountains; it was different in the days of Theocritus, who sang of this amiable fowl when the climate was colder and the woodlands reached as far as the now barren seashore. To the firs succeeded long stretches of odorous pines interspersed with Mediterranean heath (bruyère), which here grows to a height of twelve feet; one thinks of the number of briar pipes that could be cut out of its knotty roots. A British Vice-Consul at Reggio, Mr. Kerrich, started this industry about the year 1899; he collected the roots, which were sawn into blocks and then sent to France and America to be made into pipes. This Calabrian briar was considered superior to the French kind, and Mr. Kerrich had large sales on both sides of the Atlantic; his chief difficulty was want of labour owing to emigration.

We passed, by the wayside, several rude crosses marking the site of accidents or murders, as well as a large heap of stones, whereunder lie the bones of a man who attempted to traverse these mountains in winter-time and was frozen to death.

"They found him," the guide told me, "in spring, when the snow melted from off his body. There he lay, all fresh and comely! It looked as if he would presently wake up and continue his march; but he neither spoke nor stirred. Then they knew he was dead. And they piled all these stones over him, to prevent the wolves, you understand——

Aspromonte deserves its name. It is an incredibly harsh agglomeration of hill and dale, and the geology of the district, as I learned long ago from my friend Professor Cortese, reveals a perfect chaos of rocks of every age, torn into gullies by earthquakes and other cataclysms of the past—at one place, near Scido, is an old stream of lava. Once the higher ground, the nucleus of the group, is left behind, the wanderer finds himself lost in a maze of contorted ravines, winding about without any apparent system of watershed. Does the liquid flow north or south? Who can tell! The track crawls in and out of valleys, mounts upwards to heights of sun-scorched bracken and cistus, descends once more into dewy glades hemmed in by precipices and overhung by drooping fernery. It crosses streams of crystal clearness, rises afresh in endless gyrations under the pines only to vanish, yet again, into the twilight of deeper abysses, where it skirts the rivulet along precarious ledges, until some new obstruction blocks the way—so it writhes about for long, long hours. . . .

Here, on the spot, one can understand how an outlaw like Musolino was enabled to defy justice, helped, as he was, by the fact that the officer in charge of his pursuers was paid a fixed sum for every day he spent in the chase and presumably found it convenient not to discover his whereabouts. *

---

* See next chapter.

We rested awhile, during these interminable meanderings, under the shadow of a group of pines.

"Do you see that square patch yonder?" said my man. "It is a cornfield. There Musolino shot one of his enemies, whom he suspected of giving information to the police. It was well done."

"How many did he shoot, altogether?"

"Only eighteen. And three of them recovered, more or less; enough to limp about, at all events. Ah, if you could have seen him, sir! He was young, with curly fair hair, and a face like a rose. God alone can tell how many poor people he helped in their distress. And any young girl he met in the mountains he would help with her load and accompany as far as her home, right into her father's house, which none of us would have risked, however much we might have liked it. But every one knew that he was pure as an angel."

"And there was a young fellow here," he went on, "who thought he could profit by pretending to be Musolino. So one day he challenged a proprietor with his gun, and took all his money. When it came to Musolino's ears, he was furious—furious! He lay in wait for him, caught him, and said: "How dare you touch fathers of children? Where's that money you took from Don Antonio?" Then the boy began to cry and tremble for his life. "Bring it," said Musolino, "every penny, at midday next Monday, to such and such a spot, or else——" Of course he brought it. Then he marched him straight into the proprietor's house. "Here's this wretched boy, who robbed you in my name. And here's the money: please count it. Now, what shall we do with him?" So Don Antonio counted the money. "It's all there," he said; "let him off this time." Then Musolino turned to the lad: "You have behaved like a mannerless puppy," he said, "without shame or knowledge of the world. Be reasonable in future, and understand clearly: I will have no brigandage in these mountains. Leave that to the syndics and judges in the towns."

We did not traverse Musolino's natal village, Santo Stefano; indeed, we passed through no villages at all. But after issuing from the labyrinth, we saw a few of them, perched in improbable situations— Roccaforte and Roghudi on our right; on the other side, Africo and Casalnuovo. Salis Marschlins says that the inhabitants of these regions are so wild and innocent that money is unknown; everything is done by barter. That comes of copying without discrimination. For this statement he utilized the report of a Government official, a certain Leoni, who was sent hither after the earthquake of 1783, and found the use of money not unknown, but forgotten, in consequence of this terrible catastrophe.

These vales of Aspromonte are one of the last refuges of living Byzantinism. Greek is still spoken in some places, such as Roccaforte and Roghudi. Earlier travellers confused the natives with the Albanians; Niehbuhr, who had an obsession on the subject of Hellenism, imagined they were relics of old Dorian and Achæan colonies. Scholars are apparently not yet quite decided upon certain smaller matters. So Lenormant (Vol. II, p. 433) thinks they came hither after the Turkish conquest, as did the Albanians; Batiffol argues that they were chased into Calabria from Sicily by the Arabs after the second half of the seventh century; Morosi, who treats mostly of their Apulian settlements, says that they came from the East between the sixth and tenth centuries. Many students, such as Morelli and Comparetti, have garnered their songs, language, customs and lore, and whoever wants a convenient résumé of these earlier researches will find it in Pellegrini's book which was written in 1873 (printed 1880). He gives the number of Greek inhabitants of these places—Roghudi, for example, had 535 in his day; he has also noted down these villages, like Africo and Casalnuova, in which the Byzantine speech has lately been lost. Bova and Condofuri are now the head-quarters of mediæval Greek in these parts.

From afar we had already descried a green range of hills that shut out the seaward view. This we now began to climb, in wearisome ascension; it is called *Piè d'Impisa*, because "your feet are all the time on a steep incline." Telegraph wires here accompany the track, a survival of the war between the Italian Government and Musolino. On the summit lies a lonely Alp, Campo di Bova, where a herd of cattle were pasturing under the care of a golden-haired youth who lay supine on the grass, gazing at the clouds as they drifted in stately procession across the firmament. Save for a dusky charcoal-burner crouching in a cave, this boy was the only living person we encountered on our march—so deserted are these mountain tracks.

At Campo di Bova a path branches off to Staiti; the sea is visible once more, and there are fine glimpses, on the left, towards Staiti (or is it Ferruzzano?) and, down the right, into the destructive and dangerous torrent of Amendolea. Far beyond it, rises the mountain peak of Pentedattilo, a most singular landmark which looks exactly like a molar tooth turned upside down, with fangs in air. The road passes through a gateway in the rock whence, suddenly, a full view is disclosed of Bova on its hill-top, the houses nestling among huge blocks of stone that make one think of some cyclopean citadel of past ages. My guide stoutly denied that this was Bova; the town, he declared, lay in quite another direction. I imagine he had never been beyond the foot of the "Piè d'Impisa."

Here, once more, the late earthquake has done some damage, and there is a row of trim wooden shelters near the entrance of the town. I may add, as a picturesque detail, that about one-third of them have never been inhabited, and are never likely to be. They were erected in the heat of enthusiasm, and there they will stay, empty and abandoned, until some energetic mayor shall pull them down and cook his maccheroni with their timber.

Evening was drawing on apace, and whether it was due to the joy of having accomplished an arduous journey, or to inconsiderate potations of the Bacchus of Bova, one of the most remarkable wines in Italy, I very soon found myself on excellent terms with the chief citizens of this rather sordid-looking little place. A good deal has been written concerning Bova and its inhabitants, but I should say there is still a mine of information to be exploited on the spot. They are bilingual, but while clinging stubbornly to their old speech, they have now embraced Catholicism. The town kept its Greek religious rites till the latter half of the sixteenth century; and Rodotà has described the "vigorous resistance" that was made to the introduction of Romanism, and the ceremonies which finally accompanied that event.

Mine hostess obligingly sang me two or three songs in her native language; the priest furnished me with curious statistics of folklore and criminology; and the notary, with whom I conversed awhile on the tiny piazza that overlooks the coastlands and distant Ionian, was a most affable gentleman. Seeing that the Christian names of the populace are purely Italian, I enquired as to their surnames, and learned what I expected, namely, that a good many Greek family names survive among the people. His own name, he said, was unquestionably Greek: *Condemi*; if I liked, he would go through the local archives and prepare me a list of all such surnames as appeared to him to be non-Italian; we could thus obtain some idea of the percentage of Greek families still living here. My best thanks to the good Signor!

After some further liquid refreshment, a youthful native volunteered to guide me by short cuts to the remote railway station. We stepped blithely into the twilight, and during the long descent I discoursed with him, in fluent Byzantine Greek, of the affairs of his village.

It is my theory that among a populace of this kind the words relative to agricultural pursuits will be those which are least likely to suffer change with lapse of years, or to be replaced by others. Acting on this principle, I put him through a catechism on the subject as soon as we reached our destination, and was surprised at the relative scarcity of Italian terms—barely 25 per cent I should say. Needless to add, I omitted to note them down. Such as it is, be that my contribution to the literature of these sporadic islets of mediæval Hellenism, whose outstanding features are being gnawed away by the waves of military conscription, governmental schooling, and emigration.

Caulonia, my next halting-place, lay far off the line. I had therefore the choice of spending the night at Gerace (old Locri) or Rocella Ionica—intermediate stations. Both of them, to my knowledge, possessing indifferent accommodation, I chose the former as being the nearest, and slept there, not amiss; far better than on a previous occasion, when certain things occurred which need not be set down here.

The trip from Delianuova over the summit of Montalto to Bova railway station is by no means to be recommended to young boys or persons in delicate health. Allowing for only forty-five minutes' rest, it took me fourteen hours to walk to the town of Bova, and the railway station lies nearly three hours apart from that place. There is hardly a level yard of ground along the whole route, and though my "guide" twice took the wrong track and thereby probably lost me some little time, I question whether the best walker, provided (as I was) with the best maps, will be able to traverse the distance in less than fifteen hours.

Whoever he is, I wish him joy of his journey. Pleasant to recall, assuredly; the scenery and the mountain flowers are wondrously beautiful; but I have fully realized what the men of Delianuova meant, when they said:

"To Montalto, Yes; to Bova, No."

XXXIII

MUSOLINO AND THE LAW

MUSOLINO will remain a hero for many long years to come. "He did his duty": such is the popular verdict on his career. He was not a brigand, but an unfortunate—a martyr, a victim of the law. So he is described not only by his country-people, but by the writers of many hundred serious pamphlets in every province of Italy.

At any bookstall you may buy cheap illustrated tracts and poems setting forth his achievements. In Cosenza I saw a play of which he was the leading figure, depicted as a pale, long-suffering gentleman of the "misunderstood" type—friend of the fatherless, champion of widows and orphans, rectifier of all wrongs; in fact, as the embodiment of those virtues which we are apt to associate with Prometheus or the founder of Christianity.

Only to those who know nothing of local conditions will it seem strange to say that Italian law is one of the factors that contribute to the disintegration of family life throughout the country, and to the production of creatures like Musolino. There are few villages which do not contain some notorious assassins who have escaped punishment under sentimental pleas, and now terrorize the neighbourhood. This is one of the evils which derange patriarchalism; the decent-minded living in fear of their lives, the others with a conspicuous example before their eyes of the advantages of evil-doing. And another is that the innocent often suffer, country-bred lads being locked up for months and years in prison on the flimsiest pretexts—often on the mere word of some malevolent local policeman—among hardened habitual offenders. If they survive the treatment, which is not always the case, they return home completely demoralized and a source of infection to others.

It is hardly surprising if, under such conditions, rich and poor alike are ready to hide a picturesque fugitive from justice. A sad state of affairs, but—as an unsavoury Italian proverb correctly says—*il pesce puzza dal capo.*

For the fault lies not only in the fundamental perversity of all Roman Law. It lies also in the local administration of that law, which is inefficient and marked by that elaborate brutality characteristic of all "philosophic" and tender-hearted nations. One thinks of the Byzantines. . . . That justices should be well-salaried gentlemen, cognizant of their duties to society; that carbineers and other police-functionaries should be civilly responsible for outrages upon the public; that a so-called "habeas-corpus" Act might be as useful here as among certain savages of the north; that the Baghdad system of delays leads to corruption of underpaid officials and witnesses alike (not to speak of judges)—in a word, that the method pursued hereabouts is calculated to create rather than to repress crime: these are truths of too elementary a nature to find their way into the brains of the megalomaniac rhetoricians who control their country's fate. They will never endorse that saying of Stendhal's: "In Italy, with the exception of Milan, the death-penalty is the preface of all civilization." (To this day, the proportion of murders is still 13 per cent higher in Palermo than in Milan.)

Speak to the wisest judges of the horrors of cellular confinement such as Musolino was enduring up to a short time ago, as opposed to capital punishment, and you will learn that they invoke the humanitarian Beccaria in justification of it. Theorists!

For less formidable criminals there exists that wondrous institution of *domicilio coatto*, which I have studied in the islands of Lipari and Ponza. These evil-doers seldom try to escape; life is far too comfortable, and the wine good and cheap; often, on completing their sentences, they get themselves condemned anew, in order to return. The hard-working man may well envy their lot, for they receive free lodging from the Government, a daily allowance of money, and two new suits of clothes a year—they are not asked to do a stroke of work in return, but may lie in bed all day long, if so disposed. The law-abiding citizen, meanwhile, pays for the upkeep of this horde of malefactors, as well as for the army of officials who are deputed to attend to their wants. This institution of *domicilio coatto* is one of those things which would be incredible, were it not actually in existence. It is a school, a State-fostered school, for the promotion of criminality.

But what shall be expected? Where judges sob like children, and jurors swoon away with emotionalism; where floods of bombast—go to the courts, and listen!—take the place of cross-examination and duly-sworn affidavits; where perjury is a humanly venial and almost praiseworthy failing—how shall the code, defective as it is, be administered? Rhetoric, and rhetoric alone sways the decision of the courts. Scholars are only now beginning to realize to what an extent the ancient sense of veracity was tainted with this vice—how deeply all classical history is permeated with elegant partisan non-truth. And this evil legacy from Greco-Roman days has been augmented by the more recent teachings of jesuitry and the Catholic theory of "peccato veniale." Rhetoric alone counts; rhetoric alone is "art." The rest is mere facts; and your "penalista" has a constitutional horror of a bald fact, because *there it is*, and there is nothing to be done with it. It is too crude a thing for cultured men to handle. If a local barrister were forced to state in court a plain fact, without varnish, he would die of cerebral congestion; the judge, of boredom.

In early times, these provinces had a rough-and-ready cowboy justice which answered simple needs, and when, in Bourbon days, things became more centralized, there was still a never-failing expedient: each judge having a fixed and publicly acknowledged tariff, the village elders, in deserving cases, subscribed the requisite sum and released their prisoner. But Italy is now paying the penalty of ambition. With one foot in the ferocity of her past, and the other on a quicksand of dream-nurtured idealism, she contrives to combine the disadvantages of both. She, who was the light o' love of all Europe for long ages, and in her poverty denied nothing to her clientèle, has now laid aside a little money, repenting of her frivolous and mercenary deeds (they sometimes do), and becoming puritanically zealous of good works in her old age—all this, however, as might have been expected from her antecedent career, without much discrimination.

It is certainly remarkable that a race of men who have been such ardent opponents of many forms of tyranny in the past, should still endure a system of criminal procedure worthy of Torquemada. High and low cry out against it, but—*pazienza!* where shall grievances be ventilated? In Parliament? A good joke, that! In the press? Better still! Italian newspapers nowise reflect the opinions of civilized Italy; they are mere cheese-wrappers; in the whole kingdom there are only three self-respecting dailies. The people have learnt to despair of their rulers—to regard them with cynical suspicion. Public opinion has been crushed out of the country. What goes by that name is the gossip of the town-concierge, or obscure village cabals and schemings.

I am quite aware that the law-abiding spirit is the slow growth of ages, and that a serious mischief like this cannot be repaired in a short generation. I know that even now the Italian code of criminal procedure, that tragic farce, is under revision. I know, moreover, that there are stipendiary magistrates in south Italy whose discernment and integrity would do honour to our British courts. But—take the case out of their hands into a higher tribunal, and you may put your trust in God, or in your purse. Justice hereabouts is in the same condition as it was in Egypt at the time of Lord Dufferin's report: a mockery.

It may be said that it does not concern aliens to make such criticism. A fatuous observation! Everything concerns everybody. The foreigner in Italy, if he is wise, will familiarize himself not only with the cathedrals to be visited, but also, and primarily, with the technique of legal bribery and subterfuge—with the methods locally employed for escaping out of the meshes of the law. Otherwise he may find unpleasant surprises in store for him. Had Mr. Mercer made it his business to acquire some rudiments of this useful knowledge, he would never have undergone that outrageous official ill-treatment which has become a byword in the annals of international amenities. And if these strictures be considered too severe, let us see what Italians themselves have to say. In 1900 was published a book called "La Quistione Meridionale" (What's Wrong with the South), that throws a flood of light upon local conditions. It contains the views of twenty-seven of the most prominent men in the country as to how south Italian problems should be faced and solved. Nearly all of them deplore the lack of justice. Says Professor Colajanni: "To heal the south, we require an honest, intelligent and sagacious government, *which we have not got.*" And Lombroso: "In the south it is necessary to introduce justice, *which does not exist, save in favour of certain classes.*"

I am tempted to linger on this subject, not without reason. These people and their attitude towards life will remain an enigma to the traveller, until he has acquainted himself with the law of the land and seen with his own eyes something of the atrocious misery which its administration involves. A murderer like Musolino, crowned with an aureole of saintliness, would be an anomaly in England. We should think it rather paradoxical to hear a respectable old farmer recommending his boys to shoot a policeman, whenever they safely can. On the spot, things begin to wear a different aspect. Musolino is no more to be blamed than a child who has been systematically misguided by his parents; and if these people, much as they love their homes and families, are all potential Musolinos, they have good reasons for it—excellent reasons.

No south Italian living at this present moment, be he of what social class you please—be he of the gentlest blood or most refined culture—is *a priori* on the side of the policeman. No; not *a priori*. The abuses of the executive are too terrific to warrant such an attitude. Has not the entire police force of Naples, up to its very head, been lately proved to be in the pay of the camorra; to say nothing of its connection with what Messrs. King and Okey euphemistically call "the unseen hand at Rome"—a hand which is held out for blackmail, and not vainly, from the highest ministerial benches? Under such conditions, the populace becomes profoundly distrustful of the powers that be, and such distrust breeds bad citizens. But so things will remain, until the bag-and-baggage policy is applied to the whole code of criminal procedure, and to a good half of its present administrators.

The best of law-systems, no doubt, is but a compromise. Science being one thing, and public order another, the most enlightened of legislators may well tremble to engraft the fruits of modern psychological research upon the tree of law, lest the scion prove too vigorous for the aged vegetable. But some compromises are better than others; and the Italian code, which reads like a fairy tale and works like a Fury, is as bad a one as human ingenuity can devise. If a prisoner escape punishment, it is due not so much to his innocence as to some access of sanity or benevolence on the part of the judge, who courageously twists the law in his favour. Fortunately, such humane exponents of the code are common enough; were it otherwise, the prisons, extensive as they are, would have to be considerably enlarged. But that ideal judge who shall be paid as befits his grave calling, who shall combine the honesty and common sense of the north with the analytical acumen of the south, has yet to be evolved. What interests the student of history is that things hereabouts have not changed by a hair since the days of Demosthenes and those preposterous old Hellenic tribunals. Not by a single hair! On the one hand, we have a deluge of subtle disquisitions on "jurisprudence," "personal responsibility" and so forth; on the other, the sinister tomfoolery known as *law*—that is, babble, corruption, palæolithic ideas of what constitutes evidence, and a court-procedure that reminds one of Gilbert and Sullivan at their best.

There was a report in the papers not long ago of the trial of an old married couple, on the charge of murdering a young girl. The bench dismissed the case, remarking that there was not a particle of evidence against them; they had plainly been exemplary citizens all their long lives. They had spent five years in prison awaiting trial. Five years, and innocent! It stands to reason that such abuses disorganize the family, especially in Italy, where the "family" means much more than it does in England; the land lies barren, and savings are wasted in paying lawyers and bribing greedy court officials. What are this worthy couple to think of *Avanti, Savoia!* once they have issued from their dungeon?

I read, in yesterday's Parliamentary Proceedings, of an honourable member (Aprile) rising to ask the Minister of Justice (Gallini) whether the time has not come to proceed with the trial of "Signori Camerano and their co-accused," who have been in prison for six years, charged with voluntary homicide. Whereto His Excellency sagely replies that "la magistratura ha avuto i suoi motivi"—the magistrates have had their reasons. Six years in confinement, and perhaps innocent! Can one wonder, under such circumstances, at the anarchist schools of Prato and elsewhere? Can one wonder if even a vindictive and corrupt rag like the socialistic "Avanti" occasionally prints frantic protests of quasi-righteous indignation? And not a hundredth part of such accused persons can cause a Minister of the Crown to be interpellated on their behalf. The others suffer silently and often die, forgotten, in their cells.

And yet—how seriously we take this nation! Almost as seriously as we take ourselves. The reason is that most of us come to Italy too undiscerning, too reverent; in the pre-critical and pre-humorous stages. We arrive here, stuffed with Renaissance ideals or classical lore, and viewing the present through coloured spectacles. We arrive here, above all things, too young; for youth loves to lean on tradition and to draw inspiration from what has gone before; youth finds nothing more difficult than to follow Goethe's advice about grasping that living life which shifts and fluctuates about us. Few writers are sufficiently detached to laugh at these people as they, together with ourselves, so often and so richly deserve. I spoke of the buffoonery of Italian law; I might have called it a burlesque. The trial of the ex-minister Nasi: here was a *cause célèbre* conducted by the highest tribunal of the land; and if it was not a burlesque—why, we must coin a new word for what is.

XXXIV

MALARIA

A BLACK snake of alarming dimensions, one of the monsters that still infest the Calabrian lowlands, glided across the roadway while I was waiting for the post carriage to drive me to Caulonia from its railway station. Auspicious omen! It carried my thought from old Æsculapius to his modern representatives—to that school of wise and disinterested healers who are ridding these regions of their curse, and with whom I was soon to have some nearer acquaintance.

We started at last, in the hot hours of the morning, and the road at first skirts the banks of the Alaro, the Sagra of old, on whose banks was fought the fabled battle between the men of Croton and Locri. Then it begins to climb upwards. My companion was a poor peasant woman, nearly blind (from malaria, possibly). Full of my impressions of yesterday, I promptly led the conversation towards the subject of Musolino. She had never spoken to him, she said, or even seen him. But she got ten francs from him, all the same. In dire distress, some years ago, she had asked a friend in the mountains to approach the brigand on her behalf. The money was long in coming, she added, but of course it came in the end. He always helped poor people, even those outside his own country.

The site of the original Caulonia is quite uncertain. Excavations now going on at Monasterace, some ten miles further on, may decide that the town lay there. Some are in favour of the miserable village of Focà, near at hand; or of other sites. The name of Focà seems to point, rather, to a settlement of the regenerator Nicephorus Phocas. Be that as it may, the present town of Caulonia used to be called Castelvetere, and it appropriated the Greek name in accordance with a custom which has been largely followed hereabouts.*

* It is represented with two towers in Peutinger's Tables. But these, says an editor, should have been given to the neighbouring Scilatio, for Caulon was in ruins at the time of Pliny, and is not even mentioned by Ptolemy. Servius makes another mistake; he confuses the Calabrian Caulon with a locality of the same name near Capua.

It contains some ten thousand inhabitants, amiable, intelligent and distinguished by a *philoxenia* befitting the traditions of men who sheltered Pythagoras in his hour of need. As at Rossano, Catanzaro and many other Calabrian towns, there used to be a ghetto of Jews here; the district is still called "La Giudeca"; their synagogue was duly changed into a church of the Madonna.

So much I learn from Montorio, who further informs me that the ubiquitous Saint Peter preached here on his way to Rome, and converted the people to Christianity; and that the town can boast of three authentic portraits of the Mother of God painted by Saint Luke ("Lukas me pinxit"). One is rather bewildered by the number of these masterpieces in Italy, until one realizes, as an old ecclesiastical writer has pointed out, that "the Saint, being excellent in his art, could make several of them in a few days, to correspond to the great devotion of those early Christians, fervent in their love to the Great Mother of God. Whence we may believe that to satisfy their ardent desires he was continually applying himself to this task of so much glory to Mary and her blessed Son." But the sacristan of the church at Caulonia, to whom I applied for information regarding these local treasures, knew nothing about them, and his comments gave me the impression that he has relapsed into a somewhat pagan way of regarding such matters.

You may obtain a fairly good view of Caulonia from the southeast; or again, from the neighbouring hillock of San Vito. The town lies some 300 metres above sea-level on a platform commanding the valleys of the Amusa and Alaro. This position, which was clearly chosen for its strategic value, unfortunately does not allow it to expand, and so the inhabitants are deprived of that public garden which they amply deserve. At the highest point lies a celebrated old castle wherein, according to tradition, Campanella was imprisoned for a while. In the days of Pacicchelli, it was a fine place—"magnifico nelle regole di Fortezza, con cinque baloardi provveduti di cannoni di bronzo, ed una riccha Armeria, degna habitazione di don Carlo Maria Carrafa, Prencipe della Roccella, che se ne intitola Marchese." Mingled with the stones of its old walls they have recently found skeletons—victims, possibly, of the same macabre superstition to which the blood-drenched masonry of the Tower of London bears witness. Here, too, have been unearthed terra-cotta lamps and other antiquities. What are we to surmise from this? That it was a Roman foundation? Or that the malaria in older times forced Caulonia to wander towards healthier inland heights after the example of Sybaris-Terranova, and that the Romans continued to occupy this same site? Or, assuming Castelvetere to date only from mediæval times, that these ancient relics found their way into it accidentally? The low-lying district of Foca, at this day, is certainly very malarious, whereas the death-rate up here is only about 12 per 1000.

Dr. Francesco Genovese of Caulonia, to whom I am indebted for much kindness and who is himself a distinguished worker in the humanitarian mission of combating malaria, has published, among other interesting pamphlets, one which deals with this village of Focà, a small place of about 200 inhabitants, surrounded by fertile orange and vine plantations near the mouth of the Alaro. His researches into its vital statistics for the half-century ending 1902 reveal an appalling state of affairs. Briefly summarized, they amount to this, that during this period there were 391 births and 516 deaths. In other words, the village, which in 1902 ought to have contained between 600 and 800 inhabitants, not only failed to progress, but devoured its original population of 200; and not only them, but also 125 fresh immigrants who had entered the region from the healthy uplands, lured by the hope of gaining a little money during the vintage season.

A veritable Moloch!

Had the old city of Caulonia, numbering perhaps 20,000 inhabitants, stood here under such conditions of hygiene, it would have been expunged off the face of the earth in fifty years.

Yet—speaking of malaria in general—a good deal of evidence has been brought together to show that the disease has been endemic in Magna Græcia for two thousand years, and the customs of the Sybarites seem to prove that they had some acquaintance with marsh fever, and tried to guard against it. "Whoever would live long," so ran their proverb, "must see neither the rising nor the setting sun." A queer piece of advice, intelligible only if the land was infested with malaria. Many of their luxurious habits assume another import, on this hypothesis. Like the inhabitants of the malarious Etruscan region, they were adepts at draining, and their river is described, in one of the minor works attributed to Galen, as "rendering men infertile"—a characteristic result of malaria. What is still more significant is that their new town Thurii, built on the heights, was soon infected, and though twice repeopled, decayed away. And that they had chosen the heights for their relative healthfulness we can infer from Strabo, who says that Paestum, a colony from Sybaris, was removed further inland from the shore, on account of the pestilential climate of the lowlands. But the Ionian shores cannot have been as deadly as they now are. We calculate, for example, that the town walls of Croton measured eighteen kilometres in circumference, a figure which the modern visitor to Cotrone only brings himself to believe when he remembers what can be actually proved of other Hellenic colonies, such as Syracuse. Well, the populace of so large a city requires a surrounding district to supply it with agricultural produce. The Marchesato, the vast tract bordering on Cotrone, is now practically uninhabitable; the population (including the town) has sunk to 45 to the square kilometre. That is malaria.

Or rather, only one side of the evil. For these coastlands attract rural labourers who descend from the mountains during the season of hay-making or fruit-harvest, and then return infected to their homes. One single malarious patient may inoculate an entire village, hitherto immune, granted the anophelines are there to propagate the mischief. By means of these annual migrations the scourge has spread, in the past. And so it spreads to-day, whenever possible. Of forty labourers that left Caulonia for Cotrone in 1908 all returned infected save two, who had made liberal use of quinine as a prophylactic. Fortunately, there are no anophelines at Caulonia.

Greatly, indeed, must this country have changed since olden days; and gleaning here and there among the ancients, Dr. Genovese has garnered some interesting facts on this head. The coast-line, now unbroken sand, is called *rocky*, in several regions, by Strabo, Virgil and Persius Flaccus; of the two harbours of Locri, of that of Metapontum, Caulonia and other cities, nothing remains; the promontory of Cocynthum (Stilo)—described as the longest promontory in Italy— together with other capes, has been washed away by the waves or submerged under silt carried down from the hills; islands, like that of Calypso which is described in Vincenzo Pascale's book (1796), and mentioned by G. Castaldi (1842), have clean vanished from the map.

The woodlands have retired far inland; yet here at Caulonia, says Thucydides, was prepared the timber for the fleets of Athens. The rivers, irregular and spasmodic torrents, must have flowed with more equal and deeper current, since Pliny mentions five of them as navigable; snow, very likely, covered the mountain tops; the rainfall was clearly more abundant—one of the sights of Locri was its daily rainbow; the cicadas of the territory of Reggio are said to have been "dumb," on account of the dampness of the climate. They are anything but dumb nowadays.

Earth-movements, too, have tilted the coast-line up and down, and there is evidence to show that while the Tyrrhenian shore has been raised by these oscillations, the Ionian has sunk. Not long ago four columns were found in the sea at Cotrone two hundred yards from the beach; old sailors remember another group of columns visible at low tide near Caulonia. It is quite possible that the Ionian used to be as rocky as the other shore, and this gradual sinking of the coast must have retarded the rapid outflow of the rivers, as it has done in the plain of Paestum and in the Pontine marshes, favouring malarious conditions. Earthquakes have helped in the work; that of 1908 lowered certain parts of the Calabrian shore opposite Messina by about one metre. Indeed, though earthquakes have been known to raise the soil and thereby improve it, the Calabrian ones have generally had a contrary effect. The terrific upheavals of 1783-1787 produced two hundred and fifteen lakes in the country; they were drained away in a style most creditable to the Bourbons, but there followed an epidemic of malaria which carried off 18,000 people!

These Calabrian conditions are only part of a general change of climate which seems to have taken place all over Italy; a change to which Columella refers when, quoting Saserna, he says that formerly the vine and olive could not prosper "by reason of the severe winter" in certain places where they have since become abundant, "thanks to a milder temperature." We never hear of the frozen Tiber nowadays, and many remarks of the ancients as to the moist and cold climate seem strange to us. Pliny praises the chestnuts of Tarentum; I question whether the tree could survive the hot climate of to-day. Nobody could induce "splendid beeches" to grow in the *lowlands* of Latium, yet Theophrastus, a botanist, says that they were drawn from this region for shipbuilding purposes. This gradual desiccation has probably gone on for long ages; so Signor Cavara has discovered old trunks of white fir in districts of the Apennines where such a plant could not possibly grow to-day.

A change to a dry and warm atmosphere is naturally propitious to malaria, granted sufficient water remains to propagate the mosquito. And the mosquito contents itself with very little—the merest teacupful.

Returning to old Calabria, we find the woods of Locri praised by Proclus—woods that must have been of coniferous timber, since

Virgil lauds their resinous pitch. Now the Aleppo pine produces pitch, and would still flourish there, as it does in the lowlands between Taranto and Metaponto; the classical Sila pitch-trees, however, could not grow at this level any more. Corroborative evidence can be drawn from Theocritus, who mentions heath and arbutus as thriving in the marine thickets near Cotrone—mountain shrubs, nowadays, that have taken refuge in cooler uplands, together with the wood-pigeon which haunted the same jungles. It is true that he hints at marshes near Cotrone, and, indeed, large tracts of south Italy are described as marshy by the ancients; they may well have harboured the anopheles mosquito from time immemorial, but it does not follow that they were malarious.

Much of the healthy physical conditions may have remained into the Middle Ages or even later; it is strange to read, for example, in Edrisius, of the pitch and tar that were exported to all parts from the Bradano river, or of the torrential Sinno that "ships enter this river—it offers excellent anchorage"; odd, too, to hear of coral fisheries as late as the seventeenth century at Rocella Ionica, where the waves now slumber on an even and sandy beach.

But malaria had made insidious strides, meanwhile. Dr. Genovese thinks that by the year 1691 the entire coast was malarious and abandoned like now, though only within the last two centuries has man actively co-operated in its dissemination. So long as the woodlands on the plains are cut down or grazed by goats, relatively little damage is done; but it spells ruin to denude, in a country like this, the steep slopes of their timber. Whoever wishes to know what mischief the goats, those picturesque but pernicious quadrupeds, can do to a mountainous country, should study the history of St. Helena.* Man, with his charcoal-burning, has completed the disaster. What happens? The friable rock, no longer sustained by plant-life, crashes down with each thunderstorm, blocks up the valleys, devastating large tracts of fertile land; it creates swamps in the lowlands, and impedes the outflow of water to the sea. These ravenous *fiumare* have become a feature in Calabrian scenery; underneath one of the most terrible of them lies the birthplace of Praxiteles. Dry or half-dry during the warm months, and of formidable breadth, such torrent-beds—the stagnant water at their skirts—are ideal breeding-places for the anophelines from their

---

* By J.C. Melliss (London, 1875). Thanks to the goats, Maltese fever has lately been introduced into Calabria.

mouth up to a height of 250 metres. So it comes about that, within recent times, rivers have grown to be the main arteries of malaria. And there are rivers galore in Calabria. The patriotic Barrius enumerates 110 of them—Father Fiore, less learned, or more prudent, not quite so many. Deforestation and malaria have gone hand in hand here, as in Greece, Asia Minor, North Africa, and other countries.

Thus year after year, from one cause or another, the conditions have become more favourable for the disease to do its fatal work.

That much of this harm has been done quite lately can often be proved. At Caulonia, for instance, the woodlands are known to have reached the shore a hundred years ago, and there are bare tracts of land still bearing the name of "foresta." In a single summer (1807) a French regiment stationed at Cosenza lost 800 men from fever, and when Rath visited the town in 1871 it was described to him as a "vast hospital" during the hot months; nevertheless, says he, the disease has only been so destructive during the last two centuries, for up to that time the forests touched the outskirts of the town and regulated the Crati-bed, preventing the formation of marshes. The literary record of Cosenza is one of exceptional brilliance; for acute and original thought this town can hardly be surpassed by any other of its size on earth. Were statistics available, I have not the slightest doubt that fever could be shown to be largely responsible for the withering of its spiritual life.

The same fate—the same relapse from prosperity to decay—and for the same reasons, has overtaken many other riverside villages, among them that of Tarsia, the Caprasia of the Antonine Itinerary. "It was described to us," says Rath, "as the most miserable and dirty village in Calabria; but we found it worse." It remains, to-day, a highly infected and altogether pitiable place, concerning which I have made certain modest researches that would require, none the less, a chapter to themselves. . . .

Perhaps I have already said over-much on the subject. An Englishman unacquainted with malaria might think so, oblivious of the fact that Sir Ronald Ross has called it "perhaps the most important of human diseases." But let him go to a malarious country and see with his own eyes something of the degradation it involves; how it stamps its accursed imprimatur upon man and nature alike! It is the blight of youth—the desert-maker. A well-known Italian senator has declared that the story of south Italy is, was, and will be the story of malaria; and the greater part of Calabria will certainly remain an enigma to the traveller who ignores what is meant by this plague.

Malaria is the key to a correct understanding of the landscape; it explains the inhabitants, their mode of life, their habits, their history.

XXXV

CAULONIA TO SERRA

"HOW do you treat your malaria patients?" I once enquired of a doctor in India.

A few good stiff doses, he said, when the attack is on; that generally settles them. If not, they can begin again. To take quinine as a prophylactic, he considered folly. It might grow into a habit; you never know. . . .

It is to be hoped that such types are extinct, out there. They are extinct hereabouts. None but an ignorant person would now traverse malarious tracts in summer without previous quininization; or, if infected, deal with the disease otherwise than by an amply protracted treatment of cure. Yet it is only quite lately that we have gained our knowledge of a proper use of the drug; and this accounts for the great mortality long after its specific effects had been recognized by the profession. It was given both inefficiently and insufficiently. It was sold at a prohibitive price. The country people were distrustful; so-and-so had taken it for three or four days; he had improved, yes; but the fever was on him once more. Why waste money on such experiments?

I remember accosting a lad, anæmic, shivering with the tertian, and marked by that untimely senility which is the sign-manual of malaria. I suggested quinine.

"I don't take doctors' stuff," he said. "Even if I wanted to, my father would not let me. And if he did, there's no money to pay for it. And if there were, it would do no good. He's tried it himself."

"Well, but how are you feeling?"

"Oh, all right. There's nothing much the matter with me. Just the bad air."

Such types, too, are practically extinct nowadays; the people are being educated to recognize their peril and how to avoid it; they begin to follow Professor Celli's advice in the matter of regarding quinine as their "daily bread." For since the discovery of the anophelic origin of malaria many devices have been put into execution to combat the disease, not the least of them being a popularized teaching of its causes and consequences by means of pamphlets, lectures to school-children, and so forth.

Now, you may either fight the anopheles—the vehicle, or the disease itself. The first entails putting the country into such a state that the mosquito finds it unpleasant to live there, a labour of Hercules. Yet large sums are being expended in draining marshy tracts, regulating river-beds and afforesting bare spaces; and if you are interested in such works, you will do well to see what is going on at Metaponto at this moment. (A considerable portion of the Government grant for these purposes has lately been deflected for use in the Tripolitan war.) Exemplary fines are also imposed for illicit timber-cutting and grazing—in those towns, at least, where the magistrate has sufficient sense to perceive the ulterior benefits to be derived from what certainly entails a good deal of temporary hardship on poor people. Certain economic changes are helping in this work; so the wealth imported from America helps to break up the big properties, those latifundia which, says an Italian authority, "are synonymous with malaria." The ideal condition—the extirpation of anophelines—will never be attained; nor is it of vital importance that it should be.

Far more pressing is the protection of man against their attacks. Wonderful success has crowned the wire-netting of the windows—an outcome of the classical experiments of 1899, in the Roman Campagna.

But chiefest and most urgent of all is the cure of the infected population. In this direction, results astonishing—results well-nigh incredible—have attended the recently introduced governmental sale of quinine. In the year 1895 there were 16,464 deaths from malaria throughout Italy. By 1908 the number had sunk to 3463. Eloquent figures, that require no comment! And, despite the fact that the drug is now sold at a merely nominal rate or freely given away to the needy—nay, thrust down the very throats of the afflicted peasantry by devoted gentlemen who scour the plains with ambulances during the deadly season—despite this, the yearly profits from its sale are amounting to about three-quarters of a million francs.

So these forlorn regions are at last beginning to revive.

And returning to Focà, of whose dreadful condition up to 1902 (year of the introduction of Government quinine) I have just spoken, we find that a revolution has taken place. Between that year and

1908 the birth-rate more than doubled the death-rate. In 1908 some two hundred poor folks frequented the ambulance, nearly six kilogrammes of quinine being gratuitously distributed; not one of the natives of the place was attacked by the disease; and there was a single death—an old woman of eighty, who succumbed to senile decay.*

This is an example of what the new quinine-policy has done for Italy, in briefest space of time. Well may the nation be proud of the men who conceived this genial and beneficial measure and carried it through Parliament, and of those local doctors without whose enlightened zeal such a triumph could not have been achieved. . . .

Sir Ronald Ross's discovery, by the way, has been fruitful not only in practical humanitarian results. For instance, it has reduced North's laborious "Roman Fever" to something little better than a curiosity. And here, on these deserted shores that were once resplendent with a great civilization—here is the place to peruse Mr. W. M. Jones's studies on this subject. I will not give even the shortest précis of his conscientious researches nor attempt to picture their effect upon a mind trained in the old school of thought; suffice to say, that the author would persuade us that malaria is implicated, to an hitherto unsuspected extent, in the decline of ancient Greece and Rome. And he succeeds. Yes; a man accustomed to weigh evidence will admit, I think, that he has made out a suggestively strong case.

How puzzled we were to explain why the brilliant life of Magna Graecia was snuffed out suddenly, like a candle, without any appreciably efficient cause—how we listened to our preachers cackling about the inevitable consequences of Sybaritic luxury, and to the warnings of sage politicians concerning the dangers of mere town-patriotism as opposed to worthier systems of confederation! How we drank it all in! And how it warmed the cockles of our hearts to think that we were not vicious, narrow-minded heathens, such as these!

And now a vulgar gnat is declared to be at the bottom of the whole mystery.

Crudely disconcerting, these scientific discoveries. Or is it not rather hard to be dragged to earth in this callous fashion, while soaring heavenward on the wings of our edifying reflections? For the

---

* Doctor Genovese's statistical investigations have brought an interesting little fact to light. In the debilitating pre-quinine period there was a surplus of female births; now, with increased healthfulness, those of the males preponderate.

rest—the old, old story; a simple, physical explanation of what used to be an enigma brimful of moral significance.

That Mr. Jones's facts and arguments will be found applicable to other decayed races in the old and new worlds is highly probable. Meanwhile, it takes one's breath away quite sufficiently to realize that they apply to Hellas and her old colonies on these shores.

" 'Autos. Strange! My interest waxes. Tell me then, what affliction, God or Devil, wiped away the fair life upon the globe, the beasts, the birds, the delectable plantations, and all the blithe millions of the human race? What calamity fell upon them?'

" 'Eschata. A gnat.'

" 'Autos. A gnat?'

" 'Eschata. Even so.' "

Thus I wrote, while yet unaware that such pests as anophelines existed on earth. . . .

At the same time, I think we must be cautious in following certain deductions of our author; that theory of brutality, for example, as resulting from malaria. Speaking of Calabria, I would almost undertake to prove, from the archives of law-courts, that certain of the most malarial tracts are precisely those in which there is least brutality of any kind. Cotrone, for instance. . . . The *delegato* (head of the police) of that town is so young—a mere boy—that I marvelled how he could possibly have obtained a position which is usually filled by seasoned and experienced officers. He was a "son of the white hen," they told me; that is, a socially favoured individual, who was given this job for the simple reason that there was hardly any serious work for him to do. Cosenza, on the other hand, has a very different reputation nowadays. And it is perfectly easy to explain how malaria might have contributed to this end. For the disease—and herein lies its curse—lowers both the physical and social standard of a people; it breeds misery, poverty and ignorance—fit soil for callous rapacity.

But how about his theory of "pessimism" infecting the outlook of generations of malaria-weakened sages? I find no trace of pessimism here, not even in its mild Buddhistic form. The most salient mental trait of cultured Calabrians is a subtle detachment and contempt of illusions—whence their time-honoured renown as abstract thinkers and speculators. This derives from a philosophic view of life and entails, naturally enough, the outward semblance of gravity—a Spanish gravity, due not so much to a strong graft of Spanish blood and customs during the viceregal period, as to actual affinities with the race of Spain. But this gravity has nothing in common with pessimism, antagonistic though it be to those outbursts of irresponsible optimism engendered under northern skies by copious food, or beer.

To reach the uplands of Fabbrizia and Serra, whither I was now bound, I might have utilized the driving road from Gioioso, on the Reggio side of Caulonia. But that was everybody's route. Or I might have gone *via* Stilo, on the other side. But Stilo with its memories of Campanella—a Spanish type, this!—and of Otho II, its winding track into the beech-clad heights of Ferdinandea, was already familiar to me. I elected to penetrate straight inland by the shortest way; a capable muleteer at once presented himself.

We passed through one single village, Ragona; leaving those of S. Nicola and Nardo di Pace on the right. The first of them is celebrated for its annual miracle of the burning olive, when, armed to the teeth (for some ancient reason), the populace repairs to the walls of a certain convent out of which there grows an olive tree: at its foot is kindled a fire whose flames are sufficient to scorch all the leaves, but behold! next day the foliage is seen to glow more bravely green than ever. Perhaps the roots of the tree are near some cistern. These mountain villages, hidden under oaks and vines, with waters trickling through their lanes, a fine climate and a soil that bears everything needful for life, must be ideal habitations for simple folks. In some of them, the death-rate is as low as 7 : 1000. Malaria is unknown here: they seem to fulfil all the conditions of a terrestrial paradise.

There is a note of joyous vigour in this landscape. The muletrack winds in and out among the heights, through flowery meadows grazed by cattle and full of buzzing insects and butterflies, and along hill-sides cunningly irrigated; it climbs up to heathery summits and down again through glades of chestnut and ilex with mossy trunks, whose shadow fosters strange sensations of chill and gloom. Then out again, into the sunshine of waving corn and poppies.

For a short while we stumbled along a torrent-bed, and I grew rather sad to think that it might be the last I should see for some time to come, my days in this country being now numbered. This one was narrow. But there are others, interminable in length and breadth. Interminable! No breeze stirs in those deep depressions through which the merest thread of milky water trickles disconsolately. The sun blazes overhead and hours pass, while you trudge through the fiery inferno; scintillations of heat rise from the stones and still you crawl onwards, breathless and footsore, till eyes are dazed and senses reel. One may well say bad things of these torrid deserts of pebbles which, up till lately, were the only highways from the lowlands into the mountainous parts. But they are sweet in memory. One calls to mind the wild savours that hang in the stagnant air; the cloven hill-sides, seamed with gorgeous patches of russet and purple and green; the spectral tamarisks, and the glory of coral-tinted oleanders rising in solitary tufts of beauty, or flaming congregations, out of the pallid waste of boulders.

After exactly six hours Fabbrizia was reached—a large place whose name, like that of Borgia, Savelli, Carafa and other villages on these southern hills, calls up associations utterly non-Calabrian; Fabbrizia, with pretentious new church and fantastically dirty side-streets. It lies at the respectable elevation of 900 metres, on the summit of a monstrous landslide which has disfigured the country.

While ascending along the flank of this deformity I was able to see how the authorities have attempted to cope with the mischief and arrest further collapses. This is what they have done. The minute channels of water, that might contribute to the disintegration of the soil by running into this gaping wound from the sides or above, have been artfully diverted from their natural courses; trees and shrubs are planted at its outskirts in order to uphold the earth at these spots by their roots—they have been protected by barbed wire from the grazing of cattle; furthermore, a multitude of wickerwork dykes are thrown across the accessible portions of the scar, to collect the downward-rushing material and tempt winged plant-seeds to establish themselves on the ledges thus formed. To bridle this runaway mountain is no mean task, for such *frane* are like rodent ulcers, ever enlarging at the edges. With the heat, with every shower of rain, with every breath of wind, the earth crumbles away; there is an eternal trickling, day and night, until some huge boulder is exposed which crashes down, loosening everything in its wild career; a single tempest may disrupture what the patience and ingenuity of years have contrived.

Three more hours or thereabouts will take you to Serra San Bruno along the backbone of southern Italy, through cultivated lands and pasture and lonely stretches of bracken, once covered by woodlands.

It may well be that the townlet has grown up around, or rather near, the far-famed Carthusian monastery. I know nothing of its history save that it has the reputation of being one of the most bigoted places in Calabria—a fact of which the sagacious General

Manhes availed himself when he devised his original and effective plan of chastising the inhabitants for a piece of atrocious conduct on their part. He caused all the local priests to be arrested and imprisoned; the churches were closed, and the town placed under what might be called an interdict. The natives took it quietly at first, but soon the terror of the situation dawned upon them. No religious marriages, no baptisms, no funerals—the comforts of heaven refused to living and dead alike. . . . The strain grew intolerable and, in a panic of remorse, the populace hunted down their own brigand-relations and handed them over to Manhes, who duly executed them, one and all. Then the interdict was taken off and the priests set at liberty; and a certain writer tells us that the people were so charmed with the General's humane and business-like methods that they forthwith christened him "Saint Manhes," a name which, he avers, has clung to him ever since.

The monastery lies about a mile distant; near at hand is a little artificial lake and the renowned chapel of Santa Maria. There was a time when I would have dilated lovingly upon this structure—a time when I probably knew as much about Carthusian convents as is needful for any of their inmates; when I studied Tromby's ponderous work and God knows how many more—ay, and spent two precious weeks of my life in deciphering certain crabbed MSS. of Tutini in the Brancacciana library—ay, and tested the spleenful Perrey's Ragioni del Regio Fisco, etc.," as to alleged land-grabbing propensities of this order—ay, and even pilgrimaged to Rome to consult the present general of the Carthusians (his predecessor, more likely) as to some administrative detail, all-important, which has wholly escaped my memory. Gone are those days of studious gropings into blind alleys! The current of zeal has slowed down or turned aside, maybe, into other channels. They who wish, will find a description of the pristine splendour of this monastery in various books by Pacicchelli; the catastrophe of 1783 was described by Keppel Craven and reported upon, with illustrations, by the Commission of the Naples Academy; and if you are of a romantic turn of mind, you will find a good story of the place, as it looked during the ruinous days of desolation, in Misasi's "Calabrian Tales."

It is now rebuilt on modern lines and not much of the original structure remains upright. I wandered about the precincts in the company of two white-robed French monks, endeavouring to reconstruct not the convent as it was in its younger days, but *them*. That older one, especially—he had known the world. . . .

Meat being forbidden, the godly brethren have a contract for fish to be brought up every day by the post-carriage from the distant Soverato. And what happens, I asked, when none are caught? "Eh bien, nous mangeons des macaroni!" Such a diet would never suit me. Let me retire to a monkery where carnivorous leanings may be indulged. Methinks I could pray more cheerfully with the prospect of a rational *déjeuner à la fourchette* looming ahead.

At the back of the monastery lies a majestic forest of white firs— nothing but firs; a unique region, so far as south and central Italy are concerned. I was there in the golden hour after sunset, and yet again in the twilight of dew-drenched morning; and it seemed to me that in this temple not made by hands there dwelt an enchantment more elemental, and more holy, than in the cloistered aisles hard by. This assemblage of solemn trees has survived, thanks to rare conditions of soil and climate. The land lies high; the ground is perennially moist and intersected by a horde of hills that join their waters to form the river Ancinale; frequent showers descend from above. Serra San Bruno has an uncommonly heavy rainfall. It lies in a vale occupying the site of a pleistocene lake, and the forest, now restricted to one side of the basin, encircled it entirely in olden days. At its margin they have established a manufactory which converts the wood into paper—blissful sight for the utilitarian.

Finding little else of interest in Serra, and hungering for the fleshpots of Cotrone, I descended by the postal diligence to Soverato, nearly a day's journey. Old Soverato is in ruins, but the new town seems to thrive in spite of being surrounded by deserts of malaria. While waiting for supper and the train to Cotrone, I strolled along the beach, and soon found myself sitting beside the bleached anatomy of some stranded leviathan, and gazing at the mountains of Squillace that glowed in the soft lights of sunset. The shore was deserted save for myself and a portly dogana-official who was playing with his little son—trying to amuse him by elephantine gambols on the sand, regardless of his uniform and manly dignity. Notwithstanding his rotundity, he was an active and resourceful parent, and enjoyed himself vastly; the boy pretending, as polite children sometimes do, to enter into the fun of the game.

XXXVI

MEMORIES OF GISSING

TWO new hotels have recently sprung up at Cotrone. With laudable patriotism, they are called after its great local champions, athletic and spiritual, in ancient days—Hotel Milo and Hotel Pythagoras. As such, they might be expected to make a strong appeal to the muscles and brains of their respective clients. I rather fancy that the chief customers of both are commercial travellers who have as little of the one as of the other, and to whom these fine names are Greek.

As for myself, I remain faithful to the "Concordia" which has twice already sheltered me within it walls.

The shade of George Gissing haunts these chambers and passages. It was in 1897 that he lodged here with that worthy trio: Gibbon, Lenormant and Cassiodorus. The chapters devoted to Cotrone are the most lively and characteristic in his "Ionian Sea." Strangely does the description of his arrival in the town, and his reception in the "Concordia," resemble that in Bourget's "Sensations."

The establishment has vastly improved since those days. The food is good and varied, the charges moderate; the place is spotlessly clean in every part—I could only wish that the hotels in some of our English country towns were up to the standard of the "Concordia" in this respect. "One cannot live without cleanliness," as the housemaid, assiduously scrubbing, remarked to me. It is also enlarged; the old dining-room, whose guests are so humorously described by him, is now my favourite bedroom, while those wretched oil-lamps sputtering on the wall have been replaced by a lavish use of electricity. One is hardly safe, however, in praising these inns over-much; they are so apt to change hands. So long as competition with the two others continues, the "Concordia" will presumably keep to its present level.

Of freaks in the dining-room, I have so far only observed one whom Gissing might have added to his collection. He is a *director* of some kind, and his method of devouring maccheroni I unreservedly admire—it displays that lack of all effort which distinguishes true art from false. He does not eat them with deliberate mastication; he does not even—like your ordinary amateur—drink them in separate gulps; but he contrives, by some swiftly-adroit process of levitation, that the whole plateful shall rise in a noiseless and unbroken flood from the table to his mouth, whence it glides down his gullet with the relentless ease of a river pouring into a cavern. Altogether, a series of films depicting him at work upon a meal would make the fortune of a picture-show company—in England. Not here, however; such types are too common to be remarked, the reason being that boys are seldom sent to boarding schools where stereotyped conventions of "good form" are held up for their imitation, but brought up at home by adoring mothers who care little for such externals or, if they do, have no great authority to enforce their views. On entering the world, these eccentricities in manner are proudly clung to, as a sign of manly independence.

Death has made hideous gaps in the short interval. The kindly Vice-Consul at Catanzaro is no more; the mayor of Cotrone, whose permit enabled Gissing to visit that orchard by the riverside, has likewise joined the majority; the housemaid of the "Concordia," the domestic serf with dark and fiercely flashing eyes—dead! And dead is mine hostess, "the stout, slatternly, sleepy woman, who seemed surprised at my demand for food, but at length complied with it."

But the little waiter is alive and now married; and Doctor Sculco still resides in his aristocratic *palazzo* up that winding way in the old town, with the escutcheon of a scorpion—portentous emblem for a doctor—over its entrance. He is a little greyer, no doubt; but the same genial and alert personage as in those days.

I called on this gentleman, hoping to obtain from him some reminiscences of Gissing, whom he attended during a serious illness.

"Yes," he replied, to my enquiries, "I remember him quite well; the young English poet who was ill here. I prescribed for him. Yes—yes! He wore his hair long."

And that was all I could draw from him. I have noticed more than once that Italian physicians have a stern conception of the Hippocratic oath: the affairs of their patients, dead or alive, are a sacred trust in perpetuity.

The town, furthermore, has undergone manifold improvements in those few years. Trees are being planted by the roadsides; electric light is everywhere and, best of all, an excellent water-supply has been led down from the cool heights of the Sila, bringing cleanliness, health and prosperity in its train. And a stately cement-bridge is being built over the Esaro, that "all but stagnant and wholly pestilential stream." The Esaro *glides pleasantly,* says the chronicler Nola Molisi. Perhaps it really glided, in his day.

One might do worse than spend a quiet month or two at Cotrone in the spring, for the place grows upon one: it is so reposeful and orderly. But not in winter. Gissing committed the common error of visiting south Italy at that season when, even if the weather will pass, the country and its inhabitants are not true to themselves. You must not come to these parts in winter time.

Nor yet in the autumn, for the surrounding district is highly malarious. Thucydides already speaks of these coastlands as depopulated (relatively speaking, I suppose), and under the Romans they recovered but little; they have only begun to revive quite lately.* Yet this town must have looked well enough in the twelfth century, since it is described by Edrisius as "a very old city, primitive and beautiful, prosperous and populated, in a smiling position, with walls of defence and an ample port for anchorage." I suspect that the history of Cotrone will be found to bear out Professor Celli's theory of the periodical recrudescences and abatements of malaria. However that may be, the place used to be in a deplorable state. Riedesel (1771) calls it "la ville la plus affreuse de l'Italie, et peut-être du monde entier"; twenty years later, it is described as "sehr ungesund . . . so ärmlich als möglich"; in 1808 it was "réduite à une population de trois mille habitants rongés par la misère, et les maladies qu'occasionne la stagnation des eaux qui autrefois fertilisaient ces belles campagnes." In 1828, says Vespoli, it contained only 3932 souls.

I rejoice to cite such figures. They show how vastly Cotrone, together with the rest of Calabria, has improved since the Bourbons were ousted. The sack of the town by their hero Cardinal Ruffo, described by Pepe and others, must have left long traces. "Horrible was the carnage perpetrated by these ferocious bands. Neither age nor sex nor condition was spared.... After two days of pillage accompanied by a multitude of excesses and cruelties, they erected, on the third day, a magnificent alter in the middle of a large square"—and here the Cardinal, clothed in his sacred purple, praised the good deeds of the past two days and then, raising his arms, displayed a

---

* Between 1815–1843, and in this single province of Catanzaro, there was an actual decline in the population of thirty-six towns and villages. Malaria!

crucifix, absolving his crew from the faults committed during the ardour of the sack, and blessed them.

I shall be sorry to leave these regions for the north, as leave them I must, in shortest time. The bathing alone would tempt me to prolong my stay, were it possible. Whereas Taranto, despite its situation, possesses no convenient beach, there are here, on either side of the town, leagues of shimmering sand lapped by tepid and caressing waves; it is a sunlit solitude; the land is your own, the sea your own, as far as eye can reach. One may well become an amphibian, at Cotrone.

The inhabitants of this town are well-mannered and devoid of the "ineffable" air of the Tarentines. But they are not a handsome race. Gissing says, à propos of the products of a local photographer, that it was "a hideous exhibition; some of the visages attained an incredible degree of vulgar ugliness." That is quite true. Old authors praise the beauty of the women of Cotrone, Bagnara, and other southern towns; for my part, I have seldom found good-looking women in the coastlands of Calabria; the matrons, especially, seem to favour that ideal of the Hottentot Venus which you may study in the Jardin des Plantes; they are decidedly centripetal. Of the girls and boys one notices only those who possess a peculiar trait: the eyebrows pencilled in a dead straight line, which gives them an almost hieratic aspect. I cannot guess from what race is derived this marked feature which fades away with age as the brows wax thicker and irregular in contour. We may call it Hellenic on the old-fashioned principle that everything attractive comes from the Greeks, while its opposite is ascribed to those unfortunate "Arabs" who, as a matter of fact, are a sufficiently fine-looking breed.

And there must be very little Greek blood left here. The town— among many similar vicissitudes—was peopled largely by Bruttians, after Hannibal had established himself here. In the Viceregal period, again, there was a great infusion of Spanish elements. A number of Spanish surnames still linger on the spot.

And what of Gissing's other friend, the amiable guardian of the cemetery? "His simple good nature and intelligence greatly won upon me. I like to think of him as still quietly happy amid his garden walls, tending flowers that grow over the dead at Cotrone."

Dead, like those whose graves he tended; like Gissing himself. He expired in February 1901—the year of the publication of the "Ionian Sea," and they showed me his tomb near the right side of the entrance; a poor little grave, with a wooden cross bearing a number, which will soon be removed to make room for another one.

This cemetery by the sea is a fair green spot, enclosed in a high wall and set with flowering plants and comely cypresses that look well against their background of barren clay-hills. Wandering here, I called to mind the decent cemetery of Lucera, and that of Manfredonia, built in a sleepy hollow at the back of the town which the monks in olden days had utilized as their kitchen garden (it is one of the few localities where deep soil can be found on that thirsty limestone plain); I remembered the Venosa burial-ground near the site of the Roman amphitheatre, among the tombs of which I had vainly endeavoured to find proofs that the name of Horace is as common here as that of Manfred in those other two towns; the Taranto cemetery, beyond the railway quarter, somewhat overloaded with pretentious ornaments; I thought of many cities of the dead, in places recently explored—that of Rossano, ill-kept within, but splendidly situated on a projecting spur that dominates the Ionian; of Caulonia, secluded among ravines at the back of the town. . . .

They are all full of character; a note in the landscape, with their cypresses darkly towering amid the pale and lowly olives; one would think the populace had thrown its whole poetic feeling into the choice of these sites and their embellishments. But this is not the case; they are chosen merely for convenience—not too far from habitations, and yet on ground that is comparatively cheap. Nor are they truly venerable, like ours. They date, for the most part, from the time when the Government abolished the old system of inhumation in churches—a system which, for the rest, still survives; there are over six hundred of these *fosse carnarie* in use at this moment, most of them in churches.

And a sad thought obtrudes itself in these oases of peace and verdure. The Italian law requires that the body shall be buried within twenty-four hours after decease (the French consider forty-eight hours too short a term, and are thinking of modifying their regulations in this respect): a doctor's certificate of death is necessary but often impossible to procure, since some five hundred Italian communities possess no medical man whatever. Add to this, the superstitions of ignorant country people towards the dead, testified to by extraordinary beliefs and customs which you will find in Pitré and other collectors of native lore—their mingled fear and hatred of a corpse, which prompts them to thrust it underground at the earliest possible opportunity. . . . Premature burial must be all too frequent here. I will not enlarge upon the theme of horror by relating what gravediggers have seen with their own eyes on disturbing old coffins; if only half what they tell me is true, it reveals a state of affairs not to be contemplated without shuddering pity, and one that calls for prompt legislation. Only last year a frightful case came to light in Sicily. *Videant Consules.*

Here, at the cemetery, the driving road abruptly ends; thenceforward there is merely a track along the sea that leads, ultimately, to Capo Nau, where stands a solitary column, last relic of the great temple of Hera. I sometimes follow it as far as certain wells that are sunk, Arab-fashion, into the sand, and dedicated to Saint Anne. Goats and cows recline here after their meagre repast of scorched grasses, and the shepherds in charge have voices so soft, and manners so gentle, as to call up suggestions of the Golden Age. These pastoral folk are the primitives of Cotrone. From father to son, for untold ages before Theocritus hymned them, they have kept up their peculiar habits and traditions; between them and the agricultural classes is a gulf as deep as between these and the citizens. Conversing with them, one marvels how the same occupation can produce creatures so unlike as these and the goat-boys of Naples, the most desperate *camorristi.*

The cows may well be descendants of the sacred cattle of Hera that browsed under the pines which are known to have clothed the bleak promontory. You may encounter them every day, wandering on the way to the town which they supply with milk; to avoid the dusty road, they march sedately through the soft wet sand at the water's edge, their silvery bodies outlined against a cærulean flood of sky and sea.

On this promenade I yesterday observed, slow-pacing beside the waves, a meditative priest, who gave me some details regarding the ruined church of which Gissing speaks. It lies in the direction of the cemetery, outside the town; "its lonely position," he says, "made it interesting, and the cupola of coloured tiles (like that of the cathedral of Amalfi) remained intact, a bright spot against the grey hills behind." This cupola has recently been removed, but part of the old walls serve as foundation for a new sanctuary, a sordid-looking structure with red-tiled roof: I am glad to have taken a view of it, some years ago, ere its transformation. Its patroness is the Madonna del Carmine—the same whose church in Naples is frequented by thieves and cut-throats, who make a special cult of this Virgin

Mother and invoke Her blessing on their nefarious undertakings.

The old church, he told me, was built in the middle of the seventeenth century; this new one, he agreed, might have been constructed on more ambitious lines, "but nowadays——" and he broke off, with eloquent aposiopesis.

It was the same, he went on, with the road to the cemetery; why should it not be continued right up to the cape of the Column as in olden days, over ground *dove ogni passo è una memoria*: where every footstep is a memory?

"Rich Italians," he said, "sometimes give away money to benefit the public. But the very rich—never! And at Cotrone, you must remember, every one belongs to the latter class."

We spoke of the Sila, which he had occasionally visited.

"What?" he asked incredulously, "you have crossed the whole of that country, where there is nothing to eat—nothing in the purest and most literal sense of that word? My dear sir! You must feel like Hannibal, after his passage of the Alps."

Those barren clay-hills on our right of which Gissing speaks (they are like the *balze* of the Apennines) annoyed him considerably; they were the malediction of the town, he declared. At the same time, they supplied him with the groundwork of a theory for which there is a good deal to be said. The old Greek city, he conjectured, must have been largely built of bricks made from their clay, which is once more being utilized for this purpose. How else account for its utter disappearance? Much of the finer buildings were doubtless of stone, and these have been worked into the fort, the harbour and *palazzi* of new Cotrone; but this would never account for the vanishing of a town nearly twelve miles in circumference. Bricks, he said, would explain the mystery; they had crumbled into dust ere yet the Romans rebuilt, with old Greek stones, the city on the promontory now occupied by the new settlement.

The modern palaces on the rising ground of the citadel are worthy of a visit; they are inhabited by some half-dozen "millionaires" who have given Cotrone the reputation of being the richest town of its size in Italy. So far as I can judge, the histories of some of these wealthy families would be curious reading.

"Gentlemen," said the Shepherd, "if you have designs of Trading, you must go another way; but if you're of the admired sort of Men, that have the thriving qualifications of Lying and Cheating, you're in the direct path to Business; for in this City no Learning flourisheth; Eloquence finds no room here; nor can Temperance, Good Manners, or any Vertue meet with a Reward; assure yourselves of finding but two sorts of Men, and those are the Cheated, and those that Cheat."

If gossip at Naples and elsewhere is to be trusted, old Petronius seems to have had a prophetic glimpse of the *dessus du panier* of modern Cotrone.

XXXVII

COTRONE

THE sun has entered the Lion. But the temperature at Cotrone is not excessive—five degrees lower than Taranto or Milan or London. One grows weary, none the less, of the deluge of implacable light that descends, day after day, from the æther. The glistering streets are all but deserted after the early hours of the morning. A few busy folks move about till midday on the pavements; and so do I—in the water. But the long hours following luncheon are consecrated to meditation and repose.

A bundle of Italian newspapers has preceded me hither; upon these I browse dispersedly, while awaiting the soft call to slumber. Here are some provincial sheets—the "Movement" of Castrovillari—the "New Rossano"—the "Bruttian" of Corigliano, with strong literary flavour. Astonishing how decentralized Italy still is, how brimful of purely local partriotism: what conception have these men of Rome as their capital? These articles often reflect a lively turmoil of ideas, well-expressed. Who pays for such journalistic ventures? Typography is cheap, and contributors naturally content themselves with the ample remuneration of appearing in print before their fellow-citizens; a considerable number of copies are exported to America. Yet I question whether the circulation of the "New Rossano," a fortnightly in its sixth year, can exceed five hundred copies.

But these venial and vapid Neapolitan dailies are my pet aversion. We know them, *nous autres*, with their odious personalities and playful blackmailing tactics; many "distinguished foreigners," myself included, could tell a tale anent that subject. Instead of descending to such matters, let me copy—it is too good to translate—a thrilling item of news from the chiefest of them, the *Mattino*, which touches, furthermore, upon the all-important subject of Calabrian progress.

"CETRARO. Per le continuate premure ed insistenze di questo egregio uffiziale postale Signor Rocca Francesco—che nulla lascia pel bene avviamento del nostro uffizio—presso l'on. Direzione delle poste di Cosenza, si è ottenuta una cassetta postale, che affissa lungo il Corso Carlo Pancaso, ci dà la bella commodità di imbucare le nostre corrispondenze per essere rilevate tre volte al giorno non solo, quanto ci evita persino la dolorosa e lunga via crucis che dovevamo percorrere qualvolta si era costretti d' imbuccare una lettera, essendo il nostro uffizio situato all' estremità del paese.

"Tributiamo perciò sincera lode al nostro caro uffiziale postale Sig. Rocca, e ci auguriamo che egli continui ancora al miglioramento dell' uffizio istesso, e mercè l' opera sua costante ed indefessa siamo sicuri che l' uffizio postale di Cetraro assurgerà fra non molto ad un' importanza maggiore di quella che attualmente."

The erection of a letter-box in the street of a small place of which 80 per cent of the readers have never so much as heard. . . . I begin to understand why the cultured Tarentines do not read these journals.

By far the best part of all such papers is the richly-tinted personal column, wherein lovers communicate with each other, or endeavour to do so. I read it conscientiously from beginning to end, admiring, in my physical capacity, the throbbing passion that prompts such public outbursts of confidence and, from a literary point of view, their lapidary style, model of condensation, impossible to render in English and conditioned by the hard fact that every word costs two sous. Under this painful material stress, indeed, the messages are sometimes crushed into a conciseness which the females concerned must have some difficulty in unperplexing: what on earth does the parsimonious *Flower* mean by his Delphic fourpenny worth, thus punctuated—

"(You have) not received. How. Safety."

One cannot help smiling at this circuitous and unromantic method of touching the hearts of ladies who take one's fancy; at the same time, it testifies to a resourceful vitality, striving to break through the barriers of Hispano-Arabic convention which surround the fair sex in this country. They are nothing if not poetic, these love-sick swains. *Arrow* murmurs: "My soul lies on your pillow, caressing you softly"; *Strawberry* laments that "as bird outside nest, I am alone and lost. What sadness," and *Star* finds the "Days eternal, till Thursday." And yet they often choose rather prosaic pseudonyms. Here is *Sahara* who "suffers from your silence," while *Asthma* is "anticipating one endless kiss," and *Old England* observing, more in sorrow than in anger, that he "waited vainly one whole hour."

But the sagacious *Cooked Lobster* desires, before commiting himself further, "a personal interview." He has perhaps been cooked once before.

Letters and numbers are best, after all. So thinks F. N. 13, who is utterly disgusted with his flame—

"Your silence speaks. Useless saying anything. Ça ira." And likewise 7776—B, a designing rogue and plainly a spendthrift, who wastes ninepence in making it clear that he "wishes to marry rich young lady, forgiving youthful errors." If I were the girl, I would prefer to take my chances with "Cooked Lobster."

"Will much-admired young-lady cherries-in-black-hat indicate method possible correspondence 10211, Post-Office?"

How many of these arrows, I wonder, reach their mark?

Ah, here are politics and News of the World, at last. A promising article on the "Direttissimo Roma-Napoli"—the railway line that is to connect the two towns by way of the Pontine Marshes. . . . Dear me! This reads very familiarly. . . . Why, to be sure, it is the identical dissertation, with a few changes by the office-boy, that has cropped up periodically in these pages for the last half-century, or whenever the railway was first projected. The line, as usual, is being projected more strenuously than before, and certain members of the government have gone so far as to declare. . . H'm! Let me try something else: "The Feminist Movement in England" by Our London Correspondent (who lives in a little side street off the Toledo); that sounds stimulating. . . . The advanced English Feminists—so it runs—are taking the lead in encouraging their torpid sisters on the Continent. . . . Hardly a day passes, that some new manifestation of the Feminist Movement. . . in fact, it may be avowed that the Feminist Movement in England . . .

The air is cooler, as I awake, and looking out of the window I perceive from the mellow light-effects that day is declining.

Towards this sunset hour the unbroken dome of the sky often undergoes a brief transformation. High-piled masses of cloud may then be seen accumulating over the Sila heights and gathering auxiliaries from every quarter; lightning is soon playing about the livid and murky vapours—you can hear the thunders muttering, up yonder, to some drenching downpour. But on the plain the sun continues to shine in vacuously benevolent fashion; nothing is felt of the tempest save unquiet breaths of wind that raise dust-eddies from the country roads and lash the sea into a mock frenzy of crisp little waves. It is the merest interlude. Soon the blue-black drifts have fled away from the mountains that stand out, clear and refreshed, in the twilight. The wind has died down, the storm is over and Cotrone thirsts, as ever, for rain that never comes. Yet they have a Madonna-picture here—a celebrated *black* Madonna, painted by Saint Luke—who "always procures rain, when prayed to."

Once indeed the tail of a shower must have passed overhead, for there fell a few sad drops. I hurried abroad, together with some other citizens to observe the phenomenon. There was no doubt about the matter; it was genuine rain; the drops lay, at respectable intervals, on the white dust of the station turnpike. A boy, who happened to be passing in a cart, remarked that if the shower could have been collected into a saucer or some other small receptacle, it might have sufficed to quench the thirst of a puppy-dog.

I usually take a final dip in the sea, at this time of the evening. After that, it is advisable to absorb an ice or two—they are excellent, at Cotrone—and a glass of Strega liqueur, to ward off the effects of over-work. Next, a brief promenade through the clean, well-lighted streets and now populous streets, or along the boulevard Margherita to view the rank and fashion taking the air by the murmuring waves, under the cliff-like battlements of Charles the Fifth's castle; and so to dinner.

This meal marks the termination of my daily tasks; nothing serious is allowed to engage my attention, once that repast is ended; I call for a chair and sit down at one of the small marble-topped tables in the open street and watch the crowd as it floats around me, smoking a Neapolitan cigar and imbibing, alternately, ices and black coffee until, towards midnight, a final bottle of *vino di Cirò* is uncorked—fit seal for the labours of the day.

One might say much in praise of Calabrian wine. The land is full of pleasant surprises for the œnophilist, and one of these days I hope to embody my experiences in the publication of a wine-chart of the province with descriptive text running alongside—the purchasers of which, if few, will certainly be of the right kind. The good Dr. Barth—all praise to him!—has already done something of the kind for certain parts of Italy, but does not so much as mention Calabria. And yet here nearly every village has its own type of wine and every self-respecting family its own peculiar method of preparation, little known though they be outside the place of production, on account of the octroi laws which strangle internal trade and remove all stimulus to manufacture a good article for export. This wine of Cirò, for instance, is purest nectar, and so is that which grows still nearer at hand in the classical vale of the Neto and was praised, long ago, by old Pliny; and so are at least two dozen more. For even as Gregorovius says that the smallest Italian community possesses its duly informed antiquarian, if you can but put your hand upon him, so, I may be allowed to add, every little place hereabouts can boast of at least one individual who will give you good wine, provided—provided you go properly to work to find him.

Now although, when young, the Calabrian Bacchus has a wild eyed *beauté du diable* which appeals to one's expansive moods, he already begins to totter, at seven years of age, in sour, decrepit eld. To pounce upon him at the psychological moment, to discover in whose cool cobwebby cellar he is dreaming out his golden summer of manhood—that is what a foreigner can never, never hope to achieve, without competent local aid.

To this end, I generally apply to the priests; not because they are the greatest drunkards (far from it; they are mildly epicurean, or even abstemious) but by reason of their unrivalled knowledge of personalities. They know exactly who has been able to keep his liquor of such and such a year, and who has been obliged to sell or partially adulterate it; they know, from the confessional of the wives, the why and wherefore of all such private family affairs and share, with the chemist, the gift of seeing furthest into the tangled web of home life. They are "gialosi," however, of these acquirements, and must be approached in the right spirit—a spirit of humility. But if you tactfully lead up to the subject by telling of the manifold hardships of travel in foreign lands, the discomfort of life in hostelries, the food that leaves so much to be desired and, above all, the coarse wine that is already beginning, you greatly fear, to injure your sensitive spleen (an important organ, in Calabria), inducing a hypochondriacal tendency to see all the beauties of this fair land in an odious and sombre light—turning your day into night, as it were—it must be an odd priest, indeed, who is not compassionately moved to impart the desired information regarding the whereabouts of the best *vino di famiglia* at that moment obtainable. After all, it costs him nothing to do a double favour—one to yourself and another to the proprietor of the wine, doubtless an old friend of his, who will be able to sell his stuff to a foreigner 20 per cent dearer than to a native.

And failing the priests, I go to an elderly individual of that tribe of red-nosed connaisseurs, the coachmen, ever thirsty and mercenary souls, who for a small consideration may be able to disclose not only this secret, but others far more mysterious.

As to your host at the inn—he raises not the least objection to your importing alien liquor into his house. His own wine, he tells you, is last year's vintage and somewhat harsh (slightly watered, he might add)—and why not? The ordinary customers are gentlemen of commerce who don't care a fig what they eat and drink, so long as there is enough of it. No horrible suggestions are proffered concerning corkage; on the contrary, he tests your wine, smacks his lips, and thanks you for communicating a valuable discovery. He thinks he will buy a bottle or two for the use of himself and a few particular friends. . . .

Midnight has come and gone. The street is emptying; the footsteps of passengers begin to ring hollow. I arise, for my customary stroll in the direction of the cemetery, to attune myself to repose by shaking off those restlessly trivial images of humanity which might otherwise haunt my slumbers.

Town visions are soon left behind; it is very quiet here under the hot, starlit heavens; nothing speaks of man save the lighthouse flashing in ghostly activity—no, it is a fixed light—on the distant Cape of the Column. And nothing breaks the stillness save the rhythmic breathing of the waves, and a solitary cricket that has yet to finish his daily task of instrumental music, far away, in some warm crevice of the hills.

A suave odour rises up from the narrow patch of olives, and figs loaded with fruit, and ripening vines, that skirts the path by the beach. *The fig tree putteth forth her green figs, and the vines with the tender grape give a good smell.*

And so I plough my way through the sand, in the darkness, encompassed by tepid exhalations of earth and sea. Another spirit has fallen upon me—a spirit of biblical calm. Here, then, stood *the rejoicing city that dwelt carelessly, that said in her heart, I am, and there is none beside me: how is she become a desolation!* It is indeed hard to realize that a town thronged with citizens covered all this area. Yet so it is . Every footstep is a memory. Along this very track walked the sumptuous ladies of Croton on their way to deposit their vain jewels before the goddess Hera, at the bidding of Pythagoras. On this spot, maybe, stood that public hall which was specially built for the delivery of his lectures.

No doubt the townsfolk had been sunk in apathetic luxury; the time was ripe for a Messiah.

And lo! he appeared.

XXXVIII

THE SAGE OF CROTON

THE popularity of this sage at Croton offers no problem: the inhabitants had become sufficiently civilized to appreciate the charm of being regenerated. We all do. Renunciation has always exercised an irresistible attraction for good society; it makes us feel so comfortable, to be told we are going to hell—and Pythagoras was very eloquent on the subject of Tartarus as a punishment. The Crotoniates discovered in repentance of sins a new and subtle form of pleasure; exactly as did the Florentines, when Savonarola appeared on the scene.

Next: his doctrines found a ready soil in Magna Graecia which was already impregnated with certain vague notions akin to those he introduced. And then—he permitted and even encouraged the emotional sex to participate in the mysteries; the same tactics that later on materially helped the triumph of Christianity over the more exclusive and rational cult of Mithra. Lastly, he came with a "message," like the Apostle of the Gentiles; and in those times a preaching reformer was a novelty. That added a zest.

We know them a little better, nowadays.

He enjoyed the specious and short-lived success that has attended, elsewhere, such efforts to cultivate the *ego* at the expense of its environment. "A type of aspiring humanity," says Gissing, echoing the sentiments of many of us, "a sweet and noble figure, moving as a dim radiance through legendary Hellas." I fancy that the mist of centuries of undiscriminating admiration has magnified this figure out of all proportion and contrived, furthermore, to fix an iridescent nimbus of sanctity about its head. Such things have been know to happen, in foggy weather.

Was Greece so very legendary, in those times? Why, on the contrary, it was full of real personages, of true sages to whom it seemed as if no secrets of heaven or earth were past fathoming; far from being legendary, the country had never attained a higher plane of intellectual curiosity than when Pythagoras made his appearance.

And it cannot be gainsaid that he and his disciples gave the impetus away from these wise and beneficial researches into the arid regions of metaphysics. It is so much more gentlemanly (and so much easier) to talk bland balderdash about soul-migrations than to calculate an eclipse of the moon or bother about the circulation of the blood.

That a man of his speculative vigour, knowing so many extra-Hellenic races, should have hit upon one or two good things adventitiously is only to be expected. But they were mere by-products. One might as well praise John Knox for creating the commons of Scotland with a view to the future prosperity of that country—a consummation which his black fanaticism assuredly never foresaw.

The chief practical doctrine of Pythagoras, that mankind are to be governed on the principle of a community of eastern monks, makes for the disintegration of rational civic life.

And his chief theoretical doctrines, of metempsychosis and the reduction of everything to a system of numbers*—these are sheer lunacy.

Was it not something of a relapse, after the rigorous mental discipline of old, to have a man gravely assuring his fellows that he is the son of Hermes and the divinely appointed messenger of Apollo; treating diseases, like an Eskimo Angekok, by incantation; recording veracious incidents of his experiences during a previous life in Hell which he seems to have explored almost as thoroughly as Swedenborg; dabbling in magic, and consulting dreams, birds and the smoke of incense as oracles? And in the exotic conglomerate of his teachings are to be found the *prima stamina* of much that is worse: the theory of the pious fraud which has infected Latin countries to this day; the Jesuitical maxim of the end justifying the means; the insanity of preferring deductions to facts which has degraded philosophy up to the days of Kant; mysticism, demon-worship and much else of pernicious mettle—they are all there, embryonically embedded in Pythagoras.

We are told much of his charity; indeed, an English author has

---

* Vincenzo Dorsa, an Albanian, has written two pamphlets on the survival of Greco-Roman traditions in Calabria. They are difficult to procure, but whoever is lucky enough to find them will be much helped in his understanding of the common people. In one place, he speaks of the charm-formula of *Otto-Nove!* (Eight-Nine) It is considered meet and proper, in the presence of a suckling infant, to spit thrice and then call out three times, Otto-Nove! This brings luck; and the practice, he thinks, is an echo of the number-system of Pythagoras.

written a learned work to prove that Pythagoreanism has close affinities with Christianity. Charity has now been tried on an ample scale, and has proved a dismal failure. To give, they say, is more blessed than to receive. It is certainly far easier, for the most part, to give than to refrain from giving. We are at last shaking off the form of self-indulgence called charity; we realize that if mankind is to profit, sterner conceptions must prevail. The apotheosis of the god-favoured loafer is drawing to a close.

For the rest, there was the inevitable admixture of quackery about our reforming sage; his warmest admirers cannot but admit that he savours somewhat strongly of the holy impostor. Those charms and amulets, those dark gnomic aphorisms which constitute the stock-in-trade of all religious cheap-jacks, the bribe of future life, the sacerdotal tinge with its complement of mendacity, the secrecy of doctrine, the pretentiously-mysterious self-retirement, the "sacred quaternion," the bean-humbug . . .

He had the true maraboutic note.

And for me, this regenerator crowned with a saintly aureole remains a glorified marabout—an intellectual dissolvent; the importer of that oriental introspectiveness which culminated in the idly-splendid yearnings of Plato, paved the way for the quaint Alexandrian *tutti-frutti* known as Christianity, and tainted the well-springs of honest research for two thousand years. But their works ye shall known them. It was the Pythagoreans who, not content with a just victory over the Sybarites, annihilated their city amid anathemas worthy of those old Chaldeans (past masters in the art of pious cursing); a crime against their common traditions and common interests; a piece of savagery which wrecked Hellenic civilization in Italy. It is ever thus, when the soul is appointed arbiter over reason. It is ever thus, when gentle, god-fearing dreamers meddle with worldly affairs. Beware of the wrath of the lamb!

So rapidly did the virus act, that soon we find Plato declaring that all the useful arts are *degrading*; that "so long as a man tries to study any sensible object, he can never be said to be learning anything"; in other words, that the kind of person to whom one looks for common sense should be excluded from the management of his most refined republic. It needed courage of a rather droll kind to make such propositions in Greece, under the shadow of the Parthenon. And hand in hand with this feudalism in philosophy there began that unhealthy preoccupation with the morals of our fellow-creatures, that miasma of puritanism, which has infected life and literature up to this moments.

The Renaissance brought many fine things to England. But the wicked fairy was there with her gift: Pythagoras and Plato. We were not like the Italians who, after the first rapture of discovery was over, soon outgrew these distracted dialectics; we stuck fast in them. Hence our Platonic touch: our *demi-vierge* attitude in matters of the mind, our academic horror of clean thinking. How Plato hated a fact! He could find no place for it in his twilight world of abstractions. Was it not he who wished to burn the works of Democritus of Abdera, most exact and reasonable of old sages?

They are all alike, these humanitarian lovers of first causes. Always ready to burn something, or somebody; always ready with their cheerful Hell-fire and gnashing of teeth.

Know thyself: to what depths of vain, egocentric brooding has that dictum led! But we are discarding, now, such a mischievously narrow view of the cosmos, though our upbringing is still too rhetorical and mediæval to appraise its authors at their true worth. Youth is prone to judge with the heart rather than the head; youth thrives on vaporous ideas, and there was a time when I would have yielded to none in my enthusiasm for these mellifluous babblers; one had a blind, sentimental regard for their great names. It seems to me, now, that we take them somewhat too seriously; that a healthy adult has nothing to learn from their teachings, save by way of warning example. Plato is food for adolescents. And a comfort, possibly, in old age, when the judicial faculties of the mind are breaking up and primitive man, the visionary, reasserts his ancient rights. For questioning moods grow burdensome with years; after a strain of virile doubt we are glad to acquiesce once more—to relapse into Platonic animism, the logic of valetudinarians. The dog to his vomit.

And after Plato—the deluge. Neo-platonism. . . .

Yet it was quite good sport, while it lasted. To "make men better" by choice dissertations about utopias, to sit in marble halls and have a fair and fondly ardent *jeunesse dorée* reclining about your knees while you discourse, in rounded periods, concerning the salvation of their souls by means of transcendental Love—it would suit me well enough, at this present moment; far better than croaking, forlorn as the night-raven, among the ruins of their radiant lives.

Meanwhile, and despite our Universities, new conceptions are prevailing. Aristotle is winning the day. A fresh kind of thinker has arisen, whose chief idea of "virtue" is to investigate patiently the facts of life; men of the type of Lister, any one of whom have done more to regenerate mankind, and to increase the sum of human happiness, than a wilderness of the amiably-hazy old doctrinaires who professed the same object. I call to mind those physicians engaged in their malaria-campaign, and wonder what Plato would have thought of them. Would he have recognized the significance of their researches which, while allaying pain and misery, are furthering the prosperity of the country, causing waters to flow in dry places and villages to spring up in deserts—strengthening its political resources, improving its very appearance? Not likely. Plato's opinion of doctors was on a par with the rest of his mentality. Yet these are the men who are taking up the thread where it was dropped, perforce, by those veritable Greek sages, whelmed under turbid floods of Pythagorean irrationalism.

And are such things purely utilitarian? Are they so grossly mundane? Is there really no "philosophy" in the choice of such a healing career, no romance in its studious self-denial, no beauty in its results? If so, we must revise that classic adage which connects vigour with beauty—not to speak of several others.

XXXIX

MIDDAY AT PETELIA

DAY after day, I look across the six miles of sea to the Lacinian promontory and its column. How reach it?
The boatmen are eager for the voyage: it all depends, they say, upon the wind.

Day after day—a dead calm.

"Two hours—three hours—four hours—according!" And they point to the sky. A little breeze, they add, sometimes makes itself felt in the early mornings; one might fix up a sail.

"And for returning at midday?"

"Three hours—four hours—five hours—according!"

The prospect of rocking about for half a day in a small boat under a blazing sky is not my ideal of enjoyment, the novelty of such an experience having worn off a good many years ago. I decide to wait; to make an attack, meanwhile, upon old Petelia—the "Stromboli" of my lady-friend at the Catanzaro Museum. . . .

It is an easy day's excursion from Cotrone to Strongoli, which is supposed to lie on the site of that ancient, much-besieged town. It sits upon a hill-top, and the diligence which awaits the traveller at the little railway-station takes about two hours to reach the place, climbing up the olive-covered slopes in ample loops and windings.

Of Strongoli my memories, even at this short distance of time, are confused and blurred. The drive up under the glowing beams of morning, the great heat of the last few days, and two or three nights' sleeplessness at Cotrone had considerably blunted my appetite for new things. I remember seeing some Roman marbles in the church, and being thence conducted into a castle.

Afterwards I reposed awhile in the upper regions, under an olive, and looked down towards the valley of the Neto, which flows not far from here into the Ionian. I thought upon Theocritus, trying to picture his vale of Neaithos as it appeared to him and his shepherds. The woodlands are gone, and the rains of winter, streaming down the earthen slopes, have remodelled the whole face of the country.

Yet, be nature what it may, men will always turn to one who sings so melodiously of eternal verities—of those human tasks and needs which no lapse of years can change. How modern he reads to us, who have been brought into contact with the true spirit by men like Johnson-Cory and Lefroy! And how unbelievably remote is that Bartolozzi-Hellenism which went before! What, for example—what of the renowned pseudo-Theocritus, Salamon Gessner, who sang of this same vale of Neto in his "Daphnis"? Alas, the good Salamon has gone the way of all derivative bores; he is dead—deader than King Psammeticus; he is now moralizing in some decorous Paradise amid flocks of Dresden-China sheep and sugar-watery youths and maidens. Who can read his much-translated masterpiece without unpleasant twinges? Dead as a doornail!

So far as I can recollect, there is an infinity of kissing in "Daphnis." It was an age of sentimentality, and the Greek pastoral ideal, transfused into a Swiss environment of 1810, could not but end in slobber and *Gefühlsduselei*. True it is that shepherds have ample opportunities of sporting with Amaryllis in the shade; opportunities which, to my certain knowledge, they do not neglect. Theocritus knew it well enough. But, in a general way, he is niggardly with the precious commodity of kisses; he seems to have thought that in literature, if not in real life, one can have too much of a good thing. Also, being a southerner, he could not have trusted his young folks to remain eternally at the kissing-stage, after the pattern of our fish-like English lovers. Such behaviour would have struck him as improbable; possibly immoral. . . .

From where I sat one may trace a road that winds upwards into the Sila, past Pallagorio. Along its sides are certain mounded heaps and the smoke of refining works. These are mines of that dusky sulphur which I had observed being drawn in carts through the streets of Cotrone. There are some eight or ten of them, they tell me, discovered about thirty years ago—this is all wrong: they are mentioned in 1571—and employing several hundred workmen. It had been my intention to visit these excavations. But now, in the heat of day, I wavered; the distance, even to the nearest of them, seemed inordinately great; and just as I had decided to look for a carriage with a view of being driven there (that curse of conscientiousness!) an amiable citizen snatched me up as his guest for luncheon. He led me, weakly resisting, to a vaulted chamber where, amid a repast of rural delicacies and the converse of his spouse, all such fond projects were straightway forgotten. Instead of sulphur-statistics, I learnt a little piece of local history.

"You were speaking about the emptiness of our streets of Strongoli," my host said. "And yet, up to a short time ago, there was no emigration from this place. Then a change came about: I'll tell you how it was. There was a *guardia di finanze* here—a miserable octroi official. To keep up the name of his family, he married an heiress; not for the sake of having progeny, but—well! He began buying up all the land round about—slowly, systematically, cautiously—till, by dint of threats and intrigues, he absorbed nearly all the surrounding country. Inch by inch, he ate it up; with his wife's money. That was his idea of perpetuating his memory. All the small proprietors were driven from their domains and fled to America to escape starvation; immense tracts of well-cultivated land are now almost desert. Look at the country! But some day he will get his reward; under the ribs, you know."

By this purposeful re-creation of those feudal conditions of olden days, this man has become the best-hated person in the district.

Soon it was time to leave the friendly shelter and inspect in the glaring sunshine the remaining antiquities of Petelia. Never have I felt less inclined for such antiquarian exploits. How much better the hours would have passed in some cool tavern! I went forth, none the less; and was delighted to discover that there are practically no antiquities left—nothing save a few walls standing near a now ruined convent, which is largely built of Roman stone-blocks and bricks. Up to a few years ago, the municipality carried on excavations here and unearthed a few relics which were promptly dispersed. Perhaps some of these are what one sees in the Catanzaro Museum. The paternal government, hearing of this enterprise, claimed the site and sat down upon it; the exposed remains were once more covered up with soil.

A goat-boy, a sad little fellow, sprang out of the earth as I dutifully wandered about here. He volunteered to show me not only Strongoli, but all Calabria; in fact, his heart's desire was soon manifest: to escape from home and find his way to America under my passport and protection. Here was his chance—a foreigner (American) returning sooner or later to his own country! He pressed the matter with naïf forcefulness. Vainly I told him that there were other lands on earth; that I was not going to America. He shook his head and sagely remarked:

"I have understood. You think my journey would cost too much.

But you, also, must understand. Once I get work there, I will repay you every farthing."

As a consolation, I offered him some cigarettes. He accepted one; pensive, unresigned.

The goat-herds had no such cravings—in the days of Theocritus.

XL

THE COLUMN

"TWO hours—three hours—four hours: according!"
The boatmen are still eager for the voyage. It all depends, as before, upon the wind.

And day after day the Ionian lies before us—immaculate, immutable.

I determined to approach the column by land. A mule was discovered, and starting from the "Concordia" rather late in the morning, reached the temple-ruin in two hours to the minute. I might have been tempted to linger by the way but for the intense sunshine and for the fact that the muleteer was an exceptionally dull dog—a dusky youth of the taciturn and wooden-faced Spanish variety, whose anti-Hellenic profile irked me, in that landscape. The driving road ends at the cemetery. Thence onward a pathway skirts the sea at the foot of the clay-hills; passes the sunken wells; climbs up and down steepish gradients and so attains the plateau at whose extremity stands the lighthouse, the column, and a few white bungalows—summer-residences of Cotrone citizens.

A day of shimmering heat. . . .

The ground is parched. Altogether, it is a poor and thinly peopled stretch of land between Cotrone and Capo Rizzuto. No wonder the wolves are famished. Nine days ago one of them actually ventured upon the road near the cemetery, in daylight.

Yet there is some plant-life, and I was pleased to see, emerging from the bleak sand-dunes, the tufts of the well-known and conspicuous sea lily in full flower. Wishful to obtain a few blossoms, I asked the boy to descend from his mule, but he objected.

"Non si toccano questi fiori," he said. These flowers are not to be touched.

Their odour displeased him. Like the Arab, the uncultivated Italian is insensitive to certain smells that revolt us; while he cannot endure, on the other hand, the scent of some flowers. I have seen a man professing to feel faint at the odour of crushed geranium leaves.

They are *fiori di morti*, he says: planted (sometimes) in graveyards.

The last remarkable antiquity found at this site, to my knowledge, is a stone vase, fished up some years ago out of the sea, into which it may have fallen while being carried off by pious marauders for the purpose of figuring as font in some church (unless, indeed, the land has sunk at this point, as there is some evidence to show). I saw it, shortly after its return to dry land, in a shed near the harbour of Cotrone; the Taranto museum has now claimed it. It is a basin of purple-veined pavonazzetto marble. Originally a monolith, it now consists of two fragments; the third and smallest is still missing. This noble relic stands about 85 centimetres in height and measures some 215 centimetres in circumference; it was never completed, as can be seen by the rim, which is still partially in the rough. A similar vessel is figured, I believe, in Tischbein.

The small villa-settlement on this promontory is deserted owing to lack of water, every drop of which has to be brought hither by sea from Cotrone. One wonders why they have not thought of building a cistern to catch the winter rains, if there are any; for a respectable stone crops up at this end of the peninsula.

One often wonders at things. . . .

The column has been underpinned and strengthened by a foundation of cement; rains of centuries had begun to threaten its base, and there was some risk of a catastrophe. Near at hand are a few ancient walls of reticulated masonry in strangely leaning attitudes, peopled by black goats; on the ground I picked up some chips of amphoræ and vases, as well as a fragment of the limb of a marble statue. The site of this pillar, fronting the waves, is impressively forlorn. And it was rather thoughtful, after all, of the despoiling Bishop Lucifero to leave two of the forty-eight columns standing upright on the spot, as a sample of the local Doric style. One has fallen to earth since his day. Nobody would have complained at the time, if he had stolen all of them, instead of only forty-six. I took a picture of the survivor; then wandered a little apart, in the direction of the shore, and soon found myself in a solitude of burning stones, a miniature Sahara.

The temple has vanished, together with the sacred grove that once embowered it; the island of Calypso, where Swinburne took his ease (if such it was), has sunk into the purple realms of Glaucus; the corals and sea-beasts that writhed among its crevices are engulphed under mounds of submarine sand. There was life, once, at this promontory. Argosies touched here, leaving priceless gifts; fountains flowed, and cornfields waved in the genial sunshine. Doubtless there will be life again; earth and sea are only waiting for the enchanter's wand.

All now lies bare, swooning in summer stagnation.

Calabria is not a land to traverse alone. It is too wistful and stricken; too deficient in those externals that conduce to comfort. Its charms do not appeal to the eye of romance, and the man who would perambulate Magna Graecia as he does the Alps would soon regret his choice. One needs something of that "human element" which delighted the genteel photographer of Morano—comrades, in short; if only those sages, like old Nola Molisi, who have fallen under the spell of its ancient glories. The joys of Calabria are not to be bought, like those of Switzerland, for gold.

Sir Giovan Battista di Nola Molisi, the last of his family and name, having no sons and being come to old age without further hope of offspring, has desired in the place of children to leave of himself an eternal memory to mankind—to wit, this Chronicle of the most Ancient, Magnificent, and Faithful City of Cotrone. A worthier effort at self-perpetuation than that of Strongoli. . . .

A sturgeon, he notes, was caught in 1593 by the Spanish Castellan of the town. This nobleman, puzzling whom he could best honour with so rare a dainty, despatched it by means of a man on horseback to the Duke of Nocera. The Duke was no less surprised than pleased; he thought mighty well of the sturgeon and of the respectful consideration which prompted the gift; and then, by another horseman, sent it to Nola Molisi's own uncle accompanied, we may conjecture, by some ceremonious compliment befitting the occasion.

A man of parts, therefore, our author's uncle, to whom his Lordship of Nocera sends table-delicacies by mounted messenger; and himself a mellow comrade whom I am loath to leave; his pages are distinguished by a pleasing absence of those saintly paraphernalia which hang like a fog athwart the fair sky of the south.

Yet to him and to all of them I must bid good-bye, here and now. At this hour to-morrow I shall be far from Cotrone.

Farewell to Capialbi, inspired bookworm! And to Lenormant.

On a day like this, the scholar sailed at Bivona over a sea so unruffled that the barque seemed to be suspended in air. The water's surface, he tells us, is "unie comme une glace." He sees the vitreous depths invaded by piercing sunbeams that light up its mysterious forests of algæ, its rock-headlands and silvery stretches of sand; he peers down into these "prairies pélagiennes" and beholds all their wondrous fauna—the urchins, the crabs, the floating fishes and translucent medusæ "semblables à des clochettes d'opale." Then, realizing how this "population pullulante des petits animaux marins" must have impressed the observing ancients, he goes on to touch—ever so lightly!—upon those old local arts of ornamentation whereby sea-beasts and molluscs and aquatic plants were reverently copied by master-hand, not from dead specimens, but "pris sur le vif et observés au milieu des eaux"; he explains how an entire school grew up, which drew its inspiration from the dainty shapes and movements of these frail creatures. This is *du meilleur Lenormant.* His was a full-blooded yet discriminating zest of knowledge. One wonders what more was fermenting in that restlessly curious brain, when a miserable accident ended his short life, after 120 days of suffering.

So Italy proved fatal to him, as Greece to his father. But one of his happiest moments must have been spent on the sea at Bivona, on that clear summer day—a day such as this, when every nerve tingles with joy of life.

Meanwhile it is good to rest here, immovable but alert, in the breathless hush of noon. Showers of benevolent heat stream down upon this desolation; not the faintest wisp of vapour floats upon the horizon; not a sail, not a ripple, disquiets the waters. The silence can be felt. Slumber is brooding over the things of earth;

> Asleep are the peaks of the hills, and the vales,
> The promotories, the clefts,
> And all the creatures that move upon the black earth. . . .

Such torrid splendour, drenching a land of austerest simplicity, decomposes the mind into corresponding states of primal contentment and resilience. There arises before our phantasy a new perspective of human affairs; a suggestion of well-being wherein the futile complexities and disharmonies of our age shall have no place. To discard these wrappings, to claim kinship with some elemental and robust archetype, lover of earth and sun——

How fair they are, these moments of golden equipoise!

Yes; it is good to be merged awhile into these harshly-vibrant surroundings, into the meridian glow of all things. This noontide is the "heavy" hour of the Greeks, when temples are untrodden by priest or worshipper. *Controra* they now call it—the ominous hour. Man and beast are fettered in sleep, while spirits walk abroad, as at midnight. *Non timebis a timore nocturno: a sagitta volante in die: a negotio perambulante in tenebris: ab incursu et demonio meridiano.* The midday demon—that southern Haunter of calm blue spaces. . . .

So may some enchantment of kindlier intent have crept over Phaedrus and his friend, at converse in the noontide under the whispering plane-tree. And the genius dwelling about this old headland of the Column is candid and benign.

This corner of Magna Graecia is a severely parsimonious manifestation of nature. Rocks and waters! But these rocks and waters are actualities; the stuff whereof man is made. A landscape so luminous, so resolutely scornful of accessories, hints at brave and simple forms of expression; it brings us to the ground, where we belong; it medicines to the disease of introspection and stimulates a capacity which we are in danger of unlearning amid our morbid hyperborean gloom—the capacity for honest contempt: contempt of that scarecrow of a theory which would have us neglect what is earthly, tangible. What is life well lived but a blithe discarding of primordial husks, of those comfortable intangibilities that lurk about us, waiting for our weak moments?

The sage, that perfect savage, will be the last to withdraw himself from the influence of these radiant realities. He will strive to knit closer the bond, and to devise a more durable and affectionate relationship between himself and them. Let him open his eyes. For a reasonable adjustment lies at his feet. From these brown stones that seam the tranquil Ionian, from this gracious solitude, he can carve out, and bear away into the cheerful din of cities, the rudiments of something clean and veracious and wholly terrestrial—some tonic philosophy that shall foster sunny mischiefs and farewell regret.

COSIMO is a specialty publisher of books and publications that inspire, inform and engage readers. Our mission is to offer unique books to niche audiences around the world.

COSIMO CLASSICS offers a collection of distinctive titles by the great authors and thinkers throughout the ages. At COSIMO CLASSICS timeless classics find a new life as affordable books, covering a variety of subjects including: *Biographies, Business, History, Mythology, Personal Development, Philosophy, Religion and Spirituality,* and much more!

COSIMO-on-DEMAND publishes books and publications for innovative authors, non-profit organizations and businesses. COSIMO-on-DEMAND specializes in bringing books back into print, publishing new books quickly and effectively, and making these publications available to readers around the world.

COSIMO REPORTS publishes public reports that affect your world: from global trends to the economy, and from health to geo-politics.

FOR MORE INFORMATION CONTACT US AT
INFO@COSIMOBOOKS.COM

❋ If you are a book-lover interested in our current catalog of books.

❋ If you are an author who wants to get published

❋ If you represent an organization or business seeking to reach your members, donors or customers with your own books and publications

**COSIMO BOOKS ARE ALWAYS
AVAILABLE AT ONLINE BOOKSTORES**

VISIT COSIMOBOOKS.COM
BE INSPIRED, BE INFORMED

Printed in the United States
86912LV00002B/250-255/A

9 781602 063761